Cultural Representations of Piracy in England, Spain, and the Caribbean

This book examines the concept of piracy as an instrument for the advancement of legal, economic, and political agendas associated with early modern imperial conflicts in the Caribbean.

Drawing on historical accounts, literary texts, legal treatises, and maps, the book traces the visual and narrative representations of Sir Francis Drake, who serves as a case study to understand the various usages of the terms "pirate" and "corsair." Through a comparative analysis, the book considers the connotations of the categories related to maritime predation—pirate, corsair, buccaneer, and filibuster—and nationalistic and religious denominations—Lutheran, Catholic, heretic, Spaniard, English, and Creole—to argue that the flexible usage of these terms corresponds to unequal colonial and imperial relations and ideological struggles.

The book chronologically records the process by which piracy changed from an unregulated phenomenon to becoming legally defined after the Treaty of London (1604) and the Treaty of Westphalia (1648). The research demonstrates that as piracy grew less ambiguous through legal and linguistic standardization, the concept of piracy lost its polemical utility.

This interdisciplinary volume is ideal for researchers working in piracy studies, early modern history, and imperial history.

Mariana Cecilia Velázquez received her PhD in Latin American and Iberian Cultures from Columbia University. She is a Professor in the Department of World Languages and Literatures at the University of Nevada-Reno. Her research focuses on the early modern transatlantic relations and colonial piracy in Spain, England, and the Caribbean.

Routledge Studies in Cultural History

Academia and Trade
The Numismatic World in the Long Nineteenth Century, Volume 1
Edited by Stefan Krmnicek and Hadrien Rambach

Institutions and Individuals
The Numismatic World in the Long Nineteenth Century, Volume 2
Edited by Stefan Krmnicek and Hadrien Rambach

Cultural Representations of Piracy in England, Spain, and the Caribbean
Travelers, Traders, and Traitors, 1570 to 1604
Mariana Cecilia Velázquez

Sport and the Pursuit of War and Peace from the Nineteenth Century to the Present
War Minus the Shooting?
Edited by Martin Hurcombe and Philip Dine

Staging Slavery
Performances of Colonial Slavery and Race from International Perspectives, 1770–1850
Edited by Sarah J. Adams, Jenna M. Gibbs, and Wendy Sutherland

Honor and Shame in Western History
Edited by Jörg Wettlaufer, David Nash and Jan Frode Hatlen

Modern Murders
The Turn-of-the-Century's Backlash Against Melodramatic and Sensational Representations of Murder, 1880–1914
Lee Michael-Berger

For more information about this series, please visit: https://www.routledge.com/Routledge-Studies-in-Cultural-History/book-series/SE0367

Cultural Representations of Piracy in England, Spain, and the Caribbean

Travelers, Traders, and Traitors, 1570 to 1604

Mariana Cecilia Velázquez

First published 2023
by Routledge
605 Third Avenue, New York, NY 10158

and by Routledge
4 Park Square, Milton Park, Abingdon, Oxon OX14 4RN

Routledge is an imprint of the Taylor & Francis Group, an informa business

© 2023 Mariana Cecilia Velázquez

The right of Mariana Cecilia Velázquez to be identified as author of this work has been asserted in accordance with sections 77 and 78 of the Copyright, Designs and Patents Act 1988.

All rights reserved. No part of this book may be reprinted or reproduced or utilized in any form or by any electronic, mechanical, or other means, now known or hereafter invented, including photocopying and recording, or in any information storage or retrieval system, without permission in writing from the publishers.

Trademark notice: Product or corporate names may be trademarks or registered trademarks, and are used only for identification and explanation without intent to infringe.

Library of Congress Cataloging-in-Publication Data
A catalog record for this title has been requested

ISBN: 978-0-367-69356-5 (hbk)
ISBN: 978-0-367-69357-2 (pbk)
ISBN: 978-1-003-14149-5 (ebk)

DOI: 10.4324/9781003141495

Typeset in Sabon
by Taylor & Francis Books

Contents

List of Figures   vii
Acknowledgments   x

Introduction: Reading Piracy between the Lines   1

1   Navigating Conflicting Waters: Francis Drake's Circumnavigation (1577–1580)   19

   The English Captain Francis Drake: Birth of a Maritime Knight 19
   Society of Speculation and the Anglo-Spanish Rivalry 31

2   Setting Sails to the Narrative of Piracy: Francis Drake's Caribbean Raid (1585–1586)   50

   Pirate or Entrepreneur? English Justifications of the Attack 53
   Who Is to Blame? Peninsular and Caribbean Explanations of the Attack 63

3   Dangerous Representations of the Caribbean in the Sixteenth Century   83

   Giving Birth to the Caribbean Islands: Narratives of Infection and Infestation 84
   Caribbean Ports and Infestations 85
   European Waters and Infestations 90
   The Construction of Piratical Spaces: Caribbean Cartographies 93
      Mapping "Our" Islands 96
      Mapping "Their" Islands 103

4 Dropping Anchor: Francis Drake's Three Deaths and the
  Beginnings of an End   128

  Criminalizing False Historical Claims Made by the Spanish 129
    Faking Drake's Death and the Spanish Armada's Defeat
      (1588) 129
    Drake's Multiple Deaths and His Last Raid
      (1595–1596) 135
  *Criminalizing Spanish Literary Production—The Spanish
    Armada's Defeat (1588) and Drake's Last Raid
    (1595–1996)* 139
    Drake and the Spanish Armada's Defeat: An
      Entertainment 139
    Drake's Last Raid (1595–1596): Literary and Historical
      Accounts from the Islands 142
    Drake's Death in Lope de Vega's *La Dragontea* 143

5 The Changing Winds of Piracy (1570–1604)   159

  *Manipulation of Piracy: Issues of Property, Space, and
    Sovereignty* 161
  *New Legal Understandings of Piracy and the End of the
    Anglo-Spanish Rivalry* 169

6 The Aftermath: The Emergence of New Models of Piracy in the
  Caribbean Buccaneers and Freebooters (Conclusion)   187

  *Drake's Revival in Caribbean Historical Narratives and
    Geopolitics* 191
  *The Lack of Proper Defense: Intrapraesidia Spaces and
    Corruption* 193
  Contraband and Suspicious "Dutiful Subjects" 199

  Bibliography   213
  Index   230

Figures

0.1 Detail from Claudius Ptolemy's *Geographia* (1525 ed.). South East (RB) EXKA Ptolemy. Firestone Library, Princeton University   7

0.2 Detail from Claudius Ptolemy's *Claudii Ptholomaei Alexandrini Liber geographiae cum tabulis et uniuersali figura* (1511 ed.) displaying the region *Piratae* between *Ariaca* and *Limirica*. B911. 3 P951.Rare Book & Manuscript Library, Columbia University in the City of New York   7

0.3 Detail from Claudius Ptolemy's *Geographia vniversalis, vetus et nova complectens Clavdii Ptolemi Alexandrini enarrationis libros VIII* (1545 ed.) displaying the region *Pyratae*. 1549 P959. Rare Book & Manuscript Library, Columbia University in the City of New York   8

0.4 Detail from Abraham Ortelius's Abrahami Ortelii Theatri orbis terrarvm parergon (1624 ed.). This map, entitled *Erythraei Sive Rubri Maris Periplus. Olim ab arriano descriptvs, nvnc vero ab Abrah. Ortelio … (c1597)* is included in the section dedicated to Ulysses's wanderings. It displays the region Piratae below Limyrica. B912 Or85 F. Rare Book & Manuscript Library, Columbia University in the City of New York   9

0.5 Detail from Abraham Ortelius's *Abrahami Ortelii Theatri orbis terrarvm parergon* (1624 ed.). This map, engraved around 1598, was included in the section of tables of old itineraries (*Tabvla itineraria antiqva*) of Mark Welser ("Marcus Velsero"). It displays the region *Pirate* in the eighth segment (*Segmentvm octavvm*). B912 Or85 F. Rare Book & Manuscript Library, Columbia University in the City of New York   10

1.1 Nicola Van Sype's map of Drake's circumnavigation (c1591). Library of Congress   29

1.2 Jodocus Hondius's *Broadside Map* commemorating Drake's and Thomas Cavendish's circumnavigations (c1593–1595). Library of Congress   34

viii *List of Figures*

1.3 Drake's circumnavigation map in Theodor de Bry's *Grand Voyages*, Latin edition (1599) and German edition (1600). Library of Congress 35

1.4 Drake's islands in the southern hemisphere of Levinus Hulsius's map *Nova et exacta delineatio Americae partis avstralis. qve est: Brasilia, Caribana, Gviana regnũm noũũm, Castilia del Oro, Nicaragva, insũlae Antillas et Perv. Et sub Tropico Capricorni, Chile, Rio della Plata, Patagonṽ, & Fretṽ Magellanicṽ* (1602). Library of Congress 37

1.5 Jodocus Hondius's depiction of Drake's Nova Albion (c1590). Library of Congress 39

3.1 Mercator's map of the Caribbean archipelago (c1590). Note the close up of Havana's Port on the upper right side. Also note the topographical detail. Copy available at the Archivo General de la Nación, M28 (1350), Santo Domingo, DR 105

3.2 Mercator's map depicting a ship with a flag the design of which resembles the Dutch tricolor flag from 1572. Note the close up of Havana's port on the upper-right side with the inscription "*Portus celeberimus totius India Occidentalis*" ("The most famous port in all the West Indies") and also note the other inscription in lower-left side that reads "*Portus Regius Salinas Scatens Spontaneis in valle solo laboris pretio petitur*" ("Royal Port with plentiful salt located in a valley available for the price of labour").Copy available at the Archivo General de la Nación, M8 (384), 1590-c. 1630, Santo Domingo, DR 106

3.3 Mercator's engraving of the Caribbean archipelago, depicting a ship in the western part of Hispaniola with a Spanish burgundy-cross flag and what resembles a Dutch Triple Prince Flag (c1590). Note the close up of Havana's port on the upper-right side with the inscription "*Portus celeberimus totius India Occidentalis*" ("The most famous port in all the West Indies") and the inscription located in the northern part of Venezuela – very close to the Island of Margarita – that reads "*Portus Regius Salinas Scatens Spontaneis in valle solo laboris pretio petitur*" ("Royal Port with plentiful salt located in a valley available for the price of labour"). Copy available at the Archivo General de la Nación, M31(1353), Santo Domingo, DR 107

3.4 Gerardus Mercator's and Jodocus Hondius' engraving of Hispaniola Insula (c1578–1590). Copy available at the Centro Eduardo León Jimenes, Mapoteca MC-01–0008, Santiago, DR 108

3.5 Detail from Mercator's map showing a ship hoisting what resembles a Dutch Triple Prince Flag. Copy available at the Centro Eduardo León Jimenes, Mapoteca MC-01–0008, Santiago, DR 109

3.6	Giovanni Battista Boazio's engraving of Drake's Caribbean raid (1585–1586) represented by a line marking Drake's navigational trajectory that also encloses part of the Atlantic Ocean along with the Caribbean archipelago connected with England. This engraving was included in Bigges's published narrative. The text (written in English) recounts the dates when the English fleet arrived to the Caribbean islands and which they either, "spoiled," "landed and refreshed the sick men" or "fought." Kraus Collection, Library of Congress. Another copy available at the Archivo General de la Nación, M 26 (1348), Santo Domingo, DR	110
3.7	Boazio's engraving of Drake's attack in Santo Domingo (1588) with a French translation of the original Latin note that emphasizes the relationship between England and Santo Domingo. Kraus Collection, Library of Congress	111
3.8	Boazio's engraving of Drake's attack in Cartagena de Indias with the chronological narrative of the event from De Bry's *Grand Voyages*, Latin edition (1599). Kraus Collection, Library of Congress	112
3.9	Matthäus Merian's engraving of 1649, representing the city of Santo Domingo. Archivo General de la Nación, M43 (1363), Santo Domingo, DR	115
3.10	City plan of the of Santo Domingo by Alain Manesson Mallet, *Description de l'Univers* (c1683). Copy available at Centro Eduardo León Jimenes, Mapoteca, MC-01–0002, Santiago, DR	116

Acknowledgments

My heartfelt gratitude to Columbia University and the mentorship I received throughout my doctoral studies and the acceptance of my dissertation which lay the groundwork for this book. First and foremost, I wish to deeply thank my advisor, Patricia E. Grieve, for her seminars, continuous support, and enduring guidance to me as a graduate student. I am also profoundly indebted to Seth R. Kimmel for his insightful commentaries, that were seminal to this project and to embrace the challenges that came along with it. I am extremely grateful to Orlando Bentancor, Jean Howard, and Caterina Pizzigoni for being part of my committee of readers and for spurring this book.

In the halls of Columbia and through seminars and workshops, I met extraordinary people who gave me invaluable advice to develop this intellectual project. In this context, I am enormously thankful to Carlos Alonso, Eunice Rodríguez Ferguson, Jesús Rodríguez-Velasco, Alessandra Russo, Alberto Medina, and Susan Boynton who taught me unique lessons that fortified my background and gave me essential guidance. I am very grateful to Wendy Muñiz, Guillermo Zouain, Agnese Codebò, Miguel Ibáñez-Aristondo, Noel Blanco-Mourelle, Caroline Egan, David H. Colmenares, Nicole T. Hughes, Adrián Espinoza-Staines, Lexie Cook, and Deneb Kozikoski for the numerous conversations we held as graduate students about early modern culture and the several methodological approaches which were salutary in forming my vision of this book. I also want to specially thank Ana Méndez Oliver and Antonio Arraiza with whom I shared a marvelous journey from the University of Puerto Rico and its professors, and who walked by my side throughout the graduate school experience in the United States.

Special mention to Clayton McCarl who became an instrumental mentor and colleague while my investigation began to take form. During my time as a graduate student, he pointed me in the right direction and gave me the opportunity to coordinate my first panel in an academic conference. In that context, I met María Gracia Ríos Taboada who became an immediate accomplice and colleague due to our shared interest in Francis Drake. I am deeply grateful for her unbound intellectual generosity throughout the years. Later on, McCarl entrusted me with co-founding the "Grupo de Estudio Internacional de la Piratería de la Edad Moderna Temprana," an international collective of scholars whose research addresses the intersections between maritime piracy and the history and culture of Latin America from the fifteenth to nineteenth centuries.

Through our collaboration, I met extraordinary scholars in the fields of history and literature who shared a contagious interest in early modern piracy. Special thanks to Kris Lane, Raúl Marrero-Fente, Jason McCloskey, and Leonor Taiano-Campoverde. Gratitude goes also to the librarians and archivists who helped me locate rare books and documentary materials at the several consulted archives and for Chet Van Duzer, and other investigators, with whom I crossed paths during my archival research and supported me in that process. I am also grateful to the University of Nevada, and especially to Wifredo de Ràfols, a faculty colleague whose support has been vital to me from the beginning of my career as a Professor.

Finally, I want to thank my family and beloved friends for always believing in me and encouraging to follow my dreams. I wish to express my deepest gratitude to my father, for always being there and willing to talk about pirates, and to my mother, for her unconditional support. In loving memory of my brother Francisco and *Doña* Adi, whose presence in my life explain who I am.

Introduction
Reading Piracy between the Lines

On December 10, 1982, the Caribbean island of Jamaica became a diplomatic scenario to discuss and agree upon issues related to maritime law. The United Nations (UN) Convention on the Law of the Sea was held in the city of Montego Bay, and the result of this event remains the global standard of the law of the sea. The official document of this convention addresses topics ranging from the definition of contemporary piracy and the traffic in illicit drugs to the assertion of sovereign and jurisdictional powers over bodies of water and aquatic natural resources. The regulations, contained in 320 articles, are based on an international consensus upon several categories that render the perception of nautical order by structuring the maritime space. Among these categories, we find "high seas," "territorial seas," "contiguous zones," and "exclusive economic zones." The document does not dispute these terms, but rather supports their authority by providing the specific meanings acknowledged in past UN conferences held at Geneva in 1958 and 1960.[1]

The document also provides a brief definition of piracy as well as several articles dealing with the "retention or loss of the nationality of a pirate ship" (Article 104) and the right of "seizure on account of piracy" (Article 107), among other topics related to piracy and freedom of navigation, such as the "right of hot pursuit" (Article 111) and the right of "freedom of the high seas" (Article 87).[2] Certainly, unlike sixteenth- and seventeenth-century legal disputes, the UN document defines piracy and freedom of navigation in both maritime and air spaces, in ships and in aircraft: "the high seas are open to all States, whether coastal or land-locked. Freedom of the high seas is exercised under the conditions laid down by this Convention and by other rules of international law" comprising both "freedom of navigation" and "freedom of overflight" (*id.*). Regarding sovereignty and military conflicts, Articles 88 and 89 establish that "the high seas shall be preserved for peaceful purposes" and that "no State may validly purport to subject any part of the high seas to its sovereignty." By the same token, "ships have the nationality of the State whose flag they are entitled to fly" (Article 91).

Four hundred years before the 1982 convention, the Caribbean archipelago was far from being a diplomatic geographical space with stable, internationally acknowledged categories and regulations related to maritime law. Relying

DOI: 10.4324/9781003141495-1

primarily on classical and theological sources, sixteenth- and seventeenth-century jurists and legal theorists such as Balthazar Ayala (1548–1584), Alberico Gentili (1552–1608), William Welwod (1578–1622), and Hugo Grotius (1583–1645), debated and attempted to define the legal and jurisdictional status of the seas in order to enforce regulations related to trade, contraband, and piracy. These authors arranged their arguments around different categories that would eventually resonate with the core value of the 1982 UN Convention, namely the notion of order and stability in the fluid and unpredictable maritime space. For instance, the classical term "fortified lines" appears in Grotius's and Gentili's work to denominate a maritime space in which the illicit capture of booty becomes legitimate if the ship or the stolen property remains there for three days (see, e.g., Gentili, 5–10). On the other hand, Ayala emphasizes the distinction between "movable things" and "immovable things" to assert the nature of property and territory, the right of ownership, and the extent of a sovereign's power (Ayala, 36–37). Openly criticizing Grotius's *Mare liberum* (1609), Welwod concludes his treatise, *An Abridgment of All Sea-Lawes* (1613), by stating that he ultimately agrees with the author's claim of freedom of the seas insofar as that means "seas" close to our modern understanding of "high seas." In Welwod's words, he believes in the free right of navigation on the "main sea or great ocean which is far removed from the just and due bonds ... properly pertaining to the nearest lands of every nation" (Grotius, 74).[3]

In this book, acknowledging the continuing impact of those centuries (i.e., the early modern period) on the foundation of categories and procedures of the present-day maritime law, I trace the role of piracy and the repercussions of its semantic and linguistic plasticity in the formulation of notions related to geographical space, ownership, and both national and local narratives of geopolitical identities across the Atlantic Ocean. Let's take a closer look at one specific event that exacerbated an international discussion on issues related to the right of property, sovereignty, and jurisdiction of the oceans among Dutch and English jurists such as Grotius (*Mare liberum*, 1609, and *De jure praedae*, 1605), Welwod (*An Abridgment of All Sea-Lawes*, 1613), and John Selden (*Mare clausum*, 1635), and the Portuguese friar Serafim de Freitas (*Do justo império asiático dos Portugueses*, 1625).[4]

In February 1603, Dutch maritime predators commanded by Admiral Jacob van Heemskerk seized a Portuguese ship, the *Santa Catarina*, in the Straits of Singapore, and its cargo was sold in Amsterdam. Drawing on classical conceptions of just war, just cause, and right of ownership, Grotius's unpublished *De jure praedae* (written in 1609) attempts to legitimize the ship's capture while criticizing the Portuguese market monopoly in the East Indies. In so doing, Grotius, a Dutch jurist, places the Portuguese merchants in the category of "pirates" (*piratas*) because they hindered the expansion of an international market by excluding other European nations from benefiting and profiting from the East Indies.[5] Tapping into precepts and perceptions of sovereignty, Grotius asserts Heemskerk's right of ownership over his booty because, according to him, Heemskerk acted in the best interests of his sovereign country, the Low Countries (now the Netherlands, Belgium, and Luxembourg) (Feenstra & Vervliet, 452). Grotius bases this argument on two primary laws of nature: self-defense and self-preservation.[6] In this way Grotius introduces the discussion of piracy into that of space and market, referring to the issue of political and economic competition between the Low Countries and the rest of Europe. Without alluding to the *Santa Catarina*'s seizure, a great part of the twelfth chapter of *De jure praedae* was published in 1609 under the title *Mare liberum*, where Grotius argues against exclusive Portuguese access to the East Indies by asserting and defining the right of possession, the right of navigation, and the right of trade (Grotius, xv).

Welwod's critique of the then-anonymous *Mare liberum*, contained in the 27th chapter of his treatise, revolves around three main points. First, Welwod argues that *Mare liberum*'s defense of free navigation is not that controversial but, rather, is only a façade to abolish the "undoubted right and propriety of fishing" (*id.*, 66). Second, he calls into question the essay's use of classical authors (poets, orators, and philosophers of old) instead of Holy Scripture to support its arguments. Lastly, Welwod claims that the author "wrested" the work of the Roman jurists, such as Aelius Marcianus and Aemilius Papinianus, to serve his purpose of protecting freedom of navigation and trade (*commeandi commercandique libertas*) (*id.*, 72). In sum, Welwod believes that a prince should be entitled to control the waters because "immediately after the creation God saith to man, 'Subdue the earth, and rule over the fish,' which could not be but a subduing of the water" (*id.*, 66).

A few years later, around 1615, Grotius acknowledged his authorship of *Mare liberum* in his unpublished response to Welwod's critique. Aside from counterarguing Welwod's main points, the self-taught lawyer focuses on the natural distinction between land and sea to demonstrate that "the sea cannot become the property of anyone, but owes forever to all men a use which is common to all" (*id.*, 78). Dwelling on the notions of private property and communal property, Grotius draws on both theological and classical sources. For instance, he stresses Ulpian's viewpoint on property to assert that "one who fishes in the sea does not fish on his own property, but makes the fish his own by the law of nations" (*id.*, 84). On the other hand, he dismantles Welwod's argument about the right of ownership over nature during Adam and Eve's era by stating that several theologians have agreed that during that time "there was no property, that is, as distinct from use, and ... there would not have been, had not sin intervened" (*id.*, 86). By tracing the origins of individual right, Grotius reveals that "even after sin entered the world, many things remained common" (*id.*, 87). Several decades later, Selden's *Mare clausum* echoed Welwod's critique when arguing against Grotius's freedom of navigation and trade by emphasizing Grotius's personal economic interests as an active functionary of the Dutch East India Company.[7] However, Selden's proclivity to support policies against the "free seas" and the "free right of navigation" was influenced by his view about the role played by jurisdictional power over the seas in the process of consolidating the British empire.[8] More than 40 years earlier, such an international discussion was just beginning. The protagonists then were the Spanish Crown and the English Captain Francis Drake (c1540–1596)—and by extension Queen Elizabeth I's regime—after his circumnavigation of the globe, accomplished 1577–80. *Cultural Representations of Piracy in England, Spain, and the Caribbean: Travelers, Traders, and Traitors (1570–1604)* focuses precisely on that period before the Peace of Westphalia (1648) when there was not yet an international community officially constituted to agree on the regulation of freedom of navigation and criminalization of piracy.

Today "pirates" are commonly understood as outlaw figures who, during the early modern period, circumvented the rules of trade and evaded entrenched political values. By contrast, "corsairs" were sponsored by states and, although they engaged in similar "outlaw" practices, they are seen as protectors of stability on behalf of their sovereign regimes. However, such a distinction was more complex than we usually tend to acknowledge today. Therefore, I focus on the linguistic and semantic nuances of the terms "pirate" and "corsair" to show that their interchangeable usage was a useful stage for political, economic, and religious polemics. I must clarify that is not a book about the history of Francis Drake. Rather, I trace the visual and narrative representations of this colorful and politically shrewd captain because he serves as a case study to understand the wide spectrum of usages of the terms "pirate" and "corsair." My contention is that, from the 1570s to the early 1600s, an array of early modern authors—lawyers, diplomats, European and colonial officials, as well as marginal Creole individuals—wrote about piracy to discuss the meanings of property, articulate jurisdictional boundaries of geographical space, and negotiate the limits of sovereignty and commercial exchange.

Cultural Representations of Piracy explores the use of the concept of piracy as an instrument for the advancement of agendas associated with imperial conflicts in the Caribbean. Certainly, the Mediterranean region with its historical Barbary corsairs and renegados provides a crucial referent to understand the fluidity of national and religious identities grounded in economic interests. Although I analyze several primary sources that touch on Mediterranean piracy, this project primarily revolves around transatlantic piracy without losing sight of the contextual parallel between the Caribbean and the Mediterranean. Thus, my comparative analysis examines the various usages, connotations, and meanings of the categories related to maritime predation—pirate, corsair, buccaneer, and filibuster—and nationalist and religious denominations—Lutheran, Catholic, heretic, Spanish, English, and Creole—to present a nuanced perspective on the discourse of piracy, showing that the flexible usage of these terms corresponds to unequal colonial and imperial relations and ideological struggles. Drawing on an interdisciplinary and international corpus that includes historical accounts, literary texts, legal treatises, and maps, I focus on Caribbean and European authors, who depicted pirates and corsairs as travelers, traders, or traitors, giving us a hint of the tensions and conflicting notions that contributed to the prevailing heterogenous notion of the phenomenon of piracy. In this context, Drake embodies a distinct transatlantic model of piracy because he forced negotiations with Spanish colonial authorities as well as participating in English campaigns of war during a time in which the discourse of piracy was both timely and flexible.

The main theoretical assumption behind this book is that the terms and concepts related to piracy became useful tools during the second half of the sixteenth century and the beginning of the seventeenth, as evinced by Gentili, Grotius, Welwod, and Selden. Therefore, the six chapters of this book trace the usefulness and repercussions of the categories of piracy whose instability, I argue, lies in the discursive entanglement among the political, religious, and economic realms. By the same token, this book does not focus on articulating historical reconstructions of each event analyzed. Rather, it brings forth the usefulness of concepts of piracy found in the descriptions of the historical events. However, a question remains unanswered: Who, then, is a pirate in the sixteenth century?

Historian Kris Lane has divided English maritime activity and its presence in the Caribbean into three periods, each with a different focus: contraband (1558–1568), piracy (1568–1585), and privateering (1585–1603).[9] To justify or to condemn Drake's actions, several historians have defined him as anything from a pirate, corsair, or privateer to a smuggler, thief, or bandit.[10] For instance, Harry Kelsey, in his pivotal work on Drake, underscores that at the beginning of his maritime career, Drake was a smuggler rather than a pirate because his first voyage to the Caribbean was primarily intended to buy African slaves from the Portuguese. Touching on the malleability of the category of corsair or "privateer," Gonçal López Nadal underscores the superficial distinction between merchants and corsairs because men "were sometimes one, sometimes the other, sometimes both simultaneously" (López Nadal, 132).[11] Overall, it is worth noting that the flexible implementation of these categories during the sixteenth century corresponds to the lack of an officially constituted international community to agree on the regulation of navigation and the criminalization of maritime predation. A more stable scenario was eventually provided by the Peace of Westphalia, 1648, and the emergence of European sovereign nation-states. According to Fabio López Lázaro, in the period between 1648 and 1750 "European states reached mutual recognition, in principle, of each other's internal jurisdictions, external boundaries and monopolization of violence, including legally differentiating piracy from privateering" (López Lázaro, 252).[12]

Therefore, I consider that one of the main issues that has troubled historians so far is the methodological approach to define piracy through an exclusionary and binary lens when classifying maritime predators. For instance, outlining legal precepts such as "letters of marque" or royal

6 *Introduction: Reading Piracy between the Lines*

commissions is another traditional strategy to clarify the differences between the aforementioned categories related to piracy. Letters of marque and reprisal, initially issued during the late middle ages, were intended to prevent wars among kingdoms. These documents granted permission to recover stolen goods or to replace them. The *licentia marcandi* (issued around 1295) allowed the retrieval of stolen goods, whether from the hands of the original thief or a relative, friend, or neighbor. However, as Alfred Rubin has argued, over the course of the sixteenth century the letters of marque lost their original purpose of preventing wars and rather, were issued during wartime to underscore the belligerency among European countries and nascent powers (Rubin, 21).

Considering the linguistic and etymological nature of the term *peirato*, Rubin asserts that it appears in Polybius's *Historiae* (c140 BCE) referring to the Eastern communities established in the Mediterranean, who were potential military allies to fight against political leaders from that geographical zone (Rubin, 5).[13] Later on, Plutarch (100 CE) mentions that pirates were a community based in Asia Minor and describes the process by which that community became labeled as rebels due to the establishment of the Roman hegemony and sovereignty during Pompey's rule. As Roman power strengthened, the category of piracy, according to Plutarch, designated an anachronistic lifestyle that did not correspond to the Roman political and commercial order. Hence, pirates became those individuals who did not acknowledge Roman supremacy and political hegemony (Rubin, 5–8). In this way, besides the conceptualization of the categories related to piracy found in Greek and Roman traditions, the term "piracy" became attached to a specific geographical space, as several editions of Ptolemy's *Geographia* display in the sixteenth century.

An example of mapping and territorializing piratical spaces (Fig. 0.1) is found in Ptolemy's *Geographia*, 1525 edition. An annotation that reads "*Feracissime. Insuli. Pyratarum*" ("Very fertile islands of pirates")[14] is located in the gutter of the two-page modern (post-Ptolemaic) map of Italy in the Mediterranean region.[15] By contrast, two other editions of *Geographia*—from 1511 and 1545 respectively—(Figs. 0.2 and 0.3) display a coastal region labelled as "Pyrate" or "Piratae" in the western part of ancient India next to the region of Lymirica (today's Konkan) and close to what was the island of Peperina.[16] Therefore, these examples found in sixteenth-century editions of Ptolemy's work showcase the conformation of a piratical space grounded in the act of "territorialization"—to use the concept as defined by Emily Sohmer Tai, in which depicting the space was tantamount to owning it— through cartographical production, on which I elaborate in Chapter 3.[17] The landing and conquering entailed the representation of physical territorialization through which the Spanish jurisdictional power and order were established in the newly discovered territories. Stressing the distinction between land and sea, Ptolemy's *Geographia* displays a fiction of a limited piratical territory. In this context, the category of piracy nonetheless remains unstable as it refers to both individuals and geographical spaces.

Introduction: Reading Piracy between the Lines   7

Fig. 0.1 Detail from Claudius Ptolemy's *Geographia* (1525 ed.). South East (RB) EXKA Ptolemy. Firestone Library, Princeton University.

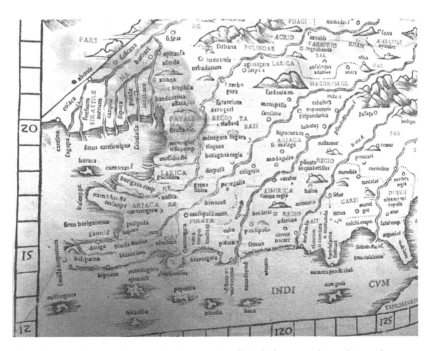

Fig. 0.2 Detail from Claudius Ptolemy's *Claudii Ptholomaei Alexandrini Liber geographiae cum tabulis et uniuersali figura* (1511 ed.) displaying the region *Piratae* between *Ariaca* and *Limirica*. B911. 3 P951.Rare Book & Manuscript Library, Columbia University in the City of New York.

8   Introduction: Reading Piracy between the Lines

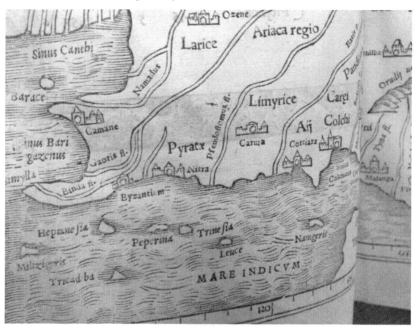

Fig. 0.3 Detail from Claudius Ptolemy's *Geographia vniversalis, vetvs et nova complectens Clavdii Ptolemi Alexandrini enarrationis libros VIII* (1545 ed.) displaying the region *Pyratae*. 1549 P959. Rare Book & Manuscript Library, Columbia University in the City of New York.

The geographical region "Piratae" or "Pirate" reappears in Abraham Ortelius's 1624 edition of *Theatri orbis terrarum parergon*, dedicated to the Spanish King Philip IV. Following the precepts proposed in the Greek historian Lucius Flavius Arrianus's descriptions (c86–140 CE) and Ptolemy's model, Ortelius located this region close to Lymirica in a 1597 map (Fig. 0.4) that describes the wanderings of Ulysses (Ortelius 1624).[18] Another map, 1598 (Fig. 0.5), depicting the old itineraries of Mark Welser ("Marco Velsero"), displays the region of "Pirate" at the northern part of the island of Taprobane, today's Sri Lanka (*id.* 1624).[19] This map depicts the Roman imperial roads and posts from Europe and North Africa to Asia. The region "Pirate" is located at the eastern limit of the Roman Empire. In Ortelius's case, the region "Piratae" or "Pirate" appears to be part of the Roman Empire's past, and corresponds to the Roman efforts to territorialize and expand their dominions. However, it is through late cartographical representations that the "Piratae" region becomes a geographical space and in turn becomes charted as part of the Roman hegemony. In the context of the sixteenth century and following Drake's transatlantic pillaging, this book considers that the sedentary nature that once characterized piracy communities traces a "piracy cycle" particular to the Caribbean region.

Fig. 0.4 Detail from Abraham Ortelius's Abrahami Ortelii Theatri orbis terrarvm parergon (1624 ed.). This map, entitled Erythraei Sive Rubri Maris Periplus. Olim ab arriano descriptvs, nvnc vero ab Abrah. Ortelio … (c1597) is included in the section dedicated to Ulysses's wanderings. It displays the region Piratae below Limyrica. B912 Or85 F. Rare Book & Manuscript Library, Columbia University in the City of New York.

10 Introduction: Reading Piracy between the Lines

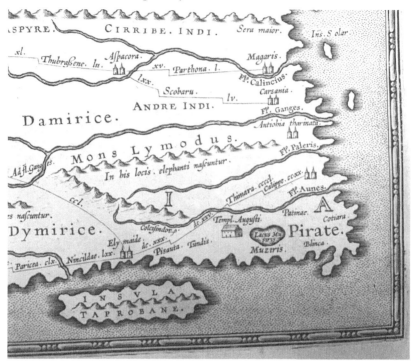

Fig. 0.5 Detail from Abraham Ortelius's *Abrahami Ortelii Theatri orbis terrarvm parergon* (1624 ed.). This map, engraved around 1598, was included in the section of tables of old itineraries (*Tabvla itineraria antiqva*) of Mark Welser ("Marcus Velsero"). It displays the region *Pirate* in the eighth segment (*Segmentvm octavvm*). B912 Or85 F. Rare Book & Manuscript Library, Columbia University in the City of New York.

The notion of piracy cycles was introduced by Philip Gosse in the 1930s and has remained a useful concept in more recent historical scholarship around piracy.[20] According to Gosse, a piracy cycle comprises a fixed story by which piracy starts at the core of disorganized and independent groups as a means of making profit, usually because they have no other economic or social choices. Later on, their success attracts the attention of other individuals who decide to join them and invest in buying larger vessels and resources. The peak of the cycle arrives when these societies manage to establish a social and political structure that holds marginal or independent economic power. Gosse argues that the two possible outcomes are: (1) the legitimation of their power by the corresponding authorities, or (2) the disintegration of such communities and their ultimate return to the original small outlawry and disorganized dynamics that once gave birth to a "mercenary navy, paid by plunder."[21] While incorporating Gosse's notion of piracy cycles, the historian Peter Galvin does not explain such cycles in terms of economic and social conditions; rather, he argues that geographical peculiarities foster piratical activities and behaviors.[22] Hence, he states that the Caribbean's insular holography played a major role in piracy because it allowed pirates to take care of their ships, such as the practice of careening, without being troubled by Spanish colonial authorities (Galvin, 84).

Furthermore, while historicizing the evolution of the legal definition of piracy, Rubin registers another piracy cycle stemming from Roman attempts to enforce political hegemony. In this case, pirates were those individuals who became dissidents against the Roman power and thus were denied the right of *postliminium*, or the right to be granted any postwar restitution. As mentioned earlier, the use of the term *peirato* consequently arose as a concept to designate or classify individuals or communities whose religious, economic, and political practices differed from those disseminated by the dominant power. Therefore, at the beginning, the pirate was part of a sedentary community whose marginality emerged from religious, economic, or political discrepancy vis-à-vis the authoritative order. This book incorporates the notion of piracy cycles to register a heterogeneously oriented kind of piracy in the Caribbean that accounts for the chameleon-like nature of the pirate, being considered a smuggler, a trader, an adventurer, or a maritime predator according to the specific agenda underlying the primary source that describes piracy attacks. This book, moreover, traces an inversion of the paradigm of piracy cycles as it registers the process through which pirates went from being transatlantic individuals attached to a specific royal regime, in the sixteenth century, to becoming marginal and outlaw figures who established sedentary communities in the Caribbean islands during the seventeenth century.

This book will advance our understanding of the cultural history of early modern piracy in three ways. First, by focusing on the language and vocabulary employed by imperial, national, and especially colonial stakeholders to describe piracy, it will tackle the multifaceted and elastic quality of the concept of piracy. Recent studies variously have explored the rhetorical dimensions of piracy, its imperial context, and the characters of the main subjects. Bridging the disciplines of history and literature, Emiro Martínez-Osorio (2016) focuses on the role of piracy in epic and heroic poetry projects produced in Spanish America to support an elite class constituted by earlier conquistadors and settlers; Barbara Fuchs (2001, 2013) traces the mimetic correspondences in Anglo-Spanish imperial narratives and the figures of the renegade and the privateer in the European landscape; and Claire Jowitt (2010) centers on the transformations of the descriptions of English and non-Hispanic maritime predators contingent to specific English projects of nationhood and empire. More recently and through the insertion of Drake's figure in the debate of what Rolena Adorno (2007) calls "the polemics of possession," María Gracia Ríos Taboada (2021) showcases the ways in which both English and Spaniards authors exploited the same rhetorical devices and literary references to achieve specific agendas. For instance, stressing the complex Anglo-Spanish dynamics of discursive exchange and translations, Ríos Taboada demonstrates that by following the Spanish narrative models intended to justify their presence in the Americas, the English articulated Drake's image as a "corrected" or improved version of Spanish conquistadors (2021, 21).

Combining these geographical and methodological approaches, this book proposes that, while the Caribbean lacked some of these categories, it nonetheless was the stage for essential geopolitical struggles between Spain and England in the Atlantic, allowing us to appreciate the flaws and strengths of imperial narratives of power during this period. I focus on the dyad of pirate/corsair because these are the predominant categories found in Hispano-Caribbean and English historical documentation and literature at the time. Second, although scholars have proposed global approaches to the study of piracy from both a multiregional and an interdisciplinary lens, they have nonetheless framed transatlantic piracy as an asymmetrical relationship between European powers and colonial territories. My analysis emphasizes the impact of the Caribbean region as the common denominator of European and American interactions that transformed the conceptualization of piracy itself. Third, traditional histories of piracy presume that their object of analysis is more stable than it was, and thus, scholars tend to define piracy as solely a consequence of European rivalries. My book refocuses this scholarship by proposing a new explanation that regards piracy as an unstable category. Its ambiguity was exploited as a rhetorical weapon to advance both the collective and individual aspirations of imperial and marginal agents. The book proposes that the period 1570–1604 is crucial to understanding the malleability of the discourse on piracy; I argue that this period ended as the political conditions shifted with the cessation of hostilities between England and Spain. It was followed by more settled models of Caribbean piracy, such as the buccaneers and filibusters, closer to our modern understanding of the ruthless and nationless figure of the pirate.

Chapter 1, "Navigating Conflicting Waters: Francis Drake's Circumnavigation (1577–80)," focuses on the relation between piracy, property, and the geographical space represented in English and Spanish cultural productions of the sixteenth century. I examine English chronicles by Samuel Purchas and William Camden, comparing them with Spanish diplomatic correspondence, as well as visual imagery (maps and portraits) that celebrate—and occasionally debate—Drake's legacy after his circumnavigation. The chapter charts the cultural construction Drake's image as a "knight of the seas" and the way piracy became an ambivalent spatial category that reformulated the parameters of property and space as Drake opened up the possibility of English maritime domination.[23] Moving to another transatlantic attack by Drake, Chapter 2, "Setting Sails to the Narrative of Piracy: Francis Drake's Caribbean Raid (1585–86)," builds on the fact that although the intermittent military conflict between England and Spain lasted almost two decades (1585–1604), Drake's first Caribbean raid started within the framework of an as-yet-undeclared open war between Spain and

England. Through the analysis of Richard Hakluyt's *Principall Navigations* (1598–1600 edition), Walter Bigges's travelogue *A Summarie and True Discourse of Francis Drake's West Indian Voyage* (1589), and Juan de Castellanos's heroic poem *Discurso del capitán Francisco Draque* (c1587), the chapter examines the narrative mechanisms employed by Spanish colonial and English authors who ultimately took advantage of Drake's raid to craft imperial narratives of power and insert the West Indies into the larger Anglo-Spanish conflict.

Chapter 3, "Dangerous Representations of the Caribbean in the Sixteenth Century," explores how, from scholarly work to contemporary popular culture, the Caribbean islands remain a mythical space characterized by foreign agents who undertake unlawful practices driven by economic scarcity, political incompetence, and the absence of traditional continental frontiers. However, such a conception calls for a different cultural narrative that reexamines the rhetorical devices employed by early modern authors within the context of the global eagerness of European imperial expansions and rivalries. This chapter analyzes the articulation of European territorial claims in cartographical representations of the Caribbean archipelago and the sixteenth-century geopolitical consequences of such assertions.

Following the end of Drake's career as a maritime predator, Chapter 4, "Dropping Anchor: Sir Francis Drake's Three Deaths and the Beginning of an End," analyzes the aftermath of the defeat of King Philip II's Armada (1588) and Sir Francis Drake's last Caribbean raid (1595–1596), when the Spanish released inaccurate historical accounts of Drake's whereabouts. Besides these factually inconsistent reports, several Spanish poems and ballads distorting Drake's image were published. The English claimed that these defamed Drake, employing the terms "lies" and "libels." This chapter traces the correlation between piracy and libel by demonstrating that the English accusations showcased an entangled narrative—stressing the Spaniards' moral misbehavior, financial ambitions, and military weakness—that ultimately reproduced the Spanish rhetorical model for describing Drake's maritime and territorial predation in Spanish America in the sixteenth century.

Chapter 5, "The Changing Winds of Piracy (1570–1604)," highlights the flexibility of the category of piracy through comparative analysis of sixteenth- and early seventeenth-century primary sources, such as European and colonial legal treatises, historical accounts, royal documents, and Caribbean epic poetry. The chapter demonstrates that the plasticity of the concept of piracy stems from an entanglement of the economic, political, legal, and religious realms. Considering seventeenth-century treatises against piracy and juridical agreements between England and Spain that took place after the deaths of Drake, Philip II, and Queen Elizabeth I, the chapter registers the legal standardization of piracy and its repercussions in the Caribbean. Through the analysis of Spanish peninsular (sometimes called "Iberian") settlers and Caribbean-born authors, the chapter traces the adoption of picaresque undertones to justify piracy and rationalize its prevalence.

Chapter 6, "The Aftermath: The Emergence of New Models of Piracy in the Caribbean: Buccaneers and Freebooters," discusses the emergence of a new pattern of imperial competition in the Caribbean. After the establishment of peace between King James I (1603–25) and King Philip III (1598–1621) in 1604, new categories of piracy such as Buccaneers and Filibusters emerged due to the lack of efficient Spanish policing. In one trend, former English maritime predators, having lost their private income, joined Barbary corsairs in the Mediterranean. In another, individuals like Captain Henry Mainwaring were hired by the English Crown to police and capture their former accomplices. In the Caribbean, Dutch and French sailors who had previously engaged in contraband trade, mostly related to the illegal purchase of tobacco and salt, continued to carry out their illegitimate businesses. However, due to the lack of efficient Spanish policing, they encountered an even more geopolitically divided Caribbean marked by the increasing establishment of English, French, and Dutch individuals on several islands. The conclusion discusses the emergence of a new pattern of imperial competition as these nations made the Caribbean archipelago their main base of operations, eventually claiming sovereign territories.

Overall, *Cultural Representations of Piracy* demonstrates how English, Spanish, and Caribbean individuals and institutions used "the pirate" as a dynamic concept with constantly changing meanings to define and question the boundaries of property, space, and sovereignty in the configuration of geopolitical identities and European imperial narratives of power. The broad cast of pirates—as patriots and even heroic figures, enemies, traitors, travelers, or traders—illustrates the lack of a unanimous conception of the phenomenon and elucidates the tensions that permeate the narrative and visual cultures produced around English Caribbean raids. This work chronologically registers the process by which piracy went from being an unregulated phenomenon to becoming legally defined after the Treaty of London (1604), to demonstrate that as piracy grew less ambiguous through legal and linguistic standardization, the concept of piracy lost its polemical utility.

More broadly, the book contributes to a growing scholarship that explores how ideas and people circulated across the formal boundaries of empires and nations in the early modern Atlantic world. During the sixteenth century, English pirates of the Caribbean also attacked and torched villages in other Spanish strongholds in America, such as Venezuela, Colombia, and Mexico. Despite the different contexts, writing about piracy shaped and reinforced a collective imagination of the conditions in the New World, in which the Caribbean remained a geographical referent of disarray and chaos marked by the preeminence of piratical events. Drawing on Matejka Volosinov's notion of "multiaccentual," denoting a term whose definition varies according to peoples and times, Sean Johnson Andrews's analysis proposes that:

> Piracy is a perfect example of this problem, particularly because different disciplines often accentuate certain meanings of the term so

that piracy—and the pirate—will fit into their already developed disciplinary framework. And, perhaps more to the point, its long genealogy makes for a chaotic category.

(Andrews 2018, 36)

This book builds upon this premise by tapping into the nuances of piracy to show its condition as a social construct that lies in the eye of the beholder. In all, the early modern manipulation of the discourse on piracy and its unstable quality provides a cultural framework to understand the configuration and limits of national, economic, and political institutions. While pirates and other marginal figures have been the subject of much historical scholarship, this book brings together the rhetorical uses and repercussions found in the descriptions of these characters. In sum, *Cultural Representations of Piracy* unveils the relation between the outlaws and their opposed lawful (or established) communities based on the interpretation of individual and, occasionally, marginal characters who challenge conventional norms or stipulations and affect the development of nations, empires, and sovereignty.

Notes

1 The document containing the agreements of the 1982-UN convention may be found at www.un.org/depts/los/convention_agreements/texts/unclos/unclos_e.pdf.
2 Article 101 defines piracy as "(a) any illegal acts of violence or detention, or any act of depredation, committed for private ends by the crew or the passengers of a private ship or a private aircraft, and directed: (i) on the high seas, against another ship or aircraft, or against persons or property on board such ship or aircraft; (ii) against a ship, aircraft, persons or property in a place outside the jurisdiction of any State; (b) any act of voluntary participation in the operation of a ship or of an aircraft with knowledge of facts making it a pirate ship or aircraft; (c) any act of inciting or of intentionally facilitating an act described in subparagraph (a) or (b)" (Convention on the Law of the Sea at 60–61).
3 Unless otherwise indicated, David Armitage's 2004 edition of *Mare liberum (The Free Sea)* is the source used in this study when quoting the English translation of *Mare liberum*, as well as Welwod's critique and Grotius's response.
4 Grotius's *Mare liberum* (which means *The Free Sea*) was originally the twelfth chapter of *De jure praedae* (*On the Law of Prize and Booty*). The former was published in 1609, but the latter was not released until the nineteenth-century because its content was not considered appropriate by the Dutch East India Company (VOC), founded in 1602, due to the 1609 truce between Spain and the Low Countries. The first English translation of *Mare liberum* was undertaken by Richard Hakluyt between 1609 and 1616. Hakluyt's translation remained unpublished during his lifetime (MS Petyt 529, Inner Temple Library, London). For more about the discussion among Grotius, Freitas, and Selden, see Monica Brito Vieira's article "Mare Liberum vs. Mare Clausum: Grotius, Freitas, and Selden's Debate on Dominium over the Seas" in *Journal of the History of Ideas*, 64(3): 361–377, 2003.
5 Grotius's first mention of the word "pirates" is at the end of the first chapter of *Mare liberum* when asserting the right of commerce held by the Dutch in the East Indies, which is being threatened by the Portuguese: "[T]here is no stronger reason

16 *Introduction: Reading Piracy between the Lines*

underlying our abhorrence even of robbers and pirates than the fact that they besiege and render unsafe the thoroughfares of human intercourse" (Robert Feenstra and Jeroen Vervliet, eds.-trans., *Hugo Grotius Mare Liberum 1609–2009: Original Latin Text and English Translation,* Leiden: Brill, 2009).

6 Armitage argues that Grotius derived this set of natural laws from the divine will (Grotius, xiii). Self-preservation, according to Armitage's analysis, meant to acquire and retain something "useful for life." The process of acquiring and retaining anything legitimately entails physical seizure (*possessio*) and use (*usus*), which lead to ownership (*dominium*) (*id.*).

7 "[D]isputing for the Profits and Interests of his Countrie, hee draw's them into his own partie; and so endeavor's to prove that the Sea is not capable of private Dominion" (Selden, 172).

8 "[T]he very Shores or Ports of the Neighbor-Princes beyond Sea, are Bounds of the Sea-Territoire of the *British* Empire to the Southward and Eastward; but that in the vast Ocean of the North and West, they are to be placed at the utmost extent of those most spacious Seas, which are possest by the *English, Scots,* and *Irish*" (Selden, 459).

9 Lane (2016 [1998], 33). By the same token, Kenneth Andrews locates both pirates and privateers in the years 1570 to 1603, arguing there were not so many adventurers or pirates until 1585 in the Caribbean (K. Andrews, 1978, 135). Drawing on Philip Gosse's methodological approach to piracy cycles, Lane emphasizes the following early modern/privateering cycles: French corsairs (1500–59); Elizabethan corsairs (1568–1603); Dutch and Flemish corsairs (1559–1648); buccaneers of all nations (1671–95); privateers, mostly English (1703–1743); Anglo-American freebooters (1697–1725); and Barbary corsairs (c1453–1830). For a more detailed story of these categories, see the following chapters of Gosse's *History of Piracy*: "The Barbarossas" (Gosse, 10–29), "The Seventeenth Century" (*id.*, 48–69), "The Elizabethan Corsairs" (*id.*, 104–115), and "The Buccaneers" (*id.* 141–175). On the other hand, historian José Bravo Ugarte proposes that the nationalities of maritime predators in the Caribbean correspond to military rivalries between European countries and Spain in four distinct periods. The first period (1521–1524) is dominated by the French, the second (1568–1596) by the English, the third (1621–1650) by the Dutch, and the last one (until 1750) by buccaneers and freebooters (filibusters) who came from different nations and controlled certain strategic places in the Caribbean region (Bravo Ugarte, 286).

10 Claire Jowitt's study highlights several identity shifts attached to specific maritime figures that enclose different categories: "From privateer to pirate (Drake); from merchant-adventurer to enemy of the State (Walter Raleigh); from failed adventurers to national heroes (both Drake and Raleigh); from delinquent pirate to government official (Henry Mainwaring); from pirate to celebrated explorer (Martin Frobisher)" (Jowitt, 33). Even Philip Gosse—more than half of a century ago—pointed out the difficulty of defining piracy in his preface to *The History of Piracy* when citing Webster's definition of a pirate as a "robber of high seas, one who by open violence takes property of another on the high seas," or someone who makes a business out of robbery and plunder. Along these lines, Gosse concludes, "[I]t is hard to determine … whether Francis Drake was a pirate or not" (Gosse, viii).

11 Even though sometimes the terms "corsair" and "privateer" have been used interchangeably, Alfred Rubin in *The Law of Piracy* presents evidence demonstrating that the term "privateer" was not introduced into English legal discourse until the seventeenth century (Rubin, 18).

12 Marcus Rediker, in *Villains of All Nations*, focuses on the "Golden Age" of Atlantic Piracy (1716–1726) through the study of several figures such as "Blackbeard," who turned to piracy after enduring difficult working conditions, and he examines their

Introduction: Reading Piracy between the Lines   17

independent organizational systems and collective communities. Along these lines, Rediker's *Outlaws of the Atlantic* (2014) focuses on the role played by marginal and multiethnic figures, such as sailors and slaves, in conquest and political and economic dominance during the "age of sail" (1500–1850). Primarily concentrating on the late seventeenth to mid-eighteenth centuries, Guy Chet's *The Ocean is a Wilderness* (2014) reveals the limits of British power on both land and sea—as a result of their ineffective anti-piracy campaign—and how this influenced their particular understanding of sovereignty and jurisdiction through the assessment of the early modern state and communities. In contrast, I focus on Drake, who identified himself with Queen Elizabeth I's royal authority, and on the geographical representation of "the islands" during the sixteenth century.

13 According to Rubin, Diodorus Siculus (60 BCE) and Livy (29 BCE) employed the term in the same fashion.
14 Even though the first Latin declension of *insula* (island) in its plural nominative form is *insulae*, here the author may have written *insuli* instead to fit the second-declension pattern of the nominative plural.
15 *Claudii Ptolemaei Geographicae enarrationis libri octo / Bilibaldo Pirckeymhero interprete; annotationes Ioannis de Regio / Monte in errores commissos a Iacobo Angelo in translatione sua.* Published/Created: Argentoragi [Strasbourg]: Iohannes Grieningerus, communibus Iohannis Koberger impensis excudebat, 1525. The maps are the same as in the 1522 edition. Books: South East (RB) EXKA Ptolemy 1525. Firestone Library, Princeton University.
16 The region "Piratae" appears in Table X of Asia in the 1511 edition *Claudii Ptholomaei Alexandrini Liber geographiae cum tabulis et uniuersali figura*, B911.3 P951, held in the Rare Book and Manuscript Collection (RBML) at Columbia University. The same region ("Pyratae") is found in the 1545 edition: *Geographia vniversalis, vetvs et nova complectens Clavdii Ptolemi Alexandrini enarrationis libros VIII*, 1549 P959, held in the same collection. In a 1564 edition translated by Geronimo Ruscelli, the term *pirati* appears in the index but is not depicted in the corresponding map of Asia (*La Geografia Di Clavdio Tolomeo Alessandrino, Nuouamente tradotta di Greco in Italiano Da Ieronimo Rvscelli*, B911.3 P952, RBML, Columbia University).
17 In the context of the Pre-Modern West, Tai argues that "territorialization" is the process by which maps became valuable tools for possessing geographical space. I argue that the process of territorialization of the New World was authorized and legitimized by the terms of Pope Alexander VI's 1493 bull *Inter caetera*, which divided the world beyond the bounds of Europe linearly between Spain (west) and Portugal (east). The line was rearranged by these two countries in Tordesillas, Spain, and ratified by Pope Julius II in 1506 (Brendecke, 160–163).
18 The 1597 map, titled "Erythraei Sive Rubri Maris Periplus. Olim ab arriano descriptvs, nvnc vero ab Abrah. Ortelio ex eodem delneatus," appears in *Abrahami Ortelii Theatri orbis terrarvm parergon*, 1624, printed by Balthasar Moretus, B912 Or85; F, RBML, Columbia University. The map includes a note stating that Ortelius followed Arrianus's descriptions.
19 The 1598 map appears in the "Segmentvm Octavvm" of the *Tabvla itineraria antiqva*. Ortelius based this map on a thirteenth-century map known as the Peutinger Table, now held in the Vienna National Library.
20 Gosse introduced this concept in *The History of Piracy*, New York: Tudor Publishing Co., 1934, 1–10.
21 For more about this description of the piracy cycle, see J.L. Anderson's article "Piracy and World History" (1995).

22 For more about Galvin's piracy cycles, see *Patterns of Pillage: A Geography of Caribbean-based Piracy in Spanish America, 1536–1718* (1999).
23 Regarding this notion of "knight of the seas" that I explore in Chapter 1, Marco Nievergelt—drawing on Jennifer Goodman's study of the role played by chivalric values in colonial writing related to exploration and colonization—argues that the rebranding of "Drake as an errant knight in his quest reveals the malleability of chivalric rhetoric and imagination, often reinvented to articulate new experiences of exploration and discovery" (Nievergelt, 58).

1 Navigating Conflicting Waters

Francis Drake's Circumnavigation (1577–1580)

The English Captain Francis Drake: Birth of a Maritime Knight

Captain Francis Drake sailed the world for three years (1577–1580), commanding a fleet under the flag of his native land, England. When he finally returned to the harbor of Plymouth, bearing treasure plundered from Spanish ships and colonies, his queen, Elizabeth I, was so impressed that she had his flagship, the *Golden Hind*, moved into the Thames River near Deptford so that everyone would remember the captain's great deed—not the capture of the treasure (which was kept a state secret), but his feat of sailing around the world. The vessel was moored as a public icon for the perpetual memory of Drake's deed. Soon afterward, the queen had Drake knighted in an unconventional ceremony: it took place on his ship, with so many attending that the small bridge by which they boarded collapsed under the weight of the multitude. More than a hundred persons fell into the Thames (Stow, 9). That same day, many verses were recited praising and honoring the newly dubbed Sir Francis Drake in front of his ship. Unlike some nobles and officials of the royal court, who wished to reject Drake's spoils, the commoners applauded him with all praise and admiration.

Drake's celebrated deed was to be the first captain to sail around the globe and, unlike Ferdinand Magellan, survive to tell the story.[1] The scene described earlier—found in William Camden's *Annales the True and Royal History of the Famous Empresse Elizabeth*—was written more than two decades after the event when, according to the English historian, the ship was still standing there "where to this houre the body thereof is seene" (Camden, 426).[2] I stress the narrative importance given to the ship because, in my opinion, it became a distinctive benchmark of Drake's career that inaugurated his close relationship with maritime space. The description of Drake's knighting ceremony brings forth the convoluted jurisdictional relationship between land and sea, where he stood allegorically as a "Sir" of the latter. By becoming a "knight of the seas," Drake figured in the discussion about the construction of maritime jurisdictions that remained under European debate until the Peace of Westphalia was enforced during the second half of the next century. The various historical and literary representations

DOI: 10.4324/9781003141495-2

of Drake's behavior and his rapport with both land and sea hindered the stable characterization of this historical figure. Exploring the particularities of Drake as a social construct, the first part of this chapter focuses on the representations, omissions, and inclusions of Drake's knighting scene and his ship as a monument for remembrance in different textual and visual environments. As we shall see, the puzzle of Drake—constituted by his malleable portrayals as a "thief" or "hero," "plunderer" or "adventurer"—demonstrates the famous/infamous character of the captain. Such a dichotomy, which also corresponds to the shift in the status of discoverers and adventurers of his time, contributed to the process of distinguishing the conquest and possession of both maritime and land spaces over the last two decades of the sixteenth century. The second part of this chapter touches on the subsequent atmosphere of secrecy created around Drake's collected booty, the visual and narrative details about the expedition, as well as the Spanish efforts to prevent the English from acquiring navigational information about the Strait of Magellan, and thereby bridges the notions of cosmography and property that accentuated the Anglo-Spanish rivalry. In this process, I will explore several strategies of claims and counterclaims that relied on the construction of "imaginary geographies" and emphasized the spatial aspect that structured the concept of piracy.

The representation of Drake's ship permeated cultural registers related to the articulation of the Englishman's fame in light of pre-imperial ambitions. Camden's description of the ship and the knighting scene is included in Samuel Purchas's compilation, *Purchas His Pilgrimes* (London 1625).[3] In the introductory letter to Volume 4, the author mentions Drake's *Golden Hind*, stressing the fact that it was preserved as a material-eternal memory of his fame and exploits:

> Sir Francis Drake a Ministers sonne, after a happy inuironing of the Globe, feasted Queene Elisabeth aboord his Argo, and then *laid her vp at Deptford, deuoting her Carkasse to Time*, Her (or rather his) exploits to Fame and Eternitie.
>
> (emphasis added)

Through an analogical comparison, Purchas fashions Drake and himself as pilots and parallels Drake's galleon with his book, considering them both tangible memories for future generations. He proposes that his compilation be laid up in the "Libraries of Saint James, Yorke-house, Westminster, and Lambith" just as the queen ordered Drake's ship to be laid up at Deptford to remember his deed.[4] Although Purchas's compilation includes four later English circumnavigations, in this letter he does not allude to any of them—perhaps because Drake's was the first and his ship the only one preserved for the sake of posterity, or because he was ultimately the only "Sir" knighted onboard. However, another question remains: Why does Purchas equate himself with Drake—as a pilot—and his compilation of travel narratives with the captain's deeds?

Purchas's parallelism underpins two main notions of the time: the growing status held by pilots and the increased interest in collecting and weaponizing cosmographical information. For instance, even before Drake's return from his circumnavigation, Purchas's mentor Richard Hakluyt proposed the importance of controlling the Strait of Magellan.[5] In the third volume's dedicatory of the second edition of his *Principall Navigations* (1599–1600), addressed to the queen's secretary Robert Cecil, Hakluyt stresses that the English must publish the secret Spanish navigations (Ríos Taboada 2017, 165–67). Regarding the binomial of hero/cartographer, the Spanish author Juan de Miramontes (1567–1610) in his epic poem *Armas Antárticas* (finished around 1609), depicts Drake as a sort of cosmographer, insinuating "that cosmography could be weaponized against threats to the Spanish Empire" and thus, "cosmographer-pilots could be considered heroic in their own right" (McCloskey 2020, 179).[6] Along these lines, Leo Braudy's comprehensive study of fame demonstrates that the advent of printing prompted mapmakers and engravers, such as Hendrik Hondius and Gerardus Mercator, to portray themselves as heroes as well as those captains who, like Drake, became discoverers (Braudy, 303). In this regard, Purchas's comparison evinces the emerging perception of the hero that encapsulated the individuals who navigated and compiled cosmographical information based on their experiences *ad hoc* along with those armchair travelers who collected and assembled their narratives.

Historians have argued about Drake's portrayal as a "famous" or "infamous" character, yet I am interested in understanding how this binomial related to the notion of piracy as a malleable signifier that permeated both Spanish peninsular and Spanish American cultures. While Drake might have been widely considered an infamous character and antihero by his contemporaries in English and Spanish eyes, this figure was also attached to specific shifts in English identity whereby "merchants" of the sixteenth century transitioned to becoming "gentlemen" during the next century. According to Jowitt's study, the portrayal of Drake's circumnavigation was modified and transformed to produce these two notions of "Englishness." On the one hand, we find that Hakluyt in the sixteenth century emphasized the "merchant" aspect of Drake's actions as a means to put forward an imperialistic propaganda and promote a "mercantile nationalism" that criticized the Spanish closed markets in their transatlantic and transpacific territories (Helgerson 187).[7] In this way, as Jowitt remarks, under Elizabeth's reign "the strategic value of piracy was recognized as the Queen authorised expeditions that ostensibly were to develop and expand trade routes, but in reality, were aimed at attacking foreign—especially Spanish—shipping" (Jowitt, 36–37). In the next century, the revamping of Drake's story about his circumnavigation by his nephew Drake "the Younger" entailed the introduction of other behavioral patterns linked to "quasi-chivalric" attitudes and "knightly venture, instead of commercial venture" (*id.*, 48). On the other hand, María Gracia Ríos Taboada argues that Drake was seen by his contemporary fellowmen as potential reformatory agent of Elizabethan social hierarchies after his circumnavigation which resulted in the depiction of Drake as both a mercantile hero and conqueror (2021, 72).[8] Building upon these arguments, it is not surprising, then, to find seventeenth-century authors such as Purchas—Hakluyt's protégé—and Camden emphasizing Drake's knighting scene as a pivotal accomplishment in the captain's career and his galleon as a memorial of English achievements to support a notion of "Englishness" and its potential pre-imperial aspirations.[9]

Whereas the ship and the water epitomize the symbolic level of Drake's title, it is worth noting that he nevertheless had to buy Buckland Abbey to fulfill the requirements of becoming a knight, as stressed by the Spanish ambassador to England, Bernardino de Mendoza.[10] Several months later, he was appointed Lord Mayor of Plymouth, becoming one of the biggest landowners of Plymouth along with the Hawkins family and the Plymouth Corporation.[11] Drake's knighting ceremony brought forth the struggle of defining the power of ownership over land and sea: the Spanish ambassador and a great number of noblemen were not pleased with either the ceremony or the celebration. In several letters to his king, Philip II, Mendoza employed the phrase "Drake's theft" (*el robo de Draques*) instead of "Drake's voyage" and reminded Philip that he had been working on the retrieval of the goods stolen by Drake's fleet during the circumnavigation.[12] The fact that Drake was knighted onboard in 1580 speaks to an emerging cultural geography marked by maritime flow and circulation. In this regard, the knighting scene also foreshadows future English endeavors aiming to challenge Spanish-controlled routes of commerce and exploration.[13]

During the sixteenth century, however, Drake's knighting scene and the importance attributed to his ship as monument for remembrance were omitted in several English sources, such as Hakluyt's compilation and Raphael Holinshed's *Chronicles of England, Scotland, and Ireland* (published in 1587).[14] In this latter case, only two paragraphs described Drake's voyage to Hispaniola (modern-day Haiti and the Dominican Republic), and Chile and the discovery of Nova Albion and Elizabeth's Island (Holinshed, 1554–1555). The following pages, 1556 through 1574, were missing from Holinshed's book. It was not until 1808, when Sir Henry Ellis published an enlarged version of Holinshed's *Chronicles*, that the excisions, which had been ordered by the Privy Council in 1587, were reincorporated.[15] Holinshed's uncut edition states that "in memorie of this gentlemans incomparable atchievement, some monument might remaine to succeeding ages: and none fitter than the brittle brake wherein he arrived safe and sound" (Holinshed 1808, 908). Afterward, he mentions that some unknown knight thought it would be appropriate to put Drake's ship "upon the stumpe of Paule's steeple in lieu of the spire" so that everyone could see it and say: "Yonder is the barke that hath sailed round about the world."[16] At the end of this section about Drake, Holinshed included several verses praising his deed and the fact that he ultimately brought glory to his country (*Perficit et patriae servit*). Although he did not delve into the details of the knighting scene, the uncensored edition portrayed Drake as a "worthy knight," underscoring his fame "in places far and neere" and describing how he was received with rejoicing at his return:

> [A]fter his arrivall and being in London, manie did flocke about him in the open streets, with admiration as a worlds woonder: yea the reports of his exploits abrode did so ravish their minds, that leaving preacher and sermon, they ran apace to behold him …
>
> (*id.*, 907)

Despite the moral concerns and judgmental reactions to his exploits, everyone left "preacher and sermon" and acknowledged his deed.[17] Thus, Drake's figure stood on a thin line that distinguished the plunderer from the adventurer. In this regard, as Jowitt demonstrates through her analysis of Drake's portrayal as found in Hakluyt's writings, "'piracy' is imaginatively recreated as a type of patriotic trade rather than illegal plunder; it is not seen as antiethical and disruptive, but rather as central, to England's imperial and commercial project" (Jowitt, 66). Holinshed's rhetorical move tinged Drake's voyage and plunder with wisdom and experience that brought wealth and richness: "And surelie as wisdome with experience is purchased by travelling; so wealth and worship is thereby obteined." The author went further and quoted the Biblical king and prophet David: "[T]hey that go downe to the sea in ships, and occupie their business in great waters: these men see the works of the Lord, and his woonders in the deepe" (Holinshed 1808, 908). Despite Holinshed's attempt to glorify Drake's expedition, to minimize his plunder, and to justify his actions through the appeal to religious figures, these parts were suppressed from the text. Another antiquarian and chronicler, John Stow—who edited the 1587 edition of Holinshed's *Chronicles*—did report Drake's knighting scene, but without commenting upon the greatness that supposedly surrounded Drake's figure, in *A Summary of the Chronicles of Englande*, published in 1590. Interestingly, after succinctly mentioning Drake's departure on page 690,[18] he recounts on the next page that seven pirates were hanged in Wapping, the place where pirates were commonly executed by orders of the Admiralty Court. Eleven pages further on, he describes the knighting scene on Drake's galleon and recounts the incident of the people who fell from the bridge:

> The 4. Of Aprill, the queene dined at Deepford, and after dinner entred the ship wherein Drake had sailed about the world, and being there, a bridge that her maiestie came over, brake, being upon the same more than 200 persons, and no hurt done by the same, and there she did make captaine Francis Drake knight in the same ship.

So far, this description remains the closest to the actual event as reported by Camden and Purchas 35 years later.[19] According to John Mack's cultural history of the sea, beaches and ports are "points of interaction between the maritime and terrestrial" characterized by the presence of liminal characters who "have become disconnected from the set of rules which sustained them in the world they have left behind" (Mack, 165). Along these lines, he argues that a port can also be understood as a "transgressive extension of the land. They are the scene of behaviours which are distinctively different either from those aboard ship or further inland" (*id.*). Ships, on the other hand, when brought to a terrestrial setting, could assert an "ideal of communal fellowship and aspiration on land" (*id.*, 203).[20] We find these elements in the representation of Drake's knighting scene: a vessel docked in a port that collapsed and a sailor being knighted on the ship. This combination embodies the celebration of an English community empathizing with transgressive navigational and commercial practices, which in turn suggests the consolidation of a liminal identity related intermittently to both land and sea. In this sense, the narrative repetition of the scene emphasizes and projects the foundation of a maritime society—in land—and the aspiration of its expansion beyond the Atlantic.

Two years after Stow's publication, the knighting scene was roundly criticized in a pamphlet attributed to the English Catholic Richard Verstegan, printed 1592 in Antwerp. Titled *A Declaration of the True Causes of the Great Troubles* ... the document attacks the English Protestant faith by denominating it as the "most repugnant to the old Catholic faith, participant of some newe heresies" (Verstegan, 12).[21] In line with the former Spanish ambassador, Verstegan's narrative casts Drake as the "fitest man to achieve an enterprize of stealing" (*id.*, 26). His brief description of the circumnavigation underscores the English spoils-taking as opposed to the good faith of the Spaniards, in the port of Valparaiso, who took the English for friends and received them onboard without suspecting their fate: the English took everything they had. While describing Drake's knighting scene on his ship, the author stresses that he was awarded with the honor of knighthood there, not because he used that ship to *circumnavigate* the globe, but because it was the place from which he *robbed* around the world: "he was at *De-ford* rewarded with the honor of knighthoode, and in the same ship, where with he had been abrode aroving" (*id.*, 27). Here the space of the ship acquires an adverse connotation produced by religious and political differences between the powers of Spain and England. The *Golden Hind* metaphorically represents the rupture of the Spanish ideological-imperial fabric as it became the vehicle that enabled the English to harm Spanish subjects, steal their property, and disrupt their commerce in both transatlantic and transpacific scenarios. Verstegan also lamented that Drake was not sent to Wapping, where other pirates had been executed for less. Unlike Holinshed's chronicle, which exalts the adventurer side of Drake's expedition and proposes the ship as the epitome of such a deed, Verstegan accuses Drake of engaging in the "enterprise of stealing," suggesting that the circumnavigation was a false adventure, a plundering service for the queen at a time when no Anglo-Spanish war had yet been officially declared.[22]

By the turn of the sixteenth century, we also find the conformation of physical and virtual geographies that entailed a religious difference to justify such geographies. For instance, within the Caribbean scope, Drake's raids triggered a religious distinction between land and sea, evinced by the superfluous consolidation of honorable terrestrial individuals against the dishonorable English and French maritime identities, as we will see in the next chapter. Theorizing upon the classification of peoples according to the differentiation between land and sea, John Mack argues that these categories should be understood as complementary instead, because "the land/sea categorization is less a distinction deployed statically in cultural contexts and more a fluid generative set of principles in whose synthesis powerful social and cultural imperatives arise" (Mack, 186). The author concludes by stating that the geographical distinction becomes a sociocultural one. The Caribbean scenario showcases such a social-cultural construction in which land and sea became devices to conform oppositional identities based on differing moral and economic values that ultimately served to reinforce allegiances to specific European powers. In official epistles sent to Spain's Council of the Indies (*Consejo de Indias*) by colonial authorities, maritime predators are mainly characterized by their "lack of shame," by their inclination "to steal," and occasionally by their efforts to introduce the "Lutheran sect" in the islands. In contrast, Caribbean individuals are described as "very honorable people committed to defending their fatherland" (*muy honrrada gente y deseosos de defender su patria*) (vol. 5 Alegría, 121 and 437).[23]

In contrast, Nicholas Breton published a laudatory text titled *A Discourse in Commendation of the Valiant as Virtuous Minded Gentleman Mister Frauncis Drake: With a Rejoicing of his Happy Adventures* (1581). Published shortly after Drake's return, Breton stresses the speculation and wonder surrounding the English circumnavigation: "[T]he world may wonder at that which I have not seene: but you have gon thorough. You have run the curse, that I cannot discourse of" (unnumbered). Using Elizabethan euphuistic prose, the author stresses the silence he will keep in order to show his esteem toward Drake: "I will say but what I thinke, and thinke that I cannot say, in commendation of your happy deserts that may well be had in great admiration …" (unnumbered). The narrative mainly revolves around the topic of fame and, in turn, Drake's fame obtained through the circumnavigation:

> Fame tels his wonders, his wonderful prowesse, his worthy praise …. When was this honour wun? In the time of three yeres, last past …. Yet having styl such a natural regard to his native countrey, such a dutifull desire to his soveraignes service, such a careful wyel, to do good to the common welth …
>
> (Breton, 11)

However, Drake's "goodwill" and "dutiful service" to his sovereign queen and the commonwealth—in Breton's representation—are rewarded with his return to England, the pleasure of the queen, the enrichment of her realm, and the admiration of all men (*id.*). The author avoids the use of the words "plunder" or "spoils," and in lieu of them we find the correlation between commonwealth and goodwill toward his "native country" along with richness and fame. Highlighting Drake's achievements without specifying how the booty was acquired, Breton justifies his collected "worldly treasure" through the emphasis placed on the perils and dangers he survived to bring it home (*id.*, 12). A few pages later, Breton admits that he does not have access to any account of the voyage, thus, he might be repeating the common knowledge of Drake's expedition: that he passed "the Gulf" homeward.[24] In this way, the text exploits the concept of fame as a way to speculate about Drake's deeds, substituting it for the necessity of giving an actual account of the facts.[25]

The author's narrative around the captain's deeds, despite his spoils and plunder, reflects a motif related to fame, recurring in Italy by the sixteenth century. According to Burckhardt, this motif emerged as a consequence of the individual's desire to acquire renown and glory in spite of the means and consequences (Burckhardt, 152). Contrasting those who stay on land with Drake's "travails" at sea, Breton declares "let him be abroad," where Drake has gained worldwide fame (Breton, 18–19). Breton's effort to immortalize Drake's figure, as well as Purchas's parallelism between the remembrance of his ship and the importance of his compilation, reproduces what Italian poet-scholars thought about Francesco Petrarch: a "giver of fame and immortality, or, if he chose, of oblivion" (Burckhardt, 151). Purchas's compilation replicates a classical and Italian-Renaissance paradigm at two levels. On one hand, his collection of narratives imitates the model of assembling written collections on famous men and women of their times while on the other, his rationalization of Drake's ship as a place and monument for remembrance reproduces the fourteenth century's emerging interest in recording new topographies where famous leaders, soldiers, or poets dwelled (Burckhardt, 145–147). In this way, the metonymical relation between Drake's ship and his fame, as well as Purchas's book of travels and his reputation, consolidates the articulation of an English maritime identity supported by pre-imperial ambitions for developing commercial ventures and establishing territorial possessions overseas.[26] Fame in this regard becomes a narrative device to overshadow claims of piracy and dissident opinions about Drake's figure; this brings us to the question of piracy understood as a malleable signifier.

But what did Drake think about fame? One of the few documents authored by Drake, is a poem that extolled Sir George Peckham's *True Report* of Sir Humphrey Gilbert's voyage to Newfoundland (1583):

> Who seekes, by worthie deedes to gaine renownme for hire:
>   Whose art, whose purse is prest: to purchase his desire
>   If anue such therebee, that thirsteth after Fame:

> Lo, heere a meane, to winne himself an everlasting name.
> Who seekes, by gaine and wealth t' advaunce his house and blood:
> Who care is great, whose toile no lesse, whose hope, is all for good
> If anie one there bee, that covettes such a trade:
> Lo, here the plot for common weath, and private gaine is made.
> Hee, that for vertues sake, will venture farre and neere:
> Whose zeale is strong, whose practize trueth, whose faith is void of feere,
> If any such there bee, inflamed with holie care.
> Heere may bee finde, a readie meane, his purpose to declare:
> So that, for each degree, this Treatise dooth unfolde:
> The path to fame, the proof of zeale, and way to purchase gold.[27]

I coincide with Ríos Taboada's argument which posits that the actions of a hero, as proposed by Drake in this poem, are less driven by a spiritual quest, as Shields has argued before (103–104), than by the quest of renown, honor, and fame. In other words, Drake emphasized the individualist venture (Ríos Taboada 2021, 83–84). By the same token, and probably perceiving himself as successful hero who, unlike Gilbert, successfully returned to England and claimed two potential English settlements (Nova Albion and Elizabeth island) in the Americas, Drake puts forth a notion of fame that incorporates an economic vocabulary that stressed potential financial profit to secure the relevance of the hero. This notion of the hero is evinced by phrases, such as, "gaine renownme for hire," "to purchase his desire," "Who seekes, by gaine and wealth t' advaunce," "private gaine is made," and "way to purchase gold."

Distinguishing a pirate from an adventurer has a long genealogy rooted in classical notions about maritime navigation and the resulting plundering. Delving into the myths of Odysseus and the Argonauts, Jason McCloskey proposes that "in the absence of any universal definition of piracy" these mythical stories "show that classical thought linked—at times—piracy, commerce, and exploration into one unified venture, and this continued to the early modern period" (McCloskey 2013, 406–407). Such a conceptual amalgam posed a challenge for sixteenth- and seventeenth-century characterizations of figures like Magellan and Drake, for both Spanish and non-Spanish audiences. As McCloskey demonstrates, the Spanish author Miramontes struggled with crafting monolithic representations of both characters in the third canto of his epic poem *Armas Antárticas*, which was finished around 1609 and remained unpublished until the twentieth century (*id.*, 407). Miramontes, a Spanish soldier who after working for the Armada del Mar del Sur settled in Lima, portrayed Drake in a surprising fashion: he suggested that Magellan was Drake's precursor not only in circumnavigating the globe but also in violating the Line of Tordesillas. In relation to this, McCloskey convincingly argues that:

> Drake's narrative poetically converts the theoretical line of demarcation, which was nearly impossible to locate in practice, into a material reality

on the beach in the Philippines. The pirate's unique version of Magellan figuratively suggests that the Portuguese mariner illicitly crossed the line of demarcation in the East Indies, much like Joao III had protested.

(*id.*, 409)[28]

This argument relates to Barbara Fuchs's study on the role of *mimesis* in the conformation of conflicting English and Spanish national ideologies during the sixteenth century (Fuchs 2001, 3–4). The two explorers and circumnavigators of the globe became representative figures of the "destabilizing effects of mimesis on the construction of national differences" (McCloskey 2013, 403). According to Fuchs, "imitation compromises the narratives of national distinction by emphasizing inconvenient similarities and shared heritages" (Fuchs 2001, 4). In the case of Miramontes, piracy remains unstable as his "epic relativizes Drake's actions by shading the distinction between authorized Iberian explorers and unauthorized pirates" (McCloskey 2013, 412). As we have seen, the struggle with providing a non-conflicting portrayal of Drake's circumnavigation does not exclusively pertain to Spanish subjects, but in this sense the Miramontes epic mirrors the heterogeneous English appropriations of the captain.

The omission of Drake's knighting scene and the ship of remembrance in sixteenth-century English chronicles might be directly related to the ideological project of putting forward the image of a "merchant" instead of that of a "gentleman" or knight. However, we find several examples where both notions circulated at the time of Drake's exploits. The crossings of these categories contributed to the complexity and nuances that surround this character. These will be addressed in Chapter 2 through the analysis of Juan de Castellanos's *Discurso del capitán Francisco Draque* (c1587). In what follows, I will delve into the visual culture that disseminated Drake's image, placing him at the intersection of both a "merchant" and a "knight" or "gentleman" and linking the cartographic representation with the portrayal of the captain.

According to Braudy, the sixteenth century staged a "humanist effort to capture a natural image of thought" that also carried the creation of images "meant to convey the iconographic meaning of an individual" without subordinating the viewer (Braudy, 302). This translated into the depiction of royal figures that, instead of looking down to us, seem to look directly to us at the same level as evinced by several portraits of Drake. Despite the English secrecy policies about the voyage, the earliest portrait is a miniature by Nicholas Hilliard with the following inscription: "Aetatis Suae, 42, Ano Domini 1581." A larger and slightly different version of this miniature (Fig. 1.1) is included in Nicola van Sype's printed map (Kelsey, 225). Thomas de Leu, based on a still-unknown painting by French artist Jean Rabel, printed another bust-length engraving of Drake ("1583, age 43") with a shield showing a naval battle scene. The round portrayal, framed by the insistence of his status (*nobilisimus eques Angliae*), is presented along with a

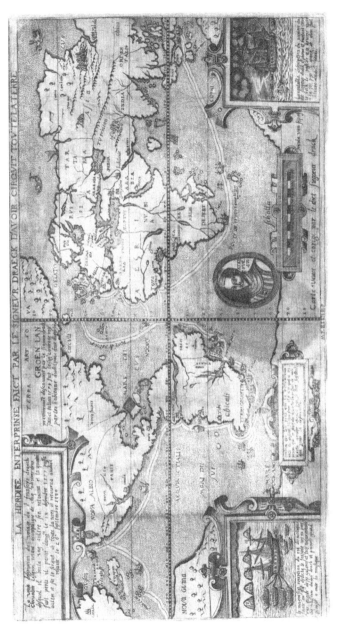

Fig. 1.1 Nicola Van Sype's map of Drake's circumnavigation (c1591). Library of Congress.

description of his greatest deed so far, the circumnavigation of the world. In another anonymous portrait, c1581, Drake's position embodies the correlation between territorial and maritime chivalry, discussed at the beginning of this section: he appears holding a terrestrial globe in his right hand and his sword in the other one. A decade later, Marcus Gheeraerts's painting of 1591[29] (probably based on an earlier one) depicts Drake with the metonymical elements that came to identify his figure: the globe, the sword, the coat of arms, and a jewel given by the queen in 1588. Within the volume titled *Effigies regum ac principum, eorum scillicet* (Cologne 1598), an engraving of Drake, based on a portrait by Hendrik Hondius, appears under the title of the "most noble English knight, very experienced in all things nautical and military." Crispin van de Passe later reproduced this engraving, depicting the captain with a two-hemisphere terrestrial map showing the itinerary of his world voyage. In the seventeenth century (1626), an engraved medallion portrait of Drake appears along with other three circumnavigators—Ferdinand Magellan, Sebastian Elcano, and Oliver van Noort—on the title page of Part IV of Levinus Hulsius's collection of voyages.

The recurrent symbols in Drake's portraits—the ship, the sword, the globe, and his knight status—pinpoint the conformation of his character as "Sir of the Seas." By the same token, the visual representations of ships can be understood as visual metaphors for imperial expansionism (Mack, 207). At that time, royal and noble portraiture also went through a transformation process that demonstrated the growing interest in "the anecdotal and the narrative—an individual's story as much as his unchanging image" (Braudy, 307). In other words, the image of an individual became accompanied by significant scenes of his/her life. Hence, rulers and the nobility were no longer the exclusive protagonists of portraiture because a new "market in faces and reputations" arose during the last decades of the sixteenth century (*id.*, 305). Reproducing the rhetoric of the English chronicles, the portraits also endorse Drake's knighthood built upon his dominion over the maritime space.

Drake's accounts of his voyage are the pieces of a puzzle whose entirety has not survived due to several factors that remain under speculation even today, namely the original purpose of the voyage, the navigational routes undertaken, and the amount of property and booty collected. There are no firsthand accounts of this travel, but in fact, they were all commented upon by clerks, copyists, and interpreters or even censored. Holinshed's *Chronicles* (1587) was recalled and censored; the account of Nuño da Silva—a Portuguese pilot abducted by Drake—was included in Hakluyt's *Principall Navigations*, 1599–1600 edition, without any authorship attributed;[30] and Jan Huygen van Linschoten's *Itinerario*, 1596, had an incomplete version of Da Silva's account. The original manuscript used by Hakluyt to publish Drake's "The Famous Voyage" in the 1589/90 edition of *Principall Navigations* has not been firmly identified.[31] What is clear is that Hakluyt did not plan to include this narrative when he wrote the introductory letter and when he compiled the book. First, he mentions in the letter that the reader would find less information about Drake's circumnavigation because he did not want to spoil the work of another mysterious author who was supposedly compiling a book based on Drake's circumnavigation (Hakluyt, A1–A3).[32] Second, the edition in question includes "The Famous Voyage" without following the pagination, as if he had inserted it after it was printed but before it was publicly circulated.[33] Among the sources that have been identified for Hakluyt's narrative, we find John Cooke's account "For Francis Drake," Francis Fletcher's version (which remained unpublished until *The World Encompassed*, 1628), and an "Anonymous Narrative."[34] Unlike Edward Cliffe's narrative, *The Voyage of M. John Winter into the South Sea by the Streight of Magellan in consort with M. Francis Drake, begun in the year 1577*, both Cooke's account and Hakluyt's narrative stated that the original purpose of the voyage was to reach Alexandria.[35] On the other hand, Camden's account (also published in Purchas's later compilation) omits this and, rather, declares that few people knew their destination.[36] The story of Drake's voyage at the time of his return, filled with uncertainties and speculations, showcases a collective English effort to blur Spanish counterclaims of piracy and stolen goods. As we shall see in the next section, the secrecy also enabled the formulation of arguments and international dissident voices about the right of property, the possession of space, and the control of commercial routes.

From censored and uncensored English chronicles, the Spanish ambassador's letters, the pamphlets, and visual representations, the depiction of Drake's knighting scene, the importance of his ship as a monument of remembrance, and the symbols associated with his circumnavigation unveil an unprecedented kind of knighthood that depends upon the maritime space. In this regard, Drake's knighthood opened up the possibility of dominating the seas and owning the booty collected onboard. As we shall see in the next section, although Spanish goods were despoiled during the voyage, as Mendoza claimed, the atmosphere of secrecy that surrounded the circumnavigation undermined potential piracy claims. The emphasis given to Drake's deed as the new "Sir" of the seas placed him and Magellan side by side. Oscillating between a discoverer and a pirate, Drake's reputation foreshadowed an imperial narrative that underscored his ability to control the seas, eclipsed his controversial attacks, and ultimately added the dominion of maritime space to the equation of territorial conquest.

Society of Speculation and the Anglo-Spanish Rivalry

The circumnavigation triggered divergent reactions in Spain, England, and the New World. From the beginning, the voyage was planned in secrecy; and Drake's return was fraught with mystery and duplicity. A diary and a planisphere, now lost, were handed to the queen, and the collected booty was locked down and guarded by 40 men.[37] Besides the restitution of stolen goods, the Spanish ambassador was interested in knowing if the English had indeed been able to circumnavigate the globe and if so, how they achieved such an enterprise.[38] The queen refused to disclose either the total amount of Drake's booty or his cartographic trajectory. Drake's feat represented an economic threat to Spain, whose property and knowledge were stolen under their very sight, and it undermined Spanish control over the cartographic representation of space.

The circumnavigation informed a growing understanding of cartographic information as property and merchandise that raised international awareness. As Benton argues in *A Search for Sovereignty*, "mapping was another technique for demonstrating possession. Settlements, including forts, were equally important symbols, both demonstrating an intent to occupy and serving as evidence of actual possession" (Benton 2010, 57). Whether Drake's voyage was intended for pillaging or for discovering new commercial routes—as several historians have argued—it certainly points up an Anglo-Spanish rivalry over the control and power of maritime space. Likewise, dominating the seas certainly became the means of dominating people, countries, and commerce. The same year of Drake's return, Flemish geographer Gerardus Mercator wrote to the Royal Cosmographer, Abraham Ortelius, that the only reason he could find to explain why English officials were "carefully concealing the course followed" by Drake and "putting out differing accounts of the route taken and areas visited" was because they must have found "very wealthy regions never yet discovered by Europeans."[39] However, as Portuondo has demonstrated, "at the time of Drake's traversing it, the waterway was poorly known to Spanish cosmographers" (Portuondo, 195). By 1569, when Alonso de Ercilla (1533–1594) wrote his epic poem *La Araucana*, there were speculations about the poor Spanish knowledge of the Strait of Magellan and the possibility of having a closed strait (*secreta senda*) (McCloskey 2020, 174).

Apparently the "secret navigation"—Magellan's route through the Pacific—was uncovered by English sailors.[40] While the English atmosphere of secrecy was intended to deceive the Spanish government by concealing details of the voyage and pretending that nothing significant had happened, such secrecy was internationally perceived to be disadvantageous, as the French Seigneur de la Popelliniere wrote soon after Drake's return.[41] Secrecy also strengthened the ties between space and property because the two principal things concealed were the total amount of Drake's booty and the cartographic information on his trajectory. While the Spanish ambassador attempted to negotiate the recovery of stolen goods by enforcing an agreement for reciprocal return of stolen property, formalized at Bristol in 1579, English authorities did not acknowledge the agreement and he was only able to negotiate the return of government property (Kelsey, 209). Thus, secrecy became a useful vehicle to placate potential piracy claims. In the end, Drake's circumnavigation not only represented an economic threat to Spanish eyes regarding the stolen property, but, as we shall see in the following lines, it challenged their control over the cartographic representation of space and emphasized its potential weaponization. For instance, the Spanish author Juan de Miramontes in his epic poem *Armas Antárticas* (1609) suggested that Drake's cosmographic knowledge came from Spanish sources, thus implying that, whereas gathering enough cosmographic information could countermeasure piracy, it could also become dangerous if placed in the wrong hands (McCloskey 2020, 175 and 182).

The production of maps contemporary with Drake's return was a mode of geographical speculation that in turn gave way to the representation of imaginary geographies to support claims of transatlantic occupation. As mentioned before, Mendoza, the Spanish ambassador, was never able to see the content of the enigmatic Drake's original planisphere; and several historians have argued that, if he'd had the chance, he then would have realized that it did not contain sufficient information to verify the new discoveries being claimed. Another reason for concealing such information might have been the English Crown's intention of securing the booty collected.[42] In relation to imaginary depictions of places supposedly visited by the English, there were several cartographical representations of the islands of the Strait of Magellan. Among these, we find Nicola van Sype's map (Fig. 1.1) from c1591; the map known as the Drake-Mellon map (c1586); Philip Gaulle's map, which appeared in Peter Martyr's *De orbe novo* (1587); and Jodocus Hondius's broadside map (Fig. 1.2) from c1593–1595. The only map that sticks to a verifiable geography is the one included in the manuscript atlas drawn by Joan Martines in 1591 (Kelsey, 129). Another version was Gerardus Mercator's Silver map and a map of Drake's circumnavigation, marked with a dotted line that indicates his journey, that appeared in several texts, such as the title page of Part VIII of De Bry's *Grand Voyages* (in the Latin edition, 1599, and the German edition, 1600), and *The World Encompassed* (1628), among others (Fig. 1.3). Drake's fifth voyage, to the West Indies, is mentioned in a section title of Blundeville's *Exercises* (1613) along with the image of a terrestrial globe. These maps and images underpin how the representation of geographical space along with the figure of Drake—displayed by the insertion of his name or a drawing of his ship—became a means of owning and claiming maritime routes and thus, Spanish booty encountered in such areas. Maintaining the secrecy of such routes—or the contrary, crafting false or imaginary routes—allowed the English to project the seas as a non-Spanish jurisdictional space.

The account of Drake's circumnavigation—written onboard and supposedly by himself—became a coveted object and a political threat. Several witnesses alluded to the existence of Drake's diary—now lost— in specific circumstances, aiming diverse purposes. For instance, to call attention to a potential English threat to Spanish overseas dominion, Ambassador Mendoza declared that Drake had "a diary of everything that happened during the three years and a great map."[43] In the interest of perhaps repeating Drake's expedition and expanding maritime knowledge, Henry of Navarre (later King Henry IV of France) wrote from Paris to Sir Francis

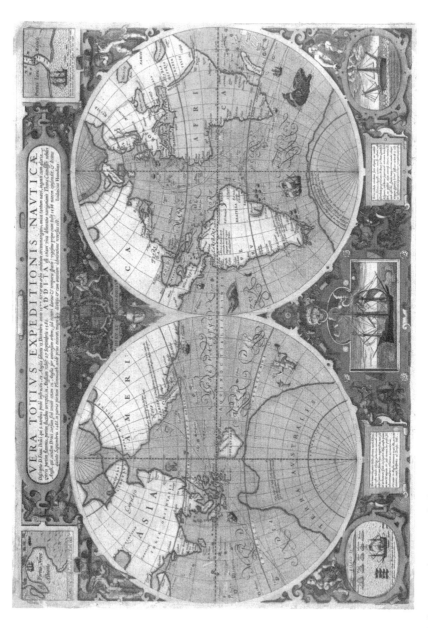

Fig. 1.2. Jodocus Hondius's *Broadside Map* commemorating Drake's and Thomas Cavendish's circumnavigations (c1593–1595). Library of Congress.

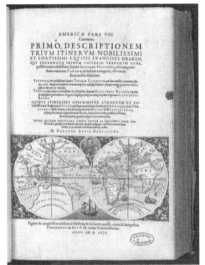 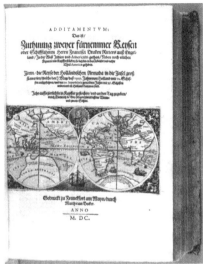

Fig. 1.3 Drake's circumnavigation map in Theodor de Bry's *Grand Voyages*, Latin edition (1599) and German edition (1600). Library of Congress.

Walsingham, Secretary of State, in 1585 asking for the "collection" (of charts) and the "discourse" of Drake's voyage.[44] Two prisoners from that expedition, the Portuguese pilot Nuño da Silva and Francisco de Zárate, were subjected to Spanish interrogation. The former claimed in an inquisitorial deposition that Drake kept a book about his course of navigation in which he depicted birds, trees, and sea lions, whereas the latter stated in a letter that Drake had painters aboard who depicted the shape of every coast.[45] In this regard, both Da Silva and Zárate suggested the existence of Drake's book as a means of evidence to support their own testimonies before the Spanish authorities.[46] As we shall see in a further discussion of the importance of "nautical charts" (*derroteros*), while there were other accounts of this voyage, the emphasis placed on the diary unveils a spirit of inquiry that favors writing onboard over and against writing on land. By the same token, the onboard diary emphasizes Drake's unparalleled circumnavigation of the globe, which, contrary to that of his predecessor supported by the Spanish Crown, stretched the line between piracy and discovery, as discussed in the previous section. For instance, more than three decades later, Peruvian viceroy Don García Hurtado de Mendoza encouraged the *adelantado* Álvaro de Mendaña to start a journey to the Solomon Islands. In so doing, García compared the efforts of past explorers and renowned discoverers such as Christopher Columbus, Hernán Cortés, Francisco Pizarro, and Magellan. He added to the list the English followers or "imitators" of Magellan. In line with Fuchs's argument on mimetic Anglo-Spanish relations, he did not praise the "imitators," such as Drake and Hawkins, like the others;

rather, he considered them the ones who came to "disturb and trouble" the seas: "Drake, Cavendish, and Hawkins, followers of Magellan, were very brave (one cannot deny it) because by navigating from North to South the Strait that bears the name of the latter, they came to trouble the seas that before were safe and pacific."[47] Thus, even in the following century, Drake's circumnavigation remained *sui generis* since it brought back the continuing debate between legitimate adventure and piracy, which in turn contributed to the sixteenth-century conceptualization of territorial and maritime space as property.

Not only was dominance over the seas at stake for the English Crown, but also the imaginary geography became a supportive strategy for backing the new claims to islands and territories supposedly discovered by Drake.[48] These problematic islands—among which was Elizabeth's Island ("Insula Elizabethae")—functioned as a means of postulating that Drake was the captain who had navigated farther south than any other sailor.[49] It is worth noting that Nuño da Silva confirms the fact that Drake reached to the southern end of the American continent but he did not mention any discovery or the taking of possessions of any island (Ríos Taboada 2021, 100). The real existence of these islands continued to be a cartographic issue and cause of dispute until the beginning of the seventeenth century (García-Redondo, 441–478). To the islands on the south side of the Strait of Magellan, Francis Fletcher gave the name *Terra australis bene cognita*, and Elizabeth's Island was the name he gave to the southernmost of that group. The group also appears as Drake's Islands in the southern hemisphere of Hulsius's map from 1602 (Fig. 1.4).[50] In the first printed edition of Sir Walter Raleigh's *History of the World*, 1614, the English explorer alludes to a conversation he had with Pedro Sarmiento de Gamboa while the latter was his prisoner in England (Book II, Chapter 23, section 4). Characterizing Sarmiento as "a worthie Spanish Gentleman, who had beene employed by his King in planting a Colonie vpon the Streights of Magellan," Raleigh states that he asked him about the island discovered by Drake in the Strait. Sarmiento replied that it should have been named "the Painters wives land," because "whilest the fellow drew that Map, his wife sitting by, desired him to put in one … for her; that she, in imagination, might haue an Island of her owne" (Raleigh, 574). In María Ríos Taboada's convincing opinion, the inclusion of this conversation discredits Drake's discoveries in the southern continent during his circumnavigation inasmuch as it suggests that Drake's map was more intended to satisfy the imperial desires of his queen than to support his claims of discovery (Ríos Taboada 2017, 167). Building upon this argument, I would like to pinpoint that Raleigh recounted this conversation with Sarmiento when discussing the "fictions" or "conjectures" found in maps from antiquity:

> Therefore the fictions (or let them be called conjectures) painted in Maps, doe serue only to mislead such discouerers as rashly beleeue them;

Navigating Conflicting Waters 37

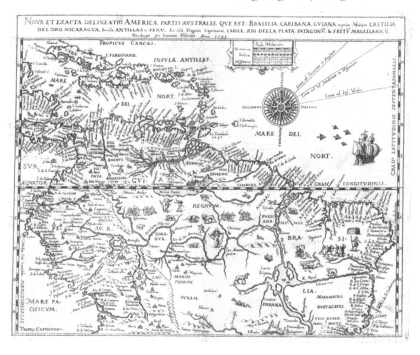

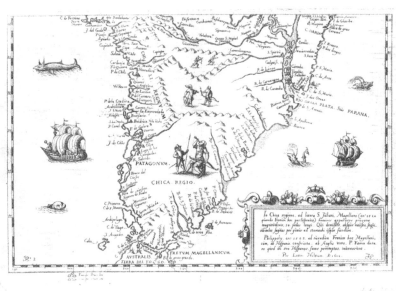

Fig. 1.4 Drake's islands in the southern hemisphere of Levinus Hulsius's map *Nova et exacta delineatio Americae partis avstralis. qve est: Brasilia, Caribana, Gviana regnùm noũum, Castilia del Oro, Nicaragva, insũlae Antillas et Perv. Et sub Tropico Capricorni, Chile, Rio della Plata, Patagonṽ, & Fretṽ Magellanicṽ* (1602). Library of Congress.

drawing vpon the publishers ... some angry curses, or well deserued scorne; but to keepe their own credit, they cannot serue always.

(Raleigh, 574)

Whereas Raleigh seemed to acknowledge the dangers of mapping "fictions," he stated that historians, like himself, did not need to be so exact or "scrupulous" when "filling vp the blankes of old Histories," because "it is not to be feared, that time should runne backward, and by restoring the things themselues to knowledge, make our conjectures appear ridiculous" (*id.*). Thus, Raleigh's position toward mapping practices of his time remains ambiguous, oscillating between the acceptance of conjectures or fictions and the historical truth.

What becomes clearer in Raleigh's fragment is the usefulness of speculative geographies and claimed places that enabled the entanglement between geography and property at two levels. On one hand, the claim that islands provided support for future English territorial establishment in the New World whereas, on the other hand, the representation of these islands articulated a different understanding of the ties between cartographic representation and property. Maps showed that the English Crown was advancing its quest of conquering new territories—whether real or imaginary— and they became valuable merchandise within the international speculation about England's economic power. Even the queen, Elizabeth I, used the term "imaginary property" to refer to Philip II's power overseas. According to Camden's narrative, when the Spanish ambassador complained about Drake's voyage and pillaging, she answered that she did not owe any obedience to the pope, who administered the lands of the New World, and added: "So that by vertue of such donation of other mens goods which in equitie is nothing worth, and of this *proprietie that is merely imaginary*, he cannot iustly hinder other Princes to negotiate in those Regions" (emphasis added) (*id.*, 429). She continued, stating that it was not against the "Lawes of Nations" to bring colonies into unoccupied areas and claiming that "the use of the Seas as of the Ayre is common to all, and publique necessitie permits not it should be possessed; that there is nor people, no particular, that can challenge or pretend any right therein" (*id.*). Two main inferences arise from the queen's discourse that link piracy with the potential colonization of unoccupied geographies. First, piracy rhetorically becomes the right of free navigation and "negotiations" (commerce). Second, such "free navigation" and "negotiation"— implying piracy and contraband—are the means of seizing territorial ownership by questioning who is entitled to such territorial possession overseas and the control upon commerce. In this regard, the queen's speech transformed the common notion associated with the pirate, as "the enemy of all," into an explorer of unclaimed territories "common to all."

Drake's discovery of Nova Albion in the upper part of California remains inconclusive because it is not yet clear if he actually arrived on the continent or if the accounts refer to an island.[51] Also, there is no other document but Hakluyt's

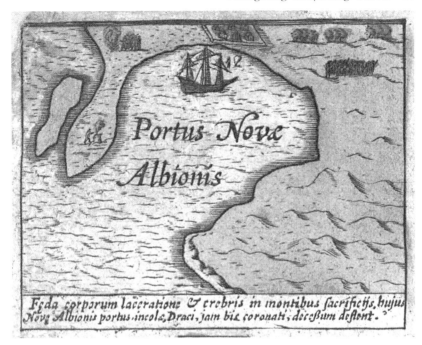

Fig. 1.5 Jodocus Hondius's depiction of Drake's Nova Albion (c1590). Library of Congress.

that records the event. Actually, there is no other account of the trajectory taken from Guatulco to Plymouth because Nuño da Silva's testimony ends when he was released from captivity in Guatulco. According to Ríos Taboada's analysis, Hakluyt might have taken advantage of this lack of information to concoct a narrative in which Drake emerges as a conqueror that follows the structure of previous Spanish texts to fill the blanks of the story of this trajectory (Ríos Taboada 2021, 108–110).[52] Hakluyt's narrative (1589) stated that the king of that region conferred his title onto Drake and declared that all the inhabitants of that land were his subjects: "[T]hey made signes to our Generall to sit downe to whom the King, and divers others made several orations, or rather supplications, that he would resigne unto him their right and title of the whole land, and become his subjects."[53] This follows the description of how the king put his crown on Drake's head and Drake accepted the crown and a scepter in the name of Queen Elizabeth. Just as Drake's ship was considered a monument—as discussed in the previous section—Drake decided to leave a monument of Queen Elizabeth's right over that territory: a plate engraved with the date of his arrival and the queen's name, a piece of English currency, and Drake's name.[54] This scene of coronation, analogous to the knighting scene, nuanced the distinction between a pirate and an adventurer because Drake became a "Sir of the seas" and a discoverer—supposedly made king.[55]

Even if Drake's ceremony of possession in Nova Albion might be "imaginary," that would not have mattered to the queen because, in the end, King Philip II's right of ownership in the New World was "imaginary" at two levels: it was decreed by the pope, who had no authority over non-Catholic countries, and it did not define the extent of territory that had not yet been discovered. In this sense, the concealing of information about Drake's voyage and the assembling of maps based on a speculative geography, supposedly discovered by Drake, reproduced the "imaginary property" held by the Spanish king because it opened up geographical space that, as Sarmiento supposedly claimed in Raleigh's story, could not be fully contained in maps or travel accounts.

Sarmiento's abduction, along with his maps and *derroteros*, by Raleigh exemplifies another dimension of commodifying cartographic information. According to Sarmiento, Drake had bought in Lisbon a maritime chart (*una carta de marear de más de dos varas de largo*) for 800 ducats. Such a chart would have allowed him to penetrate the South Sea (*la mar del sur*) and return to England.[56] The Portuguese pilot Da Silva was kidnapped and his *derrotero* was stolen; the Spanish shipmaster Juan Griego, along with his ship and *derrotero*, were also seized. Spanish pilots Alonso Sánchez Colchero and Juan Pascual, among others, were hired by Drake. Drawing on Portuondo's analysis of the combination of visual and mathematical representations vis-à-vis written descriptions as a means to construct a comprehensive cosmographic knowledge base by the middle of the sixteenth century, McCloskey emphasizes the importance that Miramontes placed on written descriptions of the navigations (i.e., *derroteros*) in his depiction of Drake in *Armas Antárticas*. In McCloskey's view, Drake convinced the queen to send him on his voyage because his plan was based on the two types of knowledge available at the time (McCloskey 2020, 175). Therefore, besides the several ships, money, and resources captured under Drake's orders, this voyage underscored the value of cartographic information as new merchandise that would be carefully stored, as it happened with Drake's diary and map. Da Silva, in his testimony before the Spanish authorities, emphasized the fact that Drake had in his possession many books of navigation, including one about Magellan's discoveries.[57]

Francisco de Toledo, viceroy of Peru, sent Sarmiento on a twofold mission to the Strait of Magellan: on the one hand he was ordered to capture Drake, while on the other he was supposed to gather geographical information about the zone to be used for developing future military defense plans. While the expedition was a failure and Sarmiento was captured by Raleigh and incarcerated in England, he was able nonetheless to compile an account that was presented before the court of King Philip II, who eventually recruited Sarmiento for the process of fortifying the Strait (Ríos Taboada 2017, 164).[58] Sarmiento's mishap not only involved his own capture, but also that of his pilot, who, according to a letter of inquiry of the War Council (*Consejo de Guerra*) addressed to the Spanish king, did not share Sarmiento's commitment to Spain, being an individual with no strong attachments to any country: "The pilot who he was with was not satisfied because he is a man who cares about serving anyone, with no fear of what they say or do."[59] More importantly, the letter stressed the fear of disclosure of the Strait of Magellan's "secret navigation," and the Council reassured the King that Sarmiento may have kept it secret by misdirecting the English:

> The loss of Pedro Sarmiento and the pilot who came with him has been considered of great importance given his knowledge of the Strait of Magellan, which the corsair has frequented. It is understood that Pedro de Sarmiento has resisted with strength and violence not to give away the secret of such navigation. It is believed that he procured to evade to speak at any cost how the forts are planted and any password that would lead to their submission.[60]

However, while incarcerated on English soil, according to the Spanish ambassador, Sarmiento inferred that the English had easy access to classified information about the Spanish security measures on American coasts (Ríos Taboada 2017, 165). According to Ríos Taboada's analysis, Sarmiento became a central figure in the transitional process by which piracy went from being an exclusive matter of interest for Spanish peninsular and colonial authorities to becoming a global issue of dispute. According to Ríos Taboada, Sarmiento's imprisonment in England enabled English authorities to get hold of classified information about the military defenses in the Strait as well as the evangelization policies of Peru's viceroy, Toledo (*id.*, 176).

Speculation contributed to the instability of the category of piracy as it supported the question of whether Drake was a pirate acting in his own interest or an individual commissioned by the queen. At the time of the voyage, there were suspicions onboard about Drake's superior authority above Thomas Doughty and John Wynter, who were originally appointed "eqwall companyons and frindly gentlemen with a fleett of fyve ships."[61] At some point, Drake assumed the whole authority of the voyage by claiming that he had a copy of a royal commission that bestowed on him the power of judging and condemning Doughty.[62] When Doughty asked to see that commission, Drake answered: "I warrant you, ... my comissyon is good enowghe."[63] Cooke, in his account, doubted the existence of Drake's royal commission. He stated that Drake pretended he had forgotten the document in his cabin; and that the only royal document he had was a letter showing that the queen had invested money in the voyage:

> "God will I have lefte in my cabyne that I shuld especially have had (as yf he had there forgotten his comyssyon, but withar he forgat his comyssyon or no he muche forgat himselfe, to set without shewing his comyssyon yf he had any) but trewly I thinke it shuld have bene shewed ... yf he had it."

(Drake 1628, 205)

Even though the document was never shown nor was its existence proved, Doughty was finally put to death. Like the controversial diary and the original planisphere of the circumnavigation, Drake's royal letter of commission remains a mysterious object.

On the other hand, speculation threatened Spanish Ambassador Mendoza's reputation a few years after Drake's return. Mendoza—who harbored deep suspicions about Drake's actions and had him under close scrutiny—was accused of plotting against Queen Elizabeth by supposedly establishing an alliance with the Queen of Scotland. The witness was Alberico Gentili, another character who will be discussed in the next chapter. A court commission was appointed to review Mendoza's case, and he was finally sent back to Spain holding a "bad reputation" in England. In a letter to King Philip, Mendoza stressed his fear caused by his infamous portrayal, crafted by all the members of the commission:

> Given the great danger that all portrayed, I have assessed not to board, without the command of your Majesty, with anyone leaving with a Minister's title nor to trust the English to sail straight back to Spain. Considering the growing outrage that everyone has against me due to my intent to murder Reyna and the bad reputation given me by a minister who preached in court in front of all these counselors that I had celebrated publicly such act, these are all fictions and lies that have deceived the people.[64]

Unlike Hugo Grotius's and John Selden's discussion during the seventeenth century about the right of free navigation and closed or open seas, Drake's circumnavigation marked a transgression over concealed, known, or unknown spaces and navigations that created new understandings of control over space. The reproduction of Drake's image along with the representation of metonymical symbols of his figure, such as the world, his ship, and a sword, reveals the notion of a new worldly space intruded upon by non-Spanish subjects. This European interloping embodied a threat to the Spanish commercial monopoly in the West Indies, just as Grotius would underscore when arguing against the Portuguese monopoly in the East Indies.

The clearest way to perceive the direct relation between cartographic information and property is through the royal decision to conceal both, namely Drake's accounts and maps of his voyage and the amount of the booty collected. Censorship over the chronicles and texts, as well as the confusion faced by the Spanish ambassador in trying to determine how much of the Spanish goods was illegitimately taken, displays this entanglement. Besides the production of Drake's circumnavigation maps, there were also maps that specifically represented his raids in the Caribbean region; these will be discussed in Chapter 3. Even if the pirate may be considered a political, religious, or economic enemy, the question of piracy is ultimately a question of space, not only in terms of concrete space but, rather, within the formulation of virtual spaces that came to define piracy. At the same time, piracy became a way of defining such spaces. Consequently, Drake's knighthood was the beginning of a process of understanding piracy as a spatial category, and his voyages would be the instrument for achieving it. In other words, the articulation of the discourse on piracy depended less on claims of robbery and illegitimate reprisals than on the transgression of specific geographical and politicized spaces. After being relieved of his duties as the Spanish ambassador, Mendoza warned King Philip about his suspicion of Drake's next voyage, for which Queen Elizabeth had given £10,000: "[O]ne can suspect that it is for building vessels for Her Majesty's orders."[65] Perhaps this warning anticipated and referred to what would become Drake's next prominent attack, in 1585–1586: the Caribbean raid. Touching on this event, in the next chapter, we will see the varying and ambiguous narratives about piracy crafted by English, Spanish peninsular, and Spanish American authors and institutions.

Notes

1 Magellan was succeeded by Juan Sebastián Elcano in the first circumnavigation, "Magellan-Elcano" (1519–1522).
2 "True faith's defenders of diuine renowned and happy memory. Wherein all such memorable things as happened during hir blessed raigne... are exactly described." William Camden, *Annales the True and Royal History of the Famous Empresse Elizabeth Queene of England France and Ireland* ... London: Printed by George Purslowe, Humphrey Lownes, and Miles Flesher, for Beniamin Fisher and are to be sould at the Talbott in Pater Noster Rowe, 1625. 426–428. Another edition in Latin, titled *Annales Rerun Anglicarum et Hibernicarum Regnate Elizabetha*, was published in Leiden by Ex Officina Elzeviriana in the same year (1625). Some critical sources claim that the English version was published in 1627.
3 See Volume 16 of *Hakluyt's Posthumus or Purchas His Pilgrimes: Containing a History of the World in Sea Voyages and Lande Travells by Englishmen and Others.* 20 vols. Glasgow: James MacLehose and Sons, 1905, 113–118.
4 The letter is addressed to the "Lord Archb. of Canterburie, Primate of all England and Metropolitan, One of His Maiesties most Honorable Privie Councell" (Purchas, 2–3).
5 Based on detailed geographical information, obtained in 1579, about the Strait of Magellan, Hakluyt wrote and addressed to the English court a pamphlet, "A Discourse of the Commodity of the Taking of the Straight of Magellanus," that underscored the strategic importance of the zone to disrupt the Spanish commercial monopoly in the Americas (Ríos Taboada, 2021, 98–99).
6 In McCloskey's words, "*Armas Antárticas* symbolically presents those who wield that science [cosmography] as a new kind of hero in a war of information" (McCloskey 2020, 176).
7 For more about the role merchants and gentlemen in projects of English nationhood during the Elizabethan era, see Helgerson, 171–181.
8 Regarding the merchant/conqueror binomial of Drake's image, on the one hand, Ríos Taboada delves into the translations of Spanish texts dealing with the conquest of the Americas by the English merchants John Frampton (1577–1581) and Thomas Nicholls (1578, 1581), among others. For instance, in Nicholls's translation of Agustín de Zárate's *Historia del descubrimiento y conquista de la*

provincia del Perú (1555), translated in 1578, the English merchant takes the opportunity to project an image of Drake that mirrors the voyages of discovery executed by Spaniards and Portuguese sailors (2021, 61–73).

9. Drawing on David Quint's definition of epic literature as a genre related to "aristocratic, martial values," Jowitt suggests that it would have been inappropriate to compose an epic after Drake's figure because of "Drake's humble origins (from yeoman stock, he was knighted only on the return from the circumnavigation)" (Jowitt, 48).

10. "Diole el título de Sr. para las tierras que ha comprado." Mendoza to the king, April 6, 1581; held at British Library (BL), Add. MS 26,056, C. fol. 138. In an earlier account from 1581, he also mentions that the ship was placed in a dock as a permanent memorial of Drake's voyage (Mendoza to the king, January 9, 1581; held at Archivo General de Simancas (AGS), Estado 835, fol. 164).

11. There is not much recorded about his career as a mayor and landowner, but there were a few construction projects like Plymouth Leat, also known as Drake's Leat, whose construction started in 1590. Among other purposes, the project was intended to provide a supply of water for naval and merchant shipping (Kelsey, 227).

12. "En la restitución del robo de draques voy siempre labrando en la conformidad que le avisado." Mendoza to the king, September 1, 1581; AGS, Estado 835, Doc. 24. Camden also mentions Mendoza's inquiry: "Bernard Mendoze, then Ambassadour for Spaine, in England, murmuring it, and as not well pleased, demands vehemently of the Queen the things taken" (Camden, 428). About the English secrecy reported by Mendoza, see Mendoza to the king, October 30, 1580; BL Add. MS 28, 420, fol. 30.

13. For more about the production of spaces and cultural geography, see Mike Crang's study (2000) and James Sutton's work (2004). For a specific approach to the English representation of water in the seventeenth century, see Julie Sanders's analysis on the representation of liquid landscapes in Caroline theatre (Sanders, 18–64).

14. Holinshed had published a previous edition of his *Chronicles of England, Scotland, and Ireland* in 1577.

15. The edition with the enlarged version of Holinshed's narrative is *Holinshed's Chronicles of England, Scotland, and Ireland*. Ed. Sir Henry Ellis. London: J. Johnson: F.C. and J. Rivington; T. Payne; Wilkie and Robinson; Longman, Hurst, Rees, and Orme; Cadell and Davies; and J. Mawman, 1808.

16. Probably the "Paule's steeple" refers to Old St. Paul's Cathedral, located in the center of the London "grapevine" where, during Elizabethan times, people would buy books and learn about current affairs mainly related to politics and religion.

17. Several members of the court openly criticized and wished to reject Drake's spoils. For instance, the Earl of Sussex and the Earl of Arundel stated at a dinner party that his captures were not honorable and that he had no shame (Kelsey, 207–217).

18. Stow's description of Drake's circumnavigation is as follows: "The 13 of December Frances Drake, John Winter, Tho[mas] Doughtie and other, to the number of 164, Gentlemen and Sailers, with a fleete of 5 ships departed from Plimmouth, making their course Southward, and to about the world as was sayd" (Stow, 690).

19. Stow published his first collection of chronicles in 1565 and 1580. He then published the *Annales of England* in 1592, in which he included John Cooke's narrative of Drake's voyage.

20. Here Mack refers to models or stone replicas of ships. The author adds that in other instances, "the idea of the ship as a vessel of transport is emphasized with other implications for the agency of the ship itself. This has two aspects: the vessel as voyaging out and the vessel as voyaging in" (Mack, 204). In relation to the representation of Drake's vessel, I argue, the *Golden Hind* stands as an

instrument of both: the solidification of a community that identifies ideologically with the agency and capability of movement provided by the vessel.
21 Source: University of Oxford, Bodleian Library, 80 L.526 BS.
22 If Verstegan was, in fact, the author of this pamphlet, it is worth noting that he was English, studied at Oxford, had to flee the country because he was a Catholic, and was a pensioner of Philip II from 1586 to 1609. Verstegan's pamphlet was rapidly contested and discredited by Francis Bacon in *Certain Observations upon a libell* (1593).
23 Quoted in Ricardo Alegría's compilation of documents pertaining to Puerto Rico from the Archivo de Indias.
24 Breton does not specify the name of the Gulf, but Drake passed through what was then known as the Pacific Gulf, specifically through the "Strait of California." Such theory has raised several myths related to Drake's entrance into the upper part of California. The Jodocus Hondius map of c1595 (BL, Maps MT, 6, A2) illustrates this route.
25 Marco Nievergelt focuses on another laudatory text related to Drake's successful circumnavigation, *The Voyage of the Wandering Knight* (London, 1581), which was a French translation made by "'William Goodyear of South-hampton, Merchant', about whom nothing else is known." Robert Norman, an instrument-maker and hydrographer, dedicated the work to Drake and according to Nievergelt, the tone of the work suggests that they Norman and Drake knew each other. Nievergelt argues that this work "paints a picture of Drake as a hero not just in general epic terms, but as entrusted with a specific mission, socio-economic as well as religious—terms ..." (55). A later work that celebrated Drake as a hero was William Gager's neo-Latin poem "In laudem fortissimo viri domini Francisci Draconis" (c1586–1588).
26 More than a decade later and before Camden's and Purchas's publications, Drake's ship is briefly mentioned in the comedy *Eastward Hoe* (London 1605), collaboratively written by Ben Jonson, George Chapman, and John Marston. In the play, Drake's ship is presented as an attraction in which one of the characters, Sir Petronel, says to another, Captain Seagull, that they will be having dinner: "Wee'll have our provided supper brought abord Sir Francis Drakes ship, that hath compast the world; where, with full cupps and banquets, we will doe sacrifice for a prosperous voyage. My mind gives me that some good spirits of the waters should hant the desart ribs of her, and be auspicious to all that honour her memorie, and will like orgies enter their voyages" (Jonson et al., v 185–194). Jonson also belonged to the web of authors discussed: he was a protégé of Camden's—who paid for his education—and he maintained a close friendship with the English jurists Francis Bacon, who wrote against Verstegan's pamphlet, and John Selden, who published *Mare Clausum* (1656) against Hugo Grotius's *Mare Liberum* (1609).
27 Quoted in Shields, 103. In 1578, Humphrey Gilbert sailed to settle a colony in America but the expedition was a failure due to a storm. He engaged in a second expedition to Newfoundland but he and his ship disappeared on his way back to England.
28 In a recent article, McCloskey emphasizes the "inspirational relationship" between Magellan and Drake as shown by Miramontes' epic poem.
29 In the Caird Library at the National Maritime Museum (NMM), Greenwich, London.
30 *Principall Navigations* also omitted certain details found in the original Spanish version of the account (*relación*) of Da Silva. Zelia Nutall translated the original documents from the Archivo General de Indias in Seville: AGI, Estado, 2–21, no. 8. Among the omitted parts found in the original, we find that Da Silva declares that Drake "carried a map of the World and other maps which, he said, had been

made in England. The map of the world which he mentioned above was made in Portugal, but he does not know by whom" (Nutall, 270).

31 David Quinn, in his essay "Early Accounts of the Famous Voyage," highlights the fact that by the time Hakluyt was compiling the 1589/90 edition of *Principall Navigations* he was employed by Sir Francis Walsingham, Queen Elizabeth's Secretary of State. Thus, he may have had access to Walsingham's documents related to the expedition, but Quinn argues that Walsingham was the original source of the omission of Drake's narrative (Quinn, 35). On the other hand, Helen Wallis argues in "The Cartography of Drake's Voyage" that Hakluyt's narrative might have been based on the following sources: Fletcher, Cooke (BL, Harley MS 540, fol. 93–110), and the "Anonymous Narrative" (BL, Harley MS 280, fols. 83–90) (Wallis, 141). *The World Encompassed* and *Sir Francis Drake Revived*—published in 1625 and 1628, respectively, by Drake's nephew—mainly included Francis Fletcher's unpublished notes from the voyage.

32 Hakluyt mentions that he would show Thomas Cavendish's circumnavigation but that from "the first made by Sir Francis Drake will be lesse: wherein I must confesse to have taken more then ordinarie paines, meaning to have inserted it in this work: but being of late (contrary to my expectation) seriously delt withall not to anticipate or prevent another mans paines and charge in drawing all the services of that worthie Knight into one volume, I have yeelded unto those my friendes which pressed me in the matter, referring the further knowledge of his proceedinges to those intended discourses."

33 The insert of "The Famous Voyage" is between pages 643 and 644. Even though several historians have argued that the insertion was later—in 1594—Quinn argues that it was by the end of 1589 or the beginning of 1590 (Quinn, 34).

34 Cooke's account (BL, Harley MS 540, fols. 93–110); "Anonymous Narrative" (BL, Harley MS 280, fols. 83–90).

35 Cliffe's narrative (Holinshed 1808, 748–53) is included in Hakluyt's third volume of the second edition of 1598/99–1600 along with two other accounts: that of Da Silva (*id.*, 742–48) and López Vaz's "A Discourse of the West Indies and South Sea" (*id.*, 778–802).

36 The Spanish ambassador, Bernardino de Mendoza, was told they were going to Alexandria but suspected that this was false.

37 Drake handed the queen a planisphere, now lost but apparently reproduced in the Drake-Mellon map, which shows an island in the Strait and another one at the southern end of Tierra del Fuego (Ríos Taboada 2017, 166).

38 María Portuondo's study *Secret Science: Spanish Cosmography and the New World* (2009) claims that maps of the New World were censored and controlled by the Spanish Crown during the reign of Philip II because they were equivalent to what we consider today a "secret of state." For this reason, royal cosmographers worked within a bureaucratic structure intended to prohibit the circulation of maps, to avoid foreign threats from the enemies of the Spanish Crown. However, selling maps outside the Spanish Crown territories during the sixteenth century was not uncommon. During the Renaissance, the transmission channels for geographic information were primarily Italian and German workshops dedicated to map production and printing. By the 1550s, Venetian ships were part of a regular trade with voyages to the Levant, the Black Sea, ports of Spain and Portugal, and the coasts of Western Europe. Such navigational circulation allowed the accumulation of geographical information, and the practice of cartography was developed through the craftsmanship of wood and copper engraving (Barrow, 133). In 1555 Christoffel Plantijn's printing house at Antwerp contributed to the spread of maps in the Low Countries and abroad. Sebastian Munster, Gerardus Mercator, Giacomo Gastaldi, and Martin Waldseemüller are

a few examples of the non-Iberian cartographic tradition that flourished at the margins of Spanish control of cartographic production.

39 Mercator's letter was written in Latin. It was translated by *The Kraus Collection of Sir Francis Drake*. Both the translation and the original document are available online: Library of Congress (LC), H.P. Kraus Collection, Sir Francis Drake no. 2a. Physical description: 1 page. Folio (310 X 249 mm).

40 The term "secret navigation" (*el secreto de aquella navegación*) was included in a letter of inquiry by the Spanish War Council (*Consejo de Guerra*), addressed to King Philip II, that stresses the fear of disclosure of the Strait of Magellan's route. See: AGS, GYM, 190, 503–504.

41 "Mais ie ne sa, s'ils not raison de ce faire: car la communication ne peut estre qu' a l'honneur de sa nation, si elles song telles que les autres peuples en puissent tired profit ou quelque commodité. Et au rebouts un desdain et mal contentement que tous et mesmement ceux qui désirent voyager en recevront centre tell qui leur envient ce bien." Quoted in Helen Wallis, "The Cartography of Drake's Voyage" in Norman J.W. Thrower, ed., *Sir Francis Drake and the Famous Voyage, 1577–1580. Essays Commemorating the Quadricentennial of Drake's Circumnavigation of the Earth*, University of California Press, 1984, 121–163.

42 Kelsey and Wallis, among others, have proposed these two theories (see, e.g., Kelsey, 179; Wallis, 133–134). On the other hand, based on the English sources, Kelsey stipulates that by 1625 the map was hanging "in His Majesties Gallerie at White Hall, near the Privie Chamber" (Kelsey, 127).

43 "[U]un diario de todo lo que le ha sucedido en los tres años y una gran carta." Mendoza to the king, October 16, 1580; BL, Add'l MS 28420, fol. 30. Helen Wallis in "The Cartography of Drake's Voyage" states that Mendoza's letter, "provides the earliest record of the two prime documents of the voyage, Drake's journal and a chart" (Wallis, 122).

44 "Je vous prie par mesme moyen me maintenir en la bonne grace dune si tres excellente Royne & la prier de commander au chevalier de Drac de m'enouyer le recueil & discours de ce quil a remarqué en son grant voyaige." BL Harleian MS 376, fol. 5, quoted in Wallis, 123.

45 "Declaración de Nuño de Silva sobre cómo cayó prisionero entre piratas ingleses en su viaje de Oporto a Brasil," May 1579. Archivo General de la Nacion de Mexico (AGN-M), Inquisicion, 85, ramo 12, fol. 86v. The English translation of Zárate's letter (April 16, 1579) is found in Zelia Nutall's *New Light on Drake* (Nutall, 201). The Spanish original is in AGI, Patronato, E.1, C.5, L 2–21, no. 19, and was transcribed by Manuel Peralta in *Costa Rica, Nicaragua y Panamá en el siglo XVI*, 569.

46 According to Wallis, both the diary and the map were destroyed in the fire at the Palace of Whitehall in 1698. The journal was not available to Hakluyt when he prepared his account of "The Famous Voyage" (1589) or to Drake's nephew when he compiled *The World Encompassed* (published in 1628) (Wallis, 124).

47 "Valientes fueron (no se niegue) los atrevimientos de Draque, Candi y Aquines, émulos de Magallanes, pues atravesaron de Norte a Sur el estrecho de su nombre, vinieron a turbar los mares que tuvieron por máxima desde infinitos años atrás, el ser seguros, y pacíficos." This letter is included in Cristóbal Suárez de Figueroa's text *Hechos de don García Hurtado* (Suárez, 277). Jason McCloskey's article "Crossing the Line in the Sand: Francis Drake Imitating Ferdinand Magellan in Juan de Miramonte's *Armas Antárticas* focuses on the rhetorical aspect of the topic of imitation in the New World's epic genre (McCloskey 2013, 393–415).

48 Among Drake's discoveries—as Helen Wallis has pointed out—he demonstrated that Tierra del Fuego was an archipelago separated from the southern continent Terra Australis. However, Kelsey states that Spanish cosmographers knew this fact from the 1560s (127). Apparently, he discovered a land on the northwestern

48 *Navigating Conflicting Waters*

coast of America that he named Nova Albion (Fig. 1.5). He corrected the shape of South America, accusing earlier Spanish and Dutch mapmakers of falsehood; furthermore, he proved a greater width for the Pacific Ocean (Wallis, 129–31). However, the English explorer Richard Madox (1546–1583) was suspicious about Drake's route and such islands. He thought that by borrowing information from Spanish maps and *derroteros* circulating in Europe at the time of the voyage, Drake would have been able to infer the existence of a free passage between the Atlantic and Pacific Oceans (Kelsey, 127).

49 Captain Richard Hawkins recalls in his narrative the story that Drake told him about that area: "And moreover, he sayd, that standing about, when the winde changed, he was not well able to double the Southermost Island, and to anchored under the lee of it; and going a-shore, carried a Compasse with him, and seeking out the Southermost part of the island, cast himselfe downe upon the uttermost poynt groveling, and so reached out his bodie over it. Presently he imbarked, and then recounted unto his people, that he had beene upon the Southermost known land in the world, and more further to the Southwards upon it then any of them, yea, or any man as yet knowne." (*The Observations of Sir Richard Hawkins knight, in His Voyage into the South Sea: Anno Domini 1593*. London: Printed by I.D. for I. Iaggard, 1622.)

50 Helen Wallis and others have proposed that Elizabeth's Island is probably today's Henderson's Island (see, e.g., Wallis, 130). Fletcher's map of this island is found in BL, Sloane MS 61, fol. 39.

51 Antonio de Herrera and Theodor de Bry considered that Nova Albion was an island, whereas Jodocus Hondius and Nicola van Sype thought it was the coast of California.

52 Kelsey has pointed out the narrative similarities between Antonio Pigafetta's account of the Magellan-Elcano circumnavigation (translated into English) and Francis Fletcher's account which was probably the source for Hakluyt's narrative (135). For a comprehensive analysis of the Hakluyt's representation of Drake and the appropriation of former Spanish narrative models of the conquest and history of the Americas (that includes the description of the indigenous populations, flora and fauna, rituals, sacrifices, and mythical legends, among others) put forth by Spanish chroniclers of Indies and explorers such as Christopher Columbus and Oviedo, see Ríos Taboada 2021, 94–115.

53 This scene is on an unnumbered page since the whole narrative was inserted after publication of the 1589/90 edition.

54 Neither Stow nor Camden recorded this event.

55 In relation to the description of Nova Albion's discovery, Ríos Taboada argues that the English missionary component of the narrative imitates the Iberian model (2021, 113).

56 García-Redondo, José María and Consuelo Varela, 442.

57 "[T]raia tres libros de navegacion uno en frances, otro en ingles y el otro era el descubrimiento de magallanes no sabe en que lengua." AGN-M, Inquisición, 85–86v.

58 Sarmiento's account was the "Relación y derrotero del viaje y descubrimiento del estrecho de la Madre de Dios, antes llamado de Magallanes" (Ríos Taboada 2017, 164). López Vaz was another sailor captured in January 1587 by the Earl of Cumberland. He wrote about Drake's circumnavigation in an account that Hakluyt called "[a] discourse of the West Indies and South Sea, written by López Vaz a Portugall, conteining divers memorable matters not to be found in any other writers, and continued unto the yere 1587." It was published in Hakluyt's *Principall Navigations* (1600 edition).

59 "[P]ero no se tiene esta satisfacion del piloto que con el iba por ser hombre que tanto le importa servir a unos como a otros y quequando no hubiera esto contemores le haran hazer y decir lo que quisieren."

60 "La pérdida de Pedro Sarmiento y el piloto que con el benia a sido de mucha consideracion por la platica que tiene del estrecho de Magallanes y ser navegacion que el cossario de deseado frequentar y se entiende que aunque a pedro de sarmiento les hagan fuerca y violencia para que les descubra el secreto de aquella navegacion y de la manera que quedan los fuertes y que con alguna contrasena se podrian apoderar dellos se cree que procurava desviarlo como pudiese." AGS, GYM, 190, 503–504.
61 Cooke's narrative starts with this description of the relationship among the three captains.
62 Under the English juridical system, disputes about incidents outside the realm were heard before the Earl Marshal and the Chief Constable. Soon after Drake's return, the latter post was vacant and Queen Elizabeth refused to appoint anyone. This represented an issue for John Doughty, whose brother Thomas had been put to death by Drake during the voyage, in 1578. He had recourse to the High Court of Chivalry and Honor, because the incident had occurred outside England, and he was finally accused of plotting against Drake (Kelsey, 232). Doughty's trial and death onboard are relevant to understanding the juridical charge and overseas command.
63 Cooke as published in the 1628 edition of *The World Encompassed* (Drake 1628, 202).
64 "[P]or estar tan peligrosos todos he juzgado no ser bien resolverme sin mandato de V.M. tomar ninguno saliendo de aquí con titulo de ministro ni fiarme en las manos de los ingleses para embarcarme derechamente para Espana teniendome todos tanta indignación que se ha acrecentado mucho mas con la fama que han echado de que me mandan salir por haver tratado de matar a la Reyna, lo qual dijo un ministro en sus predicas en la misma corte delante de todos estos consejeros y que yo havia hecho fuegos públicos de alegrías dello, por donde se ver con las ficciones y embustes que traen engañado el pueblo." AGS, Estado, 839.
65 "[S]e puede sospechar que es para armar los navios a V.M. que ponen en orden." Mendoza to the King, January 15, 1581. AGS. Estado, 835.

2 Setting Sails to the Narrative of Piracy
Francis Drake's Caribbean Raid (1585–1586)

In September 1585, Sir Francis Drake sailed from Plymouth with two dozen ships and eight pinnaces. His fleet besieged the city of Santo Domingo, capital of Hispaniola (today the Dominican Republic) on New Year's Day 1586, whereof the city paid him 25,000 ducats to end the attack. A few weeks later, he arrived in Cartagena de Indias, Colombia; he captured the city, held it 53 days, and left with a ransom of 107,000 ducats, returning to England on July 22.[1] These attacks occurred in the context of a yet-undeclared open war between Spain and England. To English eyes, Drake's raid was less a formal act of war than an expedition to the West Indies (Neale, 298; Kelsey, 241). However, the Spanish considered this event both an act of piracy and a military offense to their domains overseas.

The raid was recorded in various cultural registers, both historical and rhetorical, ranging from bureaucratic correspondence between Spanish peninsular and colonial authorities to an English travelogue and a Spanish-Caribbean heroic poem.[2] In this chapter, examining an interdisciplinary corpus that includes Juan de Castellanos's *Discurso del capitán Francisco Draque* (1586–1587), depositions conducted by colonial authorities, and inquiries (*consultas*) and other epistles sent by peninsular and colonial officials, I will compare these dissimilar descriptions of the raid and link them to the development of ambivalent narratives of blame that constructed internal enemies within the Spanish transatlantic power. The idea of a national Spanish supremacy lies at the very heart of such conflicting narratives of blame that diffuse the historical truth behind the attacks. While these narratives contradicted themselves, they converged in their effort to support an ideology of power accentuating discursive overtones attached to economic, military, and moral affairs. Providing a comparative framework to the Spanish peninsular and colonial accounts of the event, while contrasting rhetorical similarities and dissimilarities among them, I incorporate Walter Bigges's concomitant perception of the attacks, found in his *Summarie and True Discourse of Sir Drake's West Indian Voyage* (1589).[3] Through an intertextual approach that revisits the moral reiterations, political concerns, and economic interests found in the conflicting accounts of Drake's raid, I argue that authors rearranged the concepts of the enemy, the

DOI: 10.4324/9781003141495-3

pirate, and the battle, in territories marked by chaos, to reassert their authority and emphasize their contribution to the imperial ideology of both Spanish and English powers. As will be shown, the retellings of the attack also reveal the clash of economic, political, and social values of the period.

Historians have drawn upon inquiries, along with other epistolary documents, to produce historical reconstructions of piracy attacks and to identify both contradictions and narrative similarities in these sources. Delving into Drake's historical and literary representations, the works of Harry Kelsey and Claire Jowitt have shed light on the shifting narratives in the portrayal of the English captain. Kelsey's seminal study *Sir Francis Drake: The Queen's Pirate* (1998) demonstrates that Drake's adversaries tended to disguise unauthorized trading with the payment of ransoms. In *The Culture of Piracy, 1580–1630* (2010), Jowitt registers an ideological and paradigmatic shift in the representations of English maritime predation found in Hakluyt's *Principall Navigations* (c1589) and Drake the Younger's *The World Encompassed* (1628). According to Jowitt, these representations corresponded to dissimilar national and ideological projects that influenced the descriptions and narratives produced around Drake's circumnavigation of the globe, discussed in Chapter 1. Hakluyt, on his part, stressed Drake's interest in becoming a merchant against the Spanish monopoly in the West Indies, whereas Drake's nephew, "Drake the Younger," consolidated Drake's status as a gentleman by the early decades of the seventeenth century (Jowitt, 49–50). In other words, Hakluyt emphasized several qualities among the English, such as their military prowess and attempt to open new markets in the Americas, to whitewash Drake's raids by turning the attacks into legitimate economic transactions. On his part, Drake's nephew portrayed his uncle as a gentleman who, unlike his crew, was not interested in the economic profit resulting from the expedition. Upon perusal of the nuanced representations of Drake's image, I will build on this scholarship by arguing that Drake's Caribbean raid provides the grounds to establish the first notions of Drake as a gentleman and not merely a vicious merchant and violent pirate.

Regarding the colonial representations of the attack, Emiro Martínez-Osorio asserts that Castellanos's *Discurso del capitán Francisco Draque* conveys an ideology of Spanish domination that praises the warrior class that had been replaced by administrators and bureaucrats without military experience (Martínez-Osorio 2011, 26).[4] Expanding upon this argument, I will illustrate how, while fingering internal enemies to rebrand the attacks, Castellanos and the colonial depositions and epistles demonstrate that writing about piracy became a strategic weapon to target specific rivals inside the colonial administrative apparatus while—paradoxically—attempting to disseminate an idea of Spanish imperial strength. The territorial disputes during the second half of the sixteenth century are related to Rolena Adorno's concept of "polemics of possession," which bridges the geographical debate on possession of land. They are also the foundation of a narrative field in which the possession of land entails a debate about the possession of a narrative identity, authority, or voice. Space and identity converged in challenging or assuming physical and rhetorical possession over lands and authority. In line with Adorno's argument, while the sources in question may be pointing to the origins of a Creole sensibility that differentiates Spanish Americans from their peninsular counterparts (as in the case of *Espejo de paciencia*, Silvestre de Balboa's poem of 1608), this chapter posits that the varying appraisals of Drake also register the distinction of geographical spaces that reshapes specific attitudes and procedures toward maritime predation. This maneuver, primarily based on the transatlantic dichotomy of the "here" and "there," relates to the classical topos of arms and letters (*sapientia et fortitudo*).

Through the close reading of Walter Bigges's 1589 travelogue and other English primary sources, such as historical documents and dictionaries, the first part of the chapter addresses the unstable concept of piracy, evinced by the conflicting notions that describe maritime predation as an economic transaction or as a multifaceted concept that moves across religious and political realms. From the English perspective, historical accounts of Drake's raid on the Caribbean accentuate the instability of the figure of the pirate. Hakluyt's collection of testimonies of English navigations, compiled in his *Principall Navigations*, 1598–1600 edition, establishes the need to present a different perspective on pirates.[5] In his preface he states that Spanish and Portuguese writers "account all other nations for pirats, rovers and theeves, which visite any heathen cost that they have once sailed by or looked on" (Hakluyt 1598–1600, 4). Hakluyt's selected vocabulary insists on the innocence of English sailors; hence, they "visit" coasts instead of attacking them. Such use of vocabulary conforms to a specific rhetorical narrative in which "pirates," "rovers," and "thieves" are adjectives assigned to English sailors by peninsular sources. Hakluyt's preface unveils one of the main repercussions of using the concept of piracy and its related terminology, which is the geopolitical positioning of the English Crown and others against peninsular Spain and its control over territories "sailed or looked upon" by them. In this sense, a pirate in the peninsular mind is anyone who does not come from the Iberian Peninsula and thus has no right even to visit foreign territories claimed by Spain or Portugal. Further on, Hakluyt's rhetoric changes, becoming more aggressive, but still aims to justify the expedition by pointing out King Philip's poor military strategies to defend his transatlantic territories.[6]

The second part of this chapter focuses on the portrayal of tensions and differing interests between Spanish colonial functionaries and peninsular authorities pertaining to the transformation of chivalric societal values into financial concerns. In this context, the moral undertones served both to endorse the functionaries' response to the English and to promote the valiant military men who, according to colonial authorities and Castellanos's heroic poem, used to risk their lives in the past and now there remain only a few. The second part also draws on Drake's negotiations with two governors, Cristóbal de Ovalle and Pedro Fernández de Busto, to show the debate on what constituted a pirate and how the governors transformed Drake into a legitimate adversary to justify their questionable leadership decisions and conceal their military weaknesses. The Caribbean raid thus illustrates the changing values of an era in which money—instead of military altercation—becomes the vehicle to resolve a war or to respond to a violent attack. The analysis of English, Spanish peninsular, and Spanish colonial sources provides a different angle on the configuration of rhetorical culpabilities to understand the fraught and nuanced relations among these powers. Even though Castellanos and Bigges narrated the attack from different perspectives—from the attacked versus the attackers standpoints—they display rhetorical similarities within the articulation of justifications and condemnations of piracy as a multifaceted and unstable concept that moves across religious, political, and economic realms.

Pirate or Entrepreneur? English Justifications of the Attack

During wartime, in the early modern period, pirates were commonly understood as outlaw figures who betrayed their sovereign powers, while corsairs, who engaged in largely the same outlawed practices as pirates, were state sponsored and were seen as protectors of the stability of their sovereign regimes. It is worth noting that, at the time, the terms were intertwined. For instance, Sebastián Covarrubias de Orozco defines a "pirate" as a "corsair who steals on the seas" (Covarrubias, 590), and other dictionaries followed this trend of defining the term "pirate" with the word "corsair" (e.g., Minsheu 1617 and Franciosini 1620). Also, in the context of the beginning of what came to be known as the Caribbean raid of 1585–1586, we find no reference to the official larger Anglo-Spanish conflict. On the contrary, Bigges notes the lack of an official declaration of war when Drake's fleet reached the Isles of Bayona (today known as the Cíes Islands), just off northern Spain, before setting out for the New World. They came peaceably, short of supplies and seeking more to sustain them on the ocean crossing. Upon arrival, however, they found that trade was officially barred and the English merchants on shore could not be found. Bigges describes the scene that followed: an English merchant—sent by Pedro Bermúdez, governor of the islands Bayona—conferred with Captain Sampson, appointed by Drake to meet the governor and gather information about two main issues:[7] first, "if there were any warres betweene Spaine and England;" and second, why "their goods were imbarred or arrested" (Bigges 2010, 219–220).[8] Being advised by Christopher Carleill, his lieutenant general, Drake resolved not "to make any stand" before receiving news. The response was:

> First, touching peace or warres, the Gouernour sayd he knew of no warres, and that it lay not in him to make any, he being so meane a subject as he was. And as for the stay of the Marchants with their goods, it was the kings pleasure, but not with intent to endommage any

man. And that the kings conter commandement was (which had bene receaued in that place some seauennight before) that English Marchants with their goods should be discharged ...

(*id.*, 220)[9]

After this exchange the governor accommodated the fleet, providing them with refreshments including bread, wine, oil, apples, grapes, and marmalade. Another source, known as the *Tiger Journal* because it was kept aboard Carleill and Powell's ship *Tiger*, also stresses the misunderstanding between the English and the inhabitants of the isles as subjects of the Spanish Crown:

> Capt. Sampson was geven this Instruction that synce the Governor [had sent] to know what we were, he was to certyfye hym that we were [English] shipps sent from her Majestye to demavnde the cause of empryson[ing her] subiectes & takynge ther goodes from them *as yf it were open war* [and in] case it were the Intention of the Kynge of Spayn to hold them t[hus by force] and therby to geve cause of warr, then we were lykewyse redy [to proceede] accordynglye with his people and contrye as farr as wee myght ... (emphasis added).
>
> (Bigges 2010, 79–80)[10]

Captain Sampson warned Governor Bermudez that if their reasonable demands were not satisfied, the English would fight vehemently because the captain realized that they were able to proceed "when he saw theyr weakeness in every respect" (Bigges 2010, 80). Governor Bermudez replied that he did not hold the power to "make warre or peace betwine the two princes" and declared that the English merchants were not under arrest "but that they myght dispose them selves and th[eir goodes] at theyr owne pleasures" (*id.*). Emphasizing the good rapport between the sides, the *Tiger Journal* portrays all the gallantries provided to the English "as one Captaine in honest Curtesie might and owght to do one to an other, theyr [prin]ces being in league together" (*id.*). Thus, at this point there was not an official war, which means that the English sailors seemed to be considered less pirates or corsairs than sailors looking for their countrymen merchants, who presumably had been imprisoned and their goods embargoed.

I would like to focus on two main points stemming from these narratives: first, the fact that the English sailors perceived this voyage as a retrieval of goods and a potential business venture; and second, the polite rapport evinced by the depiction of the proper treatment received by the English from their Spanish counterparts.[11] This is not the last time that the sources for the Caribbean raid describe such fair Spanish behavior, intended to please the English sailors. On the contrary, as we shall see in the second part of this chapter, both Hispanic and English sources also dramatized the banquets that took place between Drake and the governor of Cartagena while negotiating the payment of ransoms a few months later when Drake attacked the cities of Cartagena and Santo Domingo. By the same token, while repeatedly alluding to economic transactions, the sources articulated a topos of wealth and money through either the celebration or the condemnation of their retrieval, gain, or loss.

Historians have claimed that the Caribbean raid of 1585–1586 was sponsored by Queen Elizabeth's policies that encouraged certain individuals to plunder any vessel sailing under the Spanish flag (Coote, 200). As seen earlier, Drake's pillaging was apparently considered justified by an earlier event in which English merchant vessels were embargoed by the Spanish Crown. Thus, the Caribbean raid, instead of being a mercantile expedition, was an aggressive act of "coordinated and official acts of random piracy" (Coote, 199). Another motive that may have spurred Queen Elizabeth's interest in sponsoring this raid was to use the English embargo as an excuse to justify pillaging against the Spanish to acquire financial resources to support the Dutch rebels' war of independence from Spain.[12] Looting Spanish goods from the New World and aggravating the Dutch–Spanish conflict became a recurrent twofold strategy employed by the English Crown to debilitate Philip II's power and enlist the Protestant religious cause against the Spanish Catholic dominion. In this way, the Caribbean raid presents an overlapping of motives and rhetorical justifications encompassing economic, political, and religious realms. The accounts of the raid entail both the questioning and the justification of Hispanic jurisdictional power in the New World, enabling either the condemnation or legitimation of English pillaging.

Bigges's account stresses the English economic pursuits as well as their allegedly diplomatic behavior before carrying out any military offensive against the Spanish territories visited throughout the voyage. His narrative allows for the understanding of the figure of the pirate as an entrepreneur and a soldier rather than solely a maritime predator. In what follows, I will delve into Bigges's specific usage of vocabulary to trace how the account articulated piracy more like a business and less like an unjustified attack. Second, my focus and analysis based on the words related to the economic and military realms unearths the construction of an economic and military discursive pattern that accounts for the classical topos of "arms and letters" (*sapientia et fortitudo*).

During the seventeenth century, as Anne J. Cruz demonstrates, these categories were far from being at odds; rather, technological advances in weaponry scattered the values commonly associated with chivalric behavior, such as a soldier's selfless courage on the battlefield (Cruz, 191). Cruz affirms that Spain witnessed the first glimpse of this social paradigm by the last decades of the sixteenth century, evinced by the increasing number of non-military men (*letrados*) appointed to run the government's bureaucracy. In exchange for their efficient administrative services, these men were often granted nobility privileges or were knighted into well-esteemed military orders (*id.*, 202). By the same token, the depictions of banquets and proper treatment among these soldiers and Spanish functionaries illustrate what Elizabeth Wright has coined the "fetish of recreation" through which courtiers disguised their economic interests by emphasizing leisure as the epitome of their respective courtly culture (Wright 2008, 31–32). Certainly neither Drake nor the governors were noblemen; however, by taking part in this courtly culture they projected a story that aligned economic affairs with recreation to efface piracy and potential military altercations.

In Bigges's narrative we never find the term "pirate" or "piracy." Conversely, Hakluyt in his 1598–1600 edition attaches to Bigges's account a document called "The Resolutions of the Land-Captains." This document does not fashion the English as pirates but, rather, depicts them as entrepreneurs who organized themselves so that "all things went forward in a due course, to the achieving of our happy enterprise" (quoted in Eliot, *Voyages and Travels*, 14). But let us take a step back and explore the multiple meanings assigned and related to the word "enterprise."

According to several dictionaries from the sixteenth and seventeenth centuries, an "enterprise" means achievement of something great and also is the physical symbol of such a deed. The Spanish translation of this word is *empresa* and its verbal form *emprender*. Covarrubias, in his *Tesoro de la lengua castellana o española (1611)*, defines both terms in the same entry: *emprender* stands for the pursuit of some difficult and arduous affair (*determinarse a tratar algún negocio ardor y dificultoso*), whereas *empresa* is the achievement of it. Drawing on the chivalric tradition, the Spanish lexicographer states that *empresa* also refers to the symbol embroidered in the banners of those knights who conquered.[13] Thus, during Bigges's time period, the word "enterprise" meant both an accomplishment and the symbol that represented it, and its usage implied a military victory as well. Another document, an English newsletter, stresses the importance given by Drake to compiling a narrative or "booke" registering the events:

> And because our generall Sir Fran[cis Drake] promised a whole and perfect booke of all such th[ings that] have happened throughout our whole voyadge ... this present will comvnycate no more then the effective tymes and manner of our procedynges, referryng the rest [to the] promysed booke.[14]

In this way, Bigges's text stands for both the achievement and the chivalric banner used to signify a military victory against the attacked Spanish territories throughout their *feliz empresa* or "happie enterprise" (Bigges, 233).[15] To describe the term "enterprise," Covarrubias also employs the word *negocio*, whose translation appeared in several of the dictionaries as "buzines," 1591 (Percival, unnumbered), "dealing," 1591 (*id.*), and "to trafficke," 1617 (Minsheu, 175).[16] In Covarrubias's definition, the word *negocio* stands for something that engages men to put some effort or disposition on it (Covarrubias, 562).[17] To some extent, Bigges's usage of the term "enterprise" in his travelogue exemplifies a discursive interaction that encompassed a polysemy built from military victory, the visual representation of such accomplishment (a banner), and an economic affair. In other words, to conduct an "enterprise" was to conquer or to accomplish a great deed; but also, such a deed—if defined as Covarrubias's *negocio*—entailed dealing in business or trafficking in merchandise. In this sense, English "piracy" or maritime predation, according to the Spanish viewpoint, becomes a hinge between chivalry and an increasingly modern understanding of capital. In other words, Bigges's emphasis on both the successful accumulation of wealth and victories against the Spanish territories places maritime predation at the center of the overlap of chivalric values and economic interests.

This is not to say that the Spanish colonial economic model embodied exclusively a feudalistic antithesis against an archetypical English approach to the accumulation of capital, as put forth by the German historian and sociologist Max Weber. Weber postulated two opposed colonial strategies of accumulation: "the feudal type in the Spanish and Portuguese colonies, the capitalistic in the Dutch and English" (Weber 1923/27, 298).[18] As demonstrated by Daniel Nemser, Weber was not the only one to formulate this binary opposition; rather, from the sixteenth and seventeenth centuries "Spain's northern European rivals began to construct and popularize a narrative of Iberian empire as superstitious, backward, greedy, and cruel in order to justify their resistance to Iberian domination and to promote their own imperial projects" (Nemser and Blanco 2019, 2).[19] Thus, I am interested in the notion of "entangled histories of capitalism," which according to Nemser opens up the possibility of exploring the "complexities and contradictions of early modern globalization as well of the logics of domination and accumulation that it set in motion" (*id.*, 10). As we shall see further on, English and Spanish colonial sources displayed both colliding and converging narratives about their perception of capital and logic of domination to justify imperial projects and coastal attacks. In so doing, they challenged the conventional ironclad notion of the "pirate" and the "corsair" by introducing the figures of the businessman and the non-military administrative manager.

For instance, Bigges reasserts and justifies at many levels the legitimacy of the expedition and enterprise through a narrative that carries an economic undertone to neutralize the arguable illegitimacy of their stay in such places as Santo Domingo and Cartagena.[20] He criticizes the Spanish colonial economic model by decrying its incompetent exploitation of natural resources evinced by the lack of people working in mines, "the gold and siluer Mines of this Island are wholie giuen ouer, and thereby they are faine in this island to vse copper money"; and the beasts that were "fed vp to a very large growth, & so killed for nothing so much" and then killed only for their hides (*id.*, 246–247). He repeatedly stresses that the Spanish were ransoming the places the fleet attacked because of their lack of military men, power, and resources. However, even though he acknowledges the legitimacy of the negotiations with the two governors of Santo Domingo and Cartagena—

Cristóbal de Ovalle and Pedro Fernández de Busto—he also criticizes colonial officials, implying that the people in charge do not live up to the expectations of the Spanish king and, instead of being ashamed, they smile (*id.*, 245–246).[21] His account also parallels Drake with governor Ovalle when stating that for "common benefit of the people and countrie" the governor of the island must present himself to their "Noble and merciful Gouernor, Sir Frances Drake" (*id.*, 230). If the governor refused, the English threatened, they would burn down the town and kill all the inhabitants. Placing Drake and Ovalle in the same category, Bigges neutralizes the piratical English attack by enabling Drake to play the role of a governor against the appointed colonial governor. Certainly Drake is not an authorized governor; nor is he acting as an official English commissioner. However, under the coordinates provided by Bigges's rhetorical configuration of the event, Drake emerges as an unauthorized political figure overseas—thus, as an extra-official agent who deals with colonial authorities by demanding ransoms and giving in exchange receipts for payment.

From the perspective of the governor of Cartagena, Pedro Fernández de Busto, Drake oscillates between being an enemy and a businessman. The governor's report to the Council of the Indies casts the figure of Drake as an enemy when explaining the English military victory, but later switches to describe him as an entrepreneur who distributed receipts for the ransoms collected: "He provided the citizens with receipts for everything and left."[22] In another report to the Audiencia of Panamá, the governor stresses the fact that the ransom was given to Drake in exchange for his promise of not returning to Cartagena: "[A]ll the inhabitants and lords have agreed to give him 100,000 ducats as long as he promises that he will never return to Cartagena, neither will another captain or England's corsair do so, during Queen Elizabeth's reign, and he will seal the pact with the queen's stamp."[23] In this sense, Drake is neither a pirate nor is he an enemy; but rather, in the governor's narrative, he becomes a legitimate dealer conducting a transnational business overseas.[24] In this regard, Michael Kempe argues that there is a distinction "between law and rhetoric in the matter of piracy" (Kempe 2010, 359). He demonstrates that piracy was instrumental in "turning the seas into a transnational realm, in which contradictory, mutually exclusive postulates competed and collided" (*id.*). While Kempe argues that the "political use of violence was thus often disguised by its legal labelling" (*id.*), I argue that in the context of the Caribbean raid it was quite the opposite. In other words, it was actually the *unstable* legal labeling of piracy that disguised the use of violence while justifying financial interests and economic transactions. For instance, the governor's letter to the Audiencia brings forth a more nuanced and less oppositional definition of maritime predation through the rhetorical decision of depicting Drake as a qualified businessman to deal with. To hold Drake accountable enabled the governor to justify the outcome of the attack—the English victory—and his role as an administrative authority, because the violent altercation became an economic transaction.

The discursive interaction of military victory and economic profit, found in the lexical and semantic realms, became manifest in the aforementioned "Resolutions of the Land-Captains" attached to the Bigges travelogue. These paratextual narratives establish a correlation between the English military deeds and financial gain—goods, money, and other wealth—taken from each island they raided:

> [W]e do therefore consider, that since all these cities, with their goods and prisoners taken in them, and the ransoms of the said cities, being all put together, are found far short to satisfy that expectation which by the generality of the enterprisers was first conceived.
>
> (Eliot, 34)

> And to say truth, we may now with much honor and reputation better be satisfied with that sum offered by them at the first, if they will now be contented to give it, than we might at that time with a great deal more; inasmuch as we have taken our full pleasure, both in the uttermost sacking and spoiling of all their household goods and merchandise, as also in that we have consumed and ruined a great part of their town with fire.
>
> (*id.*)

> This town of *Carthagena* we touched in the out parts, and consumed much with fire, as we had done *St. Domingo*, upon discontentments, and for want of agreeing with us in their first treaties touching their ransom; which at the last was concluded between us should be 110,000 ducats for that which was yet standing, the ducat valued at five shillings sixpence sterling.
>
> (*id.*, 36)

> [W]e do therefore conclude hereupon, that it is better to hold sure as we may the honour already gotten, and with the same to return towards our gracious sovereign and country, from whence, if it shall please her Majesty to set us forth again with her orderly means and entertainment, we are most ready and willing to go through with anything that the uttermost of our strength and endeavour shall be able to reach unto.
>
> (*id.*, 34)

From these resolutions derives a discursive pattern that jeopardizes the conventional understanding of the figure of the pirate both as an independent maritime predator and as an agent entirely sponsored by the English Crown. Drake thus remains somewhere in between both models, marked by the interaction of military skills and economic profit. However, the way in which economic profit was described, that is, how wealth was distributed among the soldiers and sailors who took part in the Caribbean raid—or, in the text's words, "enterprise"—discloses a notion of the pirate that stressed their skills as entrepreneurs. After distributing the ransoms and other wealth collected among the participants, they returned to their "gracious sovereign and country." This statement suggests that the English were neither pirates nor were they official corsairs—at the beginning of the voyage—demonstrating that the notion of maritime predation was ultimately associated with that of an entrepreneur who operated within the scope of a gray area between the realms of economic profit and military supremacy. Their actions did not dwell on the scope of legality or illegality because, as economic figures, they built their own rules while also maintaining an intermittent relationship with their nation of origin—in this case, England.

Drake, in his "Account to the Queen for her Share in the Venture," employed the words "adventure" and "enterprise" to allude to this voyage:

> Adventurers shall enioye their portions thereof according to the quantities of their Adventure, portion and portion alike, without anie question to be made to them for the same. And further wee are pleased, that if vpon anie consideration shall staie this enterprise, to promise hereby, that the Adventurers shall beare no losse.
>
> (Bigges 2010, 52)

Stressing a strictly economic tone, this document offers an itemized budget of the investments, expenses, and potential earnings. The reports of the Royal Commission of 1587 follow this trend by establishing that "the adventurers should be paid 15 *s.* on each pound invested, with the possibility at most of 12 *d.* The queen's dividend would be 15 *s.* for each pound ventured, with an additional amount of 350–16–4" (*id.*, 60). The lack of the terms "spoil," "plunder," or "attack," and the constant use of "adventure" and "venture" instead, elucidates the financial nature of the voyage.

Certainly the Spaniards were also interested in money or at least in preserving what they claimed was theirs for having been the discoverers of those territories. As a result, Juan de Castellanos's attempt to maintain the Spanish/English contraposition of values—moral and economic—introduces religious discourse when justifying the Spaniards' interest in safeguarding their money. Describing Hispaniola's attack, Castellanos in his historical poem *Discurso del capitán Francisco Draque* stresses the fact that nuns were running without their veils to avoid captivity, and since the inhabitants did not have great wealth, he focuses on the destruction of churches and paintings of saints. However, the little fortune they possessed was thrown into wells to conceal it from the English. Drake's ravages in the attack are measured by the money and wealth he took and also by the destruction of churches. Therefore, one of Drake's main epithets would be, in the words of Castellanos: "traitor thief, heretic, furious" (*ladrón traidor, herege, furibundo*) (Castellanos 1921, 92).[25]

On the other hand, Castellanos also combines the economic vocabulary with religious adjectives when describing the tone of the negotiations between the governor of Cartagena and Drake: "The conversation went on / *indifferent to any Catholic benefit* / and the Englishman always favoring *his right*" (emphasis added).[26] In this way Castellanos opposes English rights, indifferent to conferring any benefit to the Catholics in the transaction. The entry for *provecho* in Covarrubias's *Tesoro*, 1611, defines this word as something that "results in usefulness or utility" (*lo que resulta en utilidad*); more than a century before that, Nebrija's *Vocabulario de Romance en Latin*, 1495, points out the Latin translation: *utilitas* or *commoditas*. It is worth noting that the Latin word *commoditas*, which refers to "convenience," will appear in the English language as "commodity" or "merchandise." By highlighting the fact that Drake was exclusively interested in his "own right" or greed, Castellanos circumscribes the concept of "Catholic" to the realm of economic values. Instead of stating that the negotiations were not just profitable or economically advantageous for the Spanish authorities, Castellanos intertwines moral and economic discourses by using the phrases "Catholic advantage" or "Catholic benefit" (*católico provecho*). As a result, Castellanos neutralizes the position of the pirate along with that of the governor, because both parties participate in an economic transaction in which the "Catholic" part is subdued to particular—in this case, Protestant—economic interests. By mentioning that Drake was merely "favoring his right," Castellanos does not acknowledge any differentiation between the legality or illegality of Drake's siege of the city of Cartagena, but rather the stage of negotiations effaces Drake's condition of pirate from the main picture.

By using the term "Catholic" as both a religious and economic denomination against the "Lutherans," Castellanos defines both English and Spanish colonial nationalities. In contrast, if Castellanos were using the adjective "Catholic" to refer to its original meaning—namely "universal" and "diverse"—then he would also be projecting the Spanish Catholic power as the solely imperial narrative upon which economic value is defined. In this sense, Castellanos's "Catholic benefit" equals universal profit, which suggests an attempt at universalizing the Catholic faith while justifying peninsular jurisdiction and control overseas. In any case, by combining religious and economic discourses, Castellanos rhetorically discredits foreign English interlopers in the Spanish economy in the New World. "Catholic profit" ultimately pinpoints an entrenched and all-encompassing peninsular economic model, whereas Drake belongs to an English and Protestant approach that indulges movement, circulation, and private profit.[27]

To criminalize or decriminalize Drake's raid seems coincidentally to reformulate the limits of geographical space, property, and nationhood. Even though Drake claimed to be a representative of his queen, he acted without any ambition of conquering Spanish colonial territories to expand English territorial power, nor was he officially appointed by the Privy Council or the queen to raid the Caribbean as a military strategy. Therefore, moving across English national boundaries, Drake emerges as an agent who operates in different topologies and the import of his character becomes a unique transatlantic construct. From both sides of the Atlantic, maps, travelogues, epistles, and historical poetry broadcast the story of Drake's Caribbean raid of 1585–1586. These sources bear the struggle of demarcating the illegitimate or legitimate nature of Drake's maritime and land-based predations as they present conflicting versions when describing the same event. The instability of Drake's condition—as a pirate, an English patriot, or a Spanish enemy—and the justifications and condemnations of his actions ultimately place this figure in a gloomy area constituted by the incompatible dynamics of mobility and sedentary life, fluid economic models and restricted ones, sturdy political institutions and elastic ones, static moral values and flexible ones.

More broadly, Drake's model of piracy emerges from the fact that he operates mainly in maritime space with no particular intention of settling in the New World as the buccaneers will do afterward in the Caribbean (which we will see in Chapter 6).[28] However, by calling him a transnational figure I do not imply that he was fully sponsored by the English Crown, but rather, that he identified himself as a subject of Queen Elizabeth and occasionally received money from her and other representatives of the court. As mentioned in Chapter 1, he was openly criticized and rejected by several noblemen, such as Earl of Sussex and the Earl of Arundel. As an unintended consequence of the English concept of piracy, Drake was nonetheless the metonym of the English Crown in the eyes of the Spaniards and Spanish subjects in the Caribbean. In this way, the raid showcases a heterogeneously oriented kind of maritime predation that accounts for the chameleon-like nature of the pirate, a figure who was considered a corsair, a smuggler, a trader, or an adventurer according to the specific agenda underlying the primary source describing pirate attacks. In any case, looking at the transnational and economic aspects of Drake's figure allows for the understanding of piracy as an unstable category, because it sheds light on the nuances of national identity and the multiple layers that constituted it. In this way, Drake's representations account for the contingency nature of nationality and its direct relationship with moral behavior or misbehavior and economic interests or tendencies. In this sense, using the category of piracy or non-piracy to classify English maritime predators allows for the establishment of national identities and imperial narratives of power.

The distinction between heroic deeds and moneymaking pursuits was derived from the Renaissance ideology of discovery that considered trade and money as constitutive aspects of mercenary behavior. During the seventeenth century, the increasing merchant audience contributed to the epic model's decline and the emergence of the romance genre that had to adapt to represent a "world of money and materiality" (Quint, 263–267). This is evinced by a later Caribbean epic poem, Silvestre de Balboa's *Espejo de paciencia*, which retells the historical attack carried out by the French pirate Gilberto Girón, the abduction of Bishop Juan de las Cabezas de Altamirano, his eventual release, and the pirate's death at the hands of the residents of the city of Yara.[29] The first canto portrays the hyperbolized torture endured by the bishop, while the second canto focuses on describing how the population avenged the bishop by fighting against the French pirate. Whereas the first canto criticizes the French pirates because of their economic greediness against the moral, exemplary figure of the bishop, at the end of the canto the poetic voice emphasizes the local efficiency in collecting the ransom and extols the importance of the Indies in international commerce.[30] Here the poetic voice refers to contraband, since none of the countries listed were authorized to trade with the Indies without the intervention of peninsular authorities.[31] Unlike the first canto, in which the main conflict's resolution is mediated by the payment of the ransom, the second canto displays Cuban and colonial fighting prowess as a means to resolve the conflict. In this way the structure of the poem reasserts the conciliation of two conflicting ideologies of honor. On the one side, honor could be found in the process of collecting ransoms and engaging in contraband practices with other countries, while on the other, honor could also be achieved through conventional fighting against an overwhelming military force. This work displays the acceptance of financial transactions with chivalric and moral conventions that were previously criticized or embraced by the governors' rhetoric, Bigges's travelogue when reporting Drake's Caribbean raid, and Juan Castellanos's historical poem, which I will discuss in depth in the following section.

Who Is to Blame? Peninsular and Caribbean Explanations of the Attack

Juan de Castellanos crafted the first historical poem written in Spanish and exclusively dedicated to the portrayal of Francis Drake. Consisting of five cantos, the *Discurso del capitán Francisco Draque* (c1586–1587) was intended to function as a coda for his "History of Cartagena," contained in the third part of his *Elegies of Illustrious Men*. Finished a year after the English raid, the poem was sent to Spain along with a letter addressed to the abbot of Burgo Hondo, Melchor Pérez de Arteaga.[32] In this letter, Castellanos, a chaplain and *beneficiado* (rector) of the Cathedral of Tunja, claims to have compiled this story from several accounts and interviews with eyewitnesses and people who apparently knew the English captain before "he came to bother" the Indies (Castellanos, xiv–xv). There, Castellanos also reveals the inconsistency of some of the sources he consulted on account of different "perceptions" (*sentimientos*): "[S]ome people say more and others say less, according to each one's perceptions, as it happens in such events."[33] He also explains that because Drake was not welcome in Spain, he was advised to "amputate" (*desmembrar*) the *Discurso* from the rest of the third *Elegy*.[34] Not only did Castellanos "amputate" the text from its original place, but one of the censors of the

64 *Setting Sails to the Narrative of Piracy*

Council of the Indies, Pedro Sarmiento de Gamboa—discussed in Chapter 1—ordered its suppression sometime before 1592.[35]

In the aftermath of Drake's sieges of Cartagena and Santo Domingo, Castellanos's *Discurso* is part of a larger network of information that includes epistles, depositions, and letters of inquiry sent to the Council of the Indies and to the Spanish King Philip II. These documents questioned the military leadership, the distribution of wealth, and the undertones of the negotiations conducted between Drake and the high officials from both political and religious institutions. Martínez-Osorio and others have argued that Castellanos's intention was to assert his preeminence as a historical poet by alluding to his knowledge and to his methodology of comparing different accounts (see, e.g., Martínez-Osorio 2011, 8).[36] While concurring with this substantiated claim, I propose that Castellanos's clarification in his letter also highlights the challenge of compiling truthful sources about maritime predation that triggers the formulation of divergent factual narratives which, in this case, were crafted and manipulated according to the authors' particular interests. In this sense, the sources became a vehicle for crafting narratives to blame several authorities or individuals other than Drake.

For instance, Diego Hidalgo de Montemayor—governor of the city of Santa Marta and commissioned judge of the Real Audiencia of Santa Fe—stated that the varying culprits emerging from these narratives were primarily based on the interests of the complainant.[37] As such, these blaming narratives showcase that the specifics surrounding the attack or piracy event were mediated by the Spanish colonial sources to advance a specific agenda—condemning or celebrating the deeds of several captains or high officials.[38] To this end, rather than focusing on the historical veracities of these letters and works, I assert what Rolena Adorno has denominated as "rhetorical referentiality" in colonial writing to emphasize their role in recasting the pirate from the viewpoint of the targeted Spanish territories.[39] She argues that colonial writing—including a variety of genres and modes: chronicles, accounts, epic poetry, among others—may not be considered a truthful description of events because colonial writing becomes an event itself (Adorno, 4).

The narratives of the documents I will analyze here share four core elements: (1) the governor of Cartagena, Pedro Fernández de Busto, and the governor of Santo Domingo, Cristóbal de Ovalle, were warned about the potential attacks; (2) both governors took precautions to protect the cities, although the acting president of the Council of the Indies, Hernando de Vega y Fonseca, and others claimed that these precautions were neither efficient nor sufficient; (3) Pedro Vique, captain of galleys in Cartagena, made negligent decisions; and (4) local soldiers ran away when confronted by Drake's troops. Peninsular and colonial authorities manipulated these key details to denounce larger issues of governmental administration and corruption in the New World, the lack of military resources in the Spanish strongholds that were attacked, and the transformation of piracy into a diplomatic and financial transaction. I will examine the denunciations supported by religious and moral values that appear in the governors' descriptions of the event to conceal military incompetence and justify local defeats in Santo Domingo and Cartagena. Also, I will show how these narratives labeled internal enemies by revealing issues related to political and economic corruption that seem to transcend Drake's raids. Eschewing anti-English propaganda and highlighting peninsular and colonial administrative incompetence instead, the sources underscored Spanish supremacy by blaming military defeat on internal failures that did not account for either macro-military or administrative weaknesses in the empire.

As several scholars have posited, there was a rhetorical tendency to define piracy attacks as God's punishment for moral misbehavior during the first decades of Spanish conquest (from both Spanish and English perspectives).[40] This explains why literary and historical narratives of the Caribbean raid rationalized the English military victories by resorting to religious discourse. A concerned Pedro Fernández de Busto, governor of Cartagena, sent a letter to the king claiming: "Our Lord gave the victory to the enemy because of my sins and the sins of others."[41] Officers in Santo Domingo blamed divine sources as well: "[W]e understand that this was a punishment sent from heaven for all the sins of this town."[42] Such a moralizing view echoes what historians have coined the Decadence Tradition: writing about a wrathful God who punishes Muslims, Protestants, and Catholics alike because of their moral failings.[43] In doing so, the governors entwined economic and political affairs to align the historical facts they provided to justify the payments of ransoms based on both moral and financial considerations.[44]

In his letter, the governor of Cartagena singled out an internal moral enemy as he blamed the religious office of Cartagena's bishop, Fray Juan de Montalvo, for influencing the negotiations with Drake:

> [The person] who bothered me most and persuaded me to take your majesty's royal treasure to ransom the city was the Bishop of this province, not for the good of the City, but because it seemed to him that he could, in this way, do more harm to me and make me fail; and not only in this, but he strives to make all things go badly for me because he has a diseased heart and is out to get me.[45]

Additionally, the governor stressed the financial interests that led him to negotiate with Drake, such as the potential loss of the city as an important stronghold of trade with Seville, Nombre de Dios, and Peru. He also alleged that three monasteries would have been destroyed and more than 4,000 people would have died. Fernández de Busto cast himself as a victim by placing the bishop and Drake in the same category, painting them both as being driven by distorted morals to endanger the economic state of the city.[46]

From Castellanos's viewpoint, the decision to pay ransom was a consensus reached by the higher offices (the bishop and the governor) and common individuals such as merchants and neighbors (Castellanos, 205–207). The agreement, according to his poem, was not against "religious laws" (*leies de derecho sancto*), since the Audiencia of Santo Domingo had also struck a deal with Drake: "Nobody judged him for dementia / or for being against the Holy Law, / seeing that the members of the Audiencia / did the same thing" (Castellanos, 206).[47] On the one hand, the governor compares Drake's moral defects to those of an individual in charge of a religious office while on the other, Castellanos refers to the absence of religious laws that might intervene in these cases. In this manner, they strategically merge moral undertones and economic concerns to conceal questionable leadership skills. As we shall see further, such a moralizing view to explain the Spanish colonial economic setback and military defeat enabled authors to convey issues ranging from administrative incompetence and military weaknesses to political corruption and damaged social structures.

Besides intertwining moral considerations and military affairs, the governor of Cartagena accuses Alonso Bravo—one of the renowned captains in Castellanos's heroic poem—of corruption for trading and not paying what he owed to the residents of the city. Another culprit in the governor's letter is Dr. Guillén Chaparro, a judge of the Real Audiencia, for paying exorbitant salaries to his servants.[48] The governor displays his concern about Chaparro's intention to use Drake's raid as an excuse for squandering money by appointing several judges, such as Hidalgo Montemayor, to investigate the attack. If we saw before that the governor compared Drake's moral misbehavior with the bishop's evil intentions to damage his reputation, here the governor matches the economic bankruptcy caused by Drake's siege with the potential economic wreckage that Chaparro may cause:

> [I]t is feared in the City that this Doctor Chaparro will send many judges with excessive salaries because of everything that happened in Cartagena; and that this would be another ruin, no lighter than the one caused by the captain [Drake].[49]

Through his report of Drake's attack and by equating Drake's and Chaparro's tactics, the governor discredits the juridical apparatus of the Spanish stronghold and implies that Drake's attack was as dangerous as the internal economic corruption of the appointed judicial figures in the Indies. He thus deflects the reader's attention from Drake's successful attack by highlighting internal enemies within the Spanish colonial apparatus.

Even though Castellanos and Bigges had different views—being subjects of opposing powers—they both emphasize the deterioration of the Spanish colonial landscape by specifically alluding to colonial military flaws. As we saw in the previous section, Bigges underscores that the English were better equipped, with longer pikes, while very few Spaniards were armed (Bigges

2010, 251). Castellanos also stresses that local soldiers were "poorly armed" to protect the city of Santo Domingo and thus, most of the population ran away (Castellanos, 76–83).[50] Doctor Aliaga, for his part, does not acknowledge the English armada's supremacy; rather, he emphasizes governor Ovalle's incompetence to coordinate an effective military counterattack. He recorded in a letter addressed to his superiors that he suggested the governor provide the *Fortaleza* (fortress) with gunpowder and ammunition, and select a group of people with military experience to counsel his decisions and orders. Apparently Ovalle—also appointed president of the Real Audiencia of Santo Domingo—disregarded Aliaga's proposals before and during the attack.[51] Besides highlighting the governor's poor military leadership, Aliaga urges the Spanish peninsular authorities to send someone versed in war affairs and capable of implementing a rigorous military training among the local soldiers.[52] In his *Discurso*, Castellanos stresses Aliaga's points by displaying the governor's failure to follow advice and the inadequate performance of the disorganized troops.[53] After stating that he also found conflicting descriptions of Cartagena's attack, Hidalgo Montemayor, the governor of Santa Marta, blames the people who fled the scene because the Spanish galleys ran aground and captain Pedro Vique ordered to set them on fire—and mistakenly did not take away the artillery—so that the English would not be able to take them.[54] The governor of Cartagena accuses someone from the Spanish side who ordered the troops' withdrawal: "A voice was heard from our side: 'Withdraw, gentlemen!'"[55] Transferring the blame to local residents unable to fight produces an ambivalent narrative that delineates the chaotic state of the city and justifies the further negotiations conducted by the governors. At first glance, Castellanos's heroic poem and the Spanish peninsular and colonial documents reflect the medieval conflict of the classical rhetorical topos of arms and letters (*sapientia et fortitudo*) discussed in the previous section. This clash of social values—arms versus letters—traversed transatlantic waters and reached the Spanish colonial landscape. Referring to the English-Caribbean raid, the sources display such a conflict through the formulation of denouncing narratives that either criticize or approve the bureaucratic and military skills of high-ranking officers and the more privileged social sphere.

Even though Castellanos does not openly condemn the governors' decision to pay the ransoms, he emphasizes local flaws related to chivalric values when reporting Drake's fleet's success in looting Spanish territories. It has been argued that Castellanos rationalized the loss of the cities of Santo Domingo and Cartagena as a result of the lack of properly trained military men and chivalric values that once populated the Indies. For instance, Luis Restrepo's seminal study compares Castellanos's regret toward the absence of brave and chivalric men in the Americas with the classical verse *Ubi sunt* to restore the notion of an idealized knight and conquistador (Restrepo, 40). The values of such men, according to Restrepo, ultimately support Castellanos's foundational historical project of promoting a social order led by a martial aristocracy (*id.*, 40–41). Through his narrative representation of the conflicts among the Spanish colonial populations, Castellanos favors the conquistadors and the *encomenderos* (those who were granted portions of land along with a number of indigenous individuals under their command) (Martínez-Osorio 2011, 26). To him, the internal enemies are servants, indigenous populations, and others who have become unreliable or "harmful" over time (Martínez-Osorio 2016, 118–121).[56]

In the case of Santo Domingo, the narratives that blame the governor and local soldiers for the loss of the city, as well as those that defend their performance, reinforce the notion of a Spanish preeminence through the incorporation of the topos of arms and letters. That is, while certain authors criticize the soldiers' lack of military experience or precarious situation to repel the attack, others aggrandize chivalric values, such as their courage, and their bureaucratic competence to end the English threat. For instance, officers who accentuated colonial chivalric values stood by the work of Santo Domingo's governor and the military local resistance, declaring that their people were "not used to war affairs" (Rodríguez Demorizi, 24–25). Melchor Ochoa de Villanueva states that the governor assembled the troops well, considering the limited amount of time he had to do so.[57] The archbishop, on the other hand, declares that "despite being infamously blamed [the governor and the soldiers]," he does not know any other nation "with so much bravery that embraced and resisted the attack without ammunition and weapons."[58] These opinions pinpoint that those who blame the governor and the local soldiers, as well as those who defend them, converge in that they do not credit the English with military supremacy, nor do they condemn Queen Elizabeth I for enabling these attacks. After all, both governors, Ovalle and Fernández de Busto, manipulate their narratives to focus on their "victory," earned through negotiations with the English captain, while uncovering serious concerns about corruption within the colonial apparatus.

On his part, Cartagena's governor uncovered serious concerns about corruption; unveiled internal conflicts between colonial forces; and alluded to the transatlantic conflict between colonial and Iberian authorities. He admitted such colonial tensions when suggesting his own removal and the appointment of someone from Spain who was cognizant in matters of land and sea. He also proposed that such an individual should hold more centralized power to avoid the internal disputes that, in the end, led to Cartagena's fall.[59] In contrast, the president of the Council of the Indies, Hernando de Vega y Fonseca, emphasized the governor's shameful decision to spend the money of the royal treasury in paying Drake's ransom and financing Drake's accommodations, banquets, and conversations after the negotiations in Cartagena: "[T]he Governor shared a shameful relationship with the corsair, spending money from the Royal Treasure, your majesty, and so it is said that he enjoyed banquets and conversations with the corsair."[60] From the English perspective, as discussed in the previous section, Bigges's account confirmed the alleged good treatment provided in Cartagena and Santo Domingo by Spanish authorities:

> During our abode in this place, as also at S. DOMINGO, there passed diuerse curtesies between vs and the Spaniards. As feasting, and vsing them with all kindnesse and fauour: so as amongst others there came to see the Generall, the Gouernor of CARTAGENA, with the Bishop of the same, and diuerse other Gentlemen of the better sort.
>
> (Bigges 2010, 258)

These descriptions also support Kelsey's suspicion of unauthorized trading disguised as ransoms.[61] They nonetheless exemplify the transposed social values—from military dominance to diplomatic advantage—in the context of Spanish transatlantic territories and kingdoms.

David Quint's study on classical rival epic traditions traces two predominant patterns—the victors and the defeated—exemplified by Virgil's *Aeneid* and Lucan's *Pharsalia*, respectively. While the first model showcases a linear teleology marked by the fate of the hero inserted in a coherent narrative structure, the latter relies on wanderings and digressions that provide a vehicle for dissident voices and result in open endings ruled by chance (Quint, 8–11). Delving into Lucan's desire to project a class conflict or "a warrior nobility at odds with a central monarchy determined to limit their power," Quint analyzes the nostalgic tone toward the anachronistic military technologies and the inconclusive endings and romance digressions found in the epic poem *La Araucana* (1569, 1578, 1589). He also considers its overlapping aspects with Virgil's legitimizing narratives of imperial victors and Lucan's anti-imperial losers (*id.*, 9–18). I place Castellanos's poem in such an intersectional terrain between the two epic models, the winners and the losers, inasmuch as his poem nostalgically revamps the figure of the individual conquistador while acknowledging the importance of a centralized and incorruptible power to avoid future attacks from enemies of the Spanish Crown. Rehearsing the parameters of a local identity structured by the epic form, the *Discurso* portrays a local and transatlantic society defeated by the English military, Spanish colonial schemes, and corrupted social values.

Referring to *La Araucana*'s ending, Quint proposes that the lack of a definitive closure, aligned with Lucan's epic model of the vanquished that reinforces a political message of resistance, suggests an "ever-repeating cycle of Araucanian insurgency" (*id.*, 166). Castellanos's *Discurso* also promotes this notion of repetitive cycles in what might be considered an open ending as well. At the poem's end, he reflects on the ongoing work of historians that will register future events: "otros historiadores más enteros / dirán después sucesos venideros" (Castellanos 1921, 226). As time passes, the last verses conclude, the stronger light upon the historian's path is "hope fulfilled with uncertainty."[62] In this manner, while alluding to the unforeseeability of events and almost adopting the tone of a cautionary tale, Castellanos warns the reader that if maritime predation parallels the erosion of the social and moral fabric, the future of his society might be driven more by economic interests than by past heroic deeds.

National supremacy, in the case of the Spanish and colonial officials, was the repulsion of the incursion led by Drake—not on the battlefield, but at the negotiating table. However, Spanish national supremacy also consisted in efficiently managing a hostage situation to conceal the imperial fragility and the tensions between colonial and peninsular societies. As many have argued, distance became one of the most harmful enemies of King Philip II's empire.[63] In the context of the Caribbean raid, peninsular and colonial sources created strategic narratives for building a sort of "long-term resilience"—a term coined by Wright—to mitigate geographical distances and differences (Wright 2008, 38).[64] As we have seen and shall see further, the English and Spanish colonial sides attempted to articulate an ideology of national supremacy based either on military prowess or on economic-bureaucratic advantage (arms and letters). Although Spanish peninsular and colonial sources celebrated or condemned the financial transactions, they agreed with their English counterparts in addressing colonial administrative issues and tensions between colonial and peninsular authorities, through the configuration of narratives of culpability. While peninsular and colonial authorities looked for a scapegoat, the paradox lies in the fact that by considering Drake's attack as a symptom of internal fissures, the Spanish sources struggled to uphold and project the pursued notion of Spanish imperial and transatlantic strength.

By crafting a narrative that transforms a maritime attack into an economic transaction, the governors highlighted the efficiency of their negotiations with the English captain. They reported that the sum of money paid for the ransom was significantly less than Drake had originally demanded. In Santo Domingo's case, governor Ovalle mentioned that Drake asked for one million, then for 100,000, and finally agreed to collect 25,000 ducats.[65] The governor of Cartagena, Fernández de Busto, stated that Drake requested 400,000 ducats but that he counteroffered 20,000 ducats and, after seeing that Drake's men were willing to burn the entire city, raised the amount to 30,000 ducats. Once the bishop authorized that payment "without remorse," he ordered everyone to contribute according to their holdings and property. Finally, Drake settled for 107,000 ducats, and 79,000 ducats were borrowed from the royal treasury (Castellanos 1921, 318–319). He even mentioned that Drake provided him with a receipt for the ransom. These claims demonstrate that both governors, while formulating a narrative that portrayed them as successful leaders (or men of letters), attempted to reinforce the notion of Spanish supremacy by making it seem that they had outsmarted the English. Consequently, the governors maintained that the Spanish did not lose entirely, but prevailed through negotiation.

The two governors' efforts to benefit from the rhetorical transformation of piracy into a legitimate economic transaction was not well received by peninsular and other colonial representatives for two reasons. First, this rhetoric undermined the Spanish military reputation and capability of protecting their territories; and second, to negotiate with a pirate posed the question of who might be considered or recognized as a legitimate adversary (or a just enemy). Only a decade before Drake's Caribbean raid, Jean Bodin (1529/30–1596) debated this topic in his *Six livres de la république* (1576). Although Bodin mentioned that pirates should not be protected by the law of nations, he stated that sometimes they forced sovereign leaders to negotiate when they had brought an overwhelming military force.[66] This notion resonated in later texts dealing with the concept of diplomacy and the role and rights of ambassadors when "recognition" meant to "be acknowledged as a legitimate political agent" (Hampton, 119). In the context of Drake's Caribbean raid, it could be argued that the two governors projected this trend by characterizing their negotiation with Drake as something honorable and officially conducted. Their narratives previewed the transformation of maritime predation into a modern diplomatic and economic exchange. After all, they were not military men but, rather, skilled in letters or administrative matters.

The debate about the figure of the pirate is crucial to understanding the justifications given by the colonial officials, especially the governors, who claimed a diplomatic and economic victory in dealing with a hostage situation. To this end, they had to transform Drake's public image of a ruthless pirate into a legitimate enemy. However, the juridical distinction between the pirate and the enemy was a subject of debate among European sixteenth-century legal theorists such as Balthazar Ayala (1548–1584) and Alberico Gentili (1552–1608).[67] They posited that unlike the just enemy, who had the right of restitution and the power of negotiation, the pirate belonged to the notion of an enemy deprived of any right.[68] In the context of the New World, the Spanish sources will sometimes refer to Drake as a just enemy or as a pirate, depending on their underlying intentions. For instance, the governors, probably aware of the illegitimacy of pirates to declare war or negotiate a peaceful agreement to end military hostilities, converted Drake into a legitimate enemy to validate their negotiations.

As several scholars have pointed out, Drake defies such an ironclad classification. Jowitt underscores that in theory, a legislation that was passed by the English in 1536 defined piracy as a criminal offense, yet in praxis, English authorities failed properly to enforce it because of the flexibility between criminal piracy and legitimate reprisal (Jowitt, 50). It is precisely the semantic and linguistic ambivalence behind the terms "pirate" and "corsair" that allowed both English and colonial authorities to render Drake's figure into a legitimate enemy in the ransom negotiations. By using "corsair" and "pirate" interchangeably throughout his poem, Castellanos crafted a system of enunciation, a sort of sleight of hand, in which the figure of the pirate escaped any stable taxonomy. As mentioned in the previous section of this chapter, several dictionaries at the time linked the terms, using one to define the other.

After raiding the governor's house, Drake found several royal *cédulas* (decrees) in which King Philip II had warned the governor about the possibility of facing Drake "the corsair" (Castellanos 1921, 204). However,

Castellanos's ambivalent system of portraying Drake was also constrained by metrical concerns and the rigors of the literary device of rhyme; thus, the term *pirata* suited him better than the term *corsario*. Consequently, there is a further scene that portrays how Drake became enraged because he realized that the king had used the word "pirate" to describe him: "Because His Majesty had treated him badly / By putting upon him the name of pirate" (*id.*, 208).[69] The governor tried to calm Drake's anger by suggesting that perhaps the king had not read the *cédula*, that in fact he sometimes signed documents written by his secretaries without proofreading them. Drake threatened the governor and anyone, including the Spanish king and his secretaries, who dared to use this "base word" (*palabra baxa*) to characterize him.[70] Aside from blurring the semantic difference between the categories of pirate and corsair, Castellanos implied that Drake's concept of his own condition enabled him to justify the attack and subsequent negotiations.[71] This dramatic scene thus displays an effort to neutralize a potential legal case against both Drake and the colonial authorities who negotiated with him. The negotiation, also recorded in Spanish colonial depositions, reinforced the lack of leadership to articulate narratives of blame for the enemy within. Instead of criminalizing Drake's actions, Spanish peninsular authorities brought several legal cases against the Spanish colonial functionaries involved in the event.

To a great extent, the classical topos of arms and letters corresponded to sixteenth-century notions of the gentleman (or the knight) and the merchant, respectively. According to Quint, the merchant, unlike the knight, was considered non-heroic in the classical-epic world's code of ethics (Quint, 264). Castellanos and several Spanish peninsular and colonial authorities addressed these categories by criticizing military strategies and administrative decisions taken under Drake's siege due to the emphasis on merchant values against chivalric ones. The notion of the merchant acquired unlawful or piratical undertones whereas the knight emerged as a just enemy or corsair. However, the representations of Drake in this particular event blur the dichotomy between these categories by intermingling the notions of the pirate and the just enemy (corsair). This is evinced by Castellanos's indiscriminate use of the terms and by the governors who fashioned themselves and Drake into merchants and "just enemies" (knights and gentlemen) to justify their negotiations. Consequently, if "letters" corresponded to the category of the merchant and "arms" to that of the knight and the gentleman, these narratives showcase a conflation of such *ad hoc* dichotomies.

To save the Spanish Crown from public shame, the president of the Council of the Indies urged the king to investigate and, if guilt was found, prosecute the offending subjects.[72] In this way, his narrative warned that negotiating, whether with a corsair or a pirate, revealed the governors' inability to protect the Spanish strongholds. Also, dealing with Drake implied that colonial officials considered Drake a worthy and legitimate adversary and exonerated his piracy by closing an economic deal with him.[73]

The Council of War (*Consejo de Guerra*) sent another letter of inquiry concluding that besides the spoils, economic loss, and poor military resistance found in San Agustín (now St. Augustine, Florida), Cartagena, and Santo Domingo, the event "might have strengthened the corsairs' confidence to plan a major strike against these places, next year or every time they might want to."[74] More broadly, to regard Drake as a just enemy or legitimate rival was to acknowledge English military prowess, and then to cast piracy attacks as battles in a just war between England and Spain that—as evinced by Bigges's account (2010) discussed in the previous section—had not been officially declared.

Colonial and peninsular authorities used the attack as a pretext to blame internal enemies within the Spanish colonial apparatus. At the dawn of an age of increasing bureaucratization, the two governors of Cartagena and Santo Domingo concealed their questionable military leadership by employing moral undertones to highlight issues related to internal economic and political corruption. In doing so, they attempted to transform Drake into a legitimate adversary or a just enemy in order to justify the processes of negotiation. Meanwhile, Bigges, Castellanos, and several officials—who occasionally discredited the work of these governors—embraced the superiority of arms against letters or bureaucrats in charge of high governmental Spanish colonial offices. In the end, all Spanish colonial, peninsular, and English sources failed to condemn Queen Elizabeth I but, rather, blamed the enemy within by rationalizing the outcomes of Santo Domingo and Cartagena's attacks as if they were self-inflicted wounds.

Despite the governors' attempts to vindicate their efforts when warding off the attack through negotiation, they did not succeed and were held accountable by peninsular authorities. In the aftermath of Drake's raid, the president of the Council of the Indies ordered the arrest of both Captain Pedro Vique and Governor Fernández de Busto. The latter, who was over 70 years old, appealed his sentence by alluding to his 40 years of service to the king; and Vique continued to live in exile as late as 1598 in Oran (now in Algeria), a coastal city northwest of Algiers. Governor Ovalle died several months after Drake's siege and several measures, including the strengthening of Santo Domingo's fortresses, were ordered by peninsular authorities (Castellanos, c–cii). The report of the secret Spanish official, Ángel González, who was sent to investigate the attack on Cartagena mysteriously disappeared on its way to Spain. A Spanish representative in Cartagena, Dr. Juan Milio, stated in a letter that a friar of Cartagena, Juan González de Mendoza, believed that the local people might have stolen the documents because they proved more than the king wished to know.[75] Milio's statement confirms the peninsular suspicions of corruption in Cartagena's administrative apparatus, including the doubtful story of Drake's siege.

Divergent perceptions (*sentimientos*) of the same event foster multiple ambivalent narratives of culpability. Peninsular and colonial authorities maligned higher officials and identified internal enemies or denounced misguided military tactics. In this way they disavowed Drake's prowess and reinforced an imperial narrative of Spanish supremacy over the affected territories. Peninsular and colonial sources thereby claimed that they were defeated because they were not properly prepared, not because they were weaker. Meanwhile, the governors' depiction of their negotiations with Drake, in which they resorted to diplomacy instead of war, paradoxically asserted a Spanish victory as they tackled the timely ideological tensions between military and emerging diplomatic societies. Marginal Caribbean economies thrived on illegitimate commercial trade unbeknownst to the Spanish Crown, circumventing peninsular monopolistic restrictions. Writing about maritime predation shaped and reinforced a collective image of the conditions in the New World in which the Caribbean remained a geographical referent of chaos, marred by the constant threat of foreign attacks. The analysis of rhetorical blames and factual inconsistencies, found in both literary and historical accounts in the region, allows for a nuanced understanding of the phenomenon of maritime predation across the transatlantic borders of Spanish power. Given that there were no specific legal directives or religious laws to address a piratical siege, as Castellanos and Bigges have stated, Drake's raid provided a rhetorical scenario for rehearsing ideological premises as to the limits of war, the conception of the enemy, and the possibility of repelling attacks through negotiations and economic transactions.

Neither the English nor the Spanish fulfilled their expectations of this incident: the English did not gain the expected economic profit from the collection of ransoms, while the Spanish lost both profits and military prestige.[76] Both sides nonetheless turned the descriptions of the attacks into claims of victory. While the English transformed an economic defeat into a military victory and scored a rhetorical triumph over the Spanish empire, colonial governors cast the Spanish military defeat as an economic and diplomatic victory.[77] By exploiting the rhetorical value—evinced by the contrasting factual and literary descriptions of the attack—both the English and the Spanish crafted their descriptions to ultimately advance an ideology of national supremacy. The significance of the English narratives of military preeminence, along with Spanish and colonial narratives of blame, is neither military nor economic. The profit derived from Drake's attack is the rhetorical capital of its depictions.[78] Beyond the 132,000 ducats Drake collected from colonial ransoms, the lasting profit of this venture was the account of the raid, as English ambitions became manifest. Along these lines, although the Spanish were military defeated and economically harmed, they crafted their descriptions of the event to perpetuate their status as a dominant empire, thereby securing an ideological profit as well.

These portrayals of piracy reveal the circumstances that led England to replace ideological mercantile values with projections of empire. In the context of the Caribbean raid, however, Drake is portrayed as both a merchant and a gentleman. The analysis presented discloses that both the descriptions of the attack and the narratives of blame forged an ideology that braids the notion of imperial and national military supremacy with increasingly mercantilist early-modern values. Depictions of maritime predation, therefore, set an ideological precedent for the articulation of the military and economic values that underpinned further European projects of colonization in the Americas during the following century. However, the pirate's figure—as a literary and historical trope—will not be legally defined and will remain flexible and chameleon-like until Elizabeth I's and Philip II's deaths and the ends of their respective reigns. In the next chapter, focusing on the visual and narrative representations of the Caribbean islands, we will continue threading the ongoing impact of Drake's Caribbean raid alongside the exploration of the external foreign and Hispanic idiosyncrasies of the region.

Notes

1 There were only six investors for this voyage. The queen contributed £10,000, Drake £7,000, the Earl of Leicester £3,000, Drake's cousin John Hawkins £2,500, William Hawkins £1,000, and Sir Walter Raleigh £400 (Kelsey, 240).
2 Two other laudatory poems were composed celebrating Drake's raid of the Caribbean in 1585–1586: Henry Robarts's *A Most Friendly Farewell Given by a Welwiller to the Right Worshipful Sir Frauncis Drake Knight* (London 1585) and Thomas's Greepe *The True and Perfecte Newes of the Worthy and Valiant Exploits, Performed and Done by that Valiant Knight Syr Francis Drake* (London, 1587).
3 Bigges recorded the events that took place until he died of fever in Cartagena. While it remains unclear at which point of the attack he died, his account was apparently continued and finished by Lieutenant Croftes, another member of the expedition. The first edition of his account was published in Latin in 1588, and two editions in English appeared in 1589.
4 Among those flaws, Martínez-Osorio mentions "the absence of a more reliable system of communication, the lack of forethought by local authorities, and the military incompetence of newly arrived merchants and bureaucrats" (Martínez-Osorio, 50).
5 It is worth noting that Hakluyt also translated several Spanish accounts into English to prove his point about the Spaniards' view toward English maritime pillagers.
6 "[T]he aforesayd Francis Drake, with a strong fleet of 24 ships arrived there, and made spoile of Santo Domingo, Carthagena, and S. Augustine, things that are knowen to all the worlde. But it is likely that if the King of Spaine live, he will in time provide sufficient remedy, to keepe his countreys and subjects from the invasion of other nations" (Hakluyt 1598–1600, 68).
7 According to editor Mary Frear Keeler, in *Sir Francis Drake's West Indian Voyage* (2010), they arrived in the Cies islands close to the Vigo River (78).
8 The *Primrose Journal* (kept aboard the ship *Primrose*) states they were also looking for imprisoned Englishmen, their merchant goods, and victuals. It is included on page 181 in the compilation titled *Sir Francis Drake's West Indian Voyage 1585–86* (edited by Mary Frear Keeler).
9 Addressed to the Marquis of Santa Cruz, Bermudez's letter states that he replied to the English that "he had no power or order to make war, but that if Drake intended to levy war, 'he would find his hands full'" (quoted in Bigges 2010, 79).
10 Source: BL, Cotton MS Otho E. Viii, fols. 229–234.

11 Regarding the rapport between the English and the Spanish, the *Primrose Journal* also states that: "Now when wee came again The Spaniardes did Marvaile & fledd owt of the Towne. Then the Generall sent them woorde what the cawse was, & desired the Governor of the Towne that they mighte bake bredd there, & gave his woord to the Governoure that none shoulde come on shore but Bakers, for our shippes were five or 6 miles from the Towne .... Wee weare bakinge of Bisket there 6 or 7 Daies, & the governour of the Towne received vs with greate courtesie & made proclamation vppon paine of death that no man shoulde molest vs but to help vs with woode water & all other necessaries ..." (*Sir Francis Drake's West Indian Voyage, 1858–86*, edited by Mary Frear Keeler 2010, 203).
12 According to Kelsey (1998), the Privy Council issued general letters of marque for those English merchants whose products were embargoed in Spain. These letters allowed the forcible seizure of Spanish goods in reprisal. Also, at this point, the queen promised a delegation from the Low Countries that she would support and assist their war of independence (Kelsey, 241). On the other hand, Coote affirms that Drake might have intended to destroy the three great centers of Spanish transatlantic commerce—Santo Domingo, Cartagena, and Panamá—and seize the island of Cuba to block the passage to Mexico (Coote, 204). Sean Johnson Andrews states that Queen Elizabeth did not have imperialistic intentions at the time but rather, was interested in increasing the war treasure while debilitating the Spanish military defense (Andrews 46–47).
13 Covarrubias's definition of *empresa*: "Y de allí se dixo Empresa, el tal acometimiento: y por que los cavalleros andantes acostumbrauan pintar en sus escudos, recamar en sus sobreuestes, estos designios y sus particulares intentos se llamaron empresas y tambien los Capitanes en sus estandartes quando yuan a alguna conquista. De manera que Empresa es cierto símbolo a figura enigmática hecha con particular fin, endereçada a conseguir, o mostrar su valor y animo" (Covarrubias, 344–345).
14 This excerpt comes from "A Newsletter" (BL, Cotton MS Otho E. VIII, fols 235–236v; quoted in editor Frear Keeler's 2010 compilation of Bigges, 106). For more about the origins of this document and its apparent intended audience, see the footnote on Frear Keeler, 107.
15 "By this prouident counsell, and laying downe this good foundation before hand, all things went forward in a due course, to the atchiuing of our happie enterprise."
16 French and Italian sources included the following three words in the same entry: *azienda, obra*, or *negocio*. The definitions were: *faire trafic de merchandise* (Oudin 1607) and *negoce* or *affari*, (Vittori 1609).
17 His definition of *negocio* is "la ocupación de cosa particular, que obliga al hombre a poner en ella alguna solicitud" (Covarrubias, 562).
18 Referring to the continuing repercussions of the Black Legend, historian Jorge Cañizares-Esguerra argues that "Iberians have come to represent the antithesis of modernity" (Cañizares, 24).
19 My argument here aligns more with tendencies related to the "new history of capitalism," which, according to Nemser, provide a "flexible approach to the concept of capitalism," paving the way to bring in different stories and "situate them within new temporal and spatial horizons" (Nemser, 5–6). For more about the debates around the two genealogies that constitute the history of capitalism from an innovative lens of the "new history of capitalism," see Nemser's and Jody Blanco's Special issue of the *Journal for Early Modern Cultural Studies* (2019).
20 More on this can be found in Bigges 2010, 261, and later in note 25.
21 "[They] would shake their heads, and turn aside their countenance in some smiling sort, without aunsering any thing as greatly ashamed thereof."

22 "Él dio carta de pago de todo y se salió de la ciudad y la dexó a los vecinos." AGI, Estado 72, 6.
23 "[E]stán determinados los vezinos y señores de ellas de darle los cien mil ducados con que dé seguro de fe y palabra de no tornar sobre Cartagena, él ni capitán suyo, ni cosario ninguno de Ynglaterra, mientras él fuese general de la Reyna; e questo les dará sellado con el sello de la Reyna." AGI, Estado 2, 8–18.
24 Kempe argues that aside from the Peace of Westphalia and European colonization of newly discovered territories in the early modern period, the modern transnational order "arose from the confrontation with privateering and piracy on the high seas along various coasts" (Kempe 2010, 355).
25 All the references in Spanish from the *Discurso* come from Ángel González-Palencia's 1921 edition. Unless otherwise indicated, translations from Spanish are my own. Here is Bigges's account of Hispaniola: "Now to the satisfying of some men who maruell greatly that such as fanous & goodly builded Citie so well inhabited of gallant people, very brauely appareled (whereof our souldiers found good store for their reliefe) should afoord no greater riches then was found there, wherein it is to be vnderstood that the Indian people, which were the naturals of this whole Island of HISPANIOLA (the same being neare hand as great as England) were many years since cleane consumed by the tyrannie of the Spaniards, which was cause, for lacke of people to worke in the Mines, the gold and siluer Mines of this Island …. The chiefe trade of this place consisteth of suger & ginger, which growth in the Island, and of hides of oxen and kine …" (Bigges 2010, 261).
26 "Prosiguiéronse las conversaciones / *agenas de cathólico provecho* / y el ynglés de razones en razones/ favoresçiendo siempre *su derecho*" (emphasis added). For more about the negotiations conducted in Cartagena, see the *Leicester Journal* in *Sir Francis Drake's West Indian Voyage, 1585–86*, edited by Mary Frear Keeler, 169–174).
27 Considering Nemser's notion of "entangled histories of capitalism," here we can appreciate the intricate legacy of both tendencies.
28 Whereas Kempe mentions the emergence in the seventeenth century of a "freelance privateer" such as George Cusack, who operated on a sort of "freelance" basis marked by the increasing dissolution of national links, I argue that Drake could also be placed in this category inasmuch as the instability of piracy laws in the sixteenth century provided the conditions for a "transnational" maritime predator as a chameleon-like and unstable representative of his Crown.
29 Originally from Gran Canaria, Balboa arrived in Cuba around 1592 and worked as a notary. For more about the literary and stylistic European influences and innovations found in his epic poem, see the studies by Juana Goergen and Raúl Marrero-Fente.
30 "En estas Indias que el Oceano baña, / Rica de perlas y de plata fina. / Aquí del Anglia, Flandes y Bretaña / A tomar viene puerto en su marina / Muchos navíos a trocar por cueros / Sedas y paños y a llevar dineros" (Balboa, v 65–72).
31 Although Balboa stresses that the characters in the epic poem did not trade contraband with pirates, Marrero-Fente's research reveals that they were in fact accused of it, as was Balboa himself (Marrero-Fente 2008, 86–89).
32 A facsimile of the surviving copy of the poem and letter was published by the Instituto de Valencia de Don Juan, Madrid, 1921. According to editor González Palencia's "Noticia Biográfica," 285–287, Melchor Pérez de Arteaga was a judge (*oidor*) of the Audiencia de Santa Fe in 1557 but was later accused of several crimes that involved negligence, abuse of power, and corruption (Discurso del capitán Francisco Draque, by Juan de Castellanos, edited by Palencia in 1921).
33 "Unos dizen más y otros menos, según el sentimiento de cada uno, como en semejantes cosas acontece" (Castellanos, xv). Martínez-Osorio translates the

letter as: "I also consulted many individuals who were present, some who said more and some who said less in accordance with their sentiments, as is usual in these cases" (Martínez-Osorio, 42). The word *sentimiento* stands for *sensus* (observation, perception, view, prevailing mode of thinking) in both of Nebrija's editions of the *Vocabulario de romance en latín* (Salamanca 1495, Seville 1516).

34 Castellanos wrote the letter from Tunja on April 1, 1587: "[A]lgunos me importunaron que desmembrase este nuevo suçeso de su lugar, para que a solas passasse en Hespaña, adonde ansí él como quien lo crió es cosa notaria que no podrán hallar buena acogida ..." (Castellanos, xv)

35 The censored letter is in Madrid in the Real Academia de la Historia (RAH), Colección Muñoz, MS 71. This manuscript shows Sarmiento's suppression on two pages. The remainder of the folios was torn out. Although Sarmiento's annotations do not explain the reason for cutting the *Discurso*, it has been suggested that the censorship was intended to conceal the insufficient military defense raised by Cartagena's local authorities (Castellanos, ix). For a detailed analysis of Sarmiento's annotations, see the article by María Ríos Taboada in which she analyzes the relation between English piracy and the debate around the legitimacy of the Spanish presence in the Americas (Ríos Taboada 2017, 161–176).

36 Luis Restrepo, in his study of Castellanos's *Elegías*, overcomes the dichotomy between history and literature in the poet's work by proposing that Castellanos consciously imbricated a variety of literary genres to create the "archeology" of the foundational history of what will become viceroyalty of Nueva Granada in 1717 (Restrepo, 19–21).

37 Hidalgo de Montemayor claimed that "blame ... except as is above related, does not appear to attach to the residents ... in this city. Having all fled and deserted the city, each one lays the onus on the others and says that the others ... fled and he himself left because he found himself alone among the enemy ... and the (governor?) to exculpate himself reports that the enemy was strong ... killed many English, and other impertinent matters, declaring that ...[he heard] a voice saying: 'Withdraw, gentlemen!' and he does not know whose voice it was ... [In] trying to evade the blame which is generally laid upon him ...sought to place an excessive value on this city, more than it is worth, in order to give the impression that it was advisable to effect the ransom." (Wright, *Further English Voyages*, 136)

38 Here I draw on Jowitt's methodological approach (2010) which, albeit referring to Drake's circumnavigation, demonstrates that attitudes toward piracy change according to political and financial considerations. It is worth noting that in the context of the Caribbean raid, the sources discussed in this essay do not exclusively exaggerate Drake's prowess; rather, they also underscore the ruptures within the colonial political and military system and they justify the payment of ransoms to conceal their military defeat.

39 Here I draw on Adorno's argument on the "referentiality" of colonial writing, which "is not historical, as in the historical truth whose referent is a past event. It is instead rhetorical and polemical, with the objective of influencing readers' perceptions, royal policies, and social practices" (Adorno, 4).

40 For instance, in Castellanos's *Discurso*, English violence against the Spaniards is understood as divine punishment for past colonial injustices. A few decades later, Friar Pedro Simón revisited this leitmotif in his foundational historical project, *Noticias Historiales* (Nueva Granada, 1625) wherein he blames the Spanish, who violently took everything from the indigenous population, for Drake's attack (Martínez-Osorio 2011, 20–21). During this period, on the other hand, English poets perceived Drake's efforts to undermine Philip II's power as a conflict against evil forces (Cañizares-Esguerra, 57).

41 AGI, Estado, 76: "Dióla Nuestro Señor al enemigo por mis pecados y de otros; y aprovechan poco prevenciones, quando Dios es servido de los contrarios." (quoted in *Discurso*, edited by González Palencia, 313).
42 Letter written by the Canon Llerena and the Town Council: "[E]ntendemos que fue castigo del cielo por los muchos pecados deste pueblo, aunque la gente dél estaua tan nueva y desusada en cosas de guerra y avia tanta falta de polvora y municiones, que siempre se entendió que esta ciudad estaua puesta como por presa y despojo de qualquiera que quisiese acometerla" (quoted in Rodríguez Demorizi, 24–25).
43 Patricia Grieve in *The Eve of Spain* discusses the Decadence Tradition within the context of the peninsular authors who explained that the fall of Spain in 711 CE resulted from a wrathful God who punished their country because it was pervaded by sin and decadence (Grieve, 38–45). Nina Gerassi-Navarro in *Pirate Novels*, proposes a moralizing intention of the *Discurso*, concerning Drake's portrayal framed by the recurrent binary differentiation between Catholicism and Lutheranism, as has been highlighted (Gerassi-Navarro, 44).
44 By the same token, the *Primrose Journal* emphasizes that "God fowghte for vs, for our Shippes" (see *Sir Francis Drake's West Indian Voyage*, edited by Frear Keeler, 198).
45 AGI, Estado, 76 (quoted in Castellanos, 319).
46 Apparently, the bishop raised the amount of the ransom from a previously established 80,000 ducats to 100,000 ducats.
47 "[N]inguno lo juzgava por demençia / ni contra leies de derecho santo, / viendo que los señores del Audiençia / con él mismo hizieron otro tanto." Martínez-Osorio argues that whereas the *Discurso*'s first canto criticizes merchants and colonial administrators, the second canto focuses on the religious antagonism between Catholicism and Protestantism (Martínez-Osorio 2016, 57).
48 According to the *Leicester Journal*, Alonso Bravo's wife died at some point of the English attack on Cartagena and he asked Drake not to burn down the place where she was to be buried. "The 8th day Alonso Bravo brought his wyfe to the foresaid pryory where she was buried after their owne manner with smalle solemnity, sauing that the *generall* bestowed a volley of shott of [for] her for Alonso's sake, of smalle and great shott because he was a souldier, the which he tooke it most thankfully" (quoted in *Sir Francis Drake's West Indian Voyage*, edited by Mary Frear Keeler, 175–176).
49 AGI, Estado, 72, 6 (quoted in Castellanos, 322).
50 In Cartagena's case, Castellanos mentions: "De la manera dicha los traidores,/ como ninguno ya la defendía,/ quedaron totalmente por señores / de la ciudad y de la artillería" (Castellanos, 203). While certain authors criticized the soldiers' lack of military experience, others aggrandized chivalric values—such as their courage—and their bureaucratic competence to end the English threat. Officers who accentuated chivalric values stood by the work of Santo Domingo's governor, declaring that their people were "not used to war affairs" (*id.*, 24–25).
51 Aliaga's advice includes the following: "Yo le avisé ... que hiciese que los navios que estaban en el puerto, estuviesen a punto, y que hiciese alardes de la gente de pie y de a caballo, y que se repartiesen en las partes y lugares convenientes, y se le mandase a cada uno lo que habia de hacer y a lo que habia de acudir ... y que se proveyese la Fortaleza de pólvora y municiones; creo no lo hizo porque toda la gente de la tierra le aseguraba que por el dicho puerto de Haina era imposible entrar gente" (quoted in Rodríguez Demorizi, 20); "Cuando parecieron los dichos galeones de ingleses, le supliqué que escogiese una docena de personas de experiencia y tomase consejo con ellos, y lo que allí se ordenase se ejecutase, porque admitía el parecer de todos los de la dicha ciudad y en nada determinaba; no lo quiso hacer" (*id.*, 21).

80 Setting Sails to the Narrative of Piracy

52 About Aliaga's proposition: "[E]ntienda la guerra y disciplina en ella a la gente de la tierra, que si esto se hubiera hecho, entiendo no librara tan bien el inglés como libró, y el daño que de presente hay es que toda la gente de esta ciudad está tan amedrentada que su refugio y remedio es el monte, y es lástima que no se aúnan ni junten, antes se desparcen tanto por las estancias, hatos y campos que, seiscientos hombres y aun menos que viniesen juntos, podrían tomar y apoderarse de esta Isla" (quoted in Rodríguez Demorizi, 33).
53 About the governor of Santo Domingo's reputation after the attack, Castellanos writes: "[Y] era juez el buen doctor Ovalle, / que tenia la silla presidenta; mas por agora su bondad se calle,/ pues a dado de sí tan mala cuenta;" (Castellanos, 64). When referring to the lack of military leadership, Castellanos states the following: "Devieron faltar diestros capitanes / donde cumple que cada cual lo sea" (*id.*, 65); "Jamás abituados a pelea; / y donde faltan modos y experiencias/también suelen faltarlas diligencias" (*id.*).
54 AGI, Estado, 2, 2/21 (quoted in Castellanos, 306).
55 AGI, Estado, 72, 6: "[U]na voz de parte de los nuestros que se dixo 'retirar, cavalleros'" (quoted in Castellanos, 314).
56 Castellanos wrote to Dr. Chaparro suggesting the "appointment of generous people / loyal and trustworthy captains / who are not suspicious" (Castellanos, 118).
57 "[C]on el cual aviso el Presidente hizo tocar arma y juntar la gente de la ciudad en sus compañias y dar la orden que se pedia seguir por la brevedad del tiempo" (Rodríguez, 27).
58 "Aunque se les imputa culpa con infamia, no sé yo que gente ni nación fuera de tanto valor, que siendo tan pocos y teniendo el puerto sin munición y estando ellos sin armas, pudieran resistir a quien de todo venía tan prevenido" (Lugo, 70).
59 AGI, Estado, 72, 6 (quoted in Castellanos, 321).
60 AGI, Santa Fe, 1, 72. Although the president of the Council of the Indies may have classified Drake as a corsair to accentuate his ties with the English Crown, Drake lacked a royal commission to pillage Cartagena.
61 Kelsey argued that the Spaniards tended to exaggerate the nature of Drake's events to ask for crown subsidies, concealing the lack of efficient systems of defense (Wright 2008, 29).
62 "[M]e cumple caminar por otras vías/ que deseo correr a toda priesa,/ viendo quan abreviados son los días,/ pues en tal caso la más clara lumbre/es esperança con incertidumbre" (Castellanos, 227).
63 Wright highlights Fernand Braudel's argument that considers geographic distance a great obstacle in Philip II's territorial control (Wright 2008, 29–30).
64 Here I draw on Wright's use of the concept "long-term resilience" when she mentions that: "historians have argued that the weakness of the Spanish monarchy proved a source of long-term resilience, as individual realms and constituencies negotiated their interests with an energy that might have produced more conflicts and rebellions in a stronger, more centralized system of rule" (Wright 2008, 38).
65 "[L]e pidieron un millón, y le dijeron que no lo harían menos de cien mil ducados (…) y porque no se les dieron, comenzaron a quemar la ciudad y quemaron de tres partes la una" (quoted in Rodríguez Demorizi, 31). According to Governor Ovalle, other mayors and aldermen, and the treasurer, Alonso de Peña, agreed that the best way to save the city of Santo Domingo and stop the devastation by the English was to strike a deal with them.
66 Bodin refers to a case in which the Roman general Pompey signed a treaty with Mediterranean pirates (Hampton, 118).
67 Lauren Benton elaborates on the issues encountered by lawyers, such as Gentili, when distinguishing legitimate from illegitimate captures (Benton 2010, 104–161). Daniel Heller-Roazen's study traces the rhetoric behind the different definitions of the pirate and the just enemy from classical times.

68 Alberico Gentili—an appointed lawyer of the Spanish Crown at England's Court of Admiralty (1605–1608)—in his famous legal treatise, *Hispanicae advocationis*, posthumously published c1613, compiled specific disputes and pleas in which he defined piracy in contradictory ways depending upon whether he desired to legitimize or delegitimize an economic transaction. For a related specific analysis, see Benton's study (2011). Balthazar Ayala, a Flemish lawyer appointed by Philip II to the position of General Military Auditor, wrote *De Iure et Officiis bellicis et disciplina militari* (1584), in which he underscored the difference between the notions of a just enemy and a rebel.

69 "Su magestad tan mal lo trata/en ponelle renombre de pirata" (Castellanos 1921, 208). The English translation of this quoted episode can be found in Lane and Bialuschewski's anthology (Lane and Bialuschewski, 26). However, it is also worth noting that, according to Odin's dictionary, 1607, the word *renombre* also meant "renown" or "fame."

70 About the semantic debate, Castellanos writes: "[Y] el intérprete suyo, dicho Ionas, / en idioma propio las expuso, / a gran enojo van palabras pronas / por el nombre que nuestro Rey le puso porque dezían que cossario era, / como si por ventura no lo fuera" (Castellanos 1921, 204). "To whatever sir who invented this / Base word, should he write me, / The reply won't be long in coming / Because I will surely unmask the lie ... And there we'll make it clear one day / So that I may be vindicated / Before the Great Philip who sent it / By the secretaries he confided" (Lane and Bialuschewski, 28).

71 Edmund Spenser (see *The Complete Works in Verse and Prose of Edmund Spenser* 1882) attributed damaging and dishonorable moral attributes to the "brigants" (brigands) in "Book VI" (about courtesy) of *The Fairie Queen* (c1599). While the Elizabethan author did not employ the term "pirates," the word "brigants" encapsulated all the stereotypes conventionally associated with pirates, such as their inclination to spoil, invade, capture, and murder. For instance, in Canto X, the poetic voice remarks that they are: "A lawlesse people, Brigants hight of yore, / that neuer vsed to liue by plough nor spade, / But fed on spoile and booty, which they made / Vpon their neighbours, which did nigh them border, / The dwelling of these shepheards did inuade, / And spoyld their houses, and them selues did murder; / And droue away their flocks, with other much disorder" (Stanza 40, v 345–351). Paralleling the myth of Proserpina's abduction with Pastorella's, Alice Blitch argues that Spenser employed the term "brigands" instead of "pirates" to preserve the Italian connotation of "devil" from the word *brigante* and to stress the similarities of the encounter between the captain of the brigands and Pluto (Blitch, 18). In Castellanos's *Discurso* (1921) we see that both terms, "pirates" and "corsairs," refer to such characteristics and behavioral traits.

72 AGI, Santa Fe, 1,72: "[Q]ue conviene para lo presente y para dar exemplo en lo porvenir que enesto se haga demostracion y que una persona con autoridad y buena intelligencia vaya a aquella ciudad y haga información con diligencia y de fuerza y averigue todo lo que en esto paso y si resultaren notablemente culpados el governador y el don Pedro o alguno dellos hagan con ellos los procesos y los concluya y con sus personas presas los enbie al Consejo para que en el se vean y provea con justicia lo que convenga y quanto a lo demas particulares que dela información resultare haver sido culpados dando les traslado y haviendolos oydo sentencie las causas conforme a justicia."

73 AGI, Santa Fe, 1, 72.

74 The Spanish State Council was part of the Council of War until Philip II made the latter an independent organ between 1586 and 1592. The Council of War became an institution that dealt primarily with military conflicts in Spain and its territories overseas. AGS, Guerra y Marina, 190: "Las relaciones que an benido con las cartas del presidente, jueces y oficiales de la contratación de Sevilla delo

82 *Setting Sails to the Narrative of Piracy*

    subcedido enlas Indias se an visto en el consejo y adado mucho ciudado entender la perdida del fuerte de sant augustin en la florida y ver la poca resistencia que el cossario a allado en el y en santo domingo y Cartagena porque de mas de la perdida de estos lugares y los sacrilegios y rovos que se an hecho estima el consejo en mucho el animo y orgullo con que estos cossarios vuelven a sus tierras pareciéndoles que podian emprender mayores cosas el ano que viene y siempre que quisieren."

75 Quoted in Castellanos's *Discurso del capitán Franciso Draque*, edited by González Palencia, 377.

76 According to Alonso Bravo, Drake had promised the queen one million ducats, which he failed to amass during the raid. Kelsey states that the collected ransom was probably small because Drake insisted in conducting personal negotiations (Kelsey, 240–272).

77 Kelsey claims that England turned the voyage into a triumph over Spain through Bigges's account (Kelsey, 278).

78 Here I borrow the term "rhetorical capital" from Piki Ish-Shalom's article which states that the rhetorical capital could be used to justify the "democratic peace thesis" by reframing it "in terms of a democratic us against an autocratic them" (Ish-Shalom, 287). In the context of Drake's attack, the rhetorical capital of the narratives of piracy was used to support and project an ideology of English or Spanish global supremacy.

3 Dangerous Representations of the Caribbean in the Sixteenth Century

In 1589, one of the censors of the Council of the Indies, Agustín de Zárate, recommended the publication of Juan de Castellanos's *Elegías de varones ilustres de Indias* for its descriptions of the Caribbean islands.[1] Castellanos, a priest and *beneficiado* of a church in the city of Tunja, Colombia, had no previous publications, nor had he held political office. Probably aware of Castellanos's lack of a reputation before the Spanish court, Zárate focused on the *Elegías*'s description of Christopher Columbus's arrival in the islands. As Zárate explained, several other sources of information about Peru and New Spain had been compiled by other authors, including himself, but they had the "defect" of not addressing the beginnings of the history of European transatlantic navigation and settlement.[2] According to Zárate, Castellanos focused on telling the stories of "illustrious men" (*varones ilustres*) who conquered and converted indigenous peoples from "widespread islands … commonly known as the New World."[3] Moreover, Zárate argued that Castellanos's description of Columbus's navigational routes would be well received in Andalusian port cities or "maritime places" that would benefit from the practical navigational knowledge because they had more contact with the Indies.[4] He did not delve into the specificity of the Caribbean islands, nor did he even mention them by name, but he used his official recommendation of the text's publication to project the territorial totality of the Indies, as we will see in this chapter.

Castellanos underlined the role played by the island of Hispaniola (today Haiti and the Dominican Republic) as the first Spanish transatlantic stronghold and the launching point for New World conquests: "In this city and in this port / strong Mars has had courage / Because everyone who discovered / mainly departed from this city and this port" (Castellanos 1847, 46).[5] Creating a narrative of stabilization, he depicted the Caribbean islands as a locus of chaos where Spanish soldiers, captains, and governors, such as Fray Nicolás de Ovando y Cáceres (the second appointed governor of Hispaniola), put in motion the process of discovery, conquest, and pacification of the Taino and Carib nations. By centering the narrative of the *Elegías* on the deeds of these Spaniards, Castellanos rendered the islands unstable and unpredictable because of the calamities Ovando y Cáceres and others had had to contend with in the archipelago.

DOI: 10.4324/9781003141495-4

Representations of the Caribbean archipelago have long revolved around stereotypical notions of piracy, contraband, and political disorder. From scholarly work to contemporary popular culture, the Caribbean islands remain a mythical space inflected by foreign agents who undertake unlawful practices driven by economic scarcity, political incompetence, and the absence of traditional continental frontiers. In the face of efforts by early modern authors to define the Caribbean within the context of European imperial expansion and global rivalries, new perspectives from different cultural narratives are needed to reexamine the rhetorical tropes grounded in the sixteenth century to shape concepts of sovereignty and jurisdiction as well as spatial identities that are based on transatlantic mobility.

A particular focus of this chapter is the "grammar" of assertion and threat that challenged and contributed to the projection of dominion and control upon geographical and sovereign spaces in the sixteenth and early seventeenth centuries.[6] The term "grammar" as I use it refers to the vocabulary, syntax, and semantics used by European power structures to portray interlopers on both sides of the Atlantic, whether they were pirates, rebels, or indigenous peoples who challenged specific Spanish orders. All of these actors were cast as enemies or plagues (whether moral or physical) threatening specific European powers, and the narrative structures used to encapsulate them regularly employed the syntactic opposition of "us" (Europeans and Spanish Creoles) and "them" (Amerindians, pirates, interlopers, and dissidents).

The first section of this chapter focuses on the narrative construction of the Caribbean space inscribed within ordinances and laws addressing the transformation of the Caribbean islands into a stable and controllable locus. The geopolitical conceptualization of forces that obstructed the process of Spanish settlement relies on the notion of "others" such as pirates and indigenous nations. The rhetorical maneuvers used to spatialize property, sovereignty, and jurisdiction from the mid-sixteenth to the seventeenth century relied on connecting these others to notions of "infection" and "infestation." The second part of the chapter looks at visual narratives of the Caribbean archipelago and their articulation of European territorial claims through cartographic representations, exploring these assertions and their sixteenth-century geopolitical consequences. By analyzing the work of sixteenth-century Flemish, Italian, and Spanish cartographers and sailors—such as Giovanni Battista Boazio, Gerardus Mercator, Juan Escalante de Mendoza, and Baltasar Vellerino de Villalobos—this part of the chapter reassesses the role of piracy in depictions of Caribbean islands and identifies "contra-cartographies" that dispute the Spanish Crown's territorial order.

Giving Birth to the Caribbean Islands: Narratives of Infection and Infestation

In April 1492, the Capitulations of Santa Fe, signed by Christopher Columbus and Ferdinand II and Isabella I, known as the Catholic Monarchs, shaped what would become the first viceroyalty in the New World.[7] Known as the Viceroyalty of the Indies or the "Columbian Viceroyalty," it initially encompassed several islands discovered by Columbus. This transatlantic institution was eventually marked by disputes between the Catholic Monarchs and the Columbus family.[8] To ensure royal control and presence in these territories, the monarchs implemented a system of *audiencias* (tribunals) across the Atlantic. In 1511 the city of Santo Domingo on Hispaniola staged the first *audiencia* in the New World. By the first decades of the 1500s, Hispaniola was the hub of the first network in the Americas for emigration, contact, and cultural exchanges between the Spanish peninsula and the West Indies.[9]

In what follows, I will focus on the rhetorical moves used by early modern writers to define the Caribbean islands within the context of sixteenth-century European imperialism and rivalries over global expansion. The analysis will also approach the rhetorical solutions found in Spanish-language chronicles, historical poetry, ordinances, and laws of the time to address the problem of how to turn the Caribbean islands into a controllable, stable locus. Finally, my interpretation will address how depictions of pirates and indigenous populations as stereotypical "others" and harborers of disease and lawlessness served an agenda of Spanish settlement and hegemony over the archipelago.

Caribbean Ports and Infestations

Zárate's censorship review noted the dynamic influx of travelers between Europe and the Indies through Andalusian port cities. Castellanos was a figure of this influx himself, having at 12 or 13 years of age left his hometown (Alanis, Seville) and traveled to the Indies, making stops at the islands of Puerto Rico, Margarita, Trinidad, and Santa Marta and the continental vicinities of Venezuela and Antioquia before eventually landing in Tunja, where he became a priest and started writing the *Elegías*.[10] He constantly referred to the Caribbean islands and other coastal-continental cities as "ports" (*puertos*) or "desired ports" (*puertos deseados*).[11] Aside from the stories of calamities endured by Spaniards during the first years of Spanish occupation in the New World, Castellanos rhetorically filled the Caribbean space with the heavy presence of indigenous populations. While ports in his narrative served as staging grounds for Spanish movements of conquest, control, and exploration, Castellanos also emphasized the role of ports as places of influx. They were entrance or exit points for everyone, whether Spaniards, Caribs, or Tainos. They also functioned as emergency exits or battlefields for unpredictable attacks. For instance, in *Elegía II*, Part I, when describing how the colonist Juan de Salas plotted to escape from the Caribs holding him on the island of Cubagua, he relates how the port became the only way out and, after that, the only successful solution: "He told them that a great deed will be / to steal the canoe one night / which he would put at the port and beaches of Cubagua" (Castellanos 1847, 24).[12]

Castellanos construed the Caribbean islands as a web of port cities that provided the conditions for moving across the insular regions and reaching and controlling other strategic continental territories, as Hernán Cortés did when he sailed from Cuba and arrived at the coast of Yucatán. However, seaports also promoted dynamics of contagion and contamination from both physical and spiritual plagues. For instance, Castellanos in *Elegía II*, Part I, referred to several Caribbean islands as places "infested" by neighboring Caribs (*infestada de todos los caribes comarcanos*); as "infamous islands" (*infames islas*); and as "lands of inhumane traditions" (*tierra de costumbres inhumanas*) (*id*., 25 and 64). The Caribs, for their part, were described as "despicable and bloodthirsty people" (*Caribe gente vil, sangrienta*) and as an abhorrent pestilence (*id*., 24). In this sense, internal conflicts and war were perceived in terms of plague and infestation.

Ports were problematic places in the Caribbean archipelago because they could stand both for colonial control and for dynamics of danger and belligerence that threatened Spanish transatlantic power during the sixteenth century. According to John Mack's cultural history of the sea (see the discussion in Chapter 1), beaches and seaports were liminal spaces, inhabited by liminal characters, because they were points where the terrestrial and maritime orders converged. In the case of the Caribbean, it has been argued that European alliances and frictions helped to promote the consolidation of "translocal identities" based on individuals such as pirates who questioned the imperial order without necessarily having in mind a "national project or a communal identity based on the idea of a singular form of political or cultural belonging" (Martínez-San Miguel, 20). Ports, islands, and coasts posed political, religious, and economic threats. The political threat of ports derived from their geographical nature because they became part of an ethos of decentralized political power by connecting the corridors of layered sovereignties (Benton 2010, 32). Economically and religiously speaking, ports presented a threat by enabling different licit and illicit economic dynamics that challenged religious divides, such as those discussed in Kristen Block's study, where she stressed the relation between the impoverishment of Spanish Caribbean seaports in the early seventeenth century and the formation of "new spaces for economic cooperation across the Protestant-Catholic divide" (Block, 14). Besides these political, economic, and religious threats, the islands and the sea played a role in the religious and economic cultural domains. In the case of islands, religious agendas even came into play because, as Lauren Benton has pointed out, islands could be seen as "an invitation to an 'archipelagic imagination' already developed in medieval representation of islands as wild and holy places and as stopping points along spiritual itineraries" (*id*., 162). Elvira Vilches's seminal work on economic writing has pointed out that sixteenth-century Spanish authors relied on nautical metaphors to criticize emerging economies marked by credit and bankruptcy: Tomás de Mercado (1525–1575) compared the use of credit with "navigating the ocean in vessels of greed," and Fray Luis de León wrote that "the ocean symbolizes the boundless liquidity of entrepreneurial credit" (Vilches, 276–277). In what follows, I will discuss how ports conformed to the geopolitical architecture of the Caribbean by posing another threat: that of infection and infestation.

Ports were portrayed as enclaves of moral and physical infestation and infection from non-Catholics, pirates, and maritime predators.[13] When examining the metaphors of illness and infestation used in Spanish sixteenth-century texts, it is important to keep in mind some key questions. Which places are depicted as infested, and who are the presumed carriers of disease? Which diseases are singled out, and which doctors or individuals are entitled to identify the disease? What are the underlying interests in delivering the diagnoses?

One use of illness metaphors in describing indigenous American populations was to legitimize the role of priests in the process of civilizing the newly discovered territories. An example of this is found in *Historia general de las cosas de nueva España* (c1540–1577), commonly known as the *Florentine Codex*, by the Franciscan friar Bernardino de Sahagún. This bilingual and colorfully illustrated manuscript—written in both Spanish and Nahuatl—serves as a repository of indigenous knowledge about moral philosophy and political organization.[14] In his prologue, Sahagún stresses the relation between idolatry (or heresy) and illness, foregrounding the figure of the priest as a "spiritual healer" of "spiritual diseases"[15] and portraying the "idolatry" of the indigenous peoples as both an illness and a sin to be cured through preaching, confession, and Christian conversion[16] (Sahagún, 1). Fashioning a narrative in which an "ill" indigenous population requires a cure, Sahagún rhetorically justifies the Spaniards' presence in the Indies by portraying them as spiritual healers and effectively effacing their role as conquerors.

In the Spanish legal vocabulary from the time of King Charles I's reign (1516–1556), the threat of "infestation" was used to justify the development of a civil military body. In the legal compendium *Recopilaciones de las leyes de los reynos de Indias*, Law XIX—originally promulgated by Charles in 1540 and reinforced in 1570 by his successor Philip II—requires that people living close to a port be provided with weapons and horses so that they can protect the coast. In the language of the law, "We ordered all viceroys, presidents, and governors to take great care to provide weapons and horses to the people who live close to ports so that they are prepared to defend themselves in case anyone tries to 'infest' them" (Pérez de Soto, 25).[17] At that time the verb "to infest" mainly conveyed a religious meaning related to "powerful heretics or infidels," according to the Dominican friar Bartolomé de Las Casas in his arguments with Juan Ginés de Sepúlveda in the Valladolid debate, as reported in his *Tratados de 1552*.[18] Las Casas used the term again in his *Historia de las Indias*, c1527–1561, when alluding to Spaniards who asked permission to enter Tierra Firme (the southern part of the empire's coastal possessions) so as to "*infest*, disturb, steal, kill, capture, and destroy those people who used to live in remote parts and neither did they see or hear us; nor did they offend us" (emphasis added).[19] Later dictionaries—in French, 1604 (Palet); English, 1617 (Minsheu); and Spanish, 1679 (Henríquez)—define "to infest" to mean "to haunt" (*poursuivre*), "to be an enemy" (*être ennemi*), "to vex," or "to damage" (*dañar*). The verb "to infect," on the other hand, mainly referred to the Latin verb *inficionar*, "to infect or stain" (Minsheu); in Spanish, in Covarrubias's words (1611), it was defined as "to corrupt the air with smell" (*corromper con mal olor el ayre*). However, there is also a conflation of the terms (to infect/to infest) that became apparent in the definition of *inficionar* in the *Diccionario de autoridades*, 1734: "se toma algunas veces por lo mismo que Inficionar" (Volume 4).[20] Such a conflation in the term *inficionar*, encompassing the contagion of both physical and moral pestilence, is relevant to understanding the rhetorical solutions employed by Castellanos and other early modern Spanish writers when attempting to project Spanish control and homogenization over the New World soil, their diverse indigenous populations, and European maritime predators.

The discourse on infection, contagion, and contamination and its association with heresy had medieval roots. For instance, *Gesta romanorum* (c1300–1310) and Pietro de Tossigno's *Tractatus de pestilentia*, among other medieval texts, underscored the relation between leprosy and sin. Analyzing several case studies in France during the fourteenth century from the vantage point of the late 1990s, David Nirenberg underlined how, in that context, leprosy was understood as a disease of the soul that entailed moral corruption. The metaphors of illness, infection, and corruption corresponded to the kind of "moral economy" of the kingdom in which the body reflected moral behavior. As Nirenberg's analysis highlights, accusations of leprosy became a rhetorical strategy to expand jurisdictional power, claim property, and remove lepers from specific zones.[21] In this context, the charge of leprosy quickly expanded to include enemies, business rivals, and neighbors as a means of bending structures of royal power and also exercising that power (Nirenberg, 105). French municipalities, in turn, took advantage of accusations of leprosy to exercise their power without having to wait for a royal response. In this sense, as Nirenberg points out, the charge of leprosy provided the ideological legitimation for some actions that otherwise might have been perceived as rebellious (*id.*, 122).[22] Therefore, the metaphor of a contagious illness has a twofold function. On the one hand, accusations of leprosy provided the grounds for segregating religious communities; on the other hand, the charge of leprosy gave more jurisdictional power to the local municipalities and became a useful tool for legitimizing actions that would seem disloyal in the monarch's eyes. Castellanos reproduced this model: by casting pirates and corsairs as heretical and sources of moral infection, he justified Spain's jurisdiction over the Indies, claiming a right that was not necessarily acknowledged by other European nations.

Castellanos employed the same terms he had used to refer to Caribbean indigenous populations when describing pirates, Spaniards who betrayed the crown, and failed ultramarine governments. Just as the Caribs were "bloody" (*sangrientos*), "despicable" (*vil*), and a "pestilence" (*pestilencia*), French pirates amounted to a "French pestilence" (*francesa pestilencia*) and "despicable Lutherans" (*viles luteranos*).[23] Diego Pérez, a Spanish priest who was exiled from the Indies and joined forces with the French pirate Jacques Soria (*hizo con su pirata su concierto*), had "bloody inclinations" (*condición sanguinolenta*) and a heart full of "malicious pestilence" (*dolosa pestilencia*) (Elegía XIV, Part I, 1847, 153). Moreover, Castellanos expanded the notion of pestilence to encompass politics by underlining the suspicious liaisons between governments and people of "loose consciousness" whose claims of being Christians were only a façade.[24] By creating a network of adjectives conflating the moral and political illegitimacy of Caribs and pirates, Castellanos legitimized Spanish rights to sovereignty over the islands and coastal continental zones, contributing to the Spanish "grammar" of territorial possession.

Castellanos used *inficionar* in the medical sense to describe the effects of bats, mosquitos, and other plagues that left Spaniards with "cruel skin ulcers."[25] He also employed *infestar* to refer to the presence of pirates and indigenous populations as another kind of plague, thus anchoring Spanish order to the territorial and maritime space of the Indies. This use of language homogenized the Caribbean space as a collective entity harassed by the movement of individuals who, in the eyes of Castellanos, did not belong to the construction of that space. Disregarding the fact that the islands were inhabited before the Spaniards' arrival, Castellanos characterized the Caribs and French pirates as rebels who were outside of the Spanish political, economic, and religious order. In this way, he configured a Caribbean geography of infection and infestation to justify his main theme of Spanish exploration, conquest, and settlement.

In Castellanos's eyes, Caribs and pirates were external agents whose failure to share Spanish Catholic values rendered them devoid of any right of ownership over Caribbean territory. He described Caribs as inhumane cannibals and characterized pirates as covetous, arrogant Lutherans. In the elegy composed after the death of the second governor of Cartagena, Juan de Bustos de Villegas, Castellanos recounted Martin Cote's characterization of him as a covetous and haughty Frenchman (*Francés cudicioso y arrogante*) and a "robber corsair" (*robador cosario*).[26] Also, by his logic, Spaniards could be infected by this kind of behavior: he criticizes Columbus's younger brother Bartholomew, who, after gaining a reputation, became proud and haughty in substantial enterprises and social dealings: "Bartholomew Columbus acquired great fame, / The land stood in fear, / and he, seeing himself so far ahead of others, / became more proud and arrogant. / He used no discretion / in conducting large transactions, / and failed to show the dignity and respect / that befit prominent men."[27] In Castellanos's construction, the Caribbean was marked by a constant battle against the pestilence of pirates and indigenes, and this battle had religious, economic, and political dimensions. The association of infection and infestation with maritime and territorial predation in his *Elegías* and in the juridical treatises and ordinances cited earlier underscores the need to assign oppositional terms to piracy, rhetorically configuring the contested space of the Caribbean as constituted by contingent jurisdictions, sovereignties, and moral values. In this sense, describing piracy as a pestilence had the effect of construing the Caribbean as an infected or infested place—a spatial commodity in need of protection against external or foreign plagues.[28]

European Waters and Infestations

King Charles's ordinances from the first half of the sixteenth century used the verb *infestarlos* to condemn the presence and actions of Caribs and French pirates in the Caribbean region. In the same manner, Castellanos's use of "infestation" served to reinforce European views of the Caribbean as an unstable and volatile region. Portraying the archipelago as a place infested with lawless pirates, rebels, and indigenes helped him justify the development of Spanish settlements in a region that, by his reckoning, was in dire need of decontamination. In articulating a vision of the islands as swarming with indomitable hostiles of every persuasion, Castellanos succeeded in appealing to the sensibilities of Europeans, who readily accepted the notion that the Caribbean posed a threat to established moral and religious norms. Thus, from the sixteenth century onward, the word *infestar* moved beyond its medical meaning to occupy space in the political and economic realms, becoming a recurring word to describe maritime predation in European legal treatises and documents.

The term "to disinfest" (*desinfestar*) appears in *De iusto imperio Lusitanorum Asiatico*, 1625, by the Portuguese friar Serafim de Freitas, who at the time was teaching at the Faculty of Law in Valladolid. Following Castellanos's spatial narrative of the Indies and the Caribbean as maritime spaces that should be dominated by Spaniards against the piratical plagues that interfered or infested it, Freitas proposed the occupation of the sea as a means of protecting, dominating, and "disinfesting" Portuguese sovereignty against pirates.[29] "Dominion," in Freitas's example, meant "protection" and "jurisdiction," which stood in opposition to the Dutch rebels and justified the Iberian "disinfestation" of the seas. Both Castellanos and Freitas, almost 30 years apart, constructed a rhetorical vindication of the Iberian dominions—on which I will focus in the second part of this chapter—based on the conceptualization of maritime and territorial space as something infested that must be acquired as property by Iberian power in order to be disinfested. In short, the threat of infestation also implied the dangers of contagion or infection that could spread across the seas and unprotected coasts. Pirates, rebels, outlaws, or even rivals of the Iberians were described using metaphors of contagious diseases or viruses, ranging from religious differences and moral misbehavior to illegal trading practices and violent attacks. Freitas employed the term to describe Dutch rebels against the Iberian empires who interfered with the rights of Portuguese to conduct business and commerce in the East Indies.[30] In the dialectical relationship between the pirate and the empire, the former became what has been described as "a general term for an outlaw, simultaneously threatening and mutually constituting the legitimacy of the state" (Andrews 2018, 36). Thus, the use of the term "to infest" justified the transformation of maritime and territorial spaces, from the West to the East Indies, into property and merchandise to regulate in the interest of containing the threat of contagion and safeguarding the predominance of specific sovereign powers (Spain and Portugal, in this case).

By the same token, the debate about ownership of maritime space reached English soil, where the concept of infestation surfaced in legal discussions. For instance, John Selden, in his juridical treatise *Mare Clausum*—which contested Dutch jurist Hugo Grotius's argument, condensed in *Mare Liberum* (c1609)—justified the right of ownership over maritime space by quoting the papal bull *In Coena Domini*. According to the bull, Selden argued, the pope had his own maritime possessions, known as the Papal Sea, and he held the right to excommunicate specific types of individuals who were "infesting" these waters: "Item, we excommunicate and anathematize all Pirates, Rovers, and Robbers upon the Sea, those that haunt and infest our Sea."[31] Selden's treatise—censored in the 1630s by King James I and published in 1652—traced the history of several closed seas from the classical period to Pope Alexander's 1493 bull *Inter caetera*. Despite the fact that Selden was not Catholic, he recognized the pope's right to demarcate his own maritime religious spaces. In other words, Selden accepted the pope's religious authority as a source of legitimacy in taking possession of certain waters and excommunicating those who "infested" them since, in refusing to live by the moral values espoused by the Church, pirates and robbers were rightly being made to face both religious and economic consequences.[32]

By the time Freitas, Grotius, and Selden had written their juridical treatises and the Spanish ordinances were enforced, piracy encapsulated the experience of lawlessness, illegitimacy, and rebellion against territorial and maritime orders. However, the discussion about piracy during the previous century had remained inconclusive and mainly depended on the victim's viewpoint. For instance, English and French sailors had claimed that they were not pirates but individuals who were conducting business on foreign soil. They did not acknowledge Spanish sovereignty over the West Indies at the time. By tailoring depictions of the English and French as interlopers who infested the Caribbean, Castellanos attempted to theorize about the spatial nature of piracy and assign a set of moral, political, and economic values to these individuals. "Infestation" enabled him to classify any individual who did not follow an imposed system in a given place and, at the same time, to justify the existence of such model—in this case, Spanish sovereignty, religion, and monopolistic trade in the Indies.

Moving to the late seventeenth and eighteenth centuries, Spanish ordinances against piracy that allowed Spanish subjects to become "authorized pillagers" (*armadores*) followed justifications by Freitas and Castellanos grounded in the rhetoric of infestation. The Ordinance for Corsairs (*Ordenanza de Corso*) of 1674 allowed the *armadores* to repel piracy by attacking ships and paying a sum of money to the Spanish Crown.[33] Here the notion of infestation was used to differentiate legitimate looting from illegitimate pillaging in the West Indies:

> Considering the great damages caused to the vassals of my son, the King, by many Corsairs and Pirates that infest the Indies shores; and fair it is to help the builders to encourage them ... I declare and command that bounties must be taken away from these Pirates ....[34]

By 1734, the *Diccionario de autoridades* defined the verb *infestar* in terms of pillaging: "To create damage and hostility to the enemy on land, especially at the coasts."[35] The ordinance of 1702 and some instructions sent to General Don Pedro Mesia of Tierra Firme's coasts in 1752 displayed the same rhetoric.[36] In the latter case, the Dutch had transferred their pillaging from the East Indies to the West Indies (Tierra Firme), and the instructions urged the general not to enforce the Ordinance for Corsairs in the Mediterranean.[37] Two years later, a project for another Ordinance for Corsairs in 1754 focused on "arrivals" (*arribadas*), which were legitimate inasmuch as ships navigated close to "colonial coasts" or maritime routes allowed by the Spanish Crown in the Indies.[38] Spanish ships were not permitted to navigate waters known to be "infested" at the time of the travel, nor were the vessels protected by laws in "remote navigations" such as Santa Marta or the city of Cartagena. Therefore, the verb "to infest" functioned as a tool for marking a geography of legitimate possession across disciplines—legal, historical, and literary—and time periods, and in the end, the islands described by Castellanos in the Caribbean zone remained "infested" and at risk of contagion for almost 150 years.

In time, the nearly synonymous terms "infection" and "infestation" would become key concepts in dealing with sundry Iberian overseas sovereignty and jurisdictional issues. Freitas, in a juridical treatise with the aim of resolving the problem of Dutch rebels, exploited the concept to assert rights of property in maritime space, and Selden likewise justified the commodification of the seas by quoting a papal bull in which infestation leads to excommunication. Nowadays we associate infections with disease, and infestations with vermin or sharks. In the early modern period, however, as we have seen, "infected" also meant stained and morally corrupt, while "infestation" was associated with harm and, in Spain in particular, with enemy invaders (especially coastal ones) and a lack of racial or religious purity. Indeed, the word *infecto*, or infected person, was used to denote an individual of mixed, Moorish, or Jewish blood (*Diccionario de autoridades*,

263). Castellanos and others appropriated the same terms that had been used for more than a century to justify expelling Moors and Jews from the Iberian Peninsula and redeployed the terms to suit the needs of a new and rapidly changing overseas empire. In many ways, the same discourse the Iberian kingdoms had developed to legitimize expelling non-Christians from the peninsula now served the interests of a budding empire trying to legitimize the power it had begun to wield in an ever-expanding territorial and maritime space.

Thus, the Caribbean became a proving ground for determining not merely the best logistical, military, and administrative strategies to pursue in such far-flung spaces, but also the viability of a morally grounded rationale for seeking manifest control and further expansion of those spaces. The pirates, rebels, and indigenes of the archipelago provided the ingredients necessary for developing a rationale of domination—whose linchpin was the concept of infestation—that would be applied first in the Caribbean and thereafter around the globe. Together with the components for justifying control of overseas spaces, the Caribbean offered Europeans the first complete framework for imagining a global theater, made possible by advances in navigation and cartography, that contained not only riches and limitless possibilities but also the sovereignty, geopolitical, and jurisdictional challenges that Spain and future colonial powers would face for centuries to come. Notably, the rhetorical instruments for meeting those challenges were forged in the crucible of the Caribbean archipelago, the first Spanish transatlantic Viceroyalty of the Indies.

The Construction of Piratical Spaces: Caribbean Cartographies

Sixteenth-century Spanish chroniclers of the Indies elaborated a narrative of geographical homogenization—of both lands and peoples—to define the Viceroyalty of the Indies or the Caribbean archipelago.[39] For instance, Gonzalo Fernández de Oviedo y Valdés chose Hispaniola as a frame of reference to describe the rest of the islands in the sixteenth book of his *Historia general* (1535).[40] Likewise, Bartolomé de Las Casas cast the islands of Hispaniola, Cuba, San Juan (modern-day Puerto Rico), and Jamaica as sharing a common denominator: indigenous peoples, who (whether insular or continental) were universally humble and naturally kind "because in these Indies everything is the same."[41] While aware of distinct places and peoples encountered by other explorers during the first decades of the sixteenth century, Las Casas and Oviedo nevertheless attempted to articulate a geographical and anthropological continuity among the new territories of the Indies. Regarding an alleged continuity between the Mediterranean and the Caribbean archipelagos, Ricardo Padrón argues that Oviedo's insistence that the Caribbean islands were "Mediterranean" was part of the project of creating a "new Mediterranean" (the Caribbean) for a "new Rome"—Spain, in this case (Padrón, 147–148).

The discursive homogenization of both the geography and the peoples of the Indies reflects the transitional process from a threefold continental system to a fourfold one. The task of crafting America as a separate portion of land equivalent to the other continents challenged the conventional cosmographic order based on the old conception of the "world island" (Orbis Terrarum)—consisting of Europe, Africa, and Asia. It is worth noting that the Orbis Terrarum implied the existence of another island at the antipodes of the Southern Hemisphere (Orbis Alterius) inhabited by sapient organisms of an utterly different species (Lewis, 25–26). Las Casas's and Oviedo's homogenization of the indigenous populations of the Indies eradicated the association of the Orbis Alterius with the New World.[42]

Several Spanish cartographers echoed this homogenizing narrative of "the islands" in their depictions of the Caribbean archipelago.[43] Spanish and Portuguese efforts to restrict navigational information during the sixteenth century focused less on concealing theoretical or cosmographic information than on controlling the circulation of knowledge acquired by sailors as they navigated uncharted waters.[44] Key aspects of that experience were pirate attacks throughout the Caribbean as a result of the Spanish Crown's neglect of the region after new continental territories had been discovered and new viceroyalties instituted. Historian Kenneth Andrews has argued that, starting in the early sixteenth century, the Caribbean emerged as a fragmented region because of Spanish inefficiency, manifest in the inability to incorporate and control the zone (Andrews 1978, 1). Another factor that contributed to the economic decline of the islands was the scattering of Spanish settlers, who left the islands of Hispaniola and San Juan for the continental zones or who went to try their luck in the newly founded viceroyalties of New Spain and Peru (*id.*, 16). At this time, the phrase "*Dios me lleve al Perú*" (May God take me to Peru) became a popular refrain among those who stayed in the islands. According to Andrews, by the end of the sixteenth century, Antillean ports became minor players because most of the ships were using the Cartagena and Veracruz trading route to reach the Floridian strait (*id.*, 3).[45] As Jon Latimer noted, the depopulation of the islands and their economic ruin allowed local commerce to be controlled by the English, Dutch, and French, in whose hands "plunder and trade were never separate activities" (Latimer, 21–22). In this section, I will address three main questions: (1) What were the geopolitical consequences of the European territorial claims made in cartographic representations of the Caribbean in the sixteenth century?; (2) What role did piracy play in cartographic depictions of the Caribbean islands of this period; and (3) How are claims of Spanish sovereignty over these territories and contra-cartographies disputing those claims related to the representations of piracy by peninsular and non-peninsular cartographers?

Dangerous Representations of the Caribbean in the Sixteenth Century 95

Sixteenth-century European cartography, narrative descriptions of the islands, and Spanish navigational manuals provide a framework for understanding the Caribbean region as a geopolitical stronghold of European rivalries and antagonistic propaganda for European imperial and pre-imperial powers.[46] I will start by focusing on Spanish peninsular cosmographers and sailors—such as Alonso de Santa Cruz, Juan López de Velasco, Juan Escalante de Mendoza, and Baltasar Vellerino de Villalobos—to reexamine how the notions of maritime predation in the Americas influenced their depictions of the islands and, by extension, all of the West Indies. Overall, cosmographers in Seville gathered and employed geographical knowledge about the overseas territories to which Spain had laid claim to assist the empire in its assertion and projection of sovereignty at the same time that they worked to improve navigational routes.[47]

This section will also demonstrate that cosmographers increasingly framed the islands within a conflicting narrative that emphasized both the possibility of exploiting them for profit and the Spanish Crown's lack of interest in protecting and developing the region. Drawing on Martin Lewis's concept of "metageographies"—geographic notions that rely more on cultural factors than on scientific data—this section will parallel the lack of internal details, displayed by the Spanish cartography of the archipelagic region, with the "narrative of oblivion" or Spanish lack of interest in the islands found in Santa Cruz's and Escalante de Mendoza's portrayals. From the 1520s, the Audiencia of Santo Domingo attempted to gain the Spanish Crown's attention by emphasizing their mines, sugar plantations, and other agricultural products such as bread and corn. In 1584, before Sir Francis Drake's attack on Hispaniola, Cristóbal de Ovalle (discussed in Chapter 2) wrote a letter to the Council of the Indies in which he stressed the need for military gunpowder and munitions, also asserting he had previously written several letters without receiving any response. Later documents show this "narrative of oblivion" following Drake's 1595 attack on San Juan (Puerto Rico); the captain general and governor of the island, Pedro Suárez, wrote to the Council, "[I]t seems that Your Majesty has forgotten me and this island."[48] As we will see, Santa Cruz's and Escalante de Mendoza's works contributed to the configuration of an ideological geography of "the islands" marked by scarcity and vulnerability to maritime predation and illicit trade.[49]

Moving to the works of non-Spanish-peninsular cartographic representations of the Caribbean zone—such as those of Giovanni Battista Boazio and Gerardus Mercator (included in one of Theodor de Bry's collections and in Walter Bigges's travelogue)—in the second part of this section, I will reassess the role of maritime predation in contemporary depictions and identify contra-cartographies that disputed the Spanish Crown's territorial order.[50] Besides displaying geographic data and emphasizing the economic potential of the islands, these maps depicted the threat to Spanish claims on these possessions posed by Francis Drake's assaults in 1585–86 (discussed in

Chapter 2). The raid by Drake stands out as the only one of its time to be depicted cartographically and have its maritime routes publicly divulged. While this representation did not end Spanish dominion over the region, it certainly projected Philip II's lack of competence in protecting the cities of Cartagena and Santo Domingo.

Mapping "Our" Islands

Spain's oversight of and communications with its transatlantic territories throughout the sixteenth century and beyond required a formal bureaucratic system. Functioning largely on an epistolary basis, the system involved several political organizations whose presence served to create the impression of a direct rapport between the Spanish Crown and its subjects. In 1503 the Catholic Monarchs created the House of Trade (*Casa de la Contratación*), which replicated the model of the Portuguese House of Trade (*Casa da Índia*) and the houses of commerce along the Mediterranean zone. Their successor, Charles I, created new *audiencias reales* (high courts) in the New World and reformed those of the Canary Islands, Galicia, Seville, and Santo Domingo.[51] Under his rule, the House of Trade assembled a navigational database known as the *padrón real* (master map of the world), which was a collective effort to reach a consensus upon previous and current maps based on the experiences of pilots (Brendecke, 174–175). Charles also established the viceroyalties of New Spain (1535) and Peru (1543) and limited the powers of their viceroys.[52] Unlike the Columbian Viceroyalty, these viceroyalties were not part of a negotiated contract (Eissa-Barroso, 32).

In 1524 Charles founded the Council of the Indies, an institution responsible for coordinating any administrative, juridical, and governmental affairs related to the recently conquered territories of the Americas and the Philippines.[53] The *audiencias*, for their part, dealt with the organization of the territorial jurisdictional entities, while the captaincies general (*capitanías generales*) oversaw military affairs and the governors of the local and civil administration (Brendecke, 250).[54] Through these institutional structures, Spain functioned as a modern transatlantic state that relied on viceroyalties and *audiencias* to administer its territories overseas.[55] For Charles's successor, Philip II, maps became an essential administrative instrument for overseeing his dominions without the need for travel (Mundy, 9).[56] Borrowing Emily Sohmer Tai's concept, maps became valuable tools for "territorializing," or possessing, geographical space.[57] Conquering newly discovered territories required the representation of physical "territorialization," through which the Spanish jurisdictional power and order were established.[58] Maps played a role in placing territories within imperial concepts of domination, and these in turn materialized through visual representation.[59] As Lauren Benton argues, maps were political instruments used in intra-imperial controversies over extra-European territorial claims. Encoding ideas of law and sovereignty, maps became both a technology in the service of empire and a metaphor for colonization through

Dangerous Representations of the Caribbean in the Sixteenth Century 97

the process of accumulating and controlling knowledge (Benton 2010, 10–11). Mapping was thus incorporated into the repertoire of claim-staking practices such as building forts or founding towns. It allowed imperial powers to construct extra-European sovereignty through symbolic assertions linking legal and geographical imaginations (*id.*, 57). Considering these significative functions and usages of mapping practices, I will now focus on the works of several Spanish cosmographers and sailors to examine how they contributed to the process of configuring an image of the Caribbean archipelago that emphasized the need of the Spanish Crown's attention to the region while promoting Spanish dominion over the insular territories.

The cosmographer Alonso de Santa Cruz opened his four-volume geography *Islario general de todas las islas del mundo* (1541) with a letter addressed to King Philip II. According to the letter, Philip II had commissioned Santa Cruz's work "to have a clearer understanding of what his heart wished to place under Christ's yoke" through the "visual and narrative depictions of all the known and discovered islands" (Santa Cruz 1542–60, 17). Thus, Santa Cruz framed the depictions in his work as representations of spaces that were submitting to the authority of the Spanish Crown and the Catholic faith, becoming manifestations of the crown's territorial claims. Beyond constructing a narrative of legitimacy, the letter to the king reveals an additional agenda. With an emphasis on the islands' agricultural and mining resources, it highlights the issue of depopulation that was negatively affecting the "principal islands": Jamaica, Cuba, Hispaniola, and San Juan (*id.*, 18). Focusing on Cuba, Santa Cruz explained that many settlers had left because they were looking for new settlements on "the continent," creating an exodus that took the form of four armadas that had departed from that island and discovered Yucatán, Cozumel, Florida, and New Spain (*id.*, 483–84). In light of the important function of seaports in supplying Spanish ships bound for Spain or Tierra Firme (*id.*, 484–95), Santa Cruz stressed their value as assets and urged Philip II to pay more attention to the islands as points of passage (*como de escala y paso*) for great expeditions (*id.*, 487). The cosmographer even suggested that Spaniards "who have been oppressed by misfortune" and who "are useless to themselves, to others, and to their King" could be transferred to the islands (*id.*, 488). Underlining the archipelago's geopolitical importance, Santa Cruz contributed to the configuration of the narrative of oblivion by calling attention to the neglect of the islands under Spanish dominion.[60]

The name *isolario* (a book of islands) is a term for a cartographic genre that was prominent from 1528 to 1573 and undermined cosmographic and universalist viewpoints by emphasizing topographic perspectives.[61] Lacking the rhumb lines of nautical charts, the *isolario* was designed not to assist navigators but to show, in a fragmentary and discontinuous form, the totality of the archipelagos represented (Jacob, 127). In this spirit, Santa Cruz's maps of Cuba, Jamaica, Hispaniola, and Puerto Rico lack geographical and topographic details, focusing instead on signaling the main ports and entries to the islands and, in some cases, representing Spanish settlements through symbols. For instance, following the medieval portolan model, his maps do not portray interior cities, villages, or topographic features. What we know today as the Virgin Islands are identified as "cannibal islands," and their depiction shows even fewer internal details than the "principal islands." The representation of the Lesser Antilles correlates with Santa Cruz's descriptions of those territories as "inhabited" places with "little value" (Santa Cruz 1542–60, 438 and 441–442).[62]

Juan López de Velasco—the first appointed "principal cosmographer-chronicler" (*cosmógrafo-cronista mayor*) of the Indies in 1571—differs from Santa Cruz in his attention to the outlines and geographical locations of islands, as illustrated in his *Descripción de las Yndias del Norte* (1575).[63] He provides a larger representation of the Caribbean that encompasses the *audiencias* of Mexico, Lima, Guatemala, Nueva Galicia, and Santo Domingo and uses visual means to emphasize important information. For example, he writes the name of the Audiencia of Santo Domingo in the space occupied by the sea to indicate that the archipelagic political organization encompasses both land and sea. In his *Descripción de la Audiencia de La Española* (1575), López de Velasco underscores the transatlantic political apparatus of the *audiencias* by listing several regions, ports, and cities of Cuba, Jamaica, Hispaniola, and San Juan as constituent parts of these *audiencias*. Influenced by sixteenth-century Spanish efforts to institutionalize the science of cosmography as a political tool to legitimize the extent of the Spanish Crown's jurisdiction, López de Velasco's work exemplifies the quest to lay territorial claim through cartographic representation (Sánchez-Martínez, 729–730).[64]

The next senior chronicler, Antonio de Herrera y Tordesillas, appointed in 1596, revised and adapted López de Velasco's maps of the Indies. These maps were published in his three-volume *Historia general de los hechos de los castellanos en las islas i tierra firme del mar oceano* (1601, 1606, 1612). Like his predecessor, Herrera y Tordesillas represents the archipelago without emphasizing interior details of cities, villages, or topography. He mainly prioritizes the islands' general outlines and geographical positioning. Contrasting the private interests of conquistadors and local officials against the public good, ensured through royal laws and ordinances, Herrera's *Historia* served to legitimize Spain's empire in the New World. Even though Herrera adopts a sympathetic position toward the indigenous populations, advocating for the defense of their natural right to liberty against exploitation, his project perceives the Spanish monarchy's imperium over the Indies as something righteous and just (Kagan 2009, 179–181). Underscoring the role played by the Catholic Monarchs in establishing both spiritual and temporal order while criticizing foreign incursions in the Indies, his work claims to "document the deceit of foreign nations who have not done anything similar except to extract profits from the Indies" (quoted in *id.*, 178).

In this regard, Spanish theologian and jurist Francisco de Vitoria believed that the pope should deny everyone but the Spanish the right to travel to the New World because "the princes of Spain were the first to undertake the voyages of discovery, at their own expense and under their own banners" and therefore, "they alone [the Spanish] should enjoy the fruits of their discoveries" (Vitoria, 285). In the first issue raised in his *De Indis* (1532), "On the dominion of the barbarians," Vitoria argues that the native inhabitants of the Americas "undoubtedly possessed as true dominion both public and private, as any Christians" because they were "true masters" (*ueri domini*) before the Spaniards' arrival, and thus they could not be denied the right of ownership (*dominium rerum*) (*id.*, 250).[65] While acknowledging that the indigenes had been described as "foolish and slow witted," Vitoria states that these traits were not grounds for Spaniards to steal their property or treat them as slaves (*id.*, 251). According to him, the Spanish and the indigenous populations had an equal right of ownership. This notion of ownership justified travel and the physical presence of Spaniards in the Indies as long as they avoided confrontations with indigenous populations (*id.*, 278). Anchoring this argument in the law of nations (*ius gentium*), Vitoria validates trade between Spaniards and the "barbarians" (referring to the indigenous populations). He also defends the Spaniards' right to mine gold, pearls, and other resources that did not "belong to anyone" (*res nullius*) and were found in common land or property such as seas, rivers, and ports (*id.*, 279–280). In this case, and according to the law of nations and the law of wild animals (*ferae bestiae*), Vitoria affirms that what has no owner "becomes the property of the first taker" (*id.*, 280). However, he modifies this viewpoint by emphasizing discovery over freedom of trade and the transfer of rights of ownership.

As Vitoria's example illustrates, sixteenth- and early seventeenth-century debates about the Spanish Crown's claims to property rights (*dominium rerum*) and sovereignty (*dominium jurisdictionis*) over its kingdoms triggered a series of juridical discussions that challenged the relation between discovery, territorial claims of possession, and sovereignty. There were three main processes whereby Europeans mastered America: (1) symbolically taking possession of lands; (2) physically occupying them; and (3) peopling them.[66] Possession was based on occupation and use, while sovereignty was conditioned on an official claim, although such a claim was only valid in the eyes of those who made it (Elliott, 30). For both the Spanish and the English, symbolically taking possession entailed a ceremonial act that acknowledged the principle of *res nullius* in Roman law, whereby the first user became the owner. However, the Spanish showed less interest in this doctrine because their title in colonial America was primarily based on papal concessions granted to the Spanish Crown. Therefore, their principal concern was to rationalize their lordship over the people who inhabited the lands they wished to settle (Elliott, 30).[67] In this process, Spanish efforts to systematize the extent of their dominion over the Caribbean archipelago hinged on cartographic representations.

Benton argues that during the early modern period, the seas were perceived as space constituted by maritime passages or "jurisdictional corridors." As a result of the increasing militarization of these corridors, "[The Spaniards conceived] their maritime voyages as marking *derrotas* (routes) or *caminos* (roads) within the sea and understood the value of keeping secret any precise knowledge about such tracks" (Benton 2010, 106). With the increasing Spanish need to make public territorial claims for diplomatic purposes, the tendency grew for published maps to emphasize this aspect while suppressing new practical and navigational knowledge. Two unpublished manuals of the time, by Juan Escalante de Mendoza (*Itinerario*, 1575) and Baltasar Vellerino de Villalobos (*Luz de navegantes*, 1592),[68] illustrate the tension between secrecy and public claims that lies at the heart of cartographic production at the end of the sixteenth century.

In Vellerino's case, his manual expresses explicit awareness of its publication by including the word "light" (*luz*) in the title. *Luz* might stand for light from a lamp or lighthouse that guides sailors' way as they navigate the seas, but it also alludes to the need to bring the material to light by publishing it and making it accessible to experienced and inexperienced navigators alike. The chasm between theory and practice, or between cosmographers and pilots, resulted in the articulation of two types of knowledge about the Atlantic with different aims. On the one hand, cosmographic public knowledge—primarily expressed in latitudes and longitudes—was relevant to diplomatic discussions because both were tools for legitimizing territorial claims. On the other hand, practical and local knowledge was excluded from charts and maps because its dissemination did not confer any diplomatic advantage. Both Escalante and Vellerino convey practical and navigational knowledge in their works. In the case of Vellerino, this takes the form of handmade sketches showing the main coastal landscapes of the islands and other continental Spanish territories to orient sailors in their navigation. In the case of Escalante, practical advice appears on matters such as how to deal with piracy and what to expect when landing on Caribbean islands.[69] Consequently, neither author's navigational manual was published because neither did much to promote the expansion of the Spanish Crown's territorial possession overseas.[70] In Escalante's case, for instance, King Philip II only authorized publication of the part dedicated to the study of celestial bodies.

Both authors address the phenomenon of piracy, showcasing the relation between maritime predation and their divulgence of practical and navigational knowledge. While Vellerino alludes to English maritime predation and foreign incursions to legitimize the creation of his manual and reaffirm his authoritative voice, Escalante incorporates the topic of piracy in his description of the Caribbean in its current state.[71] In his prologue, Vellerino tackles piracy as a way to legitimize his own career as a sailor and reaffirm his authorial authority. He stresses that, after being a priest in the Colegio de San Gregorio, he began a career as a sailor when the city of Mexico

Dangerous Representations of the Caribbean in the Sixteenth Century 101

decided to send 300 men to fight against Captain Drake, who had previously ambushed the Spanish in the Strait of Magellan during his circumnavigation (Vellerino, 2–3). Because of his experience of sailing and following Drake's raid, Vellerino claims to have gained practical knowledge that previously he could only speculate about: "In this voyage I finally came to learn through practice what I had understood by speculation" (*id.*, 3). Touching on piracy enabled Vellerino to increase the relevance of his manual.

Vellerino roundly criticizes the state of navigational manuals at the time, arguing that foreign nations know more about the routes to the Indies than the Spanish, who are entitled to that knowledge as masters of those territories (*id.*, 5). Even though he lists Escalante's work as a reference, he claims to benefit only from the printed manuals—those from Abraham Ortelius, Santa Cruz, and Gerardus Mercator (the Flemish geographer discussed earlier, who was concerned with maintaining secrecy over Drake's circumnavigation). He discredits the content of Escalante's *Itinerario*, alleging that "the documents written by hand were full of inappropriate things that were too long and from which very little could be learned" (*id.*, 3). However, what probably influenced the council's decision against publishing the text was the fact that Vellerino included about 115 images that mainly represented the coastal view of the Caribbean islands and other adjacent continental territories from the viewpoint of a sailor on board. On the one hand, this manuscript renders Spanish territorial possessions visible before the rest of the nations while on the other, it also provides pirates and "unentitled" foreign sailors with local, practical navigational knowledge that can only be acquired through experience.

Echoing Santa Cruz's narrative of oblivion in the Caribbean islands, Escalante links the narrative of negligence on the part of the Spanish Crown with piracy and contraband while explaining the presence of foreign sailors in the region and specifically on the island of San Juan: "The seaports of this island are less frequented by Castilian [Spanish] ships than by the French and other foreign nations, who navigate to these places without permission" (Escalante 1985, 162).[72] Unlike Santa Cruz, who had previously recommended the transfer of new settlers to the islands, Escalante advises Spanish sailors to avoid visiting the island of San Juan if they were attempting to become wealthy. He states that "even though the name of its main seaport is 'Puerto Rico' (wealthy port), the inhabitants of the island are not that wealthy" (*id.*). Stressing the dangers posed by these islands, such as foreign sailors and indigenous rebellious populations as well as the lack of economic profit, Escalante gives this general advice on navigation to the Caribbean archipelago: "One should stay only briefly in any part of these islands" (*id.*). By underscoring the absence of Spanish ships and warning Spanish sailors about the lack of wealth in the region, Escalante's description of the islands serves as an ideological representation of the Caribbean as a space marked by the inefficiency of peninsular and colonial authorities, who failed to enhance economic development and address the issue of foreign interlopers likely to engage in illicit trade or pirate attacks. Some examples of the practical advice in Escalante's manual have to do with distinguishing pirates and corsairs from everyone else in a space where piracy and contraband were all around. Sailors on a Spanish vessel coming upon an unidentified ship are advised to pretend that theirs is a corsair ship by approaching the other vessel and hoisting all the sails. The aim is to determine if the other vessel is a merchant ship, in which case the ship would "fear the temerarious behavior and thus ... turn away" (*id.*). Conversely, if the other vessel is a corsair ship, "it [will] come closer" (*id.*, 398).

Who were those "foreign sailors" that Vellerino and Escalante referred to? Who were the pirates or entitled European citizens who navigated transatlantic waters? Let us take a look.

The sixteenth century witnessed changes in the notion of Spanish citizenship between the peninsular and American contexts. Tamar Herzog's seminal study traces this transformative process, which included the emergence of different forms of exclusion in Spanish America such as "the tendency to exclude Indians and persons of mixed blood or African descent from citizenship" and the growth of restrictions to concede citizenship to non-Spanish Europeans by the beginning of the seventeenth century (Herzog 2003, 45).[73] Several laws dating from the early sixteenth century, put in place to build a legal monopoly on the New World, decreed that "only natives of the kingdoms of Spain could immigrate, settle, and trade in Spanish America" (*id.*, 94). In the context of Escalante's work, the Spanish Crown considered "natives of the kingdom of Spain" to be those individuals who qualified as natives by birth, citizenship, or naturalization.[74] Vitoria supports the right of Spanish citizenship for children born in the Indies of Spanish parents:

> If children born in the Indies of a Spanish father wish to become citizens (*cives*) of that community, they cannot be barred from citizenship or from the advantages enjoyed by the native citizens born of parents domiciled in that community.
>
> (Vitoria, 281)[75]

By the same token, he argues, those who wish to acquire citizenship in "barbarian communities" (i.e., American ones) should not "be prohibited from doing so, any more than the other inhabitants" (*id.*). One could argue that Escalante's and Vellerino's understanding of "foreign sailors" meant those individuals who were not subjects of—or authorized by—the Spanish Crown to engage in colonial enterprise or commerce.[76] By this time, "foreigners" were those non-Spanish Europeans or non-Spanish citizens—even those naturalized individuals—who attempted to trade in and gain profit from the American markets.

By the time of Escalante's writing, several French and English sailors, such as Jacques de Sores (1555) and John Hawkins (1562, 1564, and 1567), had engaged in smuggling African slaves and occasionally attacking insular

Dangerous Representations of the Caribbean in the Sixteenth Century 103

ports in the Caribbean region.[77] J.L. Anderson has noted that Caribbean piracy reflected political and economic European rivalries in the Old World; ineffective enforcement of maritime jurisdictions, as opposed to territorial ones, hindered the legal suppression of piracy even from those territories or nation-states with a jurisdiction that was in constant dispute (Anderson, 83–84).[78] Although, in the 1550s, Portuguese dealers started to evade the rules on shipping African slaves within Spanish America that had been imposed by the House of Trade, John Hawkins was the first English sailor to circumvent exclusive Spanish regulations of trade (Andrews 1984, 118).[79] In 1566 the Spanish ambassador to England thwarted Hawkins's plans for a third transatlantic voyage; nevertheless, Hawkins sponsored three ships under Captain John Lovell's command that undertook the voyage to the Caribbean. This marked the first time Francis Drake crossed the Atlantic, commanding the *Judith*. It was also Drake's last slave-trade venture (Andrews 1984, 129). His next voyages, in 1570–71, 1572, 1577, 1585, and 1595, were more focused on raiding than on smuggling.[80]

I will now turn to the analysis of the visual representations that account for the presence in the Caribbean of those considered "foreigners" in the eyes of the Spanish Crown. These maps of the places called "principal islands" were primarily developed by non-Spanish (i.e., Flemish and Italian) cartographers. These mapmakers used the visual and narrative representation of the Caribbean geography as a tool for projecting economic interests and challenging the Spanish Crown's hegemony through the depiction of Drake's attacks.

Mapping "Their" Islands

Drawing from the Portuguese strategy and model, the Dutch also transformed maps into ownership claims, manifesting their dominion over their "possessions" through detailed descriptions (Seed, 154–165). Like their Portuguese counterparts, Dutch maps provided tangible, visible referents to the geographical discourse to claim the right of occupation over the space represented. The maps acted as signs of power in temporal, spiritual, political, commercial, military, and cultural terms. As part of the Spanish institutionalization of cartography and the imminent threat posed by foreign nations and contested territories subject to the Habsburg dynasty, Spanish peninsular cosmographers and sailors arranged a geographical representation whose main purpose was to enunciate and legitimize political and territorial claims. Italian and Flemish cartography depicting the Spanish Crown's "forgotten" Caribbean islands plagued by English piracy stressed the potential economic and geopolitical importance of what was once the first Viceroyalty of the Indies. In this way, Italian and Flemish maps of the Caribbean—those not produced for Habsburg consumption–aimed for a set of counterclaims, economic and political, that had less to do with territorial possession—the key concern of their Spanish counterparts—than with a display of opportunities presented to enemies of the Spanish Crown because of its inability to rule and protect its transatlantic and "infested" territories.

The image of the Caribbean that emerges out of these ideological and geographical representations is a diverse space under constant intervention by European agents foreign to the Spanish Crown or by citizens of its non-peninsular and contested realms. One such citizen was the Flemish geographer Gerardus Mercator, who engraved maps of the islands of Cuba, Hispaniola, San Juan, Jamaica, and Margarita that were published in 1578, c1590, 1607, and 1630 with minor alterations. One of these maps duplicates the port of Havana in a close-up next to a depiction of the island of Cuba, as if to emphasize the island's economic activity (Fig. 3.1). Two other versions of this map (Figs. 3.2 and 3.3) include Latin inscriptions that underscore the economic value of the Caribbean region.[81] Both versions read *"Portus celeberimus totius India Occidentalis"* ("the most famous port in all the West Indies") and include the close-up of the Havana seaport. They also display an inscription, at the northern part of Venezuela, that reads *"Portus Regius Salinus Scatens Spontaneis in valle solo laboris pretio petitur"* ("Royal port with plentiful salt located in a valley [and] available for the price of labor").[82]

Mercator's maps mark the political territorialization of the maritime space through their Latin inscriptions highlighting potential sources of monetary profit and through their depictions of ships.[83] By the same token, we can see a contra-cartographic effort, or the questioning of Spanish order, in three of Mercator's maps. These maps display a ship, located at the western end of Hispaniola, imprinted with a changing-flags design illustrating different political potentialities (Figs. 3.2, 3.3, and 3.4). Two of these maps show the Burgundy Cross flag of Spain (Figs. 3.3 and 3.4), introduced in naval fortresses by Charles I, while another map (Fig. 3.3) depicts a flag with a design that resembles the Dutch tricolor, first used by the Dutch in revolts against Spain led by Prince William of Orange.[84] A closer look at the map reveals that the same ship has a second flag with a design resembling the Dutch Triple Prince flag, which had different versions featuring up to eleven stripes by the end of the sixteenth century (Fig. 3.5). If the engraver had intended to depict the Dutch rebels' tricolor, hoisted during the Eighty Years' War against Spain, then this second flag heralds the later independence of the Dutch and symbolizes their eagerness to introduce themselves into Spain's commercial monopoly, projecting their capacity to navigate Caribbean waters (Fig. 3.5). Further, Mercator's engravings feature detailed topographic representations of the islands' interiors. For instance, they provide the names of the cities and regions in Spanish and Latin and also display indigenous names such as Haity, Quisqueia, Albaiamo, and Samana. Maps of Hispaniola, Cuba, Jamaica, and Margarita show more mountainous regions, towns and cities (Spanish settlements), and forest areas.[85] Other maps of Hispaniola by Italian engravers such as Giacomo Gastaldi, Giovanni Battista Ramusio, and Girolamo Ruscelli also detail the topography and provide more names of its interior neighborhoods and cities. Overall, these maps offer more information, in both symbols and words, about towns, rivers, and ports than the Spanish cartographers discussed earlier.

Dangerous Representations of the Caribbean in the Sixteenth Century 105

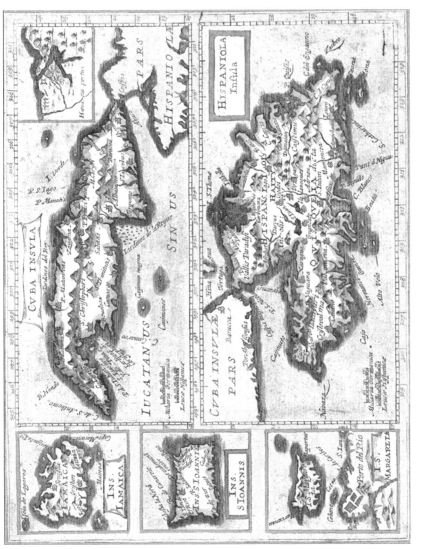

Fig. 3.1 Mercator's map of the Caribbean archipelago (c1590). Note the close up of Havana's Port on the upper right side. Also note the topographical detail. Copy available at the Archivo General de la Nación, M28 (1350), Santo Domingo, DR.

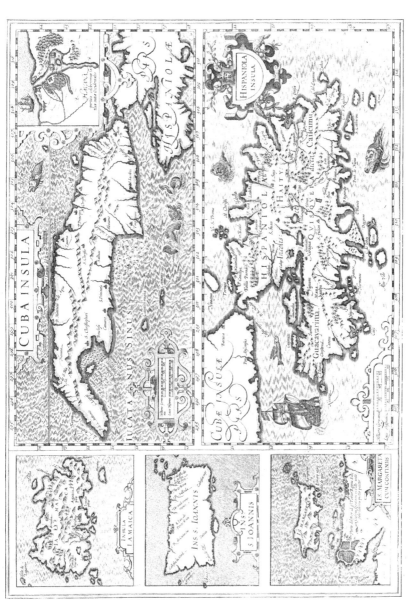

Fig. 3.2 Mercator's map depicting a ship with a flag the design of which resembles the Dutch tricolor flag from 1572. Note the close up of Havana's port on the upper-right side with the inscription "*Portus celeberimus totius India Occidentalis*" ("The most famous port in all the West Indies") and also note the other inscription in lower-left side that reads "*Portus Regius Salinas Scatens Spontaneis in valle solo laboris pretio petitur*" ("Royal Port with plentiful salt located in a valley available for the price of labour"). Copy available at the Archivo General de la Nación, M8 (384), 1590–c. 1630, Santo Domingo, DR.

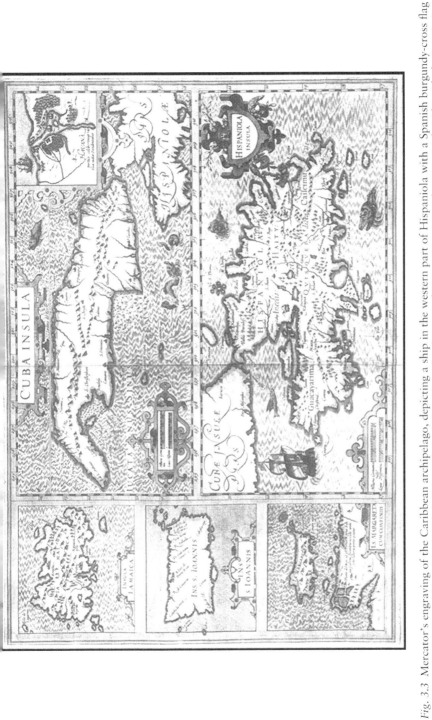

Fig. 3.3 Mercator's engraving of the Caribbean archipelago, depicting a ship in the western part of Hispaniola with a Spanish burgundy-cross flag and what resembles a Dutch Triple Prince Flag (c1590). Note the close up of Havana's port on the upper-right side with the inscription *"Portus celeberimus totius India Occidentalis"* ("The most famous port in all the West Indies") and the inscription located in the northern part of Venezuela – very close to the Island of Margarita – that reads *"Portus Regius Salinas Scatens Spontaneis in valle solo laboris pretio petitur"* ("Royal Port with plentiful salt located in a valley available for the price of labour"). Copy available at the Archivo General de la Nacion, M31(1353), Santo Domingo, DR.

108   *Dangerous Representations of the Caribbean in the Sixteenth Century*

Fig. 3.4 Gerardus Mercator's and Jodocus Hondius' engraving of Hispaniola Insula (c1578–1590). Copy available at the Centro Eduardo León Jimenes, Mapoteca MC-01–0008, Santiago, DR.

Dangerous Representations of the Caribbean in the Sixteenth Century 109

Fig. 3.5 Detail from Mercator's map showing a ship hoisting what resembles a Dutch Triple Prince Flag. Copy available at the Centro Eduardo León Jimenes, Mapoteca MC-01–0008, Santiago, DR.

Moving to the relation between cartography and maritime predation, let us examine the representations of Giovanni Battista Boazio, an Italian artist residing in London, who depicted Drake's Caribbean raid of 1585–1586, an account of which is given in Bigges's *A Summarie and True Discourse of Francis Drake's West Indian Voyage* (1589) and in De Bry's *Grand Voyages*, Latin edition (1599).[86] As discussed in Chapter 2, Drake sailed from Plymouth with 23 vessels. His fleet reached Santo Domingo, the capital of Hispaniola, on New Year's Day 1586, where they collected a ransom of 25,000 ducats. They arrived in Cartagena, Colombia, a few weeks later, where they stayed 53 days. After collecting a ransom of almost 110,000 ducats, they headed to other destinations in the Caribbean and returned to England on July 22.

The practice of depicting battles or military scenes as an aspect of cartography began in Italy during the 1520s. A school for mapmakers known as the School of War was founded in 1576. The conflation of military depictions and cartography generated maps that included annotations of military events.[87] Boazio's maps of Drake's attacks at Cape Verde, Santo Domingo, Cartagena, and St. Augustine correspond to this trend. However, Drake's Caribbean raid occurred in the framework of a yet-undeclared official war between Spain and England. To English eyes, Drake's attack was less a formal act of war than an expedition to the West Indies (Neale, 298). The

110 Dangerous Representations of the Caribbean in the Sixteenth Century

Spanish, on the other hand, considered this event both an act of piracy and a military offense to their domains overseas. In what follows, I will analyze the geopolitical repercussions of Boazio's visual depiction of the attacks through the configuration of contra-cartographies.

Boazio's world map, which uses lines to trace Drake's Caribbean raid (Fig. 3.6), presents a geopolitical representation of the Caribbean in relation to the Old World.[88] The two lines representing the movement of Drake's 23-ship fleet are labeled "the waye outwarde" and "the waye homewarde."

Fig. 3.6 Giovanni Battista Boazio's engraving of Drake's Caribbean raid (1585–1586) represented by a line marking Drake's navigational trajectory that also encloses part of the Atlantic Ocean along with the Caribbean archipelago connected with England. This engraving was included in Bigges's published narrative. The text (written in English) recounts the dates when the English fleet arrived to the Caribbean islands and which they either, "spoiled," "landed and refreshed the sick men" or "fought." Kraus Collection, Library of Congress. Another copy available at the Archivo General de la Nación, M 26 (1348), Santo Domingo, DR.

Dangerous Representations of the Caribbean in the Sixteenth Century 111

South America is identified with Spanish flags, but the Caribbean locus lacks any imperial power flag. This provides a contra-cartographic image that undermines Spanish claims of jurisdictional power over the region. Beyond contesting official perspectives, Boazio's depiction of Drake's attack on Santo Domingo (Fig. 3.7) also strategically destabilizes the Spanish conception of its territorial order overseas and in turn projects a rising spirit of English military supremacy over the Spanish—the ones entitled to rule "the islands." Boazio's representation of Drake's Caribbean raid emphasizes the economic potential of the region and depicts the cities under attack in some detail. For instance, unlike the Spanish cartographers, his engraving of Santo Domingo (Fig. 3.7) displays a detailed city map from a bird's-eye view bordered by a sea filled with ships carrying the English sixteenth-century royal banner and their naval flag depicting St. George's Cross.

In the Roman tradition, which influenced Hispanic notions of geographical order, cities were associated with the *imperium*, understood as "command" or "order." Boazio's depiction of Santo Domingo's urban grid allows the viewer to identify the locations of roads and the cathedral in the central plaza, as well as the outline of the defensive wall, the military fortress, and the positions of several Spanish cannons. The map includes Latin and French inscriptions underscoring Hispaniola's resemblance in "grandeur," "magnitude," and geographic extension to English cities. It also emphasizes the city's proximity to the roads of the rest of the neighborhoods

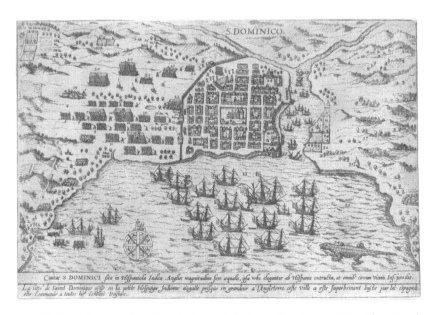

Fig. 3.7 Boazio's engraving of Drake's attack in Santo Domingo (1588) with a French translation of the original Latin note that emphasizes the relationship between England and Santo Domingo. Kraus Collection, Library of Congress.

112 *Dangerous Representations of the Caribbean in the Sixteenth Century*

on the island.[89] Boazio's representation of Drake's attack on Cartagena, which appears in De Bry's collection (1599) under the title *Franciscvs Draco Carthagenam Civitatem Expvgnat*, also shows a detailed port city's urban grid along with a depiction of an assault by English troops by land and sea. The short description that accompanies the image underscores its spatial and political importance by stating that Cartagena is the "door to all the commerce between Spain and Peru."[90] Ships labeled with English flags occupy the maritime space surrounding the territorial space (Fig. 3.8).

Fig. 3.8 Boazio's engraving of Drake's attack in Cartagena de Indias with the chronological narrative of the event from De Bry's *Grand Voyages*, Latin edition (1599). Kraus Collection, Library of Congress.

Dangerous Representations of the Caribbean in the Sixteenth Century 113

Unlike the smaller versions of these maps included in Walter Bigges's account, Boazio's maps from De Bry's later edition display numbers and captions that frame the attack within a readable chronological narration.[91] Besides recounting the events, the narration identifies the places—doors, walls, countryside, or plazas—in which the actions took place. These descriptions evoke what Padrón calls "prose cartography" employed by Spanish explorers, chroniclers, and conquerors (Hernán Cortés, Oviedo, and Las Casas, for example) through which the reader could create an image of the Americas from a bird's-eye perspective (Padrón, 145). In Boazio's map we see the same narrative strategy combined with the visual depiction of the event. Certainly, the combination of cartography and written annotations resembles the military cartography of the time, but the maps also project a single contra-cartographic spatial narrative in which Spanish jurisdiction in the New World is under threat of attack by the English. Rather than depicting a war whose outcome results in the imposition of a different regime or political order, both maps portray a city under siege (*civitatem expugnat*) by Drake. In Michel de Certeau's words, the "spatial trajectories" represented by the visual depiction of the attack, juxtaposed with the "prose cartography" exemplified by the written measures taken by the people of Cartagena and Santo Domingo during the attack by Drake's fleet, show that maritime predation is intrinsically related to the representation of space.[92] In so doing, both maps reshape the overseas perception of Hispaniola and the Caribbean continental coast of Cartagena as scenarios of European territorial dispute.

Boazio's contra-cartographies support the notion of Caribbean space as part of a fractured Spanish territorial order subject to unofficial invasion. In this respect, his maps serve as visual representations of Bigges's account of the Caribbean raid, which was critical of Philip II's territorial ambitions. Bigges underlines the relation between geographical space and political interests by emphasizing Philip II's coat of arms ("The world is not enough"), found in the governor's lodge in Santo Domingo:

> I may not omit to let the world know one very notable marke and token, of the vnsatiable ambition of the Spanish King and his nation which was found in the kings house ... wherein vpon one of the walles ... there is described & painted in a very large Scutchion, the armes of the king of Spaine, & in the lower part of the said Scutchion, there is likewise described a globe, containing in it the whole circuite of the sea and the earth, whereupon is a horse standing on his hinder part within the globe, and the other fore part without the globe lifted vp as it were to leape, with a scroll painted in his mouth, wherein was written these wordes in Latin Non Svfficit Orbis.
>
> (Bigges, 245)

In other words, the wall displayed a very large Spanish shield that included in the lower part a visual representation of the globe with a horse on top of it with a scroll containing the Spanish king's coat of arms. Bigges' ekphrastic maneuver of vividly describing the escutcheon amplifies the meaning of the act of mapping as a means of owning and possessing the space represented. In this case, the English sailor's ekphrasis served as a rhetorical device with a twofold function. First, it became a metaphorical representation of the 1570s world's geopolitical stage where Spain claimed control over the "whole circuite of the sea and the earth." Second, the act of finding such a visual representation provides Bigges with a justification for maritime predation and for dissemination of propaganda against the Spanish king and his inability to preserve what he claims to dominate:

> [I]f the Queene of England would resolutely prosecute the warres against the king of Spaine, he should be forced to lay aside that proude and vnreasonable reaching vaine of his, for he should finde more then inough to do, to keepe that which he had alreadie, as by the present example of their lost towne they might for a beginning perceaue well inough.
> (Bigges, 246)[93]

In this way, through the representation of geographical space along with its geopolitical implications, the visual and narrative description of power poses the question of who is entitled to own maritime and territorial space, and thus who is entitled to classify acts of hegemony on the part of others as piracy.

The way Boazio's map—originally intended to accompany Bigges's account— appropriates Drake's attack against Santo Domingo informs two later maps attributed to Matthäeus Merian (1648) and Allain Malleson Mallet (1683). Based on Boazio's city plan of Santo Domingo, Merian's map identifies five places: a cathedral (Templum primarium), a plaza (Forum), a castle (Castellum), a city garden (Hortus civium), and St. Barbara's Abbey (Coenobium S. Barbarae) (Fig. 3.9). Unlike Boazio's engraving, Merian's illustration excludes the Anglo-Spanish conflict: he neither depicts the English and Spanish troops fighting in the western part of the city, nor does he include the three ships burning in the Ozama River. Using stylized lines to depict the outlines of the houses, buildings, and other structures, Merian's urban design enables the viewer to discern more details than those found in Boazio's depiction (Fig. 3.10). In his description of the city, Mallet does not refer to Drake's attack, but he does mention the French pillaging of 1536 and 1638 when describing the city of Havana, Cuba. It is worth noting that, while Escalante underscores that Puerto Rico is anything but "wealthy," Mallet explains that its name comes from the "goodness of its port where the largest galleons are completely safe."[94] Even though neither engraver chooses to depict the English attack, both base their city plans of Santo Domingo on Boazio's map. In this sense, Merian's and Mallet's works bear the imprint of a previous map, the original intention of which was to represent an English raid.

Dangerous Representations of the Caribbean in the Sixteenth Century   115

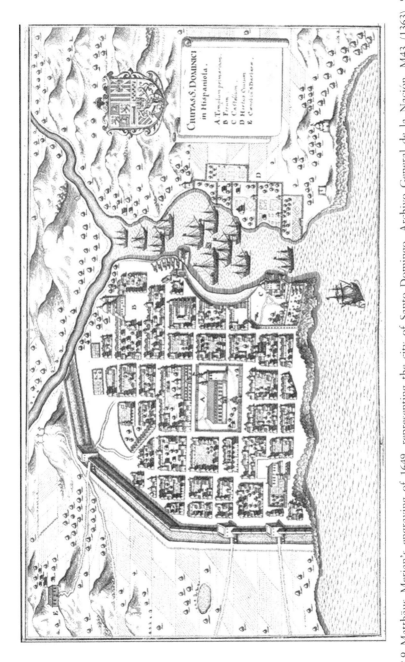

Fig. 3.9 Matthäus Merian's engraving of 1649, representing the city of Santo Domingo. Archivo General de la Nación, M43 (1363), Santo Domingo, DR.

116 *Dangerous Representations of the Caribbean in the Sixteenth Century*

Fig. 3.10 City plan of the of Santo Domingo by Alain Manesson Mallet, *Description de l'Univers* (c1683). Copy available at Centro Eduardo León Jimenes, Mapoteca, MC-01–0002, Santiago, DR.

Dangerous Representations of the Caribbean in the Sixteenth Century 117

This chapter has focused on the visual and narrative descriptions of the Caribbean islands and adjacent port cities (like Cartagena and Santo Domingo) that create a geography of danger marked by maritime predation, imperial aspirations, and metaphors of infestation. The later adoption of Boazio's maps in the works of Matthäeus Merian and Allain Malleson Mallet—from the second half of the seventeenth century—illustrates a historical context in which intra-imperial disputes over the possession of the Caribbean islands no longer concerned the legitimation of the European right to rule those territories. By the end of the sixteenth century, part of the jurisdiction of the Caribbean was transferred to the Audiencia of México, removing power from the Audiencia of Santo Domingo (capital of Hispaniola). Later maps, such as one by Vicenzo Coronelli from 1688, place the Caribbean region as part of the Mexican archipelago and no longer as an independent region.[95] The transfer not only gave more jurisdictional power to New Spain but also, as this map evinces, gave more presence to Mexico within the scope of the Caribbean region. The Caribbean archipelago changed from an independent network of islands, as depicted in the cartographic works discussed, to a component of the Mexican archipelago. Through the analysis of the instrumentalization of sixteenth-century maps, we have examined the narrative of Spain's legitimation of its power over the Caribbean islands and the contestation of this narrative through the articulation of contra-cartographies, primarily executed by rivals of the Spanish Crown. Moving to the next and last transatlantic attack by Drake and the descriptions found in literary and historical documentation, the next chapter will focus on the mechanisms employed to promote specific geopolitical narratives that questioned even the veracity of specific historic events.

Notes

1 Zárate was the censor of the first part of a four-part collection of the *Elegías*, which was first published in Madrid in 1589. After Zárate, Alonso de Ercilla and Pedro Sarmiento de Gamboa were appointed to this office. See Chapter 2 for a discussion of Castellanos's *Elegías*.
2 Zárate writes: "[T]odos estos libros quedaban defectuosos y sin principio, por no haber sabido quien tomase á su cargo declarar cómo y cuándo, y por quién se comenzó a describer tanta anchura como jay ansi norte sur." Zárate's quotes are included in the edition consulted of the *Elegías*, 2.
3 Zárate writes: "[T]rata de los ilustres varones que en compañía de Cristóbal Colón, y después dél, descubrieron la navegación del mar del norte, que los autores llaman atlántico, y conquistaron y redujeron al conocimiento de nuestra santa fe y la corona real de Castilla los indios naturales de tan estendidas ínsulas como en él conquistaron, que comúnmente se nombra el Nuevo Mundo" (*Elegías*, 2).
4 Zárate writes: "será muy bien recibida en todos estos reinos, especialmente en el Andalucía y lugares marítimos de aquella costa, donde se tiene mas noticia y comercio con las Indias y navegación ellas" (*Elegías*, 2).

5 "En aquesta ciudad y en este puerto/ ha tenido valor el duro Marte; / Pues todos los que han descubierto / De aquí salieron por la mayor parte / Y muchos en el tiempo de Ovando / De cuyas alabanzas voy tratando."
6 Here I incorporate the term "grammar" from Walter Mignolo's approach to exploring the "grammar" of epistemic decolonization (Mignolo, 470). In my case, I'm interested in exploring the grammar employed by foreign interlopers to the Spanish Crown who challenged the processes of Spanish colonization in visual and textual environments (in maps, epistles, and legal treatises, among others).
7 "Otrosi, que Vuestras Altezas fazen al dicho don Christoual su visorey e gouernador general en todas las dichas tierras firmes e yslas, que como dicho es, descubirere o ganare en las dichas mares" (Rumeu de Armas, 52). Francisco A. Eissa-Barroso emphasized the previous experience of the Crown of Aragon in creating and enforcing the title of viceroy in the Mediterranean during the late fourteenth and fifteenth centuries (Eissa-Barroso, 26–27).
8 Columbus's son and successor Diego engaged in several litigations (*pleitos colombinos*) against kings Ferdinand II and Charles I to retain the title of viceroy (Rumeu de Armas, 52). Matthew Restall has argued that Columbus's career and reputation were damaged and diminished not only by his questionable skills in administrating the territories and his fortune's decline, but also by Castilian ethnocentrism (Restall, 10).
9 Fray Nicolás de Ovando y Cáceres, second governor of Hispaniola, came from the city of Cáceres in the northeastern Extremadura region of Spain (Altman, 33). Ovando's endeavors included relocating people in cycles from his hometown by promoting the island's economic landscape. He also enforced the *encomienda* system on the island, whereby a selected group of indigenes was entrusted to colonists called *encomenderos*. Alongside the *encomienda* system was a project of maintaining two coexisting republics in Spanish America—the *república de indios* and the *república de españoles*—intended to protect the indigenous populations from Spanish influences and to prohibit Spaniards from settling in indigenous communities (Herzog 2003, 48). After complaints of abuse of the indigenes, the system was reformed under the New Laws (*Nuevas Leyes*), enforced in 1542. While in theory the indigenous populations were supposed to be protected or engage in a reciprocal relationship of rights with their *encomenderos*, in reality the latter looked upon their wards as rewards for their service in the conquest, and the safeguards of this system were commonly ignored in the Americas (Brendecke, 248–249). Regarding the cultural influences of local Taínos, Lauren Macdonald states that the Laws of Burgos (1512) protected and preserved several aspects of the indigenous culture of the Caribbean, such as the celebration of *areitos* (a type of religious pageant) and the use of the hammock (Macdonald, 18).
10 For more about the movement and circulation of colonial writers, see "The Colonial Crucible, 1580–1820" in Roberto Márquez, 11–14.
11 *Elegías* (first three volumes), 1874 edition, printed in Madrid. Some examples may be found on pages 72, 109, 253, 276, 287, 335, 337, 348, and 373.
12 "Deciales que gran cosa sería / Una noche hurtar una piragua, / La cual en breve tiempo yo pornía / En los puertos y playas de Cubagua." Salas was captured by Caribs in Borinquen (present-day Puerto Rico) and after three years of captivity returned to his mother, who resided on the island of Margarita. Martínez-Osorio relates Castellanos's depiction of the encounter between Salas and his mother to the Iberian tradition of captivity narratives because they are represented as pious Christians (Martínez-Osorio 2016, 108).
13 Here I borrow Klaus Dodds's term "geopolitical architecture" to refer to the description of "the ways in which states and non-state organizations access, manage, and regulate the intersection of territories and flows and in so doing

Dangerous Representations of the Caribbean in the Sixteenth Century 119

establish borders between inside/outside, citizen/alien, and domestic/international" (Dodds 2007, 55).
14. Sahagún's manuscript came into the possession of the House of Medici around 1588 and is currently held by the Medicea Laurenziana Library in Florence, Italy.
15. "Los predicadores, y confesores, medicos son de las animas medicinas y de las enfermedades espirituales" (Sahagún, 1).
16. "El predicador delos viçios de la republica para enderecar contra ellos su doctrina y el confessor para saver preguntar lo que conviene y entender lo que dixeren ... Ni conviene se decuyden los ministros desta conversion con dezir que entre esta gente no ay mas peccados, de borrachera, lustro y carnalidad: Porque otros muchos peccados ay entre ellos muy mas graves y que y que tienen gran necessidad de remedios los peccados de la ydolatria, y ritos ydolatricos y suspresticiones ydolatricas y agüeros, y abusiones, y ceremonias ydolatricas: no son aun perdidas del todo" (Sahagún, 1).
17. "Mandamos á los Virreyes, Presidentes y Governadores, que pongan mucho cuidado en que los vecinos de los Puertos tengan prevencion de armas y caballos conforme á la posibilidad de cada uno, para que si se ofreciere ocasion de enemigos, ú otro qualquier accidente, estén apercibidos á la defensa, resistencia y castigo de los que trataren de *infestarlos*" (emphasis added) (25). Book III, "De la guerra," Title IV, *Recopilación de las leyes de los reynos de Indias*, vol. 2, Third Edition, by Antonio Pérez de Soto, Madrid, 1774, 24–27.
18. Las Casas in the forth response to Sepúlveda argues: "Al ejemplo decimos que de los perlados es y mayormente del Summo exhortar y mandar a los reyes cristianos que defiendan la sancta Iglesia, y hagan guerra y destruyan, si fuere para esto menester, contra todos los que la ofenden e impugnan, como eran los tiranos longobardos y los poderosos herejes y cualesquiera infieles o personas grandes o chicas que presumieren de la *infestar* o fatigar" (*Controversia Las Casas - Sepúlveda*, emphasis added).
19. Las Casas, 1579, in Paulino Castañeda Delgado's edition (1994). In his *Apologética historia summaria* (1527–1550), Las Casas also employs the term in several chapters. In Chapter 148 he uses it to refer to the Romans who venerated Mars because of their inclination to "infest and disturb the world with wars and battles" (Las Casas 1994, 989).
20. The same entry alludes to another meaning related to coastal maritime predation.
21. Nirenberg refers to the case of the bishop of Dax, who arrested all the lepers of his diocese in 1320. According to Nirenberg, he was trying to preserve his jurisdiction over lepers. Later on, in 1321, the communities of Toulouse, Albi, and Carcassonne petitioned the monarchy to expel Jews and segregate lepers. One of the reasons provided by Nirenberg to explain this event is the fact that consuls were trying to gain more jurisdictional power over the autonomous property of lepers (Nirenberg, 53).
22. Several authors have stressed the relation between leprosy and sin in the Middle Ages, among them Saul Nathaniel Brody in *The Disease of the Soul*; Roger I. Moore in "Heresy as Disease" in *The Concept of Heresy in the Middle Ages*; and Jacques Le Goff and Nicolas Truong in *Una historia del cuerpo en la Edad Media*.
23. Found in *Elegía XIV* (Part I, 155) and in *Elegía a la muerte de Bustos de Villegas en un solo canto* (second governor of Cartagena) (Part III, 434).
24. "Pesado mal, terrible pestilencia, / Es en algún gobierno dalle mano/al que tiene soltura de conciencia / Y solas apariencias de cristiano" (*Elegía III*, Part II, 235).
25. "Murciélagos, mosquitos y otras plagas / Los infestaban con crüeles llagas" (*Elegía IX*, Part I, 83).
26. *Elegía de Juan de Bustos de Villegas*, Parte III, 434.
27. "Bartolomé Colon ganó gran fama, / Quedó toda la tierra temerosa, / Y el dicho, viéndose tan adelante, / Se hizo mas soberbio y arrogante. / Usaba no de términos

discretos / en algunos negocios sustanciales, / Sin aquellas decencias y respetos / Que se deben á hombres principales" (*Elegía III*, Part I, 40).

28 Regarding the relation between property and theft, and aligning with Marx and Stirner's approaches, Amedeo Policante stresses that "Property and theft, in other words, are rooted in the same soil, from which they cannot be eradicated; they are legal concepts, which are valid only where law rules" (Policante 2015, 56). Policante is quoted in Sean Johnson Andrews' who, by the same token, argues that "it is only with a change in the law and the ideology of the state that the outlaw becomes the villain, it is here that the definition of piracy—and its analogy to the present—bumps against the way law is itself a front of hegemonic struggle" (Andrews 2018, 37).

29 In the Portuguese translation, entitled, *Do justo império asiático dos Portugueses*, Freitas claims the following: "Das deduções que, com a maior brevidade possível, fizemos neste capítulo e no anterior, vêse bastantemente que é admissível a ocupação do mar, pois, embora não possamos ocupálo todo por causa da sua vastidão e da nossa impotência, todavia é ponto aceito que o podemos parcialmente proteger, *desinfestar*, dominar e ter soba nossa soberania, a fim de protegermos as nossas coisas e nos defendermos dos inimigos e piratas" (284).

30 "Os holandeses, que se haviam afastado da fidelidade e obediência a Filipe, seu príncipe próprio e natural começaram, sob o pretexto da rebelião, a infestar o direito dos Portugueses sobre os empórios da Índia e o seu competente império e como fossem muitas vezes repelidos pelos nossos" (Freitas, 104).

31 Quoted in Selden, 105.

32 The word *infestar* is used by Castellanos in the medical sense ("infect") and also as a plague ("infest"). See note 30.

33 The ordinances for corsairs are analogous to what were known as "letters of marque" or "commissions," issued by the French and English Crowns from the fifteenth century. However, Spain did not issue those official documents until the second half of the seventeenth century.

34 "Considerando los grandes daños que reciven los Vassallos del Rey mi Hijo de tantos Corsarios, y Pyratas como andan infestando las Costas de Las Indias; y siendo justo ayudar á los Armadores para que se animen … decláro, y mando, que las pressas que quitaren á los dichos Pyratas …." AGI, Contratación, 1455.

35 "Hacer daños, estragos, correrías y hostilidades el enemigo en las tierras, especialmente en las costas del mar" (*Diccionario de autoridades*, ed. 1734).

36 AGS, Estado, 4310: "Considerando los grandes daños que reciben mis vasallos y confederados de tantos Cosarios y Piratas como andad en la Mar infestandola; declaro, y mando, que las presas que quitaren á los Enemigos, y Piratas … se entienda ser buena."; AGS, Marina, 402, fol. 65, *Instrucción de lo que de orden del rey ha de observar el Gefe de Esquadra Don Pedro Mesia de La Cerda con la de su cargo en el corso de las costas de Tierra Firme*: "El desorden con que los Extrangeros, especialmente los Holandeses, infestan ilicito comercio toda la costa de Tierra Firme, faltando, faltando a esto á los tratados, y causando al legitimo comercio de los vasallos de S.M. y á su Rey herario gravisimos, perjuicios, ha obligado á S.M. á tomar la eficaz providencia … de destinar fuerzas competentes de Mar …"

37 AGS, Marina, 402, 65.

38 AGS, 6700, 198–199: "[L]as arribadas solo son legitimas en los casos expuestos en los mismos tratados con arreglo a los quales hande proceder los Jueces: que solo son contingentes en las Costas inmediatas a las Colonias ó a los tránsitos de Navegacion permitida, pero no en las remotas, como en las de Santa Marta, Carthagena, Portovelo, etc. donde ningun accidente puede licitamente conducir a los extrangeros; que debe tenerse por prueva real de malicia hallarse la Embarcación en parage despoblado, pudiendo encaminarse a puerto poblado; quela persecusion de Enemigos ó Piratas se despreciará mientras por otra parte no haya noticias ciertas ó mui probables de infestar efectivamente aquellos Mares."

39 Sixteenth-century Spanish chroniclers employed neither the term "Caribbean islands" nor the distinction between Greater and Lesser Antilles. In Alonso de Santa Cruz's *Islario*, however, we find an attempt to distinguish the Greater from the Lesser Antilles when he mentions that one of the differences between the two regions is that the main indigenous tribe of the latter (Caribs) used to attack Hispaniola, Cuba, Jamaica, and San Juan to hunt down their men and eat their bodies (Santa Cruz, 507).

40 Oviedo stated that, to avoid repetition, he would refer to Hispaniola every time he described the other islands because they were very similar in terms of flora and fauna (*Historia generale*, Oviedo, 462). In his *Sumario*, he wrote: "De la isla de Cuba y de otras, que son San Juan y Jamaica, todas estas cosas que se han dicho de la gente y otras particularidades de la isla Española, se pueden decir, aunque no tan copiosamente, porque son menores; pero en todas ellas hay lo mismo ..." (Capítulo VIII, "De la Isla de Cuba y otras," 24). For a recent analysis of Oviedo's representation of nature, see Vanina Teglia's article "Claroscuros del archivo colonial: La escritura sobre la naturaleza de Fernández de Oviedo" in *Huarte de San Juan: Geografía e Historia* 27, edited by Juan Carlos García Funes, 267–290 (2020).

41 Chapter XVLI, 243, reprinted in 1967. Ricardo Padrón argues that Oviedo's usage of "prose cartography" enabled him "to ground and organize his narrative of events, thereby suggesting that it provides the metageography of his entire historical project as developed in parts 2 and 3 of the *Historia general y natural*" (Padrón, 153). In his study, Padrón also refers to Las Casas's attempt to project the idea of America through the depiction of Hispaniola (*id.*, 178).

42 "Capítulo XVLI," *Apologética Historia Sumaria* (243).

43 Mapmakers at this time were known as cosmographers, but the discipline of cosmography encompassed more than today's "cartography," including the works of both mathematicians and chroniclers. Spain's institutionalization of cosmography produced two main currents: one focused on the mathematical scope of mapmaking, and the other centered on the descriptive aspects of geography and the peoples chronicled by historians (Portuondo, 9).

44 Alison Sandman traces the sixteenth-century Spanish debates between pilots and cosmographers on the compilation, concealment, and publication of navigational and cartographic knowledge. She makes a distinction between theoretical or cosmographic knowledge, which informed charts and planispheres that principally displayed geographical information in terms of latitude and longitude, and practical or local knowledge, i.e., all the details required "to enter ports, recognize headlands, or avoid hazards" (Sandman, 40–41).

45 According to Andrews, in the 1530s the island of Puerto Rico only had around 300 inhabitants or *vecinos* (Andrews 1978, 16).

46 Anthony Pagden has argued that although the French and English shared a rhetoric that stressed the impulse of creating an empire similar to Spain's and Portugal's—exemplified in the works of Richard Hakluyt and André Thevet—they nonetheless lacked the means or resources to undertake such a large-scale enterprise (Pagden 1995, 65). I employ the term "pre-imperial powers" to refer to those non-Iberian countries—namely, the English and the French—whose consolidation as "empires" or even as "nations"—as in the case of the Dutch—was shaped during the seventeenth century. At this point their efforts of exploration, conquest, or settlement were not entirely institutionalized or supported by a state (*status*) or an "empire." The latter terms had become synonymous by the late sixteenth century, according to Pagden (*id.*, 13).

47 Pagden's seminal study on the elusive nature of the term "empire"—evinced by its multiple meanings and usages from antiquity to the early modern period—examines the geographical, ideological, political, and cultural differences between

Spanish, British, and French imperial projects of conquest and settlement (Pagden 1995, 65–82). For instance, British forces invoked the principle of *res nullius*, or the "agriculturalist argument," to legitimize their presence in the Atlantic, while the Spanish sought to acquire rights over the inhabitants who populated their territories (Pagden 1995, 78; Elliott, 20). Although this chapter departs from such a distinction—between the idea of settlement as *dominium* over people, on one hand, and as property rights over things or lands in the practice of colonization, on the other—I incorporate Pagden's proposition in the cartographic representation of the Antilles, the "virtual devastation" of which reformulated the "laws compelling settlers to settle" on the mainland (Pagden 1995, 67).

48 "[P]arece que vuestra magestad nos tenía olvidados a mí y a esta ysla suplico a vuestra magestad mande que no se use ansi conmigo pues yo no deseo ni escrivo otra cosa sino es lo que a vuestra magestad conviene" (AGI, Santo Domingo, 169, 14).

49 Santa Cruz belonged to the scientific side, that of the "cosmographers," and in 1537 he was appointed "universal cosmographer" (Brendecke, 193). Padrón's methodological approach to cartography incorporates the concept of "metageography" to refer to the collection of texts that are not, properly speaking, maps even though they contribute to the development of an image of the world. In this case, the subject comprises America, its inhabitants, and their encounters with Europeans (Padrón, 29).

50 The term "contra-cartographies" refers to the repertoire of maps that "could challenge those in power" and were "constructed to be antagonistic to an official perspective" (Kagan and Schmidt, 674).

51 Charles I managed to control a multicultural court encompassing Spaniards, Native Americans, Austrians, Germans, Italians, Flemings, and Burgundians (Espinosa, 193). Until his abdication in 1556, such a bureaucratic apparatus required the work of both chroniclers and cosmographers (*id.*, 257–258).

52 By this time, the main function of viceroys was to represent the absent monarch and deal with several affairs related to the civil, judicial, and military administration. However, they did not have hegemonic power over all the institutions within the viceroyalty. For instance, the presidents of other *audiencias*, governors, or captains general maintained their own communications with the king or the Council of the Indies (Brendecke, 240).

53 During Charles's reign, the inquiries (*consultas*) were mainly oral (*consulta por boca*). However, his successor, Philip II, implemented written inquiries (*despacho por escrito*) to document all the assessment processes. Council members and advisors were appointed to read letters sent from the Indies and propose measures (*consultas*) to solve matters or disputes contained in those letters. Afterward the correspondence would reach the king, who ultimately approved or disapproved council members' recommendations (Brendecke, 230–232).

54 The structure of this political apparatus changed with the creation in 1600 of the Chamber of the Indies (*Cámara de Indias*), an institution that was linked to the Council of Castile (advisors to the Crown) and was placed in charge of elaborating proposals and preparing inquiries. For more about this structural and political transformation, see Brendecke, 233–234.

55 In this regard, Elliott argues: "If the 'modernity' of the modern state is defined in terms of its possession of institutional structures capable of conveying the commands of a central authority to distant localities, the government of colonial Spanish America was more 'modern' than the government of Spain, or indeed of that of almost every Early Modern European state" (Elliott, 126–127).

56 His coat of arms, which appeared on many maps, bears the Latin inscription *Non sufficit orbis* ("The world is not enough"), underscoring the political role of maps during Philip II's reign and highlighting the importance of projecting the empire's dominion over geographical space.

Dangerous Representations of the Caribbean in the Sixteenth Century 123

57 Tai stresses the role of piracy as a means of reinforcing or challenging territorial order and identifies the cartographic tradition as the grounds on which territorialization—encouraged by political and economic interests—takes place. She gives the example of late medieval portolan charts depicting banners denoting specific political loyalties along with conventional geographical information, such as mountain ranges or river passages (Tai, 207). Working with the European premodern West, she identifies a European project of "territorializing" maritime and land spaces that seeks to establish territorial order.

58 The process of territorialization of the New World was authorized and legitimized by the bull *Inter caetera* (see discussion in Chapter 1). At this juncture, cartography transcended the practice of navigation and became a tool to claim social possessions based on political and economic motives (Brendecke, 160–63). Of course, this claim was dismissed and openly criticized by the English and the French, who argued that the pope did not have jurisdiction in either the spiritual or temporal sphere (Pagden 1995, 47).

59 In *The Mapping of New Spain*, Barbara Mundy states that Philip II commissioned the production of maps to show the totality of his centralized power by displaying a bird's-eye view that configures an all-embracing notion of Spanish territory.

60 Santa Cruz uses the term "archipelago" to refer to the Caribbean and Mediterranean islands (Santa Cruz 1542–1560, 507).

61 Tom Conley (2007) argues that this genre reached its apogee during the sixteenth century and declined after Vicenzo Coronelli's *Isolario dell' Atlante Veneto* (1696).

62 By contrast, Santa Cruz's map of the city of Tenochtitlan details buildings and streets (Santa Cruz 1542–60, 341).

63 Following the structural reforms of the Council of the Indies, proposed by Juan de Ovando, the position of *cosmógrafo-cronista mayor de Indias* was created in 1571. According to Brendecke, the *cosmógrafo-cronista mayor* was an "immobile observer" who had to compile all the materials coming from the Indies into a comprehensive history of the traditions, rituals, historical events, and antiquities based on the descriptions contained in accounts (*relaciones*) and descriptions. This "general history" had to remain secret (Brendecke, 356). Referring to the English censorship and printing monopoly, the Stationers' Company (founded in 1403 and granted a royal charter in 1557), Sean Johnson Andrews argues that "the Stationers' Company were mercenaries of the ideological State Apparatus. These economic relationships were, at least in principle, still very visibly secured by political means and aimed at ideologically securing the political power of the state" (Andrews 2018, 41).

64 Nancy Van Deusen de-territorializes the concept of the "indio" by emphasizing the individual creation of an identity that is "no longer spatially bound or culturally homogenous" (Van Deusen, 409). Following this line of argument, one could argue that the mapping practices of the Caribbean islands analyzed in this essay display a twofold function. The maps by Santa Cruz and Lopez de Velasco make tangible the idea of a connected web of islands constituting a fragment of the Spanish empire, while the others de-territorialize the idea of these places by depicting piracy attacks and potential areas for economic development outside the scope of their Spanish sovereign.

65 Here I use Pagden and Jeremy Lawrence's translation and edition (Vitoria 2010).

66 Patricia Seed notes different means by which Portuguese, English, French, and Dutch powers enforced their claims of possession over land, based on their own understanding of possession. English settlements entailed the construction of fences and plantations (16–31); Portuguese claims of discovery were linked primarily to their developed nautical technology (maps, sailing devices, latitudes, etc.) (101–137); the Spanish *Requerimiento* (a ritualized and fixed speech addressed to the natives) was based on a hybrid Iberian form of a declaration of war (70–95); the French

performed a series of theatrical rituals based on royal coronations (44–67); and the Dutch claimed possession by creating detailed maps in which they thoroughly described and registered their discovered lands (149–178).

67 It is worth noting the experience of the Spanish royal intervention in the "Mediterranean Atlantic" during the fifteenth century to understand both the continuities and discontinuities of jurisdictional procedures established in the Caribbean archipelago. I refer specifically to the Portuguese–Spanish war at sea, 1474–1479, in which the Catholic Monarchs resumed the occupation of the "unconquered islands of the archipelago" (Gran Canaria, La Palma, and Tenerife) to suppress Alfonso V of Aragon's ambition of seizing the Castilian Crown and breaking Portugal's monopoly on the Guinea trade. Triggered by political and economic drives, the Catholic Monarchs were interested in opening "communications with 'the mines of Ethiopia'" (Fernández-Armesto, 203). Consequently, the geographical proximity of these islands to continental Africa made them as valuable as those in the Caribbean, the geopolitical advantage of which was measured by their close position to gold and silver mines of mainland America during the second half of the sixteenth century. Another common thread between the archipelagos was the juridical terms placed upon the Canarians that anticipated the ones placed on the American indigenous populations, based on "their apparent primitivism." However, this apparent continuity became a discontinuity because, unlike their attitude toward the Canarians, the Spanish based their conception of American natives' rights on papal donation (*id.*, 214).

68 In contrast, the British authorities used their maps to publicly promote colonization and settlement overseas during the seventeenth century (Elliott, 35).

69 Vellerino's manuscript is divided into two books: the first is titled *De las derrotas de las Indias, Islas, y Tierra Firme del mar océano*, and the second, *De las señas de las partes de las Indias, Islas, y Tierra Firme del mar Océano*. The second book includes the descriptions of the islands and Tierra Firme, with 115 images.

70 The Council of the Indies withheld Escalante's manuscript for 48 years without granting permission to publish, but it was nonetheless available for others to consult. Vellerino did so between 1590 and 1592, copying its content almost entirely. Escalante's son Alonso wrote a letter claiming that his father had spent 10,000 ducats (a large amount of his savings, which was never reimbursed) compiling the manual. The draft of this letter is attached to the manuscript at the Biblioteca Nacional de España (BNE), MSS 3104. Vellerino's manual remained unknown until 1863. Sandman argues that the route to the Indies was widely known by foreigners, whereas how to navigate in the Indies was information protected by a Spanish body of laws governing pilots, charts, and nautical instruments (Sandman, 34).

71 Because Vellerino gained experience as a sailor during his stay in the Indies, the president of the Council of the Indies, Pedro Moya de Contreras, encouraged him to write a navigational manual and provided him with several documents: "He encouraged me to bring the manual to light and gave me books and papers so that I could improve it" (Vellerino, 3). For the similarities found in both manuals, see Martín-Merás Verdejo's introduction to the 1984 edition of *Luz de navegantes*.

72 Escalante describes the sea routes that should be taken to reach the West Indies and offers general advice regarding the protection of sailors on particular islands or during sea journeys. Like Oviedo and Santa Cruz before him, Mendoza also provides descriptions of each island's natural resources and economic activity, such as gold mines and sugar mills.

73 Herzog analyzes different notions of citizenship, including as a legal category and later as a status achieved through social reputation. From the 1550s to the 1630s, it was unavailable to non-Spaniards in the cities of Caracas, Lima, and Buenos Aires (Herzog 2003, 46–56).

74 Regarding these laws, Herzog mentions, "The Spanish king specified, for example in 1561, 1562, and 1566, that foreigners (1) who were citizens of local Spanish communities, or (2) who had acted as citizens of local communities, had lived in the kingdoms for ten years with house and property, and were married to natives, or (3) those who had come to Spanish America illegally but had then lived there for at least ten years and were accompanied by their wives must be considered natives (*ser habidos*) and must be allowed to reside and trade in Spanish America. Accordingly, in the 1580s, several foreigners obtained recognition that, as citizens (*vecinos*) of Seville, they were also, by extension, natives of Spain and eligible to emigrate to and trade in the New World" (Herzog 2003, 97).

75 "On the American Indians": Question 3, Article 1. From a legal perspective, Diego de Acosta traces the incorporation of *ius solis* over *ius sanguinis* in the context of the newly founded Spanish American republics during the nineteenth century. While the source of belonging and nationality of the *ius sanguinis* originates from a specific race and/or ethnicity, the *ius solis* ensures nationality by birth in the territory. However, Acosta notes that one of the advantages of *ius solis* and its incorporation into the constitutions of countries like Peru was, on the one hand, the distinction between "nationality"—individual civil rights and obligations—and "citizenship"—Creole elite and holder of political rights—and, on the other, the rejection of those born on the Spanish peninsula who could oppose movements of Latin American independence. The author claims, moreover, that "*ius solis* was thus a principle well suited for new, still politically fragile, states that were in the process of national construction and assertion over their territories" (Acosta, 37).

76 It is worth noting that, by the end of the sixteenth and beginning of the seventeenth century, the "nativeness" of the kingdoms of Spain in the New World became increasingly defined and regulated by the commercial interests of the House of Trade and the merchant guild to protect the transatlantic trade by classifying non-Spanish European business competitors as foreigners (Herzog 2003, 95–97).

77 Also, between 1570 and 1577, 13 English expeditions to the Caribbean took place, and probably more went unreported in times of peace between Spain and England (Andrews 1984, 129).

78 Along these lines, Anne Pérotin-Dumon points out that "judicial institutions belong to land communities; consequently, they lack legal authority to judge crimes occurring in the sea" (Pérotin-Dumon, 30). By the same token, she underscores the link between war and commerce in the sixteenth century, the two main ingredients of piracy (*id.*, 29).

79 Coming from a family of businessmen interested in trading with French and Iberian ports, Hawkins learned in the Canary Islands about the profitable market for smuggling African slaves into the West Indies, specifically Hispaniola. In 1562 he embarked on his first slave-trade expedition; then again in 1564, he repeated his smuggling strategy in the Caribbean and took advantage of defenseless coastal villages. Hawkins married the daughter of Benjamin Gonson, the treasurer of the Queen's Navy, and ended up managing it (K. Andrews 1984, 116–118).

80 Kenneth Andrews notes another change in the methods employed by Drake: "By 1572, working with and learning from the French, Drake was ready to make a decisive change in the objects and methods of Panama raiding, realizing for the Spaniards their worst nightmare—an alliance of white piracy and black banditry" (K. Andrews 1984, 130).

81 The maps were found in the collection of *Mapas Antiguos y Banco Popular* at the Archivo General de la Nación in Santo Domingo, Dominican Republic, M (8) 384, dated from the 1590s to the 1630s. M 31 (1353) is dated 1590, and a map without ships that follows the same visual arrangement as the aforementioned ones is M 28 (1350), also dated 1590.

126 *Dangerous Representations of the Caribbean in the Sixteenth Century*

82 Salt was a valuable commodity, mainly exploited by the Dutch in the Caribbean during the first decades of the seventeenth century (Galvin, 11).
83 Although considered a sympathizer with the Habsburg ruler, Mercator emphasized the islands as a potential source of economic profit.
84 The former map is M 31 (1353) and the latter, M (8) 384, are both from the Archivo General de la Nación in the Dominican Republic.
85 Benton, in *A Search for Sovereignty: Law and Geography in European Empires (1400–1900)*, argues that maps were political tools used in intra-imperial controversies about the extent of power over extra-European claims. While she emphasizes the value of maps as mechanisms to consolidate authority by erasing the presence and counterclaims of indigenous populations (Benton 2010, 10–11), Elliott notes several cases in which indigenous toponyms remained or were hispanized—as in the case of Cuba (instead of Juana) or Cuzco (Qosqo) (Elliott, 33).
86 There were three Bigges editions of the Caribbean raid. The first was published in Latin (1588), and the second and third in English (1589). It is worth noting that Boazio's engraving of the St. Augustine attack is the earliest view of any city in the present territory of the modern-day United States.
87 Geoffrey Parker identifies a parallel between China's development, under Cheng of Ch'in's command (246–221 BCE), of a unified empire that lasted two millennia and the "military revolution" that enabled the European imperial expansion in the early modern period. According to Parker, this resemblance "involved a massive manpower growth, a profound change in tactics and strategy, and an intensified impact of war on society" as well as a structural and philosophical transformation of the government (Parker, 3). He also revisits the concept of sea power in the age of sail by reexamining specific infrastructural, technical, and strategic military changes during the reigns of Queen Elizabeth I, King Philip II, and their Eastern/Chinese counterparts (*id.*, 82–114).
88 M 26 (1348), Archivo General de la Nación (AGN SD), Dominican Republic.
89 "Ciuitas S. *DOMINICI* sita in Hispaniola Indica Angliae magnitudine fere aequalis, ipsa vrbs eleganter ab Hispanis extructa, et omnibus circum vicinis Ins. jura dat." "La Citte de Sainct Dominique asisse en la petite Hespaigne Indienne aegalle prisque én grandeur a l'Angleterre. ceste Ville a este superbemant bastie par lés éspagnol. elle. Commande a toutes lés Contreès Voisines."
90 "[P]ortum habet ad mercaturam inter Hispaniam et Peru."
91 It is worth noting the role played by De Bry in disseminating what has been called the Black Legend. Originally published in Seville in 1552, Las Casas's *Brevísima relación* was followed by several translations in Dutch (1578), French (1579), English (1583, 1625, 1656, 1689, 1699, and 1745), Latin (1598), and German (1599). While commending Charles I, De Bry's sons Jean Theodore and Jean Israel de Bry released the Latin and German editions "with the famous illustrations that carried to every corner of Europe the message of Spanish cruelty" (Keen, 718). For more about the surrounding circumstances and the diffusion of the Black Legend, see Benjamin Keen's "The Black Legend Revisited: Assumptions and Realities" (1969). For more about the influences and the representations of Spain from the late eighteenth to the twentieth centuries in the articulation of an Anglo-American identity, see María DeGuzmán's study *Spain's Long Shadow: The Black Legend, Off-Whiteness, and Anglo-American Empire* (DeGuzmán, 2005).
92 De Certeau argues that every travel story becomes a spatial practice by which individuals "traverse and organize places; they select and link them together; they make sentences and itineraries out of them. They are spatial trajectories" (De Certeau, 115).

93 Frear Keeler, editor of Bigges's *Sir Francis Drake's West Indian Voyage, 1585–86*, stresses that although Spanish sources claimed that Drake took the escutcheon with him, other English reports of the voyage did not contain this anecdote, whereby it is believed that it was later inserted to appear in both of the 1588 Leyden editions (2010, 245).
94 "La ville de S. Juan de Puerto Rico, ainsi nomée à cause de la bonté de son Port, où les plus grands Galions sont en toute seureté" (Mallet, 320).
95 Map found in the map collection at the archive of the Centro Eduardo León Jimenes (Dominican Republic), MC-02–0002.

4 Dropping Anchor

Francis Drake's Three Deaths and the Beginnings of an End

Recent history has clearly shown that the spread of misinformation has repercussions for societies and impacts their institutions and relations with other nations. However, as historians continually note, the effect of "fake news" on individual and collective perceptions and opinions dates back to the early modern period and the emergence of print technologies and bureaucratic apparatuses for transatlantic communications. The misinformation examined in this chapter appears in published reports and literature describing the maritime exploits of Sir Francis Drake. Two events in particular illustrate the interplay of competing accounts based on known facts versus disinformation: the naval Spanish Armada battles (1588), and Drake's final attack and subsequent death in the Caribbean (1595–1596). In the aftermath of both events, Spanish sources released inaccurate historical accounts about Drake's whereabouts. Drake's image was distorted not only in reports from that time but also in various literary works, including Spanish poems and ballads. The English responded to these Spanish narratives by releasing their own versions of the events, alleging defamation and libel while trying to set the record straight. English condemnations of Spanish "lies" and "libels" concerning Drake's maritime and territorial predations drew upon several discourses to emphasize the moral, political, and economic wrongdoings at the heart of Spanish disinformation around Drake. In this sense, the English reproduced the Spanish model for describing piracy and Drake's maritime and territorial predations, which is discussed in previous chapters of this book.

Through analysis of the anonymous English text *A Pack of Spanish Lies* (originally published in 1588 as *A Packe of Spanish Lyes*), with additional background in the form of William Hudson's and Edward Coke's juridical treatises on libel, the first part of this chapter addresses one example of a narrative attempt at condemning the falsehoods disseminated by the former Spanish ambassador in London, Bernardino de Mendoza, about Drake's whereabouts and death during the Armada battles of 1588. This section also traces the process of articulating the legal concept of libel, or defamation, by identifying and comparing narrative patterns found in English sources that give their own accounts of Drake's death and his last raid in the Caribbean.[1] These sources include Henry Savile's *A Libell of Spanish Lies* (1596), Thomas

DOI: 10.4324/9781003141495-5

Maynarde's *Sir Francis Drake, His Voyage 1595* (c1596), and the anonymous pamphlet *In memoriam celeberrimi viri Domini Francisci Drake* (c1596).[2] The second part of the chapter examines English responses to Spanish and Canarian literary treatments of both Drake's role in defeating the Spanish Armada and Drake's death in 1596. These Spanish texts include Félix Lope de Vega y Carpio's epic poem *La Dragontea* (c1598) and ballads (*romances*) by Cristóbal Bravo and Bartolomé Cairasco de Figueroa.[3] By comparing patterns in the descriptions of Drake in these Spanish texts with English characterizations of libelers, this second part analyzes the conceptual instability around historical accounts of Drake's controversial attack in the Canary Islands and his death in Caribbean waters.[4]

The overarching aim of this chapter is to show how Spanish and English manipulations of notions of libel and piracy in the seventeenth century are interrelated and create parallel processes of criminalization. My analysis suggests that English accusations of libel served a purpose similar to that of Spanish descriptions of piracy. Both types of discourse served an agenda of accentuating the Anglo-Spanish rivalry and threatening imperial reputations during the last decades of Philip II's and Elizabeth I's reigns. At the same time, as the analysis also shows, the moral, economic, and political entanglements that structured perceptions of piracy and libel served to create conceptual instability that served paradoxical agendas of decriminalizing both terms. Narratives of piracy and libel showcase divergent versions of the same events similar to the "divergent perceptions" (*sentimientos*) discussed in Chapter 2. Focusing here on textual battles waged in English political pamphlets as the underpinnings for English and Spanish disputes over power, this chapter homes in on English responses to Spanish accusations concerning Drake's Caribbean raid of 1585–86 and his final, failed raid of 1595–1596.[5] Adding to the discussion in Chapter 1 on how visual and narrative artifacts celebrating Drake's circumnavigation of the world helped to constitute an English public sphere, this chapter calls attention to how that broader English audience served as the addressee for representations of Drake's death, thereby shaping those depictions.[6] The debates over notions of piracy and libel (i.e., "lies" or "fake news" about Drake's maritime exploits) point to shared moral, political, and economic components found in Spanish and English sources from the time. The chapter's analysis of literary and historical documentation in diverse genres—including epic poetry, historical accounts (*relaciones*), satirist verses, ballads, and letters—serves to uncover the mechanisms employed to craft geopolitical narratives promoting particular versions of the historical events.

Criminalizing False Historical Claims Made by the Spanish

Faking Drake's Death and the Spanish Armada's Defeat (1588)

Francis Drake's 1587 raid in Cádiz raised concern among authorities in Spain and England alike. On the Spanish side, the Duke of Medina Sidonia,

Alonso Pérez de Guzmán y de Zúñiga Sotomayor, dispatched a letter to King Philip II highlighting the need to warn Caribbean officials about a potential attack on the islands.[7] On the English side, Drake managed to gather information about the Spanish plans to invade England and reestablish Catholic power (Kelsey, 305; Barrow, 124). Both countries prepared for war, amassing fighting galleons and galleasses and collecting private merchant ships along with royal vessels. As months went by, the strategic plans changed. At first Spain prepared to launch a small invasion of Ireland. Later the Duke of Parma offered 30,000 men from his army in Flanders, while the Marquis of Santa Cruz proposed lending 60,000 men to an invasion. He died before being able to follow through on the offer and was replaced by the Duke of Medina Sidonia, whose rheumatism, however, rendered him unfit to sail. For their part, the English were debating the role Drake should take in any attack since English officials generally considered him "capricious." In the end, Lord High Admiral Charles Howard was given command of the English navy, and Drake was placed under his authority.[8] On July 30, both fleets reached the maritime battlefield. Parallel to the military battle, a battle of polemics raged as both sides launched written attacks on specific actors involved in the events.

While the military battle lasted just under 12 days, the conflict that was waged on the printed page was much more protracted. The reasons for the English victory have been long debated by historians, who have pointed to factors such as poor strategic planning by the Spanish, adverse weather conditions, and the luck or maritime superiority of the English. But whatever the cause of the Armada's defeat in 1588, it effectively boosted England's confidence about its strength on the seas and undermined Philip II's hold on power. Still, no definitive account of Drake's precise role in the series of attacks has ever emerged. For instance, another captain of the English Navy, Martin Frobisher, criticized Drake's performance, underscoring his absence from the final battle.[9] However, whereas some English authorities questioned Drake's accomplishments in the Armada battles, the Spanish manipulated information about Drake outright, claiming that he had not even been present for the humiliating defeat of the Spanish because he had been imprisoned by Spanish sailors and died in captivity. This section will highlight the textual disputes and quest for "historical truth" that ostensibly motivated Spanish and English accounts of these events. The focus will be on attempts to conceal or expose the answers to a few key questions: Who won the Armada battles? Who lost? Who was killed? And more importantly, who was either lying or telling the truth—and to what end?

From the British perspective, one of the main sources of misinformation about these events was Bernardino de Mendoza—the former Spanish ambassador in London, later serving in France—who reported that Drake had been taken prisoner and slain. His account and other letters reporting the main events were translated into English, French, Italian, and Dutch.[10] Another report sent to the Spanish king stated that, according to "an Irish lad," it was well known in England that Drake had lost his leg while fighting the Spanish captain's ship. This Irish lad had further claimed that sources from Holland confirmed Drake's death.[11] Whether or not these accounts were intentionally false, they crafted a narrative about Drake's death that allowed Spain to claim victory in the face of unquestionable defeat.[12] The fog of diverging English and Spanish accounts of Drake's whereabouts during the battle creates a perception of him as an unstable character: he is portrayed at one and the same time as an English soldier who died at the hands of the Spaniards, and as a traitor who left the battlefield to pilfer and collect ransoms.[13]

The lie about Drake's death was soon exposed.[14] According to a Spanish account, Drake was given all the glory while Lord Howard received little credit and saw his military performance called into question: "People speak ill of the admiral upon his duty. All the glory has been for Drake and there is a conflict between both of them and it is believed that the admiral will not ever be appointed again."[15] In the same year of 1588, as mentioned, an anonymous booklet containing an English translation of the Spanish accounts and several refutations was published under the title *A Packe of Spanish Lyes* (hereafter *A Packe*).[16] This English edition was quickly translated into Dutch and printed in Amsterdam.[17] Organized in two columns— one containing English translations of Spanish documents; the other, the English condemnations—the booklet set out to clarify the truth about the Armada battles, contradicting specific accounts of events and details. In response to claims about Drake's imprisonment or death and an alleged English mutiny that compelled Queen Elizabeth to join the battlefield, the booklet has this to say: "But the truth is, Sir Francis Drake was so farre off to be a prisoner ... It is so false that there was any mutinie in the Q. Armie, that shee her selfe was there" (*A Packe*, 2). Besides attacking Mendoza, the booklet contradicts letters written by other Spanish officials such as Juan de Gamarra and Pedro de Alva. While discrediting Mendoza's false statements about Drake's fate, the booklet does not describe Drake as an exemplary soldier but rather as someone whose claim to fame was imprisoning Spanish infantry captains and other soldiers to collect a ransom of 400 crowns.[18] However, before analyzing the rhetorical content of the English booklet, it is worth reviewing the historical legal context from which this cultural artifact emerged to understand the degree to which concepts of lies and libel as criminal offenses apply in the Elizabethan and Jacobean contexts.

Within a broader context, the booklet corresponds to a culture of condemning published and unpublished lies, which the legal code termed libels. Even though in the case of the Armada battles the act of defamation was considered a crime and was punishable, legal theorization around libel was still in its early stages, and English juridical authorities faced difficulties in applying such laws. In England, the Star Chamber (1485–1642), an institution composed of the higher dignitaries of Church and State, reviewed cases on defamation.[19] The first treatise on libel, composed by the jurist and philosopher Francis Bacon a few years after the Armada battles, was titled "Certain Observations made upon a Libel Published this Present Year, 1592."[20] The treatise opens with an allusion to the rivalry between King Philip and Queen Elizabeth and highlights the proclivity of the Spanish toward undermining the queen's reputation by libeling her reign:

> [W]hat a number of libellous and defamatory books and writings, and in what variety, and with what art and cunning handled, have been allowed to pass through the world in all languages against her Majesty and her government; sometimes pretending the gravity and authority of church stories, to move belief; sometimes formed into remonstrances and advertisements of estate, to move regard; sometimes presented as it were in tragedies of the persecutions of Catholics, to move pity; sometimes contrived into pleasant pasquils and satires, to move sport …
>
> (Bacon, 147–148)[21]

Another of Bacon's main concerns about the Spanish libels was their depiction of England as a "ruinous" place and their efforts to negatively influence foreign opinion by articulating an English agenda of promoting wars and rivalries:

> For it must be understood that it hath been the general practice of this kind of men many years, of the one side, to abuse the foreign estates by making them believe that all is out of joint and ruinous here in England, and that there is a great part ready to join the invader; and on the other side, to make evil subjects of England believe of great preparations abroad and in great readiness to be put in act; and so to deceive on both sides …
>
> (*id.*, 152)

At this point, the main domestic and international repercussions of these libels were twofold. First, the pathos of Catholics toward fellow Catholics facing persecution on English soil was being exploited. Second, the specter was being raised among both English subjects and foreign states of military threats to their respective regimes.

The criminalization of libel only took shape in the seventeenth century under James I's reign. Sir Edward Coke, Attorney General during Elizabeth's and James's reigns, compiled a report on libel based on the Roman provisions of the *libellus famosus*, in which verbal injuries were treated as criminal offenses.[22] Coke's report about libel was copied almost in its entirety by William Hudson, who laid out the 1606 case *De Libellis Famosis* in his "Treatise of the Court of Star Chamber", one of the first accounts of the proceedings followed by this tribunal.[23] Hudson's Chapter XI, "Of Libeling and Scandalous Words Against Nobles," historicizes the legal precedents on libels, which, according to him, became more frequent at the end of Queen Elizabeth's reign (Hudson, 100). Overall, the treatise explains the nature of what constituted a libel by providing examples of different types of libel and how the law should address them.

Following Bacon's and Coke's notions of libel, Hudson stated that one of its main dangers was the breach of peace, both among individuals and among countries. He went further and explained that a written libel was more likely to result in a breach of peace than a spoken defamation: "[T]he reason why the law punisheth libels is, for that they intend to raise the breach of the peace, which may as well be done, and more easily, when the hand is subscribed than when it is not" (*id.*, 102). However, the intent behind the libel is what constituted its criminality. The law did not consider the falseness or truthfulness of the defamatory statement, but rather, the way in which the libel was disseminated and affected an individual's reputation: "[I]t is not the matter [content of the libel] but the manner which is punishable" (*id.*, 103). In this sense, enforcing a law against libel amounted to weighing subjective claims based upon the repercussions of the libel, particularly if it involved a breach of the peace. Hudson's seventeenth-century treatise displays the efforts at that time to establish legal standardization regarding defamation through the accumulation of legal precedents. However, although referring to an "infinite" number of such precedents, he only seemed to remember "an example or two" of each one (*id.*, 101); and although a few of the precedents pertained to the reigns of Henry VIII and Elizabeth I, the legal codification of libel clearly corresponded primarily to James I's administration since the treatise was written during that reign, when legal precedents concerning libel proliferated.

At the time of the Armada battles (1588), it was not yet a crime to lie about an event or to publish false news about it. However, the lies released by Mendoza about Drake's imprisonment and death were taken very seriously by the English. At this point, the difference between lies and libel seemed to be primarily based on the individual or institutional repercussions generated by the public dissemination of misinformation. In this sense, a lie in and of itself was not a crime, but a written or spoken lie could become a criminal act if it triggered a large and tangible impact such as a diplomatic conflict or damage to the reputation of individual subjects or higher authorities. Anticipating the later fixed legal figure of the libel, *A Packe* underscores the concept of the actionable lie. In this sense, the anonymous booklet is part of the process of conceptualizing libel that was ongoing before it became legally codified. In other words, the pamphlet became a textual space capable of transforming lies into libels. To understand the English case made against the Spanish at this historic turning point, when the Elizabethan regime wanted to position itself as the stronger of the two naval powers, we will need to examine how the booklet associated lies with moral corruption (or, as we saw in Chapter 3, "infection").

One way in which *A Packe* establishes a correlation between lying and moral misbehavior is by including psalms and Biblical verses in the front and final pages: "Thou shalt destroy them that speake lyes, the Lord wil abhorre the bloodie and deceitfull man" and "Wherefore cast off lying, and speake every man trueth vnto his neighbour: for we are members one of another."[24] In the main text, the Spanish official Gamarra is accused of giving a false account in a letter in which he misrepresented the quantity of English ships lost in battle and named a fictional location in Scotland. As in the case of Mendoza, this condemnation is accompanied by statements impugning his morals, even designating him as a follower of the Devil:

> All this is likewise as full of lyes, as lines. Iohn Gamarra may be what he is: but if there be such a man, and that hee wrote as is mentioned, except hee bee a professed member of the Devill to forge lyes, hee knoweth that he wrote falsly. Hee noteth also a Haven in Scotland called Luxaten: non-such was ever knowen there. In Vtopia there may bee such a one: no Spaniard can saye ... let Gamarra repent, or follow the Devil his master, the father of malicious lyes ...
>
> (*A Packe*, 5)

Drake, on the other hand, is described as an honorable character who successfully returned to England ready to exact revenge: "Drake is returned with honour: his shippe called the *Revenge* is in harborow, ready for a revenge by a newe service" (*id*., 4). The booklet justifies the English role in the Armada battles, attempting to criminalize the act of spreading lies and employing rhetorical flourishes and moral discourse to attack Mendoza's behavior. First, the narrative voice amplifies Mendoza's lies by hyperbolizing them: "Here followeth the Mountain of lies ... If one should make a section, or anatomie of this Mountain and body of lyes, there is no piece, nor ioynt to be found" (*id*., 7). In fact, the text clarifies, the English admiral's ship, the *Ark Royal*, had safely returned to England under Lord Howard's command. Not content to simply call out Mendoza's lie about this event, the text goes so far as to accuse Mendoza of being someone who prefers lies to the truth:

> It is reason that if there were lyars in London, they should send them to *Mendoza*; for so *Mendacia* are of more price with him then true reportes, and so was he accustomed when he was Embassadour in England, to buye more lyes, because he liked them, better then truethes ...
>
> (*id*., 7)

The quoted passage engages in etymological wordplay between the ambassador's last name and the Latin word for lie, *mendacia*, as a means of explaining his tendency to lie: "The letters from the kings Embassadour, whose name is *Mendoza*, agreeable to their Masters name, being the reporter of *mendacia mendaccisima*" (*id*., 1). The allusions to Mendoza's moral corruption, illustrated by his willingness to lie, are used to argue that he is morally infected (see Chapter 3); this narrative strategy mirrors Juan de Castellanos's attempt to segregate or exclude rivals—pirates and indigenes—who might threaten the Spanish Crown's hegemonic power. Rivals and enemies are thus positioned rhetorically as sources of infection and infestation from across the Atlantic.

This is not to say that the English conceptualization of public lies and criminalization of libels emerged solely as a consequence of the sixteenth-century Spanish peninsular and colonial discourse of piracy. Nevertheless, the boundaries between lies and libel clearly shifted within the context of imperial debates and international polemics that used the discourse of piracy as a tool for advancing certain agendas. The conceptual interplay between maritime predation and libel may have been incidental, but it was nonetheless correlational and provided a basis in moral discourse for the condemnation of defamatory speech. For instance, in defining the Spaniards' misbehavior, the booklet attacks Mendoza and others by appealing to moral discourse, thus reproducing the Spanish rhetorical strategy of defining pirates or corsairs in terms of their distortion of religion and morality. As shown in Chapter 3, Spanish authors operating under this correlation between piracy and religion, such as Castellanos, defined pirates and corsairs in terms of their "impudence" and "insolence."[25] In this way, *A Packe* echoes Spanish peninsular and colonial efforts to justify their right of ownership overseas against foreign interlopers or pirates by means of moralizing discourse. In fact, because libel and piracy were largely unregulated, moralizing discourse became one of the primary rhetorical tools that could be used to define and condemn enemies and rivals. In the process of codifying the stakes of lying, Sir Francis Drake emerged as an exemplar of the honorable individual whose reputation should be preserved and protected from false narratives. Delving next into the second historical event of this chapter—Drake's last raid (1595–96)—I will focus on the increasing deterioration of Drake's reputation as evidenced in both English and Spanish accounts. Let's not forget that characters like Drake functioned as metonymies of their respective powers, and their individual failures were interpreted as signs of collective defeat. For this reason, reports of this raid reflect an awareness of their potential to precipitate public embarrassment and international repercussions.

Drake's Multiple Deaths and His Last Raid (1595–1596)

After failing in his attack on the island of Puerto Rico, and on his way to Panamá, Drake died aboard his ship. Spanish reports about Drake's death set off a wave of misinformation that echoed the Armada battles and raised consternation among the English. However, this time the term "libel" was introduced into the title of another booklet that followed the previous model outlined in *A Packe*. Published in London and composed by the English esquire Henry Savile, and revised by Thomas Baskerville, *A Libell of Spanish Lies* (1596) refuted Bernardino Delgadillo de Avellaneda's account of the death for the royal bureaucracy that was printed in Seville and offered for sale to the general public.[26] Addressed to Pedro Flores, the president of the Spanish House of Trade at the time, Savile's pamphlet includes Avellaneda's report alongside English translations and several English accounts aimed at correcting the historical record about Drake's last voyage.

Repeating *A Packe*'s pattern regarding concerns about the worldwide circulation of false news, in the first section of *A Libell of Spanish Lies*, Savile underscores the fact that the Spanish had disseminated untruths "to the world": "Hereas, Don Bernaldino Delgadillo de Avellaneda, Generall of the Spanish fleete, hath by his Printed letters published to the worlde diverse untruthes, concerning our fleete and the Commaunders thereof, seeking thereby his owne glorie, and our disgrace" (Savile, A2).[27] Savile juxtaposed his source, the Spanish general Bernardino Delgadillo de Avellaneda, with the notorious Bernardino de Mendoza, "the olde Spanish lyer" who had reported false news about the Armada battles, thus pointing to a precedent among the Spanish for spreading untruths about such matters. According to Savile, Delgadillo's third lie was proportional to those disseminated by Mendoza, and the two of them amounted to "a payre of Spanish Lyers" (*id.*, 22).[28] Just as *A Packe* had used etymological wordplay between Mendoza's last name and the Latin word *mendacia* to suggest his proclivity for prevarication, Savile alluded to a collective understanding about the name Bernaldino, the English version of which is Barnard, or he "who does not see all":

> The General was much beholden to his godfathers who gave him the name *Barnaldino*, which we in English do take to be plaine *Barnard*, which name hath as it were a kind of privilege from being sharply reprehended when the party is thought to erre: for it is a common saying amongst the Schoolmen that *Barnardus non video omnia*, viz. *Barnard* seeth not all things …
>
> (*id.*, 32)[29]

Drake's last Caribbean raid, co-commanded with John Hawkins, ran up against financial problems and several changes of plans. Even though the Crown gave £10,000 to the expedition, Drake apparently had to sell his 71-year lease on a house called "The Herbar" to raise money for the voyage.[30] The final cost of the expedition was about £43,000. Initially planned in 1593 as a voyage to Panamá, the project took further shape in 1594, when the scheme was discussed again.[31] Queen Elizabeth openly backed this attack, which seemed doomed from the beginning and produced outcomes unfavorable to England's international reputation. The queen issued a royal commission authorizing both Hawkins and Drake to "offende our capital enemye, the Kinge of Spayne, his countries, subjectes and adherents, either on sea or lande."[32] At this place and time, which coincided with the cultural and legal theorization of lies and libel, one could argue that the use of the term "offend" in this commission refers to inflicting both material and reputational damage. Possibly the queen's strongest motivation for approving the raid, however, can be gleaned from the language of the commission itself. Captains were authorized to capture prisoners and distribute the spoils, with the Crown taking its cut of the profits:

And yf you shall, for the ease of our charge, take any persons to disburse any sommes of money to be born in adventure ... We doe by virtue hereof gyve you full power and aucthoryte to deliver unto them equall portions ... at the same rate that we ourselves shall have and receyve for our own adventure.

(Marsden, 286–287)

Despite the commission's aggressive political rhetoric against Philip II, its primary concern appears to have been making a profit from the voyage: apparently Drake and Hawkins managed to entice the queen with the possibility of capturing a stranded galleon with "two millions and a halfe of treasure" in Puerto Rico's seaport (Maynarde, 5).[33]

Before reaching the Caribbean, the English fleet was defeated in the Canary Islands. Spanish depositions of English prisoners reveal that Drake and Hawkins had kept their intention of attacking Puerto Rico a secret from crew members. Vincent Bluq, a French sailor captured in Gran Canaria who had been working for the English, stated that Drake (whom he called Francisco Draque el viejo, "old man Drake") intended to destroy Santo Domingo and Margarita Island and had enough supplies for ten months or a year.[34] Another English prisoner, Daniel Equisman, declared that they did not know where Drake was bound to, but there were rumors among the soldiers about the possibility of reaching the Indies. He claimed to have no knowledge about the appointment of Drake and Hawkins as equal commanders of this expedition, but he shared the supposition of others that the queen was responsible for putting them both in charge. A third captured prisoner from Drake's ship, one Gasparian, maintained that he did not know whether the attack was carried out under the queen's orders: he had heard that the journey to the Canaries was for more supplies. However, he added that a previously captured Spanish helmsman had revealed to them that the city on Gran Canaria (Las Palmas) would be likely to fall if they attacked it.

Savile's critique of Delgadillo's report rests mainly on the incorrect details found therein, such as a reference to the use of "oars" (ships' boats or *lanchas*) by the English during their escape. Savile ridiculed the claim, noting that the English did not use ships that required oars. According to Anne J. Cruz, Savile knew very well that Delgadillo was using *lanchas* to mean ships' boats, not oars, and he deliberately mistranslated the word to more easily debunk the report (Cruz 2002, 131). Savile also took issue with the numbers of English and Spanish captains and sailors appearing in the report. However, of all the mistakes or "lies" in the report, the account of Drake's death caused Savile the most concern. According to Delgadillo's source, Drake died of deep sorrow in Nombre de Dios after having lost a considerable number of ships and men during the Caribbean raid (*id.*, 9).[35] Savile deals with this topic in his second correction, where he clarifies the natural cause of Drake's death: "For true it is, *Sir Frauncis Drake* dyed of the Flixe which hee had grown vppon him eight daies before his death, and yeelded vp his spirit like a Christian to his creatour quietly in his Cabbin" (Savile, 20–21).[36] As in *A Packe*, which takes issue with the fabricated story of Drake's death and capture during the Armada battles, Delgadillo's narrative of Drake's death from grief over his loss to the Spanish serves as a rhetorical move that threatens the English construction of Drake as a fierce and brave captain.[37] Portraying Drake as having died from grief implies that he was weak, whereas Savile's counternarrative, in which Drake died of natural causes, acts to restore his reputation.

Nowhere but on the title page and in the headers of Savile's compilation of false and true reports does he actually employ the term "libel" even though the text served as a battle cry in response to Spanish lies in print.[38] The last document included in the book is a letter written by Sir Thomas Baskerville, who participated in the English expedition and became captain after Drake's death. In his letter, Baskerville dares Delgadillo to answer to him if he refuses to admit to his wrongdoing in printing falsehoods:

> And if Don Bernaldino Delgadillo de Avellaneda the General shal take any exceptions to this my approbation, or standing the iustification of his lying letter ... lately put in Printe: I then saye that hee falsely lyed, and the I will maintaine against him with whatsoever Armes he shall make choyce of.
>
> (Savile, 45–46)

Naming France as a possible staging ground for this hypothetical encounter (which would have to take place beyond their respective kingdoms because of their current state of war), he proposes a showdown with the armies of both their princes (*id.*, 46). This show of moral outrage has the effect of letting Drake's own maritime wrongdoings fade into the background, effectively decriminalizing the attack on the Caribbean while emphasizing the greater crime of publishing lies and libelous statements about the English captain's exploits and demise.

A pamphlet published in London and titled *In memoriam celeberrimi viri Domini Francisci Drake* (1596) takes the same position, that Drake died of natural causes: "Drake's death was a lucky one because it was caused by nature and above all, because it happened when fighting for one's country."[39] The rhetorical function of insisting on Drake's death as a natural one can be seen as a way of mitigating the humiliation of having suffered defeat at the hands of the Spanish during the final attack. A similar strategy was used by Ambassador Mendoza in playing down Spain's defeat in the Armada battles in 1588 by falsely reporting Drake's incarceration and death. Despite the contextual differences between the 1588 and 1596 events, in both instances Spanish reports about Drake's death triggered a strong reaction from the English side along with efforts to discredit the Spanish sources and establish in their stead an English version of events. Thus, the cause of Drake's death eluded the historical record and served as a polemical football between the

Spanish and the English. The variety of explanations for his death—that he died from dysentery, dropsy, "flix," grief, or poison—underscores the narrative instability around Drake and, by extension, around representations of imperial maritime powers (see Chapter 2). In other words, if piracy and Drake's previous Caribbean raid triggered "divergent perceptions" (in Castellanos's words, *sentimientos*), the various stories crafted around the English captain's death served similar ulterior purposes and agendas.

Criminalizing Spanish Literary Production—The Spanish Armada's Defeat (1588) and Drake's Last Raid (1595–1996)

Drake and the Spanish Armada's Defeat: An Entertainment

In addition to condemning "historical lies" or "fake news," *A Packe* criticizes the emerging literary culture of defamation and verse libeling that was gaining traction in the early Stuart period.[40] William Hudson, in his Jacobean "A Treatise on the Court of Star Chamber," describes the nature of literary and performance libel, which included scoffing at another person in rhyme and prose, ridiculing someone through impersonation, and "setting up horns in gates" (Hudson, 100).[41] He also explained that libel could occur in private or published letters as well as in "disgraceful or false speeches against any eminent man or public officer" (*id.*). Both the author of the libel and the publisher were subject to punishment. The definition of "publishing," according to Hudson, also encompassed both the performance of the libel and the audience who might laugh at it:

> And the *publishers* of libels are as severely punished as the makers; therefore, it is usually said, that it were a punishment to a libeler if no man would publish it. Therefore, to hear it sung or read, and to laugh at it, and to make merriment with it, hath ever been held a *publication* in law.
>
> (*id.*, 102, emphasis added)

In all likelihood, the legal theorization around criminalizing both the libeler and the publisher had to do with technological improvements and increased access to printing presses in the seventeenth century.[42] In the end, what mattered to the law was less the content of the libel than the means and channels of dissemination.

The booklet attacks two Spanish ballads written by Cristóbal Bravo, a blind man from Cordova whose verses underscore the victory of the Catholic army over the English armada (*A Packe*, 2). Drake's figure appears in the first ballad as a "pestiferous Englishman" (*pestífero inglés*).[43] Bravo's specific characterization of Drake in terms of infection, pestilence, and disease continues the tendency of several sixteenth-century authors to circumscribe pirates and piracy within a narrative of infection and infestation (see Chapter

3). The first ballad (consisting of 52 verses) emphasizes that, after the Spanish Armada had sunk 17 English ships and dismasted four more, the remaining English fleet had hastened back to London to ensure their safety.[44] The second ballad (containing 160 verses), probably based on Mendoza's written accounts, underscores several successful naval strategies used by the Spanish and describes the capture of Drake ("the great thief") and other noblemen.[45] Bravo, whose career as a versifier spanned 1572 to 1629, may well have composed his ballads about the Armada conflict before the truth about the Spanish defeat was uncovered.[46] In the third decade of the seventeenth century, Samuel Purchas, in *Purchas his Pilgrimes* (c1625), ridicules Bravo and the publication of the booklet's false Spanish accounts of an English defeat.[47] In a facetious note attached to the accounts, Purchas compares Bravo's figure with that of Homer narrating Achilles's deeds: "Like lips like lettuce. A blind Ballad maker fit Homer for Achillean conquests" (Purchas, 511).[48]

Bravo's ballads were published in Seville (1588) by Gabriel Ramos Bejaramo. They were also printed in London in 1589 alongside two anonymous English ballads written in Spanish that corrected the record about the events, entitled *Respuesta y desengaño*.[49] *A Packe* did not quote Bravo's text, but instead focused on Bravo's blindness, emphasizing that if he knew he was publishing lies, then his tongue should have been cut out, his vision restored, and his eyes plucked away so he could never lie again:

> It was meete occupation for a blinde man, tu put lyes into songs: if he knewe how false his verses were when he published them, it were to be wished that hee had his eyes restored to see his lyes, and then his tongue cutte out that uttered them, and his eyes cleane plucked out of his head, that he should never see any more written lyes.
>
> (*A Packe*, 2)[50]

In the English response to Bravo's ballads, physical senses—sight or vision, in this case—allegorically represent the diverging spectrum of perceptions that structure one's ability to distinguish whimsical thinking from historical truth. In other words, Bravo's lack of sight serves as a metaphor for an audience whose senses have been manipulated.[51] According to the booklet, his ears should be open to hearing "men call him iustly, a notable blinde liar" (*id.*). However, the primary issue taken with Bravo is not necessarily the fact that he lied. It is his awareness that he knowingly printed a falsehood. His lack of sight is taken as a sign of the moral corruption he may have displayed by lying despite knowing the historical facts. Thus, *A Packe* moralizes about the criminalization of publishing lies, whether or not they occur in literary forms such as romances and ballads, because like other kinds of accounts, lies published in literary form can be used to disseminate "fake news" and influence international opinion. The booklet does not hold back in its suggested remedies for such crimes and calls for Bravo's mutilation as punishment for his wrongdoing, even though in 1589 the criminalization of verse libeling was not standard practice in England. Also, unlike satirical writing, verse libeling, or literary libels, did not succeed as a formal literary English and Spanish baroque genre.

The anonymous English rebuttal—written in Spanish—to Bravo's ballads signals the intention of rectifying the attack on Drake's reputation from a moralizing standpoint that also accounts for the broader emerging Spanish baroque culture. By employing the word *desengaño* in its very title (*Respuesta y desengaño ... del muy ilustre valeroso caballero don Francisco Draque*) the anonymous author inscribes this text into the Spanish notion of *desengaño* (disillusionment) of the late sixteenth and early seventeenth centuries. The text articulates a close relation between lying and *desengaño*, alluding to both the lack of morality found in the act of lying and the proneness of physical senses to lead individuals to misperceive the truth.[52] The response to Bravo's first ballad also shows a moralizing undertone at many levels. First, this is evinced by the allegorical depiction of the Spanish author as a demonic vassal of Hell whose father was Lucifer, whose mother was Lie, and whose brother was Satan.[53] Second, by correlating lying and dishonor, this satiric characterization of Bravo describes him as a "blind, crazy, liar / without Christianity dishonored" whose lie caused a breach of peace among Christian kings, making him an "enemy of peace among Christian kings" and a "shameless rioter" (*Respuesta y desengaño*, quoted in Fernández-Duro, 189).[54] Even though libel had not been codified as a crime, when it did become one a couple of years later, breaching the peace was singled out as one of the main dangers of libel. In defense of Drake's reputation, the *Respuesta* criticizes Bravo's use of "ugly words" to describe such a "good soldier" and underscores Drake's role as a defender of "Faith" and "the great Britain kingdom" (*id.*, 183).[55] The *Respuesta* stresses the point that even to mention Drake's name was enough to make the universe tremble and that the Indies feared him because they had been punished by his hand.[56] By placing the emphasis on the immorality of Bravo's lies about Drake, the English response to his verses underplays Drake's crimes and aims any feelings of moral indignation at his libelers.

As was the case with *A Packe*, the response to Bravo's Spanish lies focuses on the immorality of *publishing* the misinformation about Drake and the defeat of the Spanish Armada. The blind man of Cordova is characterized as a "dog who publishes truths which are actually lies, as he bestows victory to those who were defeated" (*Publicas, perro, verdades, y mentiras vas cantando; victoria das al venzido, al venzedor deshonrrando*).[57] If stealing or attacking is, according to the Spanish authorities, a dishonorable action, then by the same token, publishing lies is an act of dishonoring someone. From the perspective of both the booklet and the *Respuesta*, the Spanish acts of manufacturing lies by writing and publishing them are no less criminal than Drake's outrages.

On the subject of Drake's historical death in 1596, Savile's *A Libell of Spanish Lies* (1596) takes a different approach, appealing to religious discourse through a proverb printed on the front page: "A false witness shall not bee unpunished, and he that speaketh lies shall perish."[58] However, contrary to *A Packe* and the English verses vilifying Bravo, *A Libell* does not delve into the immoral or dishonorable character of the author whose lies it exposes, Delgadillo de Avellaneda, but instead settles for questioning Delgadillo's judgment in amplifying the narrative of Spanish victory and glory.[59] With its inclusion of translations and eyewitness accounts, *A Libell* stands out for its attempts to codify libel as a crime and even a felony more serious than maritime predation. However, the English were not the only ones to call attention to the moral and legal issues, not to mention the dangers to individual and national reputations, associated with lies and defamation. Subjects of the Spanish Crown also joined in this international dynamic of condemning spoken and printed lies told to advance particular agendas. The next section will focus on historical and literary representations of Drake's death originating from areas in the Canary Islands and the Caribbean that sustained attacks from Drake and his men.

Drake's Last Raid (1595–1596): Literary and Historical Accounts from the Islands

The failed attack by the English on the Canary Islands inspired some inhabitants, including Bartolomé Cairasco de Figueroa,[60] to write poems and romances about the events. Cairasco's poem "El canto heroico," printed in three editions,[61] describes Drake's flight from the islands, "frightened" and "wounded." A romance by Cairasco, included in his *Templo Militante, Triumphos de Virtudes y Vidas de Santos* (Valladolid, 1603; Madrid, 1609; Lisbon 1615), recounts the victories of Gran Canaria, the site of Drake and Hawkins's 1595 defeat: "And one of the most cared for / has been the Dragon and Juanacre, / Famous generals from Britannia, / And this is how he celebrated them, / with music on this, his holy day."[62] Cairasco depicts England and Gran Canaria allegorically, as two ladies: "One is England, / The other Gran Canaria, / The first is so powerful, / So arrogant ... The second one so humble and poor, / With more weight, / And distinguished daisies / A wonderful setting."[63] By defeating the arrogant, heretical England, the poor and humble Gran Canaria became precious and beautiful in the eyes of Spain. Challenging stereotypes about Gran Canaria's population as feckless and defenseless,[64] Cairasco portrays the island as the pride of King Philip II and all of Spain, strong and rich in goods and resources.[65]

One anonymous satirist wrote a letter, in 1595, referring to the romance as too hyperbolic for widespread distribution and also citing other literary depictions that embellished several events surrounding Drake's defeat.[66] At the end, the anonymous satirist claims that everyone overstated the local victory against the English in an attempt to advance specific agendas. For instance, the author claims that there were several individuals who amplified their role played in the outcome of Drake's defeat because they aimed to become archbishops or sought presidencies (Rumeu de Armas, 987). Because of the high volume of Canary Islands military poems celebrating the battle, the author states, this battle, which spilled no blood, received more attention than the "bloody battle of Roncesvalles" (*id.*, 988). The letter commends the appellate court (*audiencia*) for taking "reasonable" measures to intervene and remove from circulation the many epigrams and stanzas being produced by "lowlife sonnet composers," even though "despite the *audiencia*'s ban, new stanzas arise every day" (*id.*).[67] One particularly curious account collected by Antonio Romero Zerpa (1726–98) described a certain Doña Ana Cibo de Sopranis, who was seen levitating in a trancelike state as the English ships suddenly disappeared without causing any loss to the islanders.[68] Now let's take a look at the link between the narratives from the Caribbean, which also sustained attacks from Drake, and those of the Canary Islands that pursue honor and glory over Drake's defeat.

In 1596 the Council of the Indies opened an investigation to clarify the facts surrounding Drake's death after attacking Puerto Rico. This body sent a questionnaire to Puerto Rico to compile "true information *ad perpetuam*."[69] The seven questions addressed different aspects of the attack, including the state of the military fortresses for which "a great amount of ducats was sent," and whether enough small boats (*lanchas*) were strategically positioned where the enemy wanted to disembark. The questions also addressed whether the governor, Pedro Suárez, used artillery to "inflict considerable damage to the enemy, killing General John Hawkins" and was able to achieve victory against the enemy.[70] Puerto Rico's reports about Drake's defeat, like the works exposed by the satirist writing about the Canary Islands, seemed to serve additional agendas. In the case of the Puerto Rican reports, these agendas ranged from accusing officials of corruption to underscoring the need for more military resources and advocating on behalf of the honorable soldiers to be exempted from the Crown's tax, the *alcábala*.[71] In the Caribbean and the Canaries alike, Drake's character, his performance in the Armada battles, and his last raid were all appropriated, whether in literary genres or historical documents, to advance local agendas.[72]

Drake's Death in Lope de Vega's La Dragontea

The representation of Drake's death in the Caribbean seas was first introduced into the Spanish peninsular literary repertoire by Félix Lope de Vega y Carpio. His epic poem *La Dragontea* showcases the problematic pendulum between epic poetry and claims of historical truth, between piracy and empire. Composed after Drake's demise in 1596, *La Dragontea* was suppressed because of its historical inaccuracies by the newly appointed principal cosmographer-chronicler (*cosmógrafo-cronista mayor de Indias*) of the Council of the Indies, Antonio de Herrera y Tordesillas.[73] According to historical documents, even though Alonso de Sotomayor was the leader of the Spanish side against Drake, Lope gave credit for the victory to Diego Suárez de Amaya.[74] The probable reason for this amendment to the historical record was the fact that Suárez de

Amaya commissioned the poem.[75] Structured in ten cantos that combined lyric and heroic poetry styles, Lope's narrative captures Drake's deeds from his circumnavigation to his last voyage. The historical accuracy of the events described by Lope became a topic of heated debate. In the prologue, Francisco de Borja y Aragón refers to the poem as an account (*relación*) and states that it was based on "reliable witnesses" (*fidedignos testigos*) drawn from the *relación* sent from the Real Audiencia of Panamá (Lope, 124).[76] Moreover, in the dedication, Lope claims that the poem's composition was driven by a desire to commemorate the Spanish victory against the English and unveil the real story (*descubrir el desengaño*) of Drake's losses before the eyes of an ordinary audience (*el vulgo*) (*id.*, 120).[77] Once again, this time from a peninsular perspective, the urge to uncover and write the historical truth surrounding Drake's life and demise was a driving force.

Lope's *La Dragontea* unleashed a controversy among the Spanish peninsular elite over its historical inaccuracy and lack of stylistic refinement. For instance, the great baroque poet Luis de Góngora y Argote wrote a sonnet—addressed to a gentleman who had sent him a copy of *La Dragontea*—in which the Cordovan poet emphasized Lope's inability to follow contemporary precepts of the epic genre. Employing the maritime metaphor of a ship poorly sailed, Góngora stressed in the sonnet that Lope was too ambitious to write in this fashion and failed because he could not control his inspiration.[78] Thus, *La Dragontea* faced rejection from both historiographic and literary circles.[79] However, beyond the historical inaccuracies and stylistic flaws of the poem, Ríos Taboada argues that Lope attempted to redefine the epic genre and used poetry as a space to propose an order upon the American world. In so doing, *La Dragontea* extrapolates the historical facts to build a discourse of just war, religious conversion, and justification of the Spanish conquest in the New World (Ríos Taboada 2021, 171–83).

In the poem, Lope uses neither "pirate" nor "corsair" to describe Drake. Instead, he explains from the start that he will refer to Drake using the term "dragon" (*dragón*) (*id.*, 142).[80] Evoking a network of intertwined political, legal, economic, spatial, and religious discourses to characterize the English captain, Lope portrays Drake as having made a pact with the Devil in the form of a written *cédula* (Spanish royal ordinance).[81] Lope reminds the reader that he also fought in the Armada battles of 1588 to stress the veracity of his account, which is allegedly based on the testimonies of soldiers who were captured from the ship he was aboard.[82] Through references to Drake's ferocity in the Armada battles of 1588 and his pact with the Devil, supported by his own and other eyewitness accounts, Lope evokes complex truths about Drake embedded in historical, religious, and legal discourses.

Why did Lope write an epic poem about a notorious English pirate and well-known enemy of the Spanish Crown? Scholars have claimed that portraying Drake as an epic protagonist was not intended to glorify Drake. Rather, it was meant to answer the requirements of the epic model, in which a struggle takes place between two monumental forces; the genre itself required an emphasis on the strength and virtues of both sides of the conflict.[83] In Lope's epic poem, the two main characters, Drake and Diego Suárez de Amaya, epitomize their respective nations by allegorically becoming a dragon and a lion battling for supremacy.[84] Some critics have suggested that Lope's poem contrasts the conduct of the two antagonists, presenting Drake as embodying a lack of prudence while Suárez embodies modesty and loyalty to the Spanish Crown.[85] Almost two decades after the publication of the epic poem in Valencia, Lope's adversaries, most notably Pedro de Torres Rámila in his *Spongia* (1617), attacked *La Dragontea* as bringing shame upon Spanish monarchs and, by extension, the Spanish empire (Fuchs, 142). The charge in *Spongia* was that *La Dragontea* was a deliberate libel against the Spanish peninsular administration and distorted the historical truth found in official accounts of the events.[86] Lope's inner circle quickly released a counterattack in which they argued that Lope had imitated Homer and Virgil, who in their epic works recounted the victories of Turnus and Hector to magnify the deeds of Achilles and Aeneas (Tubau, 313).

Despite the constraints of the epic genre on Lope's portrayal of Drake, the poem alludes to the English captain's considerable moral flaws. In the words of one English sergeant (*sargento ausente*) who questions the other crew members' support for Drake, he is a politically corrupt leader of a "vile government":

> "Until when, Britons, shall we follow / this fierce Dragon, / who by his boldness we will see / ready and tied to a cliff? / Until when shall we carry our arms for vile Francis / on our broken backs, / fire in hand and blood on our swords?"
>
> (Lope, v 5401–5408)[87]

The English sergeant attributes the pain and losses suffered by the other English crewmembers to Drake's selfishness, illustrated by his indulgence in wine, his unwillingness to pay for what he has consumed, and his greed in taking all of the gold and bounty for himself without considering his crew's sacrifices (*id.*, v 5417–5442).[88] While epic heroes represent the virtues of their nations, Lope depicts Drake as also epitomizing the individual flaws of moral and economic corruption.

This speech about Drake's wrongdoings is delivered by Alecto, an English sergeant impersonating a character from the underworld, whose indictment of Drake asserts the implicit ethical norms of his countrymen. However, accusing Drake of victimization of his crew by taking more than his share of the booty ignores the fact that the treasure was stolen from Spain in the first place. By demonizing Drake's character while humanizing his crew of English sailors, who attacked Spanish vessels, Lope leaves in place the controversial implication that not all the Englishmen are as corrupt as Drake. However, allowing this speech to be given by an Alecto (or the "English sergeant") from the underworld gave Lope some cover for contrasting Drake unfavorably with other Spanish enemies.[89]

146 *Dropping Anchor*

Lope's fictional version of the captain's death as the result of a plot by his men paints a nuanced picture of the English. According to Lope, the "English sergeant"—or the classical figure of Alecto—encouraged Drake's crew to poison him because he was already suffering from dropsy (*id.*, v 5457–5460).[90] Although other sources reported that Drake died of dysentery, Lope's medical diagnosis drew upon the coetaneous convention that linked dropsy and avarice.[91] Connecting Drake's moral misbehavior with his illness, presumably resulting from his sinfulness, enables Lope to justify Drake's death at the hands of his countrymen rather than the Spaniards. In other words, according to this version of events, fate's punishment of Drake was brought about not by his piracy, but by his tyranny. His avarice and abuse of power had led his people to poison him, subjecting him to the method of death generally recommended for tyrants.[92] Realizing that his crew intends to poison him—and following the conventional precaution taken by tyrants—he orders others to taste his food before he eats it (*id.*, v 5470–5472).[93] This raises the question of who was considered a tyrant at the time of Lope's writing and why Lope might have chosen to fashion Drake as a tyrant by including these details about Drake's demise.

Justifiable measures that can be taken against tyrants are discussed in *De Rege et Regis Institutione* (1599) by the Spanish Jesuit, theologian, and political and economic philosopher Juan de Mariana. The work was published in the city of Toledo three years after Drake's death. Although sponsored by King Philip II, the treatise appeared during the administration of his successor, King Philip III.[94] Unlike other scholastic writers at the time, Mariana does not articulate a clear distinction between usurpers, or illegitimate rulers, and legitimate or sovereign rulers whose abuse of power harms the well-being of their subjects.[95] Mariana's justifications for assassinating a tyrant include the tyrant's theft of public and private property and his contempt for public laws and the sanctity of religion (Laures, 63).[96] However, before discussing the ways in which one might kill a tyrant, Mariana emphasizes that the decision to do so should only be taken by "erudite and grave men" and not without first trying to make the tyrant aware that he has committed an abuse of power (*id.*, 65). In his discussion of whether it is lawful to poison a tyrant, Mariana notes that the tyrant should not take the poison from his own hand as "that would be cruel and contrary to natural law," but "if the tyrant were to succumb to an attempt on his life by poisoned garments or furniture or weapons, this would no longer be damnable, it always being understood that he really deserves death" (*id.* 65).[97] In light of Mariana's doctrine, Lope's representation of Drake's death at the hands of his men could be understood not as a depiction of a pirate or corsair betrayed by his ruthless countrymen but as a nuanced portrayal of Englishmen justifiably deposing a tyrant.

Lope's epic poem is the only source that gives a detailed representation of Drake on his deathbed, reliving all his voyages and conquests on land and sea and in the north and the south. He recalls the "Philippine fleets" with their thundering war machines and hears the loud cries announcing his transgressions,[98] rendered in the poem by the term *delito*, which now denotes a felony but at the time, as Covarrubias points out, was associated with sin.[99] Thus, Lope depicts Drake's fatal errors in moral rather than legal terms. This moralizing discourse extends to aspects of Drake's character, such as his "pride" and "arrogance" (Lope v 5505–10),[100] and the cause of his death, allegorically described as the "sacred Christian religion" stepping upon his "British" neck (*su planta pone en tu cerviz britana / la Religion santísima Cristiana*) (*id.*, v 5511–5512). Drake's final breath, in which "his chest spits out his obstinate soul" (*el alma pertinaz del pecho escupe*, v 5504), is worded to suggest that he dies of stubbornness in the face of religion. This shade of meaning is implicit in the word *pertinaz*, as Covarrubias underscores when defining the term as in the phrase "stubborn heretic" (*herege pertinaz*) (Covarrubias, fol. 140v).[101] According to Covarrubias, *herege* meant "in our Castilian tongue and in all the languages spoken by the Catholics who fight under the Roman Catholic Church, the desertion and separation from the Faith and from what the Sacred Mother Church believes" (*id.*, fol. 51v).[102] By emphasizing the religious and moral aspects of Drake's final moments, Lope crafts an allegorical description of Drake's death that represents the defeat of the English heresy against the Catholic Church.

At this point in Lope's narrative, the focus turns to Drake's body and the ignominious treatment it receives. His funeral consists of his body being tossed unceremoniously into the seas (Lope, v 5557–60).[103] The only creatures concerned with Drake's death are the silent fishes eating away at his body at the bottom of the sea (*id.*, v 5821–24).[104] Employing indiscriminately the terms "Huguenot" and "Lutheran" to refer to "Protestants," Lope claims that not even they had any *sufragio* to pray to ameliorate Drake's tormented soul (*id.*, v 5565–66).[105] Drake's path to Hell resembles that of other heretics (Lutherans, Calvinists, Huguenots, and Muslims), who would now become his companions (*id.*, v 5521–24).[106] Lope underscores the role of God in the final fate of Drake's soul: the allegorical figure "Christian Religion," accompanied by her daughters, "Italy," "Spain," and "America," delivers a speech highlighting God's actions against Drake, who was both killed and rejected from Heaven (*id.*, v 5785–5792).[107] After finishing the story of Drake's death and funeral at sea, Christian Religion pleads for God to intercede in the Mediterranean, where "Moorish and arrogant pirates are loaded with Catholic spoils" (*id.*, v 5825–5830).[108] This scene is very similar to another one in Claudian's classic poem *De bello Gildonico*, in which Rome and Africa seek help from Jupiter against the rebel Gildo (Jameson, 495).[109] Lope's epic poem arguably resembles Claudian's *De bello Gildonico* as well as his *In Rufinum* because of their respective portrayals of "furious invectives against public enemies" (Jameson 495). However, Lope stops short of portraying Drake monolithically as a public enemy. The poem's exploration of Drake's death as "just" (Lope, v 5630) intertwines political, economic, and religious discourses, depicting him as a tyrant without necessarily criminalizing his acts of predation.

Maynarde's *Sir Francis Drake, His Voyage, 1595* (c1596) and Lope's epic poem both portray Drake at the end of his exploits, as a defeated old man. Maynarde—Drake's protégé—creates a picture of a sea captain who made hasty decisions and was persuaded by false hopes of profit,[110] and whose main purpose was to become rich, bring gold to his Queen, and restore his reputation in her eyes with God's help. As Drake reportedly says in a final speech: "God hath many things in store for us; and I knowe many means to do Her Majestie good service and to make us rich, for we must have gould before wee see Englande" (Maynarde, 19). However, Maynarde also stresses Drake's haplessness: having supposedly confessed to Maynarde with "griefe" that "hee was as ignorant of the Indies" as Maynarde and "never thought any place could be so changed, as it were from a delitious and pleasant arbour into a vast and desarte wildernesse" (*id*.), the English captain complains about the windy weather, which is "so stormie and blusterous as hee never sawe it before" (*id*.). Reflecting upon Drake's confession, Maynarde compares him with a man living carelessly and persuading himself that the nurse who had fed him in his childhood would likewise nourish him in his old age (*id*.).[111] By employing this metaphor, Maynarde foreshadows Drake's death, stating that a man of such folly, "tormented in mind," will eventually die of starvation (*id*.). His depiction of Drake's final days even resembles the portrayal by Delgadillo that was so harshly criticized by Savile. Maynarde's text exemplifies how the narrative conventions employed to describe Drake's fate—as a defeated hero with no fortune or glory left on his side—were used by both English and Spanish writers.[112]

On the other hand, Lope's epic poem shows how talking about Drake's death became a useful tool for addressing larger issues. Drake's death allegorically represents the Catholic Church's supremacy alongside the projection of Spain's preeminence over Protestants, Lutherans, Huguenots, and Britons (*britanos*). In *La Dragontea*, Drake's death becomes a rhetorical device to exemplify the fate of an unheroic protagonist whose moral weaknesses overlap with economic ambitions. Covering almost 20 years of Drake's maritime career, Lope's epic poem is not a story about defeating piracy, but rather a narrative that casts the struggles not only between Drake—the maritime predator—and Spain but also between Drake and his men in surprisingly nuanced terms, in which economic, religious, and political competitions and ambitions are at play. Drake's death functions as a metaphor for the supposed decline of English maritime power under Queen Elizabeth and an indictment of her Protestant and mercantile values.

This chapter's comparative analysis of contrasting narrative versions of Drake's death elicits questions about the relation between literary and historical discourses and also about the enunciation of historical truth. To be sure, these questions tie in with larger sixteenth-century concerns around the limitations of poetry and historical accounts as reliable resources for understanding historical events. The Francis Drake emerging from these sources stands out as a transatlantic cultural construct whose varied descriptions and representations became narrative tools for moral, economic, and political propaganda spanning from his early attacks to his death.[113] We have seen how the uncertainty over Drake's whereabouts during the Armada battles (1588) and his last raid (1596) was used to defend individual interests and imperial objectives behind multiple and conflicting narratives. So far, we have seen how various genres—such as historical accounts, pamphlets, travelogues, epic poetry, romances, and legal treatises—served as platforms on which the justification or condemnation of Drake's acts of piracy, or libelous claims about them, could be staged. English attempts to configure the stakes and dangers of libels and their legal conceptualization coincided with the emergence of accounts of Drake's death. As we will see in the next chapter, what followed was a conceptual standardization of piracy in legal discourse.

Notes

1 Both libel and slander are types of defamation: modern legal conventions define libel as written defamation, while slander is spoken. However, during the reigns of English monarchs Elizabeth I, James I, and Charles I, the common law made no distinction between slander and libel (Veeder, 558). For more about the history of libel, see Van Vechten Veeder's article "The History and Theory of the Law of Defamation I."
2 In full, the title is *In memoriam celeberrimi viri Domini Francisci Drake militis, qui nuper in nauali expeditione contra hostes patriæ suæ, ex dysenteria laborans obijt. viz. 28 die Ianuarij Anno Dominj 1595*. S.l.: J. Windet, 1596.
3 In this context, *romances* roughly corresponds to the English word "ballads." The term is also used here to indicate narrative poems that reproduced some of the thematic and stylistic conventions found in the old Spanish romances. Among the peculiarities of this genre, we find standardization of the epic line to 16 syllables and 8-syllable lines with assonance rhymes on the even lines (*los versos pares*), no rhyme on the odd lines (*versos impares*), and no set number of lines in each strophe.
4 Unless otherwise indicated, the translations from French and Spanish colonial sources are my own.
5 Carla Rahn Phillips argues that the rhetorical language and prose found in Avellaneda's, Savile's, and Baskerville's pamphlets, which will be discussed below, were influenced by their own efforts to avoid public blame for their respective military and strategic faults (Rahn Phillips, 124–129).
6 Rahn Phillips, in "Libels and Other Weapons: The Written World as an Adjunct to Naval Warfare" (2008), analyzes the relation between English political pamphleteering revolving around Drake's death and the constitution of English public opinion as well as a broader audience "that would later be defined as the 'public sphere'" (Rahn Phillips, 124).
7 The duke's letter (May 1587) includes a list of the following authorities in the Caribbean: the governors of Havana, Cartagena, Puerto Rico, and Santo Domingo; the *Audiencias* (appellate courts) of Panamá and Santo Domingo; the islands of Jamaica and Margarita; the governor of Florida, Pedro Menéndez; and the captain of American convoys, Alvaro Flores. For more about this document, see the digitized version, "Sir Francis Drake no. 5," in the Kraus Collection, Library of Congress.

150   *Dropping Anchor*

8   For more about the history behind Drake's role in the Armada battles, see Kelsey, 307–319.

9   Frobisher's account is found in Mathew Starke's, "A note of certaine speaches spoken by Sir Martyn Frobisher," August 11, 1588. It is available at The National Archives (TNA), PRO SP Domestic, 12/214/63 and 64, fols. 139–140v, 141–142. It is also quoted in Kelsey, 335.

10 There are two French editions of 1588 and 1589 titled *La copie d'une lettre envoyee d'Angleterre a Dom Bernardin de Mendoze ambassadeur en France pour le Roy d'Espagne*; a 1589 Dutch translation from the English condemnation was titled *Een pack Spaensche levghenen, vvtghesonden alomme inde werelt*, Amsterdam, printed by C. Claesz, 1589. The Venetian ambassador in France, Giovanni Mocenigo, also reported Mendoza's misleading account; his version is found in *Calendar of State Papers Relating to English Affairs in the Archives of Venice*, Volume 8, 1581–1591, ed. Horatio F. Brown, London, 1894, pp. 372–382. Furthermore, according to Kelsey, Petrucci Ubaldino's account of the event, "Comentario della Impresa fatta contra il regno d' Inghilterra del re catholica l'anno1588," does not emphasize Drake's deeds, and a second edition was published in 1589 in both Italian and English but with minor adjustments about Drake's role (Kelsey, 336).

11 "Dize este mancebo que era fama entre los ingleses que el Drach combatiendo con nuestra nao capitana … havia perdido una pierna …. Mas dize que … por via de Holanda se confirma la muerte de Drach que en sobre estan dos correos con despachos para el rey de Francia y no les dexan passar," in "Relacion de lo que se ha podido entender de la Real Armada de su Magestad después de lo que se aviso en 29 del pasado hasta oy tres de Septiembre 1588." BL, Add. MS 26056- C, fols. 441–442, transcribed from AGS, 594,126.

12 Garrett Mattingly's historical research (*The Defeat of the Spanish Armada*, second edition, 1984) reveals another reason underlying Mendoza's unconfirmed news: "But for all that he did not abandon hope of delivering Henry III, bound hand and foot, to Guise, and Guise, bound hand and foot, to Spain; nor did he give up his dream of riding back to London a conqueror, with his old comrades of the Low Country wars behind him, just as he said he would" (Mattingly, 320). Twelve years prior, Henry III of France had signed the Edict of Beaulieu "in which he yielded to the [Catholic] League's extreme demands, including a clause ordaining that no heretic or abetter of heresy should ever be received as King of France" (*id.*, 319).

13 For more about Frobisher's account and the rumors of Drake's whereabouts, see Kelsey, 335.

14 Queen Elizabeth composed a song celebrating the Spanish Armada's defeat, sung in December 1588 "after the scattering of the Spanish Navy." In the second stanza, the queen incorporates religious discourse when claiming that God intervened on behalf of the English during the Armada battles: "And hath done wonders in my days; / He made the winds and waters rise / To scatter all mine Enemies." A contemporary copy of the song is available at the NMM, SNG/4.

15 "Del almirante se habla un poco mal que no hizo su deber. Toda la gloria se da a Drach entre los dos hay una gran pica y se piensa que el Almirante no volverá a tener cargo en la mar." BL, Add. MS 26056- C, fols. 440, transcribed from AGS, 594,132.

16 The full title is *A Packe of Spanish Lyes, Sent Abroad into the World: First Printed in Spaine in the Spanish Tongue, and Translated Out of the Originall. Now Ripp'd Up, Unfolded, and by Just Examination Condemned, as Conteyning False, Corrupt, and Detestable Wares, Worthy to be Damn'd and Burn'd*, London, Deputies of Christopher Barker, printer to the Queens Most Excellent Majestie, 1588.

17 *Een pack Spaensche levghenen, vvtghesonden alomme inde werelt*, translated from the English into Dutch, Amsterdam, C. Claesz, 1588–1589.
18 "[H]ee [Drake] was the taker: for hee tooke Pedro de Valdez, and 400 more Spanish prisoners at one time. And to prove this to be true, Mendoza shall have if hee will require it, Pedro de Valdez owne hand to shewe, that he is prisoner to Sir Francis Drake, and 400 more taken with him." Besides Valdés, the other two captains taken prisoner were Don Alonso de Zayas and Don Vasco de Mendoza y de Silva (*A Packe*, 2).
19 Veeder, 573. For more about this legal analysis, see Veeder, 546–573.
20 Francis Bacon in "Certain Observations made upon a Libel Published this Present Year, 1592," *The Works of Francis Bacon*, edited by J. Spedding, Robert Leslie Ellis, and Douglas Denon Heath, 14 vols.
21 Here Bacon refers to *A Declaration of the True Causes of the Great Troubles presupposed to be intended against the Realm of England* (1592).
22 See Veeder, 563.
23 Hudson's treatise was first published in 1792 as part of *Collectanea Juridica*, vol. 2.
24 The first verse is from Psalms 5:6, and the second is Ephesus 4:25. The last page cites John 8:44: "Ye are of your father the Devil, and the lustes of your father ye will doe: he hath bene a murtherer from the beginning, and aboade not in the truth, because there is not truth in him, when hee speaketh a lye, then speaketh hee of his owne: for hee is a lyer and the father thereof." Zachary 8:26 is included as well: "There are the things that ye shall doe: Speake ye every man the trueth vnto his neighbour."
25 The governor of Puerto Rico in 1586, Diego Menéndez de Valdez, wrote to the king of Spain discussing the military needs of the island because Drake and other corsairs had pillaged there. He characterized their acts using the words *deberguenza* and *atrevimiento*. AGI, Santo Domingo, 155.
26 Rahn Phillips argues that the publication of Avellaneda's report was not uncommon at the time because there were several other published reports concerning other events that made their way into both public and private collections (Rahn Phillips 2008, 125).
27 Henry Savile, *A Libell of Spanish Lies*, 1596.
28 "His third lye of the Generall Don Bernaldino Delgadillo de Avellaneda, (whose name for the prolixitie thereof maye be drawne somewhat neere the length of a Cable) hath no colour of protection, but it hath a iust proportion in measure to the lyes of olde Barnardino de Mendozza his Countrieman, concerning the overthrow of her Majesties Navie in the yeare 1588" (Savile, 22).
29 Thomas Lodge, an English physician and author in the Elizabethan and Jacobean periods, included this saying in his romance *Catharos: Diogenes in his Singularity* (London 1591), which criticizes usurers, false friends, and flatterers. See *The Complete Works of Thomas Lodge 1580–1623* (1963 edition).
30 The document recording Drake's sale is found in the Kraus Collection, no. 11, Library of Congress.
31 Richard Hawkins in *The Observations of Sir Richard Hawkins Knight*, printed in 1622. The current edition consulted is from 1933, edited by J.A. Williamson.
32 "Commission to Sir John Hawkins and Sir Francis Drake against the Spaniards," TNA, Patent Rolls, 37 Eliz. pt. 14, m 18. Printed in *Documents Relating to Law and Custom of the Sea*, edited by R.G. Marsden.
33 "Her Majestie's, yet many times was it very doubtfull whether the journey should proceed and had not the newes of a gallion of the King of Spaine, which was driven into St. John de Porterico with *two millions and a halfe of treasure* … it is very likely it had been broken" (Maynarde, 5, emphasis added). He stated that the queen provided six ships out of the 27 that departed August 28.

However, as Maynarde points out, the enterprise was doomed to fail from the beginning because Hawkins became sick and Drake made arbitrary decisions such as unloading and sinking the victual ship, the *Richarde,* before reaching Puerto Rico (*id.*, 8). Besides Maynarde's account about the potential economic profit, Hawkins and Drake wrote a letter to the queen in August 1595 where they emphasized their attempts at capturing a Spanish ship that had lost its mast and contained "two mylllyons and a hallf of tresure" in Puerto Rico. BL, Hatfield MS, 35, 30. Also quoted in Andrews 1959, 31.

34 The prisoners' statements are found in AGS, Guerra Antigua, 432. They were also printed by Andrews, 1959, 132–41.

35 "[I] had intelligence by an Indian, that Frances Drake dyed in Nombre de Dios, for verie grief that hee had lost so many Barkes and men, as was afterwardes more manifestlye knowne" (Savile, 9).

36 A flixe (dysentery) was a common disease among seamen.

37 Regarding the claim that Drake died of grief, Rahn Phillips notes that "the notion that someone could die of grief was fairly common at the time" (Rahn Phillips 2008, 129). Even the English historian William Camden (1551–1623), discussed in Chapter 2, reported that Drake died of "Bloudy-flux, together with Grief for his ill Fortune" (quoted in Andrews, 1978, 241 n2). As we will see further in this chapter, there are other English accounts that connect Drake's death to grief.

38 I have not found evidence that confirms Savile's authorship of the compilation's title.

39 "Fortunata igitur mors *Francisci Drake,* quae naturae debita, pro Patria potissimum est redita."

40 According to Hudson, "verse libel" became criminalized at the beginning of the seventeenth century. In the 1590s verse libel was differentiated from verse satire, and the former did not necessarily follow the neoclassical stipulations of the genre. Unlike formal verse satire, verse libel did not employ couplets in iambic pentameter and, regarding content, verse libel attacked specific individuals instead of generalized types of vice and touched upon ephemeral topics instead of enduring moral struggles. The primary purpose of verse libel, moreover, was undermining authority rather than purging evil interests from power. For more about verse libeling, see Andrew McRae's "The Literary Culture of Early Stuart Libeling" (Modern Philology, 97, no. 3, 2000, 364–392), in which he follows John Dryden's essays on satire when distinguishing both genres.

41 In the context of Hudson's treatise, "setting up horns in gates" refers to creating murals suggesting cuckoldry.

42 Hudson uses the terms "publisher" and "publications" to refer to printings and printers as well as disseminators and performances.

43 Bravo's verses and the English responses in Spanish were printed by Cesáreo Fernández-Duro in *La Armada Invencible,* vol. I, 179–191 (1884–1885).

44 "A los quales acometen / con animo no pensado / y a diez y siete navios / al profundo an enviado. … Hazia la vuelta de Dobla / sigun escripto he allado / por meterse en el gran Rio / de Londres entitulado / para bivir mas siguros" (Fernández-Duro, 181).

45 "Que es llamado *San Martin,* / aquesta es su nombradia, / aferró con el navío / donde el gran ladrón venia, / Llamado Francisco Draque, / que traxo en su compania / todos los mexores hombres / que Inglaterra avia. / Duques, condes y marqueses / gente illustre de valia, / y el gran Duque lo prendió, / sigue escripto se avia" (Fernández-Duro, 187).

46 The primary study of Bravo and his works is Antonio Rodríguez-Moñino's, "Cristóbal Bravo, ruiseñor popular del siglo XVI" (see *La transmisión de la poesía española en los siglos de oro. Doce estudios, con poesías inéditas o poco conocidas*. Edited by Edward M. Wilson. Barcelona: Ariel (Planeta de Libros), 1976, 255–283).

47 The Spanish account of the Armada battles of this booklet was published by Samuel Purchas in *Purchas his Pilgrimes* (1625), fourth volume, book ten, chapter XI.
48 The old English proverb "like lips, like lettuce," was usually employed when referring to something that happened to someone who deserved it.
49 See *Respuesta y desengaño contra las falsedades publicadas é impresas en España en vituperio de la Armada inglesa ... y del muy ilustre y valeroso caballero don Francisco Draque, y de los más nobles y caballeros, dirigida á la sacra Catholica y Real Magestad de la Reyna doña Isabel*. London, Arnoldo Hatfildo, por Thomo Cadmano, 1589. This was transcribed and printed by Fernández-Duro in *La Armada Invencible* (1884). The anonymous author uses the initials "D.F.R de M." *Respuesta y de desengaño* was translated into English and published in London in the same year under the title: *An Answer to the Untruthes, Published and Printed in Spaine, in Glorie of Their Supposed Victorie Atchieved Against our English Navie* (Ríos Taboada 2021, 88).
50 This quote relates to Bravo's work. As was the case in Hudson's treatise, the term "publishing" might refer to disseminating as well as printing because the narrative voice suggests punishments related to both "uttering" falsehoods and "seeing *written* lies" (emphasis added).
51 Here one must not forget Aristotle's sensory hierarchy that considers sight the highest of the corporeal senses (Jutte, 61). Furthermore, and drawing on classical and medieval theories, the Renaissance philosopher Marsilio Ficino (1433–1499) proposed that "fantasy" (*phantasia*) dwells upon an intermediary faculty between "imagination" (*imaginatio*) and intellect (*intellectus*). Whereas the imagination only perceives the exterior and the superficial, the fantasy enables the individual to recognize the substance of what is superficially seen. Thus, both the intellect and the fantasy (*mens* or *intellectus* and *phantasia*) become the "eyes of the soul" (Walerich, 129). The emphasis placed on Bravo's blindness pinpoints his twofold incapacity—on both exterior and interior levels—to "see the truth."
52 Here I refer to the seventeenth-century Spanish baroque aesthetic and culture of *desengaño* (disillusionment or pessimism) produced by the realization of one's own mortality, the precariousness of the senses, the fugacity of time, the ephemerality of beauty, the possession of wealth, and the enjoyment of pleasures or vices. For more, see *A History of the Spanish Novel*, edited by J.A. Garrido Ardila (2015a); Luis Rosale's work *El sentimiento del desengaño en la poesía barroca*; Enrique Valdiviesos's *El ángel admonitor del desengaño del mundo en Vanidades y desengaños en la pintura del Siglo de Oro*; and Lía Schwartz's seminal studies on Francisco de Quevedo and other Spanish baroque authors.
53 "Lucifer tienes por padre / y a Satanas por hermano, / y tu madre es la Mentira; / del Infierno eres basallo" (quoted in Fernández-Duro 1884–1885, 182).
54 "Amotinador perverso, / rebolton desvergonhado, / enemigo de ver pazes / entre los Reyes christianos. / Dime, ¿cómo osas dezir / que a vencido el Rey hispano/ a la Armada y flota Inglesas / habiendo sido al contrario?" (Fernández-Duro 1884–1885, 182).
55 "Como don Francisco Draque, / columna de el templo sancto, / y defensor de la Fee, / y del gran Reyno britano?"
56 "De quien tiembla el universo, / tan solamente en nombrallo, / temen las Indias, que han sido / castigadas de su mano" (quoted in Fernández-Duro 1884–1885, 183).
57 Fernández-Duro 1884–1885, 181.
58 Proverbs 19:9.
59 Savile even portrays the account's distortions as proof of Delgadillo's great skill "in amplifying small matters" (Savile, 36).
60 Cairasco was a clergyman of the cathedral of Santa Ana in Las Palmas.
61 Two editions were printed in J.A. Ray's *Drake dans la poésie espagnole*, 196–197.

154 *Dropping Anchor*

62 "Y uno de las que mas estima y precia / ha sido la del Dragón y de Juanacre, / Famosos generales de Britania, / Y así la celebró, con tanto acorde/ Y grave pompa, el dia deste santo." A modern version of the 1603 edition of the romance is found in J.A. Ray, *Drake dans la poésie espagnole*, 198–209. These lines appear in the section dedicated to Saint Peter Martyr, patron of Gran Canaria.

63 "Es la una Ingalaterra, / La otra Canaria grande. / La primera es tan potente, / tan altiva y arrogante ... La segunda humilde y pobre, / Mas subida de quilates, / Y de ilustres margaritas / Un maravilloso engaste" (Ray, 199).

64 "De Britania luz y esmalte, / Enseñados á victorias, / Y á rendir grandes ciudades; / En Canaria no hay defensa, / Ni saben qué cosa es Marte, / Gente ociosa y regalada, / sin experiencia, sin arte" (Ray, 203).

65 "No hay que esperar en Canaria, / Dijo en alta voz el Draque, / Valerosos hombres tiene, / De tales pueden loarse. / Mi señor el rey Filipo, / Puede muy bien gloriarse / Que tiene en Canaria gente / Briosa, fuerte, constante" (Ray, 209).

66 The anonymous letter, written in Spanish, is found in AGS, Mar y Tierra, 448. There is an English translation by K. Andrews, *Elizabethan Privateering*, 1964, 129–132. A Spanish transcription is found in Antonio Rumeu de Armas's *Piraterías y ataques navales contra las canarias*, Vol. III, 986–989. It is unknown whether the author was from the Iberian peninsula or the Canary Islands. Among the hyperbolic narratives, the author mentions one account that featured a local captain claiming that a hundred people witnessed him holding a galleon on his shoulders.

67 The *audiencia* did intervene and banned the writing or declamation of verses it had not previously authorized.

68 The account is included in Rumeu de Armas's *Piraterías*: "[A]na, retirada de su casa a la iglesia de San Francisco, puesta en oración y tan encendida en ella, que la vieron muchas personas en éxtasis suspendida en el aire, y dentro de poco se levantaron y se desaparecieron los navíos con notable pérdida suya y ninguna de los isleños" (Rumeu de Armas, 732).

69 Información hecha en la ciudad de San Juan de Puerto Rico sobre el ataque de Francis Drake a la Isla. AGI, Santo Domingo, 164.

70 AGI, Santo Domingo, 164.

71 In Puerto Rico's case, Francisco de Cid wrote to the Council of the Indies recounting the events precipitated by Drake; in his letter, Cid claimed he had been unfairly accused of corruption. Suárez, the governor of Puerto Rico, reflected a different agenda: emphasizing that Spain's soldiers had comported themselves honorably, he requested more military resources. AGI, Santo Domingo, 169. fols.1–4.

72 Recent scholarship has tackled the cultural relations between different archipelagos, including the Caribbean, the Philippines, the Azores, and the Canary Islands. For instance, Gabriel de Avilez Rocha traces connections related to slavery and trade between the Caribbean and the Azores during the sixteenth century to provide a broader image of cultural interactions in the Atlantic world. (See *The Spanish Caribbean and the Atlantic World in the Long Sixteenth Century*, edited by Ida Altman and David Wheat, 2019.) Emphasizing the experiential distinction of local identities in continental and insular Spanish colonial territories, Yolanda Martínez-San Miguel states that in the seventeenth century, "archipelagos represent a challenge to the traditional models of state formation and national configuration" and these regions also questioned models of "imperial expansion and assimilation" (Martínez-San Miguel, 21). This led to representation of characters who "engage in questionable political, social, or affective practices that are not effectively counteracted by a protagonist who plays the role of morality, justice, truth or progress" (*id.*, 22).

73 According to Brendecke and discussed in Chapter 3, the *cosmógrafo-cronista mayor* was an "immobile observer" who had to compile all the materials coming from the Indies to produce a comprehensive history of the traditions, rituals, historical events, and antiquities based on the descriptions contained in accounts (*relaciones*) and descriptions. According to Fabien Montcher, the epic poem was finally published in Valencia (1598) and another three editions appeared during Lope's lifetime (Madrid, 1602, 1604, 1605). The Duke of Lerma supported Lope and provided him with documents and reports about Drake's defeat.

74 Francisco Caro de Torres, supported by Antonio de Herrera y Tordesillas, in his *Relación de los servicios*, took issue with Lope's version of the historical events (Tubau, 312). Herrera, on his part, published his own version of the events in *Tercera parte de la historia general del mundo* (1612) and credited Sotomayor (Ríos Taboada 2021, 176).

75 See Elizabeth Wright, *Pilgrimage to Patronage. Lope de Vega and the Court of Philip III* (2001), 31. For a detailed anaylisis of politics of patronage in *La Dragontea*, see Ríos Taboada 2021, 190–203.

76 "Todo lo cual resulta en honra de nuestra nación, como se podrá ver en estos diez cantos, sacados de la relación que la Real Audiencia de Panamá hizo y autorizó con fidedignos testigos." Francisco de Borja (1582–1658), a close friend and admirer of poetry, became viceroy of Perú from 1614–21.

77 "Dos cosas me han obligado a escrebir este libro ... la primera que no cubriese el olvido tan importante victoria, y la segunda que descubriese el desengaño lo que ignoraba el vulgo, que tuvo a Francisco Draque en tal predicamento." For more about the culture of *desengaño*, see footnote 53.

78 "Para ruïdo de tan grande trueno / es relámpago chico: / no me ciega. / Soberbias velas alza: mal navega. / Potro es gallardo, pero va sin freno" (Lope, 253) "Soneto VII," in *Sonetos completos*, edited by Birute Ciplijauskaité.

79 For more about the tensions between Góngora and Lope, see Antonio Sánchez-Jimenez's introductory study of the consulted edition of *La Dragontea* (13–18).

80 "Todas las veces que se hallare este nombre Dragón, y lo que por él se dice, se ha de entender por la persona de Francisco Draque." According to Sánchez-Jimenez, the association of Drake with the figure of a dragon was not uncommon during the last two decades of the sixteenth century. For instance, it appears in Konrad Gesner's *Historia animaliaum* (1587); in the English pamphlet *In Memoriam* (1596), discussed in this chapter; and in Bernardino Beccari's *Aviso della morte* (1596). Also, Theodor de Bry usually referred to Drake as "Draco" in his *Americae*. Sánchez-Jiménez argues that unlike the previous authors, Lope circumscribed the metaphor of the dragon within a different symbolic context, placing the dragon on the infernal side of the allegorical battle against the Spanish Catholic empire (Lope, 43).

81 "Su misma patria afirma que el demonio con él tenía pacto y conveniencia, / de que era cierta prueba y testimonio / una cédula escrita en su presencia" (Lope, v 4841–4844).

82 "Soldados de la nave en que yo iba / a Ingalaterra aquí me lo han contado, / que, en ocho años de prisión esquiva / que en la corte de Londres han pasado / oyeron estas cosas que refiero" (id., v 4857–64).

83 Barbara Fuchs, in *Mimesis and Empire* (2001), argues that this poem lacks a "real hero" because of the constraints of the epic form (Fuchs, 142).

84 Around 1587–88, Lope was accused of libel because of two satirical poems attributed to him that circulated about a supposedly former lover and married woman, Elena Osorio (the daughter of a theater manager), and her family.

85 Xavier Tubau, in his article "Temas e ideas de una obra perdida: La *Spongia* (1617) de Pedro de Torres Rámila" (2010), elaborates on this topic while

addressing contemporary critics of Lope's work in the first two decades of the seventeenth century (Tubau, 312).

86   While there is no preserved copy of the *Spongia*, scholars have reconstructed the content of this publication through the response to it, entitled *Expostulatio Spongiae* (1618), published under the pseudonym Julio Columbario (Tubau, 303).

87   "¿Hasta cuándo, britanos, seguiremos / este fiero Dragón y Basilico, / que por su atrevimiento le veremos / muy presto del Caucus atado a un risco? / ¿Hasta cuándo las armas llevaremos por el gobierno de este vil Francisco / sobre nuestras cervices quebrantadas, / fuego en la mano y sangre en las espadas?"

88   "Él come la gallina y la ternera / que engorda el mar y que la tierra escota, / y bebe el vino que el sentido altera / de la aromática candiota. / Llévase el oro de la presa entera, / no viendo que la sangre nos agota, / que a peso de la nuestra lo ha comprado, / que el feroz español nos ha quitado."

89   Fuchs argues in *Mimesis and Empire* that Lope's selection of "hellish messengers" like Alecto enabled the author to underscore Spain's central role in safeguarding Christianity against heresy and Islam (Fuchs, 143).

90   "Matar podéis al Draque, pues doliente / de aquel sangriento flujo está en la cama, / con tósigo y veneno, que reviente / hinchado, como Midas, de oro y fama."

91   Lope also characterizes the English as dropsical dragons who stole Spanish gold (Lope, v 4241–4245). Among the sources that reported Drake's dysentery, we find three of Bernardino Beccaria's Italian accounts published between 1596 and 1598 (*id.*, 523). The English pamphlet *In Memoriam* (1596) mentions that Drake died of dysentery during a naval expedition against the enemies of the English: "qui nuper in navali expeditione contra hostes patriae suae, ex Dysenteria laborans obijt"; and Henry Savile (*A Libell*) mentions a "flix" (Savile, 20). Regarding the connection between greed and dropsy, see, in Covarrubias's *Tesoro*, "Algunas veces se toma por avaricia, porque el hidrópico, por mucho que beba, nunca apaga su sed, ni el avariento, por mucho que adquiera, su codicia" (Covarrubias, 686).

92   It is worth noting that Lope does not use the term "tyrant" to specifically describe Drake. Throughout the epic poem, the term appears in three different instances. First, it appears in the sixth canto to refer to the Spanish in the speech delivered by Drake when he addresses the Black populations (slaves and *cimarrones*) of Panamá and tries to recruit them to fight on his side: "El General es bueno para amigo: / tendréis en él un protector piadoso, / de cuya autoridad tema el castigo / el español, vuestro *tirano* odioso" (Lope, v 3385–88). In the seventh canto, the term refers to an English captain in a scene that emphasizes the martyrdom of the Spanish Francisco Cano, who preferred death to revealing to the English a secret route that could be used to ambush the Spanish in Panamá. The verses underscore that Cano became a martyr and in doing so liberated many souls from a "tyrant": "A nadie le parezca barbarismo / querer morir así Francisco Cano, / pues fue por morir por Dios su intento mismo, / librando tantas almas de un *tirano*" (*id.*, v 3865–3868). Finally, the term appears in the ninth canto to denominate the English in general in a scene that portrays an English captive who expresses his desire to convert to Catholicism: "Lloré, en efecto, oyéndole decirme: / Guillermo, toma el ejemplo en propia sangre; / al Vicario de Cristo adora firme / cuando el *tirano* a azotes te desangre" (*id.*, v 5001–5004).

93   Sánchez-Jimenez mentions that Covarrubias defined this practice as *salva*: the method employed by tyrants as well as illegitimate or unjust princes or kings to protect themselves from treason or to deceive (524).

94   Mariana's doctrine on tyrannicide as outlined in *De Rege* was attacked by the Society of Jesus in 1610 due to the assassination of the French King Henry IV (Laures, 2–6). Also, he came into conflict with King Philip III when the latter

debased the Spanish copper coinage and Mariana "alone had the courage to denounce the practice as robbery" (*id.*, 13).
95 Laures states that "When he [Mariana] speaks of the tyrant he means a ruler who is oppressing his people and who has, in most cases, obtained his power by force of arms or other unjust means" (Laures, 61).
96 "Si vero rempublicam pessundat, publicas privatasque fortunas praedae habet, leges publicas et sacrosanctam religionem contempt: virtutem in superbia ponit in audacia atque adversus superos impietate, dissimulandum non est" (*De Rege*, Book I, Ch. 6, 59; translated by Laures).
97 Quoted and translated in Laures.
98 "Ya con el fire tósigo basquea, / ya las heladas manos enclavija, / ya levantarse, ya dormir desea, / y apenas sabe qué remedio elija. / Con la vida frenetica pelea, / que no tiene sentido que la rica, / y en canto ve del negro camarote / mira de Dios vengativo el azote" (Lope, v 5481–87). "Allí se le presentan sus derrotas, / el oro conquistado, el mar, la tierra, / el Norte, el Sur, las filipinas flotas, / con el estruendo y máquinas de guerra" (*id.*, v 5489–5492). "Parecele que escucha grande gritos, / y publicar a voces sus delitos" (*id.*, v 5495–5496).
99 In Covarrubias's *Tesoro*, *delito* means "to fail to fulfill a duty" ("quando uno falto en hazer lo que devia"). However, he adds that Latin *delictum* and *peccatum* mean the same thing, hence, *delinquir* is to commit a *delito* (Covarrubias, 303).
100 "Miserable de ti, Dragón cogido / del cuerpo del exámine elefante / a quien la sangre frígida has bebido, / castigo a tus soberbias semejante / ya no erizas la conchas arrogante …"
101 "[E]l porfiado en mal. Herege pertinaz."
102 "Pero en nuestra lengua Castellana y en todas las de los Catolicos que militan debaxo de la Iglesia Catolica Romana, siempre significa desercion y apartamiento de la Fe, y de lo que tiene y cree la dicha Santa Madre Iglesia."
103 "Ya la gente sepulcro le apercibe, / no con la gola y la acerada malla, / no con entierro, cajas y banderas, / mas como echando cuerpo muerto a fieras."
104 "'¡Qué bien te llorarán los pieces mudos / que roen en el fondo tu litera, / al lastre mismo de las tablas presos, / para gastar tus miserables huesos!'"
105 A *sufragio* is the acknowledgment of a good deed applied to a soul in the purgatory.
106 "Mas consolarte puedes, que has tenido / penates compañeros de tu agravio, / como Conrado y Ladislao lo han sido, / Carlos francés, y Mahometo arabio … tus naves dieron como dado el turbo, / y tú seguiste del infierno el rumbo." Sánchez-Jimenez states that the names used by Lope are conventional names associated with different religious denominations: Conrado and Ladislao (German Lutherans and Calvinists), Carlos francés (Huguenot), and Mahometo arabio (Muslim) (Lope, 527).
107 "'Tú sacaste al Dragón en el anzuelo. / Su lengua ataste, y diste su cabeza / a la garganta vil del pecezuelo, / por más que estaba armada de fiereza. / Tú mismo, que le echaste de tu Cielo / al centro de la mísera bajeza, / con el armella y la acerada hebilla/agujeraste su feroz mejilla.'"
108 "'¡Oh gran Señor, que humillas al gigante, / al humilde David vuelve tus ojos! / Al moro agora, pírata arrogante, / cargado de católicos despojos/ revuelve, eterno Júpiter tonante, los rays de tus ímpetus y enojos / sobre mis enemigos y de España, / que su daño, Señor, me aflige y daña.'" Also, to transform the battle against piracy into a just war, Lope elaborates a correspondence between English pirates and Muslim Barbary corsairs who attacked Spain and Italy (Ríos Taboada 2021, 188–190).

158 *Dropping Anchor*

109 Besides Claudian's *De bello Gildonico*, A.K. Jameson, in his study of Lope's *Dragontea*, traces analogies and resemblances with Claudian's *In Rufinum*. For instance, he argues that Lope's attribution of Greed to Drake in the first canto and the gathering of infernal powers in the second canto recall *In Rufinum* (Jameson, 494). He also identifies the influence of Ovid's second book of *Metamorphoses*—specifically, when Lope in the ninth canto alludes to the story of the Arcadian nymph Callisto, who was seduced by Jove and then expelled by Diana when it was discovered that she would bear him a son (*id.*, 447). According to Jameson, Lope also drew on the Latin prose writer Pliny in cantos I, VII, and X (*id.*, 482).

110 As in Lope's epic poem, in which the English sailors realize that Drake has selfishly manipulated them, Maynarde's account states that Drake and Hawkins have deceived them. After recounting several failed attempts at plunder, Maynard acknowledges that both captains acted only in their own best interests. In this respect Maynarde's narrative resembles that of Lope in that it portrays Drake's quest for glory and treasure as coming at the expense of his crew (and Maynarde himself): "Like as upon the cominge of the sun, dewes and mistes begin to vanish, so our blinded eyes began now to open, and wee found that the glorious speeches, of an hundred places that they knew in the Indies to make us rich, was but a bite to drawe Her Majestie to give them honorable employments and us to adventure our lives for theyr glory; for now cards and mappes must bee our cheefest directors" (Maynarde, 17).

111 Maynarde proceeds to explain Drake's frustrations: "Hee had, beside his own adventure, gaged his owne reputation greatly, in promising Her Majestie to do her honorable service, and to returne her a very profitable adventure; and haveing sufficiently experienced, for seven or eight years together, how hard it was to regain favour once ill thought of, the mistress of his fortune now leaving him to yield to a disconnected mind" (Maynarde, 19).

112 As mentioned before, unlike the Spanish narratives, Maynarde's account remained unpublished until 1849.

113 In the seventeenth century, several authors retrieved and transformed Drake's image to project the short-lived English Republic's colonizing agenda by highlighting Elizabethan seafaring and power. Among these attempts, we find William Davenant's play *The History of Sir Francis Drake* (published in 1659), whose main goal, according to Janet Clare in *Drama of the English Republic, 1649–60* (2002), at 266, was to construct and project a continuum of British maritime domination from the 1580s to the 1650s while providing a distorted version of the historical facts related to Drake's enterprises largely based on *Sir Francis Drake Revived*, compiled by Philip Nichols and published in 1628 by Drake's nephew.

5 The Changing Winds of Piracy (1570–1604)

Royal documents from Philip II and Elizabeth I's reigns employ the categories of "pirate" and "corsair" without detailing their specific meaning. In 1569—before the declaration of the Anglo-Spanish war (1585–1604)—Queen Elizabeth published the "Proclamation Agaynst the Maintenance of Pirates."[1] This public document underscored that all pirates would be punished, as well as those who traded with them.[2] One cannot find a comprehensive definition of piracy therein except for the clarification that pirates were simply those who did not hold a proper license to trade. The proclamation, thus, unambiguously targeted those who engaged in contraband or unofficial trade, mainly in coastal regions and port cities.[3] To this end, the queen's proclamation indicates the institutional apparatus intended to regulate commerce and outlines the processes and protocols in place that would be followed. A few decades later and closer to the end of the Anglo-Spanish war, Spain's King Philip II circulated a royal *cédula* (1590) in which he lists the regulations to protect Spanish ships from the "corsairs" (*corsarios*). Without specifying the nationality of such corsairs, the royal *cédula* stresses that the main problem in repelling piracy is the weak Spanish defense onboard, resulting from the deteriorated state of several unqualified vessels.[4] In addition, the king highlights that foreign piracy endangers not only local Spanish peninsular trade but also the larger "universal market" (*comercio universal*). By focusing on the commercial risks and economic repercussions of piracy, these royal documents showed that both Elizabeth I and Philip II were primarily interested in protecting their respective kingdoms' finances.

The queen's proclamation forbids port authorities from providing victuals, munitions, or other "reliefe" to any "person coming from the seas." Even though the royal document underscores that those who buy or receive goods from pirates would be judged and executed "as in cases of piracies," it does not define the term, nor does it specify what constitutes a "pirate" or "piracies" in legal terms. The proclamation derived from the need for stopping those "vessels armed with certayne disordered persons mixt of sundry nations" who "do still haunt the narrow seas, and resort secretly into small Creeks and obscure places" of the queen's realm. The proclamation further states that any unregistered vessel armed and transporting ordinary

DOI: 10.4324/9781003141495-6

merchants, passengers, or "usual" fishermen will be apprehended by the corresponding port authorities.[5]

Employing an ambiguous legal vocabulary, the English Crown delegated the task of dealing with piracy to the wardens of ports, vice admirals, constables, and captains "to do theyr vttermost in their iurisdictions to enquire" following the "laws of this Realme." Besides declaring that most of these pirates were foreigners operating under the English flag who "haunt the narrow seas," the proclamation does not stipulate the nationality of those individuals or what it means by the expression of "haunting" the seas.[6] In this sense, the central issue of the proclamation was less oriented to addressing the problem of piracy on the seas than to gaining control over the potential illicit trade. Even though at this point Spain and England were not at war, the proclamation was issued in the same decade in which Drake and John Hawkins undertook several ventures in Spanish America where they carried contraband out of American ports. One must remember, then, that the proclamation did not touch upon the issue of piracy or contraband outside the English jurisdiction, nor did it refer to piracy as a phenomenon related to the Anglo-Spanish rivalry.

This chapter examines the flexibility of the discourse on piracy through the comparative analysis of sixteenth- and early seventeenth-century primary sources such as European legal treatises, historical accounts, and royal documents. In light of the absence of stable sixteenth-century definitions of what constituted a pirate, I posit that the plasticity of the concept of piracy stemmed from an interlock between the economic, political, legal, and religious realms. Drawing on Christian Bueguer's analysis of the epistemic practices behind the construction of "piracy" as an epistemic object, I consider the historical, legal, and political primary sources as epistemic practices to examine the discourses at play that framed the core and scope of maritime predation.[7] Relying on Karin Knorr Cetina's work (2001), Bueguer affirms that one of the main characteristics of objects of knowledge (*epistemes*) is "their lack of completeness" and they, thus, "continuously raise new questions" prompting reevaluations and different procedures to address them (Bueguer, 6). I incorporate these conceptions to approach sixteenth- and early seventeenth-century piracy considering the epistemic practices, namely the textual representations, involved in the creation of a coherent—though at times ambivalent—narrative around maritime predation. In the first section, I analyze how piracy was used to negotiate and articulate the limits of political wars and religious rivalries, as when European legal jurists alluded to or introduced the category of piracy to compare and articulate perceptions of private property, distribution of booty, sovereignty, just war, dominion, and the enemy. Considering Henry Mainwaring's treatise against piracy and the judicial agreements between England and Spain, such as the 1604 Treaty of London, that took place after Drake's, Queen Elizabeth I's, and King Philip II's deaths, the second part of this chapter registers a semantic taxonomy of piracy within the written legal standards implemented by England and Spain. This section also examines the development of the notion of the English "dutiful subject" and the picaresque traits adopted by those who, like Mainwaring and Captain John Smith, voiced their anxiety toward the economic turmoil resulting from James I's anti-piracy policies.

Manipulation of Piracy: Issues of Property, Space, and Sovereignty

Primarily addressing economic interests, the conventional medieval distinction between a pirate and a corsair was that while the latter had been commissioned by a state to commit maritime predation, the former had not been authorized by a sovereign power. Stemming from the postulate *ir de corso* (corsairing), the term *corsario* appeared in thirteenth- and fourteenth-century Iberian legal compilations, such as the Catalonian *Consolat de Mar* (c1258) and royal ordinances.[8] The Catalonian treatise outlined the precepts of maritime and commercial laws in the Mediterranean Sea and emphasized the corsairs' economic duties, such as the assurance of the amount loaned by private investors.[9] A century later, King Peter IV of Aragon enforced in 1356 the first royal corsairs' ordinance to strengthen the Spanish military structure against the Genoese overseas, thus incorporating a political tenor into the corsairs' financial responsibilities. After four months, sailors had to return to Aragon and hand over everything provided, whether by the king or by private investors, including the ship and its armaments.[10] Ten years after that, addressing the problem of frequent desertions, the king enforced a royal provision that compelled corsairs to return to their homeland. In cases of disobedience, if the deserters were eventually found, they would either be subjected to a monetary fine or would be publicly lashed. However, the task of capturing deserters would have required not only the existence of an effective policing apparatus, but also the royal expenditure of money and resources to enforce the regulation. The provision arguably did not delineate the Crown's logistics and active pursuit of fugitives; rather, the document stood as a deterrent policy to dissuade potential deserters. From these legal postulates emerged the figure of the corsair as a sailor whose country of origin sponsored him, whereas the pirate embodied an outlaw and marginal character. Besides the contextual political interests and military challenges encountered by the medieval powers, differentiating a corsair from a pirate rested upon the systematization of increasing and protecting economic revenues. As we shall see further, the debate around these two polemical categories continued throughout the sixteenth and seventeenth centuries as authors added more political, moral, and economic layers to the discourse on piracy, based on the viewpoints of both perpetrators and victims of maritime predation. I will focus specifically on the usefulness of the malleability of the concept of piracy arising from the lexical legal ambiguities and supposed "misunderstandings" of the categories related to maritime predation in the primary sources. In so doing, I will examine the interplay between the concept of piracy and the shifting economic and political notions that range from private property, distribution of booty, and fortified lines to sovereignty and just wars.

Let us start with the issue of the persistent "misunderstanding" of these categories as proposed and acknowledged by specific individuals, such as the English Captain Richard Hawkins. A written passage of c1593 attributed to this sailor and included in Samuel Purchas's compilation *Purchas his Pilgrimes* (1625) directly underscores the "misinterpretation of the term Pirates."[11] Hawkins states his concern toward the "nicknames" given to adventurers like him by the inhabitants "not only of Peru, but in all Spaine, and the Kingdoms thereof held all English of Warre" (Purchas, 1412). Such a "misinterpretation" or Spanish modality of calling them pirates was intertwined with issues related to religious difference. In this regard, he states that besides being identified as a pirate, he has also been called a Lutheran "both in Peru and in the Counsels of Spaine, and among the Christaines" (Purchas, 1412).[12] Attempting to clarify his status as a legitimate maritime agent and echoing past medieval ordinances, Hawkins elaborates a definition of piracy that comprehends both the figure of the pirate and the corsair, based on belligerent and political conflicts, stressing the fact that the English did have "license" and authorization to "spoil" and "pillage" the Spaniards:

> Alleging that a Pirate, or Corsair, is he which in time of peace, or truce spoyleth, or robbeth those, which have peace or truce with them: but the English have neither peace nor truce with Spaine, but warre; and therefore not to bee accounted ... Besides, Spaine broke the peace with England, and not England with Spaine ... But the English have a license, either immediately from their Prince, or from other thereunto authorized, and so cannot in any sense be comprehended under the name of Pirats, for any hostilitie undertaken against Spaine or the dependancies thereof.
>
> (Purchas, 1412)

Hawkins concludes that the confusion about the use of the terms "pirate" and "corsair" stems from the difference between Spanish and English military practices during war. The main distinction, according to him, was that the Spanish war tradition did not allow an individual to attack enemy ships without the king's permission and approval. As a consequence, the attacker had to be punished "upon paine to be reputed a Pirate, and to be chastized with the punishment due to Corsarios" (Purchas, 1412). Meanwhile, the English custom conceded permission to individuals to attack the enemy during wartime without the king's approval and thus, they should not be considered pirates: "for our greater exemption, from being comprehended with the number of Pirats" (Purchas, 1413). Instead of "law," Hawkins employs the term "custom" to legitimize English sovereignty against the Spanish power. At the time, unlike positive and prescriptive laws, customs were considered "legal" or legitimate only by those individuals who actively engaged in these "customs."[13] This example showcases that while attempting to define piracy, Hawkins conflates notions of religious identity, sovereignty, and legitimate war. In so doing, Hawkins demonstrates that, far from only being "misinterpreted words," the elusiveness of a stable distinction between the categories of pirate and corsair enabled him to delimitate the boundaries of such notions from the viewpoint of an active aggressor in Spanish eyes. In what follows, moving to the analysis of tangible economic and political repercussions, I will examine how such ambiguity of piracy proved to be useful for other coetaneous authors pertaining to the legal domain.

Alberico Gentili (1552–1608) was an Italian civilian lawyer in Perugia who, after having been suspected of heresy, fled to London in 1580 and served as the appointed lawyer of the Spanish Crown at the English Court of Admiralty (1605–08). One of his famous legal treatises, *Hispanicae advocationis*, posthumously published c1613, compiled specific disputes and pleas that allowed the theorization of the law of nations and kingdoms, based on common rules for all countries. By delving into classical sources such as Salycetus and Angelus, and contemporary ones such as Antonio de Gama and Andrea Alciato, the jurist configured a general panorama of the sixteenth-century conceptualization of property and jurisdiction. One of the main issues at the time was judging whether a specific booty's capture was legitimate. If the capture was considered illegitimate, then the right of ownership would be forfeited. Focusing on contemporary cases seen in the Court of Admiralty, the treatise evinced that the changing face of piracy underlay the pursuit of economic agendas, because the author defined piracy in contradictory ways depending upon whether he desired to legitimize or delegitimize an economic transaction.

Legal historians, such as Lauren Benton in her study on Gentili's figure, showcase the flexibility on "piracy" displayed by this lawyer when judging legitimate economic transactions (Benton 2011, 228–230). However, I am more interested in Gentili's lexical ambiguities resulting from his specific usage of the terms related to piracy. He relies on the contingent attribution of the category of piracy based on semantics suitable for specific cases. In his Chapter XII, dedicated to the "property captured by pirates and afterwards bought by friends in the enemy's country," Gentili discusses the law based on this hypothetical situation: "Robbers had stolen a slave from you. Afterward that slave had come into the hands of the Germans. Then when the Germans had been conquered in war, the slave had been sold" (Gentili, 51). Gentili's interpretation of the law governing this scenario incorporates the thought of classical authors such as Labeo, Ofilius, and Trebatius while also explaining what a pirate is. Paraphrasing these authors, Gentili states that they "assert that the buyer cannot acquire ownership of the slave by usucaption, because in reality the slave was stolen; and that this once belonging to the enemy or returning by *postliminium*[14] does not affect this rule" (*id.*). Gentili applies the core principles of this statement to the law in question, arguing that "we speak in the same way of other things" and configuring a series of comparisons based on contemporary events or disputes. He places the term "pirate" in lieu of the thief, saying "these are our pirates," substitutes "property" for "slave" because "slaves are things," and replaces "Germans" with "the enemy" (*id.*). Gentili's analogical operation of transposing terms to different contexts and agents evinces his flexible view of piracy and its changeability according to the specific scenario in which it is applied. Just as the face of the enemy changes, the term "pirate" becomes semantically replaceable.[15] This palpably overlaps the concepts of piracy, private property, and the enemy.

By the same token, notions of booty, spoils, and prizes mainly derived from unstable terms such as the Greek *leistes* (land-based maritime predators) and of conceptions of piracy encapsulated by the Latin *peirates* (Heller-Roazen, 34). These were qualities assigned to private property—individuals or things—resulting from violent acts of seizure, whether in times of war (legitimate reprisal) or of peace (illegitimate capture). In the military context, the Roman legal doctrine of *ius postliminii* (the right to be granted postwar restitution) established that if an individual was captured or enslaved during an official war, such an individual was supposed to regain previous legal status, as well as property and civil rights, when returned to the Roman jurisdiction (Rubin, 11–13). Under the frame of international law, another legal theorist, Hugo Grotius (1583–1645), discussed in Chapter 2, extends this right to individual property, arguing that pirates could not transform the status of stolen things into legitimate merchandise (Kempe, 392).

If war is the only time in which sea captures seem to be allowed and regulated, the concept of "just war" also raises questions about the clarity of its internal judicial enforcement. A "just war" implied the notion of a "just enemy" and in turn restricted the power of declaring war to the sovereign prince. However, over the course of the sixteenth century, two main currents characterized the Western European culture of just wars. One tradition, attached to the natural law, was the right to declare war (*ius ad bellum*), thus excluding religion or faith as a legitimate cause of a just war. In opposition to this naturalist approach, the theological tradition tended to legitimize religion as a just cause of war.[16] Gentili claimed that if a sovereign imposed restrictions to prevent other sovereigns' subjects from navigating, this could be considered a legitimate cause of a just war (Benton 2010, 125). Among the just causes that allow the declaration of a just war, Balthazar Ayala (1548–1584), a Flemish lawyer appointed by Philip II to the position of General Military Auditor, stressed the importance of the category of the "rebel." Intended to restore the peace in the Low Countries, Ayala's legal treatise *De Iure et Officiis bellicis et disciplina militari* (Douai 1584) underscores the difference between the notions of the just enemy and the rebel.[17] In his view, a pirate qualifies as a rebel with no right either for booty capture or a legitimate declaration of war. Enemies from a just war (*hostes*), by contrast, should receive better treatment than the rebel since their position is demarcated by fighting a just cause. Besides shifting the condition or status of the individuals involved in a military conflict, such "better treatment" also refers to private property and the right of ownership in these circumstances.

A Dominican priest and scholastic theologian of the sixteenth century, Domingo de Soto (1494–1560), proposed that although private property was not an absolute right, its nature was justifiable inasmuch as it was intended to advance the common good. Placing private property under the realm of the law of nations (*ius gentium*) and deriving its rights from natural law (*ius naturale*), Soto outlines five main arguments to support its existence. First, private property promotes a just social order; second, it is necessary for social peace; third, it is appropriated under conditions of scarcity; fourth, it improves the proper administration of material goods; and finally, it facilitates economic exchange and social cooperation (Alves and Moreira, 67–69). However, these considerations upon private property, says Soto, are trumped by cases of maritime predation. Outlining the regulations to be observed regarding property and possessions during war, Balthazar Ayala, who is quoted in Gentili's *Hispanicae*, places pirates, thieves, and bandits in the category of rebels. In doing so, Ayala removes their right to claim *postliminium* under the traditional Roman doctrine of restitution granted after war.[18] He equates the figure of the pirate and the rebel to protect Spain's sovereignty over the Low Countries. By claiming that the Dutch had no right to declare a just war, he defines them as rebels; and, as pirates or bandits, they forfeit the right to own stolen property or receive *postliminium*. Besides tracking and judging the right of ownership of previously stolen private property, another concern arises: How should one distribute such a capture? One way of justifying the fair booty distribution entailed the inclusion of the religious and political discourse evinced by a common Biblical example. Apparently, Abraham gave all the booty he captured to his king—the king of Sodom—and such action revealed diverse meanings according to each source. According to Ayala, Abraham's decision underscores the fact that the king should hold the power of booty distribution (Gentili, 38).[19] By contrast, Grotius, in *De jure praedae* (1604–08), emphasizes that Abraham's actions were also a way of acknowledging the right of *postliminium* to the people of Sodom, who were the original owners of the possessions (Grotius 2004, 86). Grotius adds that Abraham decided not to take any of the booty to avoid allegations of enriching himself, although Grotius believes he clearly deserved it, because it was not against the law, and his decision reflected his noble spirituality.

Both the right of *postliminium* and the fair distribution of booty captures derived from the determination of a just cause and a just enemy, which by extension depended on another unstable notion: that of the sovereign. Heller-Roazen argues that the phenomenon of piracy transformed the concept of war because the Roman perception of pirates as "enemies of all mankind" (*hostes humani generis*) implied the that they were "neither criminals nor belligerents in any accepted sense." Thus, actions taken against them could not be "formally identical to those employed against a lawful enemy" (Heller-Roazen, 11). During the sixteenth and seventeenth centuries the European law of nations (*ius gentium*), according to Carl Schmitt, ceased to rely exclusively on the authority of the Christian church to declare a just war. That power was transferred to the sovereignty of the states, with rights similar to those under the Church's aegis (Schmitt 2002, 110). In this way the notion of the just enemy (*iustus hostis*) outweighed that of the just cause (*iusta causa*) as a source from which the law of nations arises (*id*.). In other words, at this point the declaration of a just war had less to do with the existence of a just cause than with the presence of a just enemy against a legitimate sovereign in judicial terms.

Jean Bodin's *On Sovereignty* (1576) asserted that the monarchy conferred sovereignty to the prince, democracy to the people, and aristocracy to a limited part of the population. While legal scholars have acknowledged the flexibility of the concept of sovereignty, we find that one of the repercussions of such flexibility is the establishment of royal absolutism based on Bodin's postulates, which stressed that sovereignty must be considered an indivisible power that could only be held by an individual or a specific group. Despite the differences between the three kinds of state outlined by Bodin—monarchy, democracy, and aristocracy— he used the concept of sovereignty as a common denominator to develop a comparative legal science.[20] According to this French philosopher, the only limitation of the sovereign is that he is ultimately subject to the law of nature. While Gentili and Ayala used the figure of the pirate to articulate analogies and comparisons to define just war and the right of ownership over stolen property, Bodin explains the concept of sovereignty by employing metaphors related to property and possession. For instance, when defining the ways in which people confer sovereignty on an individual, Bodin explains that such transference of power resembles the way in which an individual waives his ownership of a particular property or possession for no other reason than generosity (Bodin, 7–8). The intangible nature of sovereignty thus seems analogous to the tangibility of individual property.[21] While it is clear that by the sixteenth century, both political and legal philosophers struggled with the task of anchoring and defining the boundaries of sovereignty, private property, just war, and the enemy, it is plausible to acknowledge the rhetorical limits at play when they attempted to conceptualize "piracy" and its relation to such conceptual network of terms that also include that of "dominion" in the wake of European imperial and pre-imperial expansion.

The Roman concept of *dominium*, traditionally understood as ownership, preceded and influenced the European notion of sovereignty in the sixteenth and seventeenth centuries. Unlike its classical precedent, sovereignty was intended to be exercised over both peoples and lands (Pagden 1995, 39–40). During the Roman period, traditional *dominium* pertained to those territories within the limits of the Roman Empire, and the external relations with the empire were mediated by the law of nations (*ius gentium*), which became what we know today as international law (*id.*, 39). Grotius has been widely considered one of the first precursors of the appropriation of *ius gentium* from the seventeenth century onward. In this context, the notion of sovereignty could be understood not only as the relation between the sovereign and its subjects, or the state and its citizens, but rather, it also became a common currency to legitimize sovereigns and sovereign states as well as their relations in the international milieu according to their designated jurisdictions.[22] This conceptualization brought forth several issues related to the extent of sovereign power.[23] For instance, focusing on the elusiveness of the term in the context of early modern empires and the relation between law and geography, Benton remarks on the emergence of uneven or "layered" sovereignties characterized by the ineffective imperial implementation of order and delegation of authority in different legal geographies or in malleable jurisdictions like the seas or far-distant and isolated territories (Benton 2010, 30–32).[24] On the other hand, examining the several distinct procedures followed by Spanish and English settlers in the Americas, Elliott stresses that while possession stemmed from occupation and use, sovereignty depended on official claims. However, such a claim was "only valid in the eyes of those who made it" (Elliott, 30). This brings us to the core of the premise from which this chapter started: that the notion of sovereignty mirrors that of piracy inasmuch as its articulation lies in the eye of the beholder.[25] In what follows, I will delve into the relation between piracy and geographical space through the analysis of the construction of European spaces based on considerations attached to time and space.

Early voyages, discoveries, and circumnavigations in the fifteenth and sixteenth centuries contributed to the rearrangement of the globe in both scientific and legal terms (Schmitt 2002, 67). Schmitt identifies four global political lines of demarcation: (1) the *Inter caetera* bull, 1493; (2) the Treaty of Tordesillas, 1494; (3) the Moluccas Line, 1526; and (4) the Treaty of Zaragoza, 1529 (*id.*, 71). Benton's reappraisal of Gentili's and Grotius's works in the face of maritime predation and fledgling international laws emerges from the distinction between ownership and jurisdiction over sea zones that these authors claimed (Benton 2010, 121). In the Roman tradition, the sea was considered common property (*res communes*) and as such was excluded from other forms of acquisition like occupation (*occupatio*). To tackle this issue, legal commentators and glossators in the fourteenth and fifteenth centuries retrieved a post-Roman-developed category of property: jurisdiction (*jurisdictio*) (Benton 2010, 121–122).[26] This notion of property opened up the possibility of asserting state control over the seas through jurisdictional claims based on laws of prescription or custom, resulting in "a kind of property right that was nominally different from dominion."[27] However, dwelling upon the muddled distinction between prescription and custom, sixteenth- and seventeenth-century jurists like Gentili and Grotius confronted the problem of defining who was entitled to restrict navigation. By employing Ciceronian arguments of natural law to address maritime pillaging, these authors differentiated jurisdiction from dominion (Benton 2010, 123–25). However, the very notion of jurisdiction would be put to the test against another legal concept that deals with the legitimization of sea captures.

Such a concept is "fortified lines" (*intra praesidia*), which appears in Gentili's discussion of booty captures (Gentili, 5).[28] While explaining the protocols in place to validate sea captures, the term highlights the relation between maritime predation and space. In theory, according to Gentili, the time spent in possession of a booty does not bestow ownership because what mattered at the time was the space where the object or capture was being held. Currently, United States laws allow "adverse possessors" to gain land or property rights over true owners after a period of seven and twenty years provided the land or the object was not stolen in the first place (because if it was, it would be considered larceny). In one of Gentili's cases, the importance of space surpasses that of time because the possession had to be held inland to acquire ownership upon it:

> Indeed time counts for nothing in this case, where booty is always of doubtful ownership so long as it has not been taken within the captor's fortified lines because time is not considered to be a space and thus, it could not be controlled with law.
>
> (*id.*)[29]

Alluding to a specific case in which a Hollander (Dutch) ship captured a Spanish vessel but failed to bring it to fortified lines, Gentili claims that ships do not constitute fortified lines and thus the capture was illegitimate.[30] Drawing on classical sources, Gentili states that unlike seas and ships, a fortified line is a "firm and steady ground" (*id.*). To claim legitimate ownership of a booty capture, Gentili argues, it must be taken to such fortified lines and remain there for a period of three days. As long as the stolen property remains on the ship or outside the fortified lines, the captor is not the legitimate owner; the right of ownership lies with the original possessor (*id.*, 10).

Whereas I will return to the concept of *intra praesidia* in the next chapter and its repercussions in the insular Caribbean context, the example just given displays the relation between piracy and space and, in turn, the articulation of a specific space—fortified lines—to define piracy by outlining the distinction between legitimate and illegitimate property. Following Gentili's argument, maritime space, because of its malleability or instability, did not qualify as an environment to legitimize new ownership over stolen property, suggesting that ownership must be land based. The concept of fortified lines thus implicates a jurisdictional formulation of a territorial space that seems to vanish when it concerns maritime space.[31] Given the fact that it was not until the seventeenth century that international discussions about maritime jurisdiction and control began, the mid-sixteenth century witnessed the conceptualization of maritime space and the rules that should be imposed upon such. Even though Gentili acknowledged that the term "territory" applied to both land and sea, he conferred maritime jurisdiction of 100 miles only to coastal territories such as those dominated by the Venetians.

The narrative fluctuation that hindered the stability of the figure of the pirate during the sixteenth century allowed the dismissal of binary oppositions. Hawkins's remark about the "misunderstandings" of the terms "pirate" and "corsair," supported by the difference between Spanish and English military practices and the European legal debate, shows the complexity of defining the concept of a pirate and the strategies and different usages of this term, primarily based on economic interests. Even though Gentili's usage of the term varied depending on the case—and even though he was particularly interested in deciding whether a booty capture was legitimate—he demonstrated that the term was interchangeable by transposing it to the place occupied by "thief" in a classical regulation. Ayala raised contemporary political conflicts related to Spain's sovereignty and "just war" with the Low Countries and declared "pirate" and "rebel" to be equal categories whereby neither has a right to *postliminium*. Bodin, on his part, attempted to define the flickering notion of sovereignty through the use of metaphors and tangible examples of property and possession. Grotius and Gentili were concerned about the spatial differences between land and sea as a means to discern a legitimate capture and a fair distribution of booty based on Roman postulates. By the same token, Queen Elizabeth I and King Philip II mentioned the concepts of pirate and corsair without defining them, but rather with the intention of emphasizing that they constituted a problem to Spanish trade—or universal trade—or to the preservation of an international English reputation. Thus, through implementation of an economic vocabulary or pursuit of financial interests, piracy became a malleable signifier, an epistemic practice, and a tool of intervention and mediation of legal demarcations and conceptualizations of notions of sovereignty, legitimate property, and the enemy. Moving to the aftermath of the Anglo-Spanish rivalry and its economic repercussions, the next section will reexamine the standardization of the legal vocabulary between the two countries and the narrative transformation of the former "pirates" into "dutiful subjects," echoing the literary picaresque model.

New Legal Understandings of Piracy and the End of the Anglo-Spanish Rivalry

Two years before Drake's death in 1596, Pedro de Valdés, who at the time was living in Brussels, wrote three letters to King Philip II reporting Queen Elizabeth I's intention to appropriate several Spanish strongholds in the Caribbean.[32] He knew the maneuvers of the English because he had been captured during the Armada battles in 1588 (discussed in Chapter 4). In the first letter, dated March 19, 1593, Valdés wrote that according to his sources an English armada would depart soon to occupy and fortify the islands of Puerto Rico and Curaçao so as to strategically gain more access to the Spanish fleets and ships coming from the ports of Havana, Nombre de Dios, New Spain, and Tierra Firme.[33] He advised the king to take the necessary measures to counter the threat. Ten days later he wrote again, emphasizing the ongoing preparations made by Drake for his next voyage to the Indies.[34]

In a third letter, written May 21, Valdés insisted on the queen's plans of capturing the Spanish ships returning from the Indies or taking the island of Puerto Rico or Cartagena. He also disclosed that George Clifford, Third Earl of Cumberland, would be in charge of a 25-ship fleet.[35] Contrary to past maritime incursions to the West Indies, the Queen's modus operandi had changed from intermittent pillaging to occupying and permanently fortifying several Caribbean islands.[36] While Drake's attack was an acute failure, as discussed in the previous chapter, three years later (1598) Cumberland managed to occupy the city of San Juan, Puerto Rico, and on July 10 the governor of the island, Antonio de Mosquera, surrendered and gave Cumberland the keys of the Castle San Felipe del Morro. The occupation lasted only until August 24 due to an outbreak of dysentery, which wreaked havoc among the English soldiers who had disembarked on the island.[37] Nevertheless, Cumberland's occupation under his queen's orders marked the beginnings of another kind of piracy based on projects of settlement in the West Indies.[38]

This form of unregulated piracy as a means of acquiring territories did not outlast Queen Elizabeth, who died in 1603; seventeenth-century economic and geopolitical ambitions dissipated rivalries between the English and Spanish Crowns. By reexamining English and Spanish royal documents—treaties of peace, proclamations, and commissions—revolving around the official condemnation of piracy between these two powers, this section will register the conceptual stabilization of piracy in the legal discourse. Considering the ambiguity of the terms as displayed by several proclamations and commissions, the first part of this section dwells upon the discussion of the relation between the discursive prohibition of piracy in English waters and potential commerce with Spain under Queen Elizabeth's reign. Contrasting the queen's policies with those of her successor, James I, I will further trace the specific shifts in language and vocabulary found in the legislations of piracy, to register the economic and political advantages resulting from its legal standardization.

In 1601, five years after Drake's death, Queen Elizabeth banned all trade and commercial activity with Spain and Portugal. While the proclamation did not explicitly allude to piracy, forbidding trade with King Philip III became the English strategy to antagonize and undermine his economic strength. Justifying this decision, the royal document incorporated both the religious and political vocabulary by stressing that Philip III, like his predecessor, claimed the throne of Ireland with support from the pope. Characterizing the pope as a "man of sin" and as "a president not to be endured by sovereign Princes," the document exemplified the entanglement of religious and political discourses: it aimed to discredit the pope's image while amplifying Philip III's threat against Elizabeth's sovereignty and her inherited right to govern Ireland.[39] From these political and religious grounds emerged an economic language aimed at blocking the commerce with Philip III to finally put an end to the war:

> [T]he stopping hinderance and impeaching of all commerce and traffick with him in his territories of Spaine and Portingall will quickly, in likelihood, give an end to these bloudie and unnatural warres, which disturbe the generall peace and quiet of all theise partes of Christendome.
> (Marsden, 315)

Besides weakening Philip's military resources by diminishing his economic resources, the proclamation served an ulterior purpose: to justify English transatlantic pillaging. This was stated explicitly:

> And to the intent that this prohibition of traffick with the Kingdoms of Spaine and Portingall may take effect, to the withdrawing of those meanes from the Spanish King, whereby hee maintaineth theise unnaturall warres, and to the speedie procurring of a generall peace and quiet, both to her Highness and also to theise partes of Christendome, her Highnes is pleased that all her loving subjects, who shall hereafter set out anie ships or vessels of war to the sea ... and by their best endeavours and means shall apprehend and take all maner of shipping whatsoever going for or to any towne, haven, citie, or place, of the King of Spaine in the Kingdomes ... or any of them, and the same shipping so taken with all the goods, marchandises, money, or jewels, laden therein, shall with all convenient speede bring or cause to be brought into some port or haven of this realm of England.
> (Marsden, 315–316)

Contrary to Elizabeth's 1601 policy of sponsoring piracy in disguise as a means of ending the Anglo-Spanish war, her successor James I changed the strategy by signing a peace agreement in London (1604) that was ratified in Philip III's courts in Valladolid (1605). Known as the Treaty of London, or Treaty of Peace, Alliance, and Commerce, it mainly revolved around the restoration of the commercial relations between the kingdoms of Spain and England.[40] Revitalization of Anglo-Spanish trade came with a price, however. On the one hand, Spain had to refrain from reestablishing Catholicism in James I's dominions of England, Ireland, and now Scotland, while on the other hand, the English had to put an end to their commercial relations and alliances with the enemies of Spain, specifically the rebels of the Low Countries (*Olanda* and *Zelanda*).[41] It has been argued that the Spanish peace treaty was part of a wider goal to resolve the European religious conflict in the long run. However, the English public became anxious and remained suspicious of James's apparent empathy toward the Spanish; this empathy was evinced by his plans for proposing marriages for his potential successors that would entail both Protestant and Catholic matches. While these eventually did not work out as expected, Sir Walter Raleigh's execution in 1618, for disobeying the king and attacking Spanish strongholds during his expedition to the Oronoco, gave rise to the mythification of the Elizabethan "good old days" when figures like Drake and Raleigh were seen as true believers of the Protestant cause against the Spanish Catholic enemy.[42]

From beginning to end, the Treaty of London addresses the issue of piracy while emphasizing several times that it applies to both sides and will be enforced on land, at sea, and in fresh waters (*tam per terram, quam per mare, et aqua dulces*). Several items found in the treaty politicize maritime space by extending the scope of the agreement to the seas, fresh waters, and ports. For instance, the second item prohibits any

> spoil, theft, offense and pillage in any kingdoms, dominions, places and estates from whether one of them or the other [Philip III and James I], located either on land, sea, or fresh water ... and the individuals will be restituted of any theft, pillage or prize ...
>
> (Berwick et al., 249)[43]

The third item repeats the same narrative pattern by establishing that neither the princes nor their successors will attack any of their countries, kingdoms, or dominions in any place in land or at sea (*id.*, 249–50).[44] Free trade, under the ninth item, will be established in the three places mentioned—land, sea, and fresh waters (*id.*, 253).[45] The kings of England, Spain, and France, the sixteenth item explains, should be able to enter and navigate freely and safely without the need of an exclusive license on land, sea, and fresh waters (*id.*, 260).

In the Spanish printed edition of this document from 1605, the term "piracies" (*piraterias*) appears in the margin of the sixth capitulation. The main body of the Spanish text revokes "any commissions and letters, either of reprisal or marque, that might allow the power to steal."[46] As I have discussed earlier, letters of marque and reprisal were initially issued during the late Middle Ages to prevent wars among small feudal kingdoms. These documents, along with the *licentia marcandi* (1295), granted permission to recover stolen goods, whether from the hands of the original thief or a relative, friend, or neighbor.[47] However, over the course of the sixteenth century, letters of marque and reprisal lost their original purpose of preventing wars and were issued during wartime, underscoring the belligerency among countries.[48] Even if the conceptual difference between the types of commission (marque or reprisal) was not clear and might be related to capricious terminology, the Spanish marginal note explicitly links "piracies" to "letters of marque for stealing." "Those who disobey," the capitulation adds, will be punished and, besides facing a criminal penalty, will be compelled to make restitution (*id.*, 8).[49]

Entirely dedicated to the issue of maritime predation (*predandi*), this agreement reveals two important aspects about piracy. First, the Spanish marginal note shows that the phenomenon of piracy was understood as something conceptually vague but attached to "sponsored stealing." Erasing any differences between the pirate and the so-called corsair, both the pirate and the sailor carrying royal commissions of marque and reprisal fell under the same Spanish perception of state-backed thievery. Second, the capitulation became the first document that seems to stabilize the category of piracy, inaugurating its entry into the legal discourse as it openly criminalizes any individual who might disobey. This is the first time in which the figure of the pirate is legally equated to that of the corsair and their conceptual stability and equalization are acknowledged by both the English and Spanish kings. In this way, the treaty leaves no room for anyone who, like Drake and others in the previous century, claims royal sponsorship or justifies maritime predation under nationalistic or religious differences. As we shall see in what follows, two former pirates had to embrace the quest to become "dutiful subjects."

To Captain John Smith (1580–1631) and Sir Henry Mainwaring (1586/7–1653), in *The True Travels, Adventures, and Observations* (1630) and *Of the Beginnings, Practices, and Suppression of Pirates* (c1617), respectively, piracy was the ultimate byproduct of James I and Philip III's peace and negligent policing of harbors and ports.[50] Both individuals were born under the reigns of Elizabeth I and Philip II, during the same decade in which Drake returned from his circumnavigation of the globe and from his first Caribbean raid. From 1612, James had started to exonerate English pirates through a general pardon (Jowitt, 152).[51] Jowitt argues that the Jacobean foreign policy was widely viewed in England—including by the Privy Council, which administered the colonies—as a symptom of weakness and a dishonorable action because it revealed the King's incapability to contain the problem of piracy (*id.*). The two policies that were enforced, namely the pirates' general pardon and the granting of "Admiralty commissions to private pirate hunters," failed to decrease maritime predation and were revoked by 1621 (*id.*). Notwithstanding James I's foreign policies—*Rex Pacificus*—they justified those seamen who undertook the path of "piracy" or "the trade" by stressing the lack of "universal employment" in the British kingdoms (Mainwaring, 41).[52]

Through the close reading of literary depictions of pirates from Elizabethan England, Jowitt underscores an attempt to rehabilitate the pirate from the position of straightforward criminality "to appreciate the strategic value of certain *types* of pirate" (Jowitt, 137). Moving to the Jacobean period, Jowitt focuses on the shift in representations of piracy, the emergence of new types of pirates, and the rise of different attitudes that shaped the perception of those systematically considered outlaws under James I's regime. In doing so, she traces what she calls "hints of Elizabethanism" in John Day, William Rowley, and George Wilkin's play *The Travels of the Three English Brothers* (1607), referring to those specific instances in the travel play that show discontent toward James I's policies (*id.*, 137–140). By the same token, she convincingly identifies the presence of Mainwaring's historical figure in the treatment of the characters of Dolimandro and Grimaldi, who appear in Mary Wroth's prose romance *Urania* (1621–c1626) and Philip Massinger's play *The Renegado* (1624) respectively. Her analysis of these works concludes that Mainwaring's historical character and career exemplify a new type of pirate marked by skillfulness, bravery, patriotism, and willingness to loyally serve the crown (Jowitt, 155–159 and 190–192). Building on Jowitt's arguments, in the following lines I will connect her notion of "hints of Elizabethanism" to Mainwaring's and Smith's incorporation of picaresque undertones to justify the origins of English pirates while they also emphasized the financial loss caused by James I's anti-piracy policies. I will also draw on her typology of the characteristics involved in the new type of pirate, embodied by Mainwaring, to establish a linkage between Mainwaring's idea of a "dutiful subject" and the financial considerations behind this conception.

Drawing on Claudio Guillén's seminal study of the characteristics of the picaresque model and how picaros transcend the very categories imposed upon them, we find that the authors in question employ several narrative patterns found in such literary genre. According to Guillén, picaros tend to conduct an itinerant life (a characteristic inherited from classical figures like Odysseus) and their narratives convey psychological and sociological interpersonal relations beyond isolation and static dynamics. By the same token, picaresque novels, mostly written as autobiographies, display a critique toward standard moral values and religious beliefs and highlight the corporeity of human existence by stressing a lack of money or food. Also, they offer a condensed viewpoint that considers the plurality of collective conditions that surrounds their characters (social classes, professions, cities or countries), thus emphasizing the international dimension of the narratives (Guillén, 76–84). One must not forget that the viewpoint of the picaro is always partial and influenced by the social and economic conditions the character had to endure, leading to the justification of his crimes and life of delinquency. In several examples, such as *Lazarillo de Tormes* and Mateo Alemán's *Guzmán de Alfarache*, the picaro pursues redemption and social acceptance that allows for the insertion of the character in the set of values and expectations pertaining to the society he once criticized.[53]

The Spanish picaresque novel was introduced to English readers as early as the 1560s with David Rowland's translation of *Lazarillo de Tormes* (1568) although the Spanish text had been placed on the Inquisition's Index of Prohibited Books in 1559.[54] More than a half-century later, an English translation of Alemán's *Guzmán de Alfarache*, titled *The Rogue*, by James Mabbe, appeared around 1621–1622. It has been argued that, while the former preyed upon the anti-Catholic viewpoints of Reformation England, the latter aimed to naturalize Alemán's work and take a political stand regarding the complex relations between England and Spain. As Paul Salzman asserts, Alemán's narrative displays both geographical and sociopolitical displacements because it "was much more concerned with vertical as well as horizontal travel, as Guzmán makes his way through Europe, as well as through a variety of professions, before returning to Spain" (Salzman, 152).

Mainwaring and Smith adopt an apologetic voice with picaresque undertones—namely the disadvantageous socioeconomic conditions and ambitions of these individuals—to explain the origins of piracy and rationalize why it prevailed in their society.[55] In their eyes, the story of an English pirate has less to do with innate ruthless traits to malign the "other" than with the need to fight the enemy or anyone else to survive and make a profit. Smith and Mainwaring were enduring an age when earlier "pirates," like Drake and Hawkins, did not align with the new diplomatic relations with Spain that had surpassed nationalistic and religious pretexts to validate maritime predation. These authors strongly believed that because of the peace agreement, former pirates or seamen became unemployed and stopped being role models for their and future generations:

> [B]ut me thinketh the best and surest way, and that which might much advance the wealth and glory of our State, were to devise some more universal employment than now we have, by which men of that spirit might not complain, as they now do, that they are forced for lack of convenient employment to enter into such unlawful courses. The proof of this is plain, for since your Highness' reign there have been more Pirates by ten for one, than were in the whole reign of the last Queen …
> (Mainwaring, 41)

> After the death of our most Gracious Queen Elizabeth of Blessed Memory, our Royal King James, who from his Infancy had Reigned in Peace with all Nations; had no imployment for those Men of Warr, so that those that were Rich relied with that they had; those that were poor and had nothing but from hand to Mouth, turned Pirates; some, because they became slighted of those for whom they had got much Wealth; some for that they could not get their Due; some that had lived bravely, would not abase themselves to Poverty; some vainly, only to get a name; others for Revenge, Covetousness, or as ill; and as they found themselves more and more oppressed, their Passions increasing with discontent, made them turn Pirates.
> (Smith, 59)

While Mainwaring was a former pirate who wrote his discourse to demonstrate his gratitude toward James I after receiving a royal pardon, Smith became the governor of Virginia and Admiral of New England and dedicated his writing to James I's successor, Charles I.[56] Their arguments to persuade their readers insert piracy into the picaresque model because they emphasize the redeemable traits of this sort of criminal at the dawn of publicly controlled markets or what would become European projects of mercantilist expansionism in the Americas. For instance, Mainwaring approaches the phenomenon of piracy from an economic perspective that links maritime predation with financial gain or loss. Unlike Spanish sources, his criminalization of piracy does not dwell upon moral misbehavior, but rather, he rationalizes piracy in economic terms. To repel piracy, he thus proposes to James I to hire those individuals:

> For by reason the Country be enriched very much by Pirates where they come, the Presidents of every place may be willing to protect and use them with all respect they may conveniently, to draw them to their quarters. All which is done under colour of sending to the State, to know if they shall be pardoned or not. In the meantime, they trim their Ships, spend their money, are well refreshed, and almost weary of the shore, so that Pardon or no Pardon they must of necessity go to Sea again, and of this there is a daily experience. These things being strictly commanded by your Highness, and duly and honestly observed by the Officers, will questionless be an infallible way to destroy all that are out, and so dishearten all that have any pretence that way that within a short time there will not be one English Pirate, nor any have encouragement to enter into it again; which though it may be some charge to your Highness, yet will the honour which your Majesty shall gain thereby, with the benefit to all Christendom, much preponderate the pressure of the expense ...
>
> (Mainwaring, 48–49)

Smith, on the other hand, compares pirates with those who worked in plantations and were initially "scorned contemned." He envisions the potential economic value of pirates—seamen and soldiers—if they were to be sent to those plantations. Through their work, Smith claims, they would regain their now lost decent reputation:

> Those Titles of Seamen and Soldiers, have been most worthily honoured and esteemed, but now regarded for the most part, but as the scum of the World; regain therefore your wonted Reputations and endeavour rather to Adventure to those fair Plantations of our English Nation; which however in the beginning were scorned contemned, yet now you see how many Rich and Gallant People come from thence, who went thither as Poor as any Soldier or Sailer, and gets more in one Year, than you by Piracy in seven. I intreat you therefore to consider how many Thousands yearly go thither; also how many Ships and Sailers are imployed to Transport them, and what Custom they Yearly pay to our most Royal King Charles, whose Prosperity and his Kingdom's good, I humbly beseech the Immortal God to preserve and increase ...
>
> (Smith, 60)

Along these lines, Mainwaring underscores their military skills and courage in battle while also stating that these individuals had spent "their whole life for the most part ... in a running prison." Instead of imprisonment—which would also require monetary investments from the Crown—or condemning them to the death penalty, he suggests the king preserve these men because "the State may hereafter want such men, who commonly are the most daring and serviceable in war of all those kind of people" (Mainwaring, 18). Also, he advises the king to provide "universal employment" to restrain individuals from engaging in piratical activities:

> [B]ut me thinketh the best and surest way, and that which might much advance the wealth and glory of our State, were to devise some more universal employment than now we have, by which men of that spirit might not complain, as they do now, that they are forced for lack of convenient employment to enter into such unlawful courses.
>
> (*id.*, 41)

The author recommends that the king either enslave pirates or take advantage of their skills and knowledge to haunt other pirates (*id.*, 44).[57] Another way to deal with pirates, he writes, is to enforce strict laws and punishments, as he did when he was a pirate (*id.*, 42–43). By the same token, English vice admirals should be carefully scrutinized because they might be accomplices of piratical activity when dealing with the proper distribution of booty (*id.*, 48).[58]

In the opening letter addressed to the king, Mainwaring underscores the assertion that he has declined several official pardons offered by foreign dukes who intended to hire his services as a pirate and as a merchant under flags overseas (*id.*, 11).[59] Besides pardons and great sums of money offered by both Christian dukes and Muslim rulers, he alleges that he has turned down several opportunities to enrich himself:

> I have abstained from doing *hurt* to any of your Majesty's subjects, where by it I might have *enriched* myself more than 100,000 pounds, being that most of the best ships that trade for the Straits, and the coast of Spain and Barbary, as also divers others have come through my fingers.
>
> (*id.*, 10)

Underlining that he was no longer a pirate enabled Mainwaring to prove that he was a "dutiful subject" who preferred to be obedient to his king and his country before his "own ends" (*id.*, 12).[60] In this way, the repeal of piracy becomes a means to define or validate someone's loyalty to his country, primarily exemplified by his ability to decline private financial profit. That is, to be a pirate in the seventeenth century is no longer to be a loyal subject making profit—private or public—out of the enemy. Mainwaring's concept of loyalty to a specific sovereign is directly associated with private financial gain or loss. Even if the pirate is considered a disloyal subject, Mainwaring hesitates when discussing whether such an individual deserves the death penalty. Although he openly asserts that pirates should not be pardoned, because if pardoned they will return to their old practices believing that they will get another pardon, Mainwaring justifies piracy by identifying its origins (*id.*, 21).[61]

The changing notion of what constitutes piracy is ultimately illustrated when Mainwaring claims that there were fewer pirates during Elizabeth I's reign: "The proof of this is plain, for since your Highness' reign there have been more Pirates by ten for one than were in the whole reign of the last Queen" (*id.*, 41).[62] Indeed, this opinion could be debatable because Queen Elizabeth's reign financially supported piratical activities like Drake's and others and therefore, there might have been even more pirates during her administration. Mainwaring's comparison demonstrates an ideological shift of the definition of piracy. That is, piracy changed from being an unstable concept due to its overlap with moral, political, religious, and economic discourses and became a legal term primarily oriented to regulating economic values related to private profit. Oscillating between condemning piracy and justifying it, Mainwaring's narrative emphasizes that piracy was not a question of immorality but of unemployment and the lack of economic resources for specific populations. In Mainwaring's eyes, to criminalize piracy was to suppress unregulated private profit, and those who declined potential financial gains followed the parameters of what constituted a dutiful subject during the first decades of the seventeenth century. By employing apologetic tones in several instances, both Smith and Mainwaring provide a nuanced picture of English and Irish pirates. In doing so, they advocate for the Crown's interference in issues related to state-run markets and the creation of a unified naval force.[63] To convert sea rogues into dutiful subjects, in their view, would positively contribute to economic burgeoning and to the political strength of their time.

In the 1590s Spanish insular authorities were also implementing measures intended to transform smugglers into dutiful subjects. For instance, in Hispaniola, Governor Diego Osorio Villegas attempted in 1598 to turn local smugglers into small militias; in exchange, they would receive full pardons for their crimes. However, following Osorio's demise in 1600, this project came to an end. As a result, such groups gained almost full control over contraband trade in the regions they used to patrol.[64] From the second half of the sixteenth century, the economic panorama in Hispaniola was at a crossroads between two types of merchant. The conflict was mainly carried on between those Spanish peninsular traders who aimed to ensure the Sevillian commercial monopoly on the island, and local merchants who were more flexible and preferred to take advantage of the lower prices, the variety of goods, and rates of exchange offered by non-Sevillian, unauthorized ships.[65] Certainly, notions of "honor" or moral misbehavior also surfaced in the discussion of contraband on the island. A great number of the Spanish peninsular prebendaries of the cathedral of the archdiocese of Santo Domingo stressed the correlation between illicit trade and the spreading of heresies and moral misbehavior in the local population by the late sixteenth and early seventeenth centuries (Ponce Vázquez, 71–73). The collective notion in Hispaniola was that smugglers did not pose a greater danger to their society than the local judges, who were paid excessive sums of money in their salaries.[66]

Moving closely to the transatlantic Caribbean geographical scenario, in the next chapter, I will further examine the debates related to sovereignty, dominion, and property, and how their rehearsal, in light of new political international developments, impacted the triangular relation between England, Spain, and the insular Caribbean. In that process, the manipulation of these issues transformed the image of the pirate and the traits conventionally attributed to this figure. In the next chapter, through the examination of the production of spaces intertwined with political and religious discourses, we will see other layers—or epistemological practices—that constituted and structured the category of piracy through its interrelation with notions of contraband based on particular peninsular and colonial economic interests in the Caribbean context during the late sixteenth and seventeenth centuries.

Notes

1 Found in Elizabeth I, *By the Queene: A Proclamation Agaynst the Maintenaunce of Pirates* (London: Powles Churchyarde by Richarde Iugge and Iohn Cawood, 1569; Early English Books Online Text Creation Partnership 2011), unnumbered, http://name.umdl.umich.edu/A21713.0001.001

2 The proclamation reads: "[n]either that any person do bye or receaue any wares or goodes of any person directly or indirectly comming from the seas, vntyll the same wares or goodes be brought and landed openly according to the lawes of the Realme in places accustomed, with consent of the officers of the customes, and that all dueties be first payde for the same, according to the vsage of marchauntes vpon payne that whosoeuer shal do the contrary, or be consenting therto, shalbe vpon due information committed to prison, there to remayne without bayle, vntyll inquisition be made (according to the lawes of the Realme) of them and their factes, *as in cases of piracies, and to be adiudged and executed as pirates, as by lawe shalbe ordered*" (emphasis added).

3 "Furthermore her Maiestie wylleth and commaundeth all maner her officers, and *specially Wardens of Portes, Uice admiralles, Constables, or Capitaines of Castles vpon the seas, and all other hauyng any office in Port townes or places of landyng*: that they shall foorthwith as they wyll aunswere at their vttermost peryll, to do their vttermost in their iurisdictions to enquire, lay wayte, and thereby apprehende all maner of persons that do haunt the seas with any kynde of vesselles armed, beyng not an apparaunt marchaunt" (emphasis added).

4 In the original wording: "*los quales con lo que roban dellos tan a su salvo, por llevar tan poca defensa*" (*cédula*, 3). Found in the *Ordenanças para remedio de los daños e inconuenientes, que se siguen de los descaminos, y arribadas maliciosas de los nauios que nauegan a las Indias occidentales*, first printed in 1569.

5 In 1577 the queen issued another commission against piracy, which was accompanied by a set of instructions detailing the legal procedures to deal with the capture of pirates, their ships, and their stolen goods. See Marsden's transcription of these instructions (Marsden, 218–219).

6 According to G.E. Manwaring in his introductory study of Sir Henry Mainwaring's work on piracy, it was not until 1635 under King Charles I's regime that a project was developed to protect the narrow seas and assert English sovereignty against the French and the Dutch. To this end, Charles created a system of policing the waters through annual "ship-money fleets" (Mainwaring, 228–229).

7 Drawing on recent Somalian piracy, Bueguer traces the generation of knowledge of piracy for the UN and the International Maritime Organization based on the analysis of three "archetypes" of epistemic practices—namely, the quantification and measurement; the interpretation of anthropological knowledge and intelligence work; and the networks of advisors combining both scientific and diplomatic knowledge. He argues that these epistemic practices "assemble different actors, knowledge, and claims, translate these, and manufacture representations to make piracy known at the UNSC. They represent different ways by which the UNSC knows piracy" (Bueguer, 14).

8 We also find the term *corsario* or *cursario* in the 15th, 16th, 17th, 18th, and later editions of King Alfonso X's thirteenth-century *Siete Partidas*. However, it is difficult to determine the exact date at which these terms were introduced into this collection since there are more than 100 earlier manuscripts, which sometimes differ in their content. The more complete and consulted compilations of this collection are the following printed editions: (1) Alonso Díaz de Montalvo's annotated incunable edition, printed in 1491 in Seville and reprinted several times (1501, 1528, 1542); (2) Gregorio López's edition, first published in 1555 and reprinted in 1565, 1576, 1587, 1598, 1610, 1829, and 1974; and (3) the Spanish Real Academia de la Historia's edition, printed in Madrid c1807. Instead of employing the conventional Spanish-language spelling of "corsair," which would be *corsario* or *cosario*, the three editions use *cursario*. The commonly quoted instance that alludes to the incorporation of corsairs into the Spanish naval forces is found in the Second *Partida* (Title XXIV, law I) in all of the Díaz de Montalvo editions, although it is ambiguous whether the words refer to the act of "corsairing" or to the "navigational course": "[L]a primera, es flota de galeas, e de naves armadas con poder de gente, bien así como la gran hueste que hace camino por la tierra; la segunda es armada de algunas galeas, o de leños corrientes, *e de naves armadas en curso*" (Díaz de Montalvo, unnumbered page, emphasis added). However, in each of the 1491, 1555, and c1807 editions, *cursario* appears twice and clearly refers to the figure of the "corsair" (Title XXVI, laws 30 and 31 of the same *Partida*). In the first case, the law emphasizes that, despite the fact that previously it was not customary to compensate *corsairs* for their labors or injuries, now they would be monetarily compensated and rewarded to increase their stimulation in the service of God and the lords who enlist them. On the other hand, the term is introduced in law XXXI, which stipulates that one who captures a corsair "who has committed depredations" is entitled to collect the corsair's booty if the captor follows specific protocols and procedures outlined by this law (Díaz de Montalvo, unnumbered page). For a modern Spanish edition, see José Sánchez-Arcilla's *Las Siete Partidas*, Editorial Reus 2004.

9 For the ordinances on corsairs, see "Ordinaciones de todo navio, que armara para ir en corso, y de toda, que se haga por mar," found in Cayetano de Palleja's Spanish edition of *Consulado del mar de Barcelona*. Barcelona: Imprenta de J. Piferrer, 1732.

10 "Primeramente, el Señor Rey ordena: que para continuar la guerra contra los Genoveses enemigos suyos, en sus Dominios seas armadas Galeras y Naos por Armadores, en la forma siguiente, es á saber: el Señor prestará á todo súbdito suyo que quiera armar Galeras, las que están carenadas, aparejadas, botadas al agua, y listas para navegar, con todas las armas … y otros pertrechos que necesiten … Item: el Señor Rey les proveerá la paga de un mes al sueldo acostumbrado, y los

The Changing Winds of Piracy (1570–1604) 181

víveres para quatro meses, si lo quisieren." Source: *Ordenanzas de las armadas navales de la Corona de Aragón, copiadas por D. Antonio de Capmany*. Madrid: Imprenta Real 1787, 63. Regarding the stipulations for corsairs who became deserters, see, in the same edition, the "Real Provisión a favor de los corsarios y armadores contra los desertores de sus embarcaciones" (*id.*, 70). Overall, sailors who decided to become corsairs were provided with ships, weapons, and other necessary resources. They received a month's pay in advance along with other privileges, such as full authority of criminal jurisdiction overseas and royal pardons, among others. See also Antonio de Capmany y de Montpalau. ed., *Memorias históricas sobre la marina, comercio y artes de la antigua ciudad de Barcelona*, Vol. 3. Barcelona: Imprenta de D. Antonio de Sancha, 1792.

11 As discussed in previous chapters, *Purchas His Pilgrimes* continued Richard Hakluyt's legacy of his *Principall Navigations*.

12 Richard Hawkins, son of John Hawkins, participated in Drake's Caribbean raid of 1585–86 and commanded one of the ships during the Armada battles in 1588. During James I's reign, he was a Member of Parliament around 1604 and vice admiral of Devon. He died in London in 1622.

13 In general terms, the "positive law" is an expression of the "natural law," which in turn is supposed to be an expression of the "eternal law." On the other hand, while "custom" is a practice considered law only by a collective of individuals who find it relevant, "prescriptive law" is a right acquired by old customs and not by "positive law." Hugo Grotius's *Mare liberum*, which was translated into English by Richard Hakluyt in 1609, establishes that a "custom" is a sort of "positive law" and, therefore, the sea should not be considered property by any specific nation or sovereign (Grotius, 43).

14 According to Rubin, "[t]here is some evidence that the Romans refused to extend the technical law of *postliminium* to them, perhaps on the ground that since they never ceased to be at war, there was no opportunity to determine the title to captured goods and no need to recognize title in those deriving rights from belligerent capture; the good remained subject to recapture by anybody, and the rights of *postliminium* would be applicable against the recaptor, just as in war goods recaptured before the end of hostilities reverted to their original owner subject only to payment of costs attributable directly to the recapturing action" (Rubin, 13).

15 "The law says 'robbers.' These are our pirates. It says 'a slave.' We speak in the same way of other things, because slaves are things. It says 'Germans,' that is, an enemy, just as the law afterwards explains, and a glossator, too. And therefore, the Berbers in this case of ours are enemies of the Spaniards in quite the same way" (Gentili, 51).

16 While discussing this religious current in relation to warfare as well as the moral viewpoint of Godfried/Godefridus Undemans (1581/2–1640) toward the military and political hostilities between Spain and the Low Countries, Joris van Eijnatten refers to the Calvinist tradition and traces back the English Puritan discourse on holy war to fifteenth-century Spanish arguments. He also mentions that among the characteristics of a holy war, according to Puritan authors from the sixteenth and seventeenth centuries, we find the following: (1) there is a religious cause; (2) it is intended to protect a religious faith and thus could be defensive or offensive, but just nonetheless; and (3) soldiers must be pious (Van Eijnatten, 194–196). However, according to Carl Schmitt's political theology, central concepts of the state are mainly secularized notions of theological concepts such as "jurisprudence," which "has an analogous meaning to that of the miracle in theology" (Schmitt 2006, 37).

17 Balthazar Ayala in *Three Books on the Law of War and on the Duties Connected with War and on Military Discipline*. Translated by John Pawley Bate, William S. Hein & Co., Inc., 1995.

18 According to Schmitt, the enemy is not necessarily an oppositional figure but can be an individual or collective that is equally capable of fighting with another individual or group. Thus, the enemy is less an *inimicus* (internal enemy) than a *hostis* (public enemy) (Schmitt 2002, 17). The pre-global-era lack of a homogeneous space contributed to the absence of a just enemy (*iustus hostis*) (Schmitt 2002, 35).

19 Specific economic interests drove the contingent legal understanding behind the legitimation of "customs." In the Spanish context, this became manifest through the traditional law of "one fifth to the Crown" that regulated the proper distribution of booty during this period. It is based on an enigmatic law denominated by the Spanish sources as: law of *delairon* or *delayron*. Diego de Encinas, in his anthology of previous laws, the *Cedulario indiano* (1596), refers to this law when describing the orders given to Pedro Arias de Ávila, governor and captain general of Tierra Firme, in 1513. José Veitía-Linage quotes the same law almost a century later in *Norte de la contratación de las Indias occidentales* (1672). However, he acknowledges that despite his research on the law's origins, he has not found anything about it. He reaffirms nonetheless that the law should be respected and followed. Even though it may appear superfluous, Veitía-Linage's observation is relevant to underline the instability and uncertainty of the legal vocabulary used and the predominance of the economic terms and conditions involved in the regulation of booty and captures.

20 See Bodin, *On Sovereignty: Four Chapters from the Six Books of the Commonwealth*. Edited and translated by Julian H. Franklin, Cambridge University Press, 1992.

21 However, according to Bodin, gifts that entail obligations and conditions are not true gifts, hence the sovereign must not have any restraints. Another interesting comparison is presented when Bodin discusses the sovereignty of a tyrant. He states that the tyrant is nonetheless a sovereign just as the violent possession of a robber is true and natural possession even though it is against the law (Bodin, 6). By the time of Bodin's writing, he clarified that Spain, France, England, and Turkey had sovereign princes.

22 Touching on the modern state, Janice Thomson asserts that sovereignty, while it organizes the political global space through territorial linkages, is a system based on ethics of exclusion (Thomson, Mercenaries, Pirates, and Sovereigns: State-Building and Extraterritorial Violence in Early Modern Europe, 13–14).

23 According to Benton, Gentili believed that a specific sovereignty could reach the space of a ship and protect its crewmembers under the parameters of such a sovereignty (Benton 2011, 229). According to Clarence Haring, it was not until 1670 that Spain acknowledged the British monarch's sovereignty upon the islands and colonies in the New World (Haring, 284).

24 In relation to Benton's conceptualization of sovereignty, she states that "Sovereignty did not have an even territorial or juridical dimension. Instead, sovereign spaces followed corridors of control, from estuary enclaves through river networks, and they depended on reinforcement through the formal incorporation of subjects in political communities, while sheer distance strained ties between subjects and sovereigns" (Benton 2010, 103). According to Schmitt, Bodin's biggest contribution to the concept of sovereignty relies on the power of decision held by the sovereign and, in turn, its capacity of signing peace, declaring war, and appointing public functionaries (Schmitt 2006, 15).

25 Analyzing Bodin's and Grotius's works, Kempe states that while Bodin opens his argument questioning the possibility whether a sovereign state or community could be distinguished from another created by pirates, Grotius "accepts that the state could have originated in a crime" (Kempe, 389–90).

26 According to Benton, before the mid-sixteenth century, authors drew their conception of property from Justinian's *Institutes*, which established four main categories:

public things (*res publicae*); common things (*res communes*); community things (*res universitatis*); and not-owned things (*res nullius*) (Benton 2010, 122).

27 Drawing on Perruso's work ("Development of the Doctrine of *Res Communes*"), Benton states that jurisdiction or "the right to collect taxes or other revenue, or even to hold court proceedings, could be attained by a state or individual in the same way that the state or the individual could acquire dominion under Roman law. Even if the sea could not be occupied, states could hold jurisdiction over it (established mainly through prescription or custom), and they could grant jurisdiction over it to others" (Benton 2010, 122).

28 The term also appears in the works of Hugo Grotius (1609) and Pedro González de Salcedo (1654).

29 "Capta, & perducta bona intra praesidia ese oportet. Nihil est tempus: de quo nihil considerat lex. Et vero nihil sit tempus hic, vbi sempre incerta est, quamdiu intra praesidia perducta non est."

30 "In quaestione, quae mihi erat pro Hispanis captis ab Hollandis, quibus erat non nihil maris arandum: errant radenda littoral inimica, eaque aduersus praedationes has intenta, & instructa: erant timendae coeli, marisque ruinae. Et merito igitur lex vult, ese bona perducta intra preaesidia. Praesidis vero non ese nauim, ad quam perducta erant bona capta, certum est: quae intermobilia numeratir: praesidia autem sunt stationes ... Praesidia sunt locus intra fines."

31 On the other hand, Ayala homogenizes land and sea by introducing a distinction between "movable things"—naval ships— and "immovable things"—land. Here, however, the definitions of both property and jurisdiction are related to the malleable notion of sovereignty discussed earlier.

32 A knight of the Order of Santiago, Valdés (sometimes spelled in primary sources as "Valdez" or "Valdéz") was captured by Drake in 1588. After his ransom was paid, he was released and went to the Netherlands, where he received news from the Elizabethan court every ten days. He was the governor of Cuba from 1602 to 1608. For more, see Gustav Ungerer, 127.

33 Valdés to the king, Brussels, March 19, 1593: "Se juntaron a parlamento y entre otras cosas las principales que pretendieron son dos. La una pedir Socorro de dineros para la armada que tienen entre manos que es la que he significado la qual tengo aviso hacen con muchos disignios y se dividira en diferentes partes a las yndias occidentales va la una y dicen con fin de tomar a Puerto Rico y fortificarle para ser señores del y hacer de alli sus salidas en la Havana y san juan de ulua tienen tambien puestos los ojos y creo estan desahuciados de poder tomar ninguna de aquellas plaças por el aviso que tienen que estan muy puestas en defensa. Tan bien antes de mi partida entendi tratavan de ocupar la ysla de curacao que esta entre nombre de Dios y Cartagena. Porque ay en ella mucha carne y oprimir desde alli a las naos que fueren y binieren a nombre de Dios. Mas yo temo que an de procurar de encontrarse con las flotas que ban a nueva hespaña y tierra firme." Found in BL, Add. MS 28420, fol. 87.

34 Valdés to the king, Brussels, March 29, 1593: "Con el primer aviso que tuviere sobre el fin que lleva y dare luego queja dello. A V.M. tambien me escriven que estando Francisco Draque adereçando y aprestando la armada por salir a la mar con mucha deligencia." Found in BL, Add. MS 28420, fol. 85.

35 Valdés to the king, Brussels, May 21, 1593: "[Y] que el conde de Conberland se apresta con mucha prisa y saldrá a la mar a fin deste y que lleua hasta veinte y cinco naos entre grandes y chicas, las ocho de la rreyna y suyas, y las demás de particulares, y que sale a uno de tres efectos: para aguardar las naos de la Yndia o para tomar a Puertorrico o Cartagena. Yo temo que dé en alguna de las flotas de Tierra Firme o Nueua España, no yendo con mejor orden de la en que hasta aquí an andado." Transcription found in Ungerer, 124–126.

184 The Changing Winds of Piracy (1570–1604)

36 For the complete transcription of Cumberland's commission to command ships against the king of Spain, invade by sea or by land, and distribute the spoils, see Reginald Godfrey Marsden's compilation *Documents Relating to Law and Custom of the Sea*, vol. I, 278–280.
37 About the history of the attack, see Enrique T. Blanco, 23–27.
38 In 1577 Sir Humphrey Gilbert proposed to seize Cuba and Hispaniola to establish an English base in the Caribbean to pressure Spanish authorities. However, the project did not materialize because the English Crown was more interested in keeping Scotland, Ireland, and the Low Countries out of Spanish control (Andrews 2018, 149). Two years later Gilbert was granted letters patent to establish a colony across the Atlantic, in Norumbega, bestowing on him the power to administer and control potential trading practices. In the sixteenth-century cartographic imagination, Norumbega occupied a place between Nova Scotia and Connecticut (Probasco, 426). For an analysis of Gilbert's voyage in 1583 and the role played by cartography as a means to promote English trans-atlantic colonization, see Probasco's article, 425–472. For an extract of his commission, see Marsden's, vol. I, 222–224. Although the scope of this book does not cover later English settlement projects involving piracy, it is worth mentioning that Cumberland's attack stands out because it was the only successful occupation in the Caribbean and also the only episode of which I have found evidence that links the English Crown directly to both maritime predation and orders for settlement.
39 For the complete transcription, see Marsden, vol. I, 313–317.
40 I will be using two editions of the treaty. The first is a version that contains a Latin transcription and Spanish translation of the original document, which is held by the AGS. It was compiled by Diego Peralta, Antonio Marin, and Juan de Zúñiga, eds., *Coleccion de los tratados de paz, alianza, neutralidad, garantia … hechos por los pueblos, reyes y principes de España con los pueblos, reyes, principes, republicas y demás potencias de Europa …* (Madrid 1740). The second is a Spanish coetaneous translation printed in Valladolid by Luis Sánchez: *Capitulaciones de la paz, entre el Rey nuestro señor, los … archiduques de Borgoña, sus hermanos y el Rey de Gran Bretaña …* (1605).
41 Two further treaties of peace between the nations were signed in 1630 and 1670.
42 See Salzman's article "Traveling or Staying in Spain and the Picaresque in the Early 1620s," (41) 1, 2011, 143–146. For a more detailed study of James's and Robert Cecil's plans, see Pauline Croft, "*Rex Pacificus*, Robert Cecil and the 1604 Peace with Spain" (140–154).
43 "[S]e abstendrán en adelante de todo genero de robo, presa, ofensa, y despojo en qualesquiera Reynos, Dominios, Lugares, y Señoríos de uno, ú otro. en cualquier parte situadas, assi en Tierra, como en Mar, y Aguas dulces … y harán restituir todo robo, despojo, y presa, y el daño que de ello se hiziere, ó causare."
44 "[N]inguno de los dichos Principes, ni de sus Herederos, y Successores qualesquiera obrara, hará, tratará, ò atentarà cosa alguna por sì, ni por otro qualquiera contra el otro, ni contra sus Reynos, Países, Dominios qualesquiera, en qualquier lugar, sea en Tierra, ò en Mar, en Puertos, ò Agua dulces con qualquiera ocasión."
45 "[S]e ha convenido, y establecido, que entre el dicho Serenísimo Rey de las Españas, y el dicho Serenísimo Rey de Inglaterra, y los Vassallos, Habitantes, y Subditos de qualquiera de ellos, tanto por Tierra, como por Mar, y Aguas dulces en todos … sea y deba ser libre el comercio en aquellos lugares."
46 "Que no se permitan piraterias, y se revoquen las comisiones y cartas de marca para salir a robar" (see *Coleccion*, edited by Peralta, Marin, and Zúñiga, 8). "[R]evoquen qualesquier comissiones y cartas, assi de repressallas como de marca, que tuvieren facultad de robar, de qualquier genero o condicion" (*id.*). The Latin version states the same: "[R]evocentque quascunque commissiones et litteras tam represaliarum

seu de marca, quam facultatem predandi continentes cuiuscumque generis aut conditionis sint" (*id.*, 251).

47 For more about the history and technical distinctions of letters of marque, letters of reprisal, and *licentia marcandi* from the late Middle Ages to the sixteenth century, see the Introduction of this book and Rubin's *The Law of Piracy*, 8–26.
48 Rubin points out that the word "reprisal" refers to French *retrieve* and that the origins of the term "marque" are as yet obscure and but that "it might have been related to a provencal technical term associated with a law of 'promise'" (Rubin, 21).
49 "[Q]ualesquiera que contravinieren sean castigados, y demas de la pena criminal, los conpelan a que restituyan los daños que huuieren hecho."
50 I refer to editor G.E. Manwaring's study and edition of one of Henry Mainwaring's copies of his manuscript (2 volumes, 1920–1922). Regarding the lack of proper monitoring, Mainwaring states that: "[E]nglish Pirates do first arm and horse themselves within your Highness' Dominions, as well England as Ireland, which the easier happens by reason that there are divers places (and chiefly such as are not capable of great shipping), that have no command, as also by the negligence of the Owners of such small Ships, that having no force to defend them keep ill watch, and leave their Sails aboard; wherein those Officers cannot be excused, that do not discreetly look into the disposition and resorts of such sea-men as either are within, or near their Harbours" (Mainwaring, 14).
51 According to Jowitt, James implemented this amnesty reluctantly. At the time, twelve pirate captains and their crews accepted his general pardon (Jowitt, 152).
52 In 1603, James I issued a proclamation recalling all letters of marque. Two years later, he forbade English sailors to work in foreign ships (Mainwaring, vol. 1, ix). The "trade" or the "trade of Brittany" refers to the illegal commercial activity carried out between English and Irish merchants and pirates in the passage of de L'Iroise and on the coasts of Spain and Barbary (see Mainwaring, vol. 2, 14). For more about the procedures and protocols involved in such "trades," see Mainwaring's description (*id.*, 17). The term "trade" appears in Robert Cawdrey's *A Table Alphabeticall* (1604) in the definitions of the words: "function" ("calling, or charge, or trade, a place wherein a man liueth"); and "vocation" ("trade of life"). See Cawdrey, 4th ed., 1617, London: Printed by W.I. for Edmund Weauer at North doore of Paules Church.
53 Garrido Ardila acknowledges that while scholarship has identified a "clear tradition" of the picaresque, he points out that "others have contended that the *picaresque novel* is merely a critical construction forged in the eighteenth century" (*The Picaresque Novel in Western Literature*, 2015b, 2). Howard Mancing, on his part, identifies three phases of the picaresque novel: (1) the first manifestations of the genre (1599–1610); (2) the height of its popularity (1610–1630); and (3) the twilight of the picaresque (1630–1650) (see *The Picaresque Novel*, 48).
54 Rowland's translation was reprinted in 1586, 1596, 1624, and 1631 (Salzman, 142).
55 According to Guillén, the character of the pícaro incorporates and transcends a previous typology of characters and traditions: (1) the errant (Odysseus, Greco-Roman); (2) the jester (*bufón*, Italian novella); and (3) the thief or the criminal (Guillén, 76). According to his analysis, the subject of Alemán's *Guzmán de Alfarache* (1599), which was also published in English (1622), is a hero who after embracing and surpassing his economic and social calamities becomes an exemplary Christian (*id.*, 88).
56 Mainwaring held several official posts such as Lieutenant of Dover Castle and Deputy Warden of the Cinque Ports (1620–1623) and Vice Admiral of the ship-money fleets (1639–1640) (Mainwaring, vol. 1, xii–xiv).
57 "Commanders as know how to work and command like a man-of-war, where to find, how to draw himself to them … with a ready wit and judgment, to do

sometimes that upon the occasion for he can have no direction or rule, which thing is only mastered by experience, particular use, and knowledge of these things."

58 "Further there must be a strict course, and duly executed, that no Vice-Admiral, or other, be suffered to speak with any of the Pirates, but to forfeit either life or goods, for so long as they have any communication with them, so long will there be indirect dealing and relieving of them."

59 Mainwaring mentions that the Duke of Medina Sidonia asked him to deliver Mamora, a pirates' stronghold, to the Spanish king; the Duke of Savoy also sent him a pardon; and the Duke of Florence even "gave leave to the ship to wait on me till I was willing to come in, which did so for a great while." The Dey of Tunis proposed that he stay with him and if he did, he promised to "divide his estate equally" and never urged him to "turn Turk" (Mainwaring, vol. II, 11).

60 "By these it may appear to your Majesty that I did not labour my Pardon as one being banished from all Christian Princes, but as a dutiful subject preferring the service of my country and my particular obedience to your Royal person before my own ends."

61 Regarding the pardons, Mainwaring claims that sometimes pirates get a pardon and then commit a crime, but have a friend who gets them another pardon. By the same token, he mentions that there are other pirates who place their hopes in another Anglo-Spanish conflict that will gain them another pardon: "They have also a conceit that there must needs be wars with Spain within a few years, and then they think they shall have a general Pardon" (Mainwaring, 21).

62 More than a decade later, Captain John Smith in *True Travels* also states that piracy increased under James I's reign for economic reasons: "some, for that they could not get their due; some, that had lived bravely, would not abase themselves to poverty; some vainly, only to get a name; others for revenge, covetousness, or as ill; and as they found themselves more and more oppressed, their passions increasing with discontent, made them turne Pirates" (Smith, 59).

63 According to editor G.E. Manwaring, the first decades of the seventeenth century witnessed the unification of the Cinque Ports, which allowed the configuration of a regular fleet that substituted medieval notions of naval militia (Mainwaring, vol. 1, ix).

64 Juan José Ponce-Vázquez elaborates on the accommodating measures for smugglers taken in Hispaniola by the end of the sixteenth century and their repercussions in the culture of contraband in the island as the epicenter of illicit trade in the circum-Caribbean region (Ponce-Vázquez 2020, 94–97).

65 Governor Ovalle (discussed in Chapter 3), in 1584, received rerouted ships bound for Brazil. In his letter, addressed to the Council of the Indies, he justifies his actions by pointing out the division between two types of merchants: (1) those who were peninsular merchants and wanted to keep Santo Domingo an exclusive market for Sevillian ships; and (2) those local merchants "who welcomed merchants who could provide them with goods at more competitive prices" (Ponce Vázquez, 60).

66 Ponce-Vázquez states that by 1585, the prosecutor of the Audiencia de Santo Domingo, Francisco de Aliaga, complained about the amount of the judges' salaries and suggested that "since the land was poor, it was better to leave some crimes unpunished and help the residents of the region than to burden them with judges" (Ponce-Vázquez 2020, 80).

6 The Aftermath
The Emergence of New Models of Piracy in the Caribbean Buccaneers and Freebooters (Conclusion)

In 1588, the celebration of Corpus Christi in the city of Santo Domingo included a "short play" (*entremés*) composed by a prebendary and teacher, Cristóbal Llerena. The main plot of Llerena's *entremés* revolved around the birth of a monster on the island of Hispaniola and the interpretations provided by four classical figures that appear to analyze this event: Edipo, Delio, Proteo, and Calcas. The monster represents the population of Santo Domingo, through which Llerena criticizes issues ranging from corrupt royal officials and contraband to changes in local currency and moral decay.[1] Above all, the satiric interlude promotes the need for better and stronger systems of defense as well as trade concessions from Spain (Johnson 1988, 41). By the same token, the *entremés* showcases the economic and political tensions between the conditions of two societies in Hispaniola: the Creoles and the peninsular Spanish.[2] In this short play, the character of Calcas, who claims to have been asked to foretell wars and attacks, interprets the monster as an omen to warn the population about a forthcoming attack.[3] Considering the fact that Francis Drake had besieged Santo Domingo (as discussed in Chapters 2 and 3) two years prior to Llerena's *entremés*, such an omen does not seem far from the truth. However, contrary to what really happened during Drake's attack and employing a satirical tone, one of the *alcaldes* replies to this prediction that they have nothing to fear because they are well equipped to repel any attack.[4] As one could expect, the drama was not well received by ecclesiastical and colonial authorities; as a result Llerena was deported for a year without a trial and was sent to Riohacha (today's eastern part of Colombia).[5] I reference this play because it became a device for Llerena, a Creole himself, to pen and even foretell the social calamities, political and military struggles, and economic crisis that will trouble the Hispanic insular Caribbean during the seventeenth century. While Drake's figure is not directly mentioned, his attack is indirectly alluded to. In this sense, the short play is a prelude to the shifting notions related to maritime predation as well as the reasons behind them, which I will discuss in this chapter.

After the establishment of peace between England's King James I (1603–25) and Spain's King Philip III (1598–1621) in 1604, new categories of piracy

DOI: 10.4324/9781003141495-7

emerged in both the Caribbean and Mediterranean geographical contexts. On the one hand, former English maritime predators, having lost their private income, joined Barbary corsairs in the Mediterranean, while others, like Captain Henry Mainwaring (discussed in Chapter 5) were hired by the English Crown to police and capture their former accomplices. In the Caribbean, Dutch and French sailors who had previously engaged in contraband trade, mostly related to the illegal purchase of tobacco and salt, continued to carry out their illegitimate businesses. However, due to the lack of efficient Spanish policing, they encountered an even more divided geopolitical Caribbean scenario marked by the increasing establishment of English, French, and Dutch colonial bases on several islands.[6] By the same token, new foreign trading institutions emerged, such as the Dutch West India Company (WIC), in 1621, an organization that sponsored sea rovers and smugglers like the Calvinist Admiral Piet Heyn.[7] The French established the French West India Company (*Compagnie francaise des Indes occidentales*), in 1635, and the English founded the Providence Island Company, in 1629, which operated in the islands of St. Christopher, Tortuga (in part), and San Andrés.[8]

These and other subsequent shifts in European powers, such as the Peace of Westphalia (1648) and the rise of merchant empires and political leaders such as Oliver Cromwell (1643–1651), who envisioned an English imperialist project in the Caribbean, coincided with the flourishing of a different kind of piracy along with new labels that defined it.[9] For instance, the Caribbean archipelago was the stage for the articulation of the figure of the Buccaneer. From the 1580s, several Spanish colonial authorities and functionaries in Hispaniola proposed the depopulation of the northern part of the island as the best solution to decreasing contraband in the region. However, it was not until 1605, under King Philip III's administration, that the several issued *cédulas* became effective and the process of depopulation of northern Hispaniola started accordingly.[10] This historic juncture proliferated the settlement of marginal societies, primarily constituting renegade Europeans and marooned sailors. Thus, the early seventeenth-century project of depopulating northern Hispaniola to deter contraband practices resulted in the increasing establishment of mainly-French sedentary communities known as the "Buccaneers." In this sense, the remedy proved worse than the disease.

Etymologically, the French term *boucanier*, from which we get "buccaneer," derives from an indigenous word *boucan* that referred to a particular wooden grate on which they cooked their meat and the particular way they prepared a kind of beef jerky or smoked meat.[11] In the seventh volume of his account titled *Nouveau voyage aux isles de l'Amérique*, Jean-Baptiste Labat (1663–1738), the "Pirate Priest," describes these practices during an exchange between "two hunters" (*deux chasseurs*) from a Caribbean island and the crewmembers of Labat's ship.[12] The two hunters brought pig meat, both fresh and smoked (*de Cochon frais & de boucané*), and were given wine and brandy, among other products, in exchange (Labat, 232). In chapter IX, Labat describes how they cooked their meat and, after sharing provisions and attending a *boucan*, stresses that this way of cooking meat was less heavy on their stomachs and that they had a good sleep and even woke up because they were hungry again.[13] These "hunters," known as *boucaniers* or buccaneers, were mainly French adventurers who "when chased by the Spanish from the smaller Caribbean islands to the larger Saint-Domingue, became hunters and *hommes de la brousse*, or bushmen" (Toczyski, 65).[14] The buccaneers mainly traded cured meat, tobacco, and sugar with non-Spanish looters known as freebooters or filibusters and lived under their own social, economic, and political code.[15] Labat describes the filibusters as "those who were navigating" (*Filibustiers, c'est ainsi qu'on apelle ceux qui vont en course*).[16] Unlike sixteenth-century pirates or corsairs like Francis Drake and John Hawkins (discussed heretofore in this book), the buccaneers established a sedentary lifestyle in the Caribbean at the margins of European sovereign powers, marking the beginning of what historians have called the Golden Age of Piracy (1650–1730).[17] This multinationally controlled Caribbean also gave rise to the advent of renowned buccaneers such as Captain Henry Morgan (1635–68), whose accounts were reported and published by Alexandre Exquemelin (1645–1707) in *The Buccaneers of America* (1684).[18] Caribbean-born sailors also joined European sea rovers, as in the case of Diego the Mulatto, a former slave from Havana, Cuba, who joined Dutch looters and after eight years of service was made a captain.[19]

The constant attacks on the colony of Hispaniola, the first significant Spanish stronghold in the Americas, led to the Peace of Ryswick (1697), by which the French were granted official permission to settle on the island. In this context Labat, the Pirate Priest, spent 12 years in the Caribbean, and in 1701 he visited Hispaniola as a missionary of the Dominican Order. Besides his descriptions of the *boucans* and other topics, Labat paid attention to the illegitimate trade conducted on the island, at the time populated and controlled by French and Spanish powers. In theory, according to Labat's description, under the buccaneers' law no one was allowed to trade with any subject of the Spanish Crown.[20] However, the Pirate Priest also recounted the ways in which this law could be evaded, including bribes and strategies of a related sort.[21] Smuggling of smaller cargoes of the English, French, and Dutch was usually conducted at night and far from the towns. No credit was allowed; the transactions were mediated by cash or products found in the region.[22] According to Labat, the guns used in the Caribbean islands were called *boucaniers* after the buccaneers because they made these weapons ubiquitous in Hispaniola.[23]

Unlike sixteenth-century pirates and corsairs, the buccaneers in the Caribbean had intermittent ties, as well as relations with European powers (France, England, and the Netherlands), that were primarily motivated by individual political and economic profit. In other words, sixteenth-century collective claims of European political and religious rivals were replaced by private economic interests and political agendas. By the same token, those

English individuals who engaged in pillaging and reprisal voyages during the seventeenth century, sponsored by a specific European national power, became "privateers," a term that did not exist in the previous century.[24] As a response to this new scenario, semi-controlled by foreign powers and marginal societies in both the Mediterranean and Caribbean regions, the Spanish Crown in 1601 enforced the first Ordinance for Corsairs, allowing armed shipowners *(armadores)* to attack and seize foreign ships and booty by paying stipulated sums of money to the Crown.[25] On the one hand, these new models of piracy entailed the articulation of different labels while on the other, sixteenth-century maritime attackers like Drake became stable national icons, revived and reframed to support narratives of emerging merchant empires.[26]

Undoubtedly, at this point Sir Francis Drake had become a brand. His infamous (or famous) legacy involved the rebranding of his image in English nationalistic projects and in Spanish peninsular and Spanish American epic poetry of the seventeenth century, as discussed in the previous chapters. The insular Hispanic Caribbean was not an exception in retrieving his figure. Both his successes and his failures were penned with several purposes that ranged from gaining the attention of the Spanish Crown and justifying certain economic measures and trading practices, to stressing the geopolitical importance of the Caribbean in light of new invaders and models of piracy—the buccaneers and freebooters. In this context, Drake's Caribbean raids of 1585–86 and 1595–96, in particular, drew the attention of several Spanish individuals relocated in the Caribbean. Colonial Caribbean authorities and individuals used the discourse on piracy to underscore the dangers produced by theft. This in turn enabled the exercise of power on several levels: political, military, economic, and religious. Among these uses, we find the illegitimacy of foreign navigation in the New World— mainly English, French, and Dutch—and the rejection of religious reformist ideas like Protestantism. However, as we shall see further, the phenomenon of contraband in the Caribbean nuanced the limits of piracy and its justifications, as several individuals—sailors, merchants, and historians—attest in their writings from the late sixteenth to mid-eighteenth centuries.

In this conclusion chapter, I will focus on three main thematic components: (1) the retrieval of the figures of Drake and later foreign interlopers to underscore the geopolitical importance of the region in historical reports; (2) the measures taken in the Caribbean to deter contraband and promote local economic activity, which included projects of enclosing the islands with walls and fortresses (called *intrapraesidia* ["within the prison"]) and their presence in epic poetry and historical accounts; and (3) the articulation of Caribbean paradoxical suspicious "dutiful subjects" that parallel those examined in the Chapter 5, such as Henry Mainwaring and John Smith. However, before delving into these issues, I would like to stress three aspects that characterize the narratives emerging from or upon the Caribbean. First, the task of writing the history of the insular Hispanic Caribbean is closely related to the history of maritime predation.[27] Second, this history shows constant efforts by colonial authorities to ask for immediate economic boosts, and to propose specific measures related to the improvement of local military defense or call out internal colonial corruption. Finally, these narratives, although marked by a lack of records and documentation in the islands, also attempted to increase the status of the region based on the continuing interest and increasing establishment of foreign powers rivaling Spain—namely the English, Dutch, and French.

Drake's Revival in Caribbean Historical Narratives and Geopolitics

It was not until the eighteenth century that Bishop Fray Íñigo Abbad y Lasierra, in his *Historia geográfica civil y natural de las islas* (1788), included Diego de Torres Vargas's (1590–1649) account and inaugurated in the official sense the historiographical Caribbean tradition that included chapters related to maritime predation in the islands carried out by the English, the French, and the Dutch.[28] Besides the attacks in the Caribbean, colonial authorities also faced another enemy: the lack of records about the history of the Spanish Caribbean strongholds. The lack of documentation for the writing of history and its relation to maritime predation are attested by Torres Vargas in his lament about the lack of documents in the archives of Puerto Rico due to two enemy attacks that devastated the main city: "la falta de papeles que tienen los archivos, con los sacos y invasiones de los enemigos, que han robado dos veces la Ciudad" (Abbad y Lasierra, 459). Delving into classical myths such as the notion of the Hesperides islands, alluding to contemporary works of history like those of Antonio de Herrera y Tordesillas, and quoting the Augustinian friar and poet Luis de León, Torres Vargas provides a comprehensive description of Puerto Rico that exhibits an enthusiastic though occasionally pessimistic tone. Prior to these historiographical efforts, we find official historical documentation contained in epistles and *relaciones* to the Council of the Indies and in Spanish questionnaires about maritime predation (discussed in Chapter 4) that dealt with Drake's 1595–1596 attack. We also have the project of *Relaciones Geográficas*, contained in Juan Melgarejo's report, which will be discussed further.

Francisco Dávila y Lugo (1588–1662) is one of the authors who exemplify the conjunction between the retrieval of Drake's figure and the geopolitical importance of Puerto Rico; he evoked Drake's 1595 attack as a framework to persuade the Spanish king about the benefits of the island (Rabell, 143). Born in Madrid, he was granted a license to travel to the Viceroyalty of Peru with a stopover in Puerto Rico. He left the peninsula in June 1620 but settled on the island instead of continuing to Peru. He remained there until 1629, when he was captured by the Dutch corsair Johann Adrián Hauspater, acting on behalf of the Dutch West India Company.[29] While the motives behind Dávila y Lugo's decision to stay on the island are unknown, it has been claimed that they might be related to family ties and contacts: he was the grandson of Francisco Bahamonde de Lugo, the first appointed governor of Puerto Rico (1564–1568), who had previous military experience (*id.*, 22). Author of *Teatro Popular* (Madrid 1622), a collection of eight novellas, Dávila y Lugo also wrote *Discurso sobre la importancia y conservación de la plaza e isla de Puerto Rico*. Addressed to King Philip IV and written in Flanders, the *Discurso* was based primarily on his experience in the island and the information he collected from the Dutch, who held him captive for 15 months.[30] Structured in nine parts,[31] Dávila y Lugo's *Discurso* revolves around several topics related to Puerto Rico—its agricultural and economic potential, its geopolitical standing, and corruption schemes carried out by high officials that contributed to its then-current deplorable scenario. Referring to Drake as a corsair—not as a pirate, like several previous sources discussed in this book—the author retrieves Drake's figure by stating that "even the English captain" was able to acknowledge the island's potential as a stronghold and he told his queen that, because of its location, it controlled all the navigational routes of the Spanish Crown.[32]

The 80-year conflict between Spain and the Dutch, initially triggered by religious differences, became a war for control of economic power. The resolution of this conflict was a strategic alliance between the Spanish monarchy and the Dutch Republic, which openly declared itself to be mercantilist. Spain tolerated the open attitude of the Dutch toward religion because of the need to protect its imperial power against France, which eventually led to the secularization of the Spanish Catholic monarchy's international policy; tolerance was prompted as well by commercial interests (Rabell, 49). According to Carmen Rabell's study on the *Discurso*, this historic juncture influenced the author's notion of pragmatism and of a secular political mentality that permeates that work.[33] The *Discurso* reached the hands of Spain's King Philip IV through his aunt, the infanta Isabel Clara Eugenia, in 1630 and had several positive repercussions ranging from the fortification of the capital city of San Juan to the auditing of high-ranking insular officials and the reformation of the position and functions of the governor.

Dávila y Lugo fashions Drake as a "great corsair," "practical," and "wise," who amassed experiential and speculative knowledge to convince his queen that by possessing the island she would become by extension the master of all navigation undertaken between the Spanish Crown and the West Indies (*id.*, 138).[34] In this sense Drake becomes a stable figure as a corsair who embodied European foreign interests to the Spanish Crown in the islands. Referring to Cumberland's 1598 attack, the author claims that not even Drake's failure and death discouraged the intention of the queen and her council to capture the island because its strategic location would have served as a military base to interlopers or enemies who aimed to control the Indies (*id.*, 155).[35] This rhetoric about the island based on its alleged geopolitical importance resurfaces where Dávila y Lugo details the specifics of Dutch Admiral Boudewijn Hendricksz's attack of 1625 and the increasing Dutch ambition to capture the island (*id.*, 153–54).

Another retrieval of Drake's figure and other interlopers is seen through the eyes of another Caribbean individual. Born in the city of San Juan, Diego de Torres Vargas (c1590–1649) wrote *Descripción de la Ciudad e Isla de Puerto Rico* (1647), a work considered the first structured historical narrative from the viewpoint of a Puerto Rican. The Salamanca-educated Creole priest touches upon diverse topics including: the conditions that had repeatedly triggered the depopulation of the island; the lives of Spanish ecclesiastical, political, and military figures; the external and inner beauty of the feminine population; and the local miracles (which had yet to be officially confirmed). He pays particular attention to several invasions undertaken by the English (Drake in 1595 and Cumberland in 1598), and the Dutch attack of 1625. He mentions Drake's failed 1595 invasion to underscore the victorious endeavors of Governor Pedro Suárez and Captain Pedro Tello, which in his view attested to the efficiency of the transatlantic system of dispatches (*avisos*) that alerted the population beforehand.[36] Contrary to this viewpoint, and referring to Hendricksz's attack, Dávila y Lugo in his *Discurso* openly accuses then-Governor Juan de Haro of being negligent, cowardly, and crooked (*id.*, 165–66).[37]

The Lack of Proper Defense: Intrapraesidia Spaces and Corruption

From the 1580s, one of the main concerns of Spanish officials was the lack of proper colonial defense in terms of military men and infrastructure. King Philip II's regime undertook the project called *Relaciones Geográficas*, whereby the colonial officials had to answer a set of questions about different topics ranging from natural resources to military defenses, among others. The governor and captain general of the island of San Juan (Puerto Rico), Juan Melgarejo, appointed the clergyman Juan Ponce de León II and the lawyer Antonio de Santa Clara to compile the required information to answer the questionnaire sent from Madrid.[38] Finished in 1582, the answering document stresses the dangers to settlements close to the sea, like town of Nueva Salamanca, which had to be moved inland because of French attackers who pillaged it several times. Besides French interlopers, the document stresses the internal threat embodied by indigenous Caribs, who also attacked the town and torched it.[39] Using Nueva Salamanca as a metonymic device to represent the totality of the island, the authors declared that the city of San Juan suffered from the same symptom: "the lack of proper defense against corsairs."[40] Later authors would allude to other attacks to emphasize both the foreign European threat and the local bravery that repelled the attacks.

Legal historian Lauren Benton, while exploring the various layers of sovereignty in several European imperial enclaves, pays particular attention to the prerogatives and limits of the legal framework in the regimes of force found in penal colonies in Caribbean slave societies from the eighteenth century. She argues that, in theory, "[i]f penal colonies were prisons, their governors could be styled as wardens. Even if some wardens might treat prisoners harshly, their prerogative to punish, and the sovereign power of the state behind them was not in dispute" (Benton 2010, 217). However, she also states that in practice

> the delegated legal authority of penal colonies was anything but simple to define. Most if not all, penal colonies had inhabitants other than convicts, and the presence of soldiers and settlers automatically posed the anomalous situation of non-convicts living under a disciplinary order not intended for them.
>
> (*id.*, 217–218)[41]

In this regard, Spanish peninsular authorities authorized additional construction of military walls and fortresses to protect the coasts of the capital cities of Cuba, Puerto Rico, and Hispaniola. For instance, after Francis Drake's 1595 attack in the term of Governor Alonso de Mercado, construction of the Castle of El Morro was begun; other fortresses were also built or repaired in Cuba and Hispaniola. Additionally, in Hispaniola, as already mentioned, the Spanish Crown ordered and enforced from 1604 to 1606 the depopulation of its northern coast in an effort to dissuade local and foreign smugglers who engaged in contraband practices in that zone. Whereas the cities of Havana, Santo Domingo, and San Juan were not technically penal colonies during the late sixteenth and seventeenth centuries, they nonetheless became enclosed cities, styled in a medieval fashion, whose prisonlike architecture had a twofold socioeconomic impact: on the one hand, the walls protected the inhabitants from maritime attacks, while on the other, they sheltered internal administrative corruption based on contraband practices.

Going back to Gentili's concept of fortified lines, these cities could also be understood as *intrapraesidia* spaces where booty captures became legitimate and the governors and high officials became "wardens" of corruption and contraband. In this sense, piracy became less of a problem than a business opportunity circumventing the Spanish peninsular commercial monopoly. By the same token, contraband increasingly disguised piracy and vice versa, as we shall see further. With this, I do not aim to provide a historical reconstruction of the events or facts described below but rather, I will trace narrative patterns, dissimilarities, metaphors, and analogies that were involved in the nuanced construction of the discourse on piracy. Drawing on reexamination of fortified lines and Benton's notion of penal colonies, I argue in what follows that the Caribbean locus emerged as a geographical *intrapraesidia* zone where one might potentially gain or lose ownership over a stolen property and where contraband disguised piracy.

As discussed in Chapter 5, Alberico Gentili stated that, unlike seas and ships, a fortified line was a firm and steady ground (Gentili, 5). To claim legitimate ownership of a booty capture, the lawyer from Perugia (relocated in London) argued that the booty or prize had to be taken to such a fortified line and remain there for three days. As long as the stolen property remained on the ship or outside the fortified line, the captor was not the legitimate owner: the right of ownership still resided with the prior possessor (*id.*, 10). Up to this point, everything seems to be crystal clear. However, what happens when such a fortified line covers the borders of a Caribbean city like San Juan, where booty captures became the main products of exchange and high-ranking officials were their distributors within its walls? Or what happens when the seacoast becomes the sole fortified line or "steady ground" where citizens, colonial authorities, and religious figures were more than willing to trade stolen property to promote the local economy—as in the cities of Manzanillo and Yara in Cuba? In all, how can we understand the European concept of fortified lines in the Hispanic Caribbean context? How do these places rearrange the notions and dynamics of contraband in Gentili's period and in later debates? What were the justifications, condemnations, or rhetorical solutions for contraband put forth by individuals, like the buccaneers described by Labat?

I will now discuss the notion of "prison" in Silvestre de Balboa Troya Quesada's epic poem, *Espejo de Paciencia* (1608). Originally from Gran Canaria, Balboa arrived in Cuba around 1592 and worked as a notary. His only known epic poem tells of the historical attack carried out by the French pirate Gilberto Girón, his abduction of Bishop Juan de las Cabezas de Altamirano, his eventual release, and the pirate's death at the hands of the residents of Yara.[42] From such a reassurance of two conflicting notions of honor (as discussed in Chapter 2), Balboa uses the notion of "prison" at several levels. First, in the opening cantos, the poet refers to the "prison" endured by the bishop in the French pirate's ship (which Gentili would call a "non-fortified line"): "Que yo en mis versos solo escribo y canto / la prisión de un obispo consagrado, / tan justo, tan benévolo, y tan quisto, / que debe ser el sucesor de Cristo (Balboa, v 5–8).[43] In subsequent verses of the first canto, Balboa makes note of the sort of enclosed port or, may I say, "imprisoned port" of Cuba that was sequestered by the Spanish Crown:

> Tiene el tercer hijo Filipo, Rey de España, / la ínsula de Cuba, o Fernandina, / en estas Indias que el océano baña, / rica de perlas y plata fina: / aquí del Anglia, Flandes y Bretaña / a tomar vienen puerto en su marina / muchos navíos a trocar por cueros / sedas y paños, y a llevar dineros.
>
> (*id.*, v 65–72)

This port, as well as others on the island, was a subject of vigilance; and the bishop, acting like a warden, was accustomed to visiting such unprotected areas to make sure they were clean of contraband or dangers:

> De los prelados es costumbre Antigua / visitar estos hatos cada año; / porque con su presencia se averigua / si malicia o incuria le hacen daño; / y si hay persona dentro, o bien contigua, / que cual polilla ruin

maltrata el paño, / la echan de la hacienda el mismo día, / y así conservan la memoria pía.

(*id.*, v 97–104)

Here the paradox inheres in the two "prisons" of Cuba: one being the enclosed port commercially controlled by the Spanish Crown's monopoly, and the other one being the heretic space or the French pirate's ship, where the bishop had to endure several calamities, including those related to his honor: "Y mandándole a voces don Gilberto / que se rindiese al fin sin más porfías: / se dio a prisión; sin duda el peor estado / a que puede llegar un hombre honrado" (*id.*, v 229–232). The bishop acknowledges the French pirate's prison because he believes God intends for him to overcome the miseries anticipated for an obedient disciple of Catholicism: "[T]e pido por las penas que pasaste / me libres hoy de esta prisión y pena, / pues un pastor para tu iglesia cobras; / que el verdadero amor se ve en las obras" (*id.*, v 317–320); "Pero si tu piedad quiere y consiente / que tenga esta prisión por beneficio, / a todo estoy sujeto y obediente" (*id.*, v 321–23).[44] The bishop is released from his imprisonment when the citizens of Manzanillo, Bayamo, and Yara agree to pay 200 ducats and 100 arrobas of meat and bacon.[45] The bishop, however, suspects that some locals might have had a hand in his capture.[46] In the second canto, a Black Creole kills the French pirate; and afterward, Girón's head is raised on a stick in the main plaza with everybody celebrating the end of the bishop's imprisonment and their role in freeing him.[47] In this poem the bishop endures two spaces of confinement: one dominated by the Spanish Crown's monopoly (granted by the Treaty of Tordesillas in 1494) and the other, the contingency of piracy and contraband that resulted from that prerogative. To some extent, the Cuban military ideological *intrapraesidia* system constituted a sort of "non-fortified line" due to the lack of a promising local economic dynamic.

The fortified lines or medieval-like walls in the Caribbean came at a high cost. However, some thought more should be spent. These walls were subjected to financial scrutiny by the pen of Dávila y Lugo, discussed earlier.[48] Not only does the poet refer to a recent historical event—the 1625 Dutch attack on Puerto Rico under Boudewijn Hendricksz ("Balduino Enrico")—to prove the political disarray of the island, but he also alludes to Drake's 1595 attack to emphasize the enemy's lust after Puerto Rico and the need to properly fortify the city of San Juan.[49] In this regard, Rabell argues that in Dávila y Lugo's eyes Puerto Rico would be a useful panopticon to meet the Spanish Crown's need to monitor, interrogate, and punish those enemies who aspired to interrupt its commercial monopoly in the West Indies (Rabell, 64–68). Such a panopticon implies the ideological closure of the island, reflected in its material walls and fortresses that the colonial administration failed to oversee and appropriately garrison.

Dávila y Lugo aspired to an enclosed island, but in his view fraud and corruption delayed the fortification of San Juan; this is evidenced, he writes, by how easily Enrico attacked and occupied the city: "El Morro está sin los bastimentos necesarios porque aunque su majestad hace el gasto que constara en su caja, éste más resulta en provecho de los gobernadores que en prevención de la Fuerza" (Rabell, 164). At the same time, he emphasizes the geopolitical importance of the "plaza," metonymically alluding to the island because of its climatic advantage and its disadvantageous geographical position due to the winds (*id*., 137).[50] Another example of corruption is Governor Juan de Haro, who was in power from 1625 to 1630 and, according to Dávila y Lugo, inflated the prices of the supplies and provisions assigned by the king to the Castle of El Morro and resold them for his own profit (*id*., 165). However, the enclosed regime of "penitentiary space" became actually the most important attribute of the island, reflecting again, metonymically, the prevailing image of Spanish control over a private cell or the "key" to such an enclosed America: "Vese evidente que el que fuese dueño de esta plaza lo es de la llave de todas las Indias Occidentales que tiene la corona de Castilla en la mar del norte" (*id*., 137). By the same token, Dávila y Lugo accuses several governors and high officials of committing fraud by squandering the money sent by the Spanish Crown to continue the building operations of the fortresses.

In addition to dealing with an inimical foreign threat, Dávila y Lugo writes, the inhabitants of the island suffer an internal threat: out of fear and terror, they do not dare accuse the governor or criticize his actions (*id*., 166).[51] In this sense, they are also prisoners of corruption and the sort of penitentiary system controlled by the governor who acts like a warden. In contrast, Diego de Larrasa's (c1580–1649) account of the same 1625 event in his *Relación* depicts a brave, selfless strategist governor who, despite being heavily injured during the attack, stood by his men and fought (Larrasa, 236–238). Though the Dutch burned the city on their way out (as Torres Vargas notes when lamenting the loss of documents from the island's archives), Larrasa presents a picture of a close community, stressing that the spirit and value of the governor, the Spaniards, and the locals should be recorded as one of the most memorable cases (*id*., 235).[52] Whereas Dávila y Lugo emphasizes the business skills of Dutch sailors (*marineros de Holanda y Zelanda*), Larrasa underscores their poor military performance compared to the Creole artillerymen who, in his eyes, only lacked proper training (*id*., 230).

Furthermore, Dávila y Lugo paradoxically admires his Dutch captors, who, according to his account, have a natural inclination toward navigational and cosmographical skills (*id*., 148). He argues that they have, therefore, managed to occupy several nearby islands, such as Tobago where, unlike the case of Puerto Rico, they have erected two fortresses to protect their commerce based on tobacco, which produces great revenues (*id*., 155–56). He asks that there be a physical inspection every two years to oversee the construction of the fortifications as well as the administration of funds; and that the governors be restored to their title of captains general. Through a hyperbolizing undertone, Dávila y Lugo also articulates an aspiration for gold mines on the island: "[O]ro si hoy quieren beneficiarle hay mucho" (*id*., 139)[53]

The geopolitical importance of Puerto Rico emerged alongside the potential for exploitation and taming of natural resources such as rivers, gold, salt, and wood, as well as livestock and other products for internal consumption and exportation. Melgarejo's report of 1582 emphasizes the abundance of gold, silver, and copper while explaining that the economic scarcity derives from the lack of manpower, slaves, and settlers who will stay a reasonable time on the island.[54] In this regard, Dávila y Lugo reflects Melgarejo's report through the emphasis he places on the deposits of gold that have been abandoned due to the increasing depopulation of the island (*id.*, 132–135).[55] Aside from this issue, Melgarejo's report outlines the city of San Juan's inclination to import salt from Margarita Island because of lower prices and the locals' incapability or indisposition to extract more from the saltpans than will fill their individual needs. Dávila y Lugo highlights the local salt's resemblance to Spain's while Melgarejo, on the other hand, remarks that it is "much saltier."[56] Melgarejo stresses the necessity of taming wild nature and building roads to strengthen the system of communication among the settlements (*vecinos*) and broaden their accessibility to commerce and products of exchange. Swinging like a pendulum between tones of optimism and criticism, both accounts articulate a narrative of economic speculation by promising wealth to potential workers and investors willing to take advantage of the natural resources available. However, ideas of autonomous circum-Caribbean exportation and importation were not well received or promoted by the Spanish Crown. Rather, the monarchs were more invested in funding projects to provide military infrastructure to enclose threatened insular coasts or depopulate certain constantly attacked regions, in turn stimulating local dynamics of contraband trade and illicit economic self-management.

Spanish commercial restrictions contributed to the physical and ideological building of walls that outlined early seventeenth-century notions of the advantages and disadvantages. The intention was to protect the territories from foreign and prohibited economic interactions, but they were exposed nevertheless. While the notion of isolation or the prevailing mentality of a penitentiary colony became part of the collective image of the Caribbean archipelago's desolation, Dávila y Lugo roundly wanted to eradicate that idea by naming a key to the imaginary geopolitical cells constituted by the American territories. Two of the Greater Antilles, Cuba and Puerto Rico, fraudulent or suspiciously corrupt as these case studies show, challenged the legitimacy of the European concept of fortified lines by using those very fortified walls or coastal frontiers to protect their local economy based on contraband, to commit fraud, and to squander the Spanish Crown's funding for reinforcement of their military defenses. While not technically penal colonies, these islands exemplify a characteristic of the *intrapraesidia* system that reflected the contrasting speed between the dilatory pace of bureaucratic procedures and the immediacy of *in situ* early modern Caribbean economic dynamics of illegitimate trading. In turn, this showcased the attempts of individuals to insert the Caribbean region into transatlantic networks that were marked by violence and corruption. Through works like Balboa's epic poem and Dávila y Lugo's account, we have seen the historical and literary representations of piracy, contraband, and fraud and their role in exploring and articulating the limits of transatlantic global spaces that might be "prisons" or "jails" built around the local needs but nonetheless were diversified and open frontiers.

Contraband and Suspicious "Dutiful Subjects"

The task of enforcing stable rules to define contraband remained a matter of dispute during the 1600s. In his *Tratado iurídico político del contra-bando* (1654), Spanish jurist Pedro González de Salcedo, known for his political writings, declares that "the topic of contraband has been for long unknown and understudied" (González de Salcedo, 4). Besides drawing on European juridical authors discussed throughout this book, such as Grotius, Ayala, and Gentili, and other classical sources, this Spanish author from Logroño uses an etymological methodology to explain the nature of the phenomenon. Through his analysis of the terms *contra* ("against") and *bando* ("order"), he underscores the unstable meanings of these words. Tracing back the origins of the terms in Spain by using the *Second Partida* as a referent to build upon a stable meaning for the concept of contraband, he resolves that contraband means "against the ruling order or supreme will of the Prince, who has criminalized something that was not previously criminal" (*id.*).[57] In this way, while providing an etymological definition of "*contra-bando*," González de Salcedo stresses the political roots of an economic practice that at the time represented an economic threat for specific European political institutions and at the same time, the contingency of what constitutes a crime.

In what follows, we shall see the manifestation of such tensions between politics and economics from the viewpoint of four characters based in the Caribbean who—despite being loyal officials of the Spanish king or other sovereigns—pushed and blurred the boundaries of "piracy" and "contraband." They wrote their personal or officially modeled stories (or they were written by others) to draw European attention to Puerto Rico in order to justify piracy or to request the Spanish Crown's recognition and resources despite being practitioners of contraband. Through the analysis of specific tropes and representations of piracy, corsairing, and contraband, I will delve into the efforts that resulted in the articulation—sometimes intentional—of the geopolitical scenario marked by the back-and-forth between economic struggle, political incompetence, and socioeconomic grappling in the insular Caribbean. Certainly, economic profit was at the heart of the tensions and impasses as well as of interrelated conspiracies between both legitimate and unlawful powers. Concomitantly with the gradual economic and military decay experienced by Dávila y Lugo, other Caribbean insular figures— Creoles and Mulattoes—surfaced in the context of shifting European rivalries. I refer in particular to the lives of Diego de los Reyes and Miguel Enríquez, who encountered and surpassed the Spanish colonial military walls and fortresses to become sailors of foreign ships and to conduct independent business with non-Spanish territories in the region. These figures reimagined and transformed the parameters of what constituted a "dutiful subject," as discussed in the previous chapter through the writings of Henry Mainwaring and John Smith. In relation to the picaresque undertones I found in their narratives, I would like to stress the confessional and political aspects of the picaresque pointed out by Alexander Samson who argues that they constitute "a form of political writing, verisimilitude as reportage, whether mediating the relationship between the individual and state power or intervening within an economy of favours and exchanges" (Garrido 2015b, 31). Miguel Enríquez and Diego de los Reyes come from the lowest echelons of society and their stories are anchored in the margins of social, political, and economic order. However, their narratives and experiences of both circumventing and benefiting from the Spanish crown's economic restrictions illustrate the complex relationship between the individual and the state (monarchical regime) becoming part of a larger political narrative during their time period.

Living an itinerant life, Diego de los Reyes, better known as Diego the Mulatto, was born in Cuba and was captured by Dutch raiders in 1632. He married the daughter of a mapmaker and returned to his homeland, the Caribbean islands, to pillage vessels indiscriminately. A former slave, he was considered a renegade by many. The governor of Cuba, Don Francisco Riaño y Gamboa, and the former Dominican English friar Thomas Gage registered his path, in 1635 and 1637 respectively.[58] In his travelogue *The English-American, His Travail by Sea and Land* (London: Richard Cotes 1648), Gage opens his portrait of Diego with a justification of his pillaging inclinations, using picaresque undertones when describing his origins:

> The captain of this Holland ship which took us was a mulatto born and bred in Havana, whose mother I saw and spoke with afterwards that same year, when the galleons struck into that port …. This mulatto, for some wrongs which had been offered unto him from some commanding Spaniards in Havana, ventured himself desperately in a boat to the sea, where were some Holland ships waiting for a prize, and with God's help getting unto them, yielded himself to their mercy, which he esteemed far better than that of his own countrymen, promising to serve them faithfully against his own nation, which had most injuriously and wrongfully abused, yea and (I was afterwards informed) whipped him in Havana.
>
> (Lane and Bialuschewski, 64)

Probably intending to reinforce old and contemporary ties between English and Dutch powers, Gage pictures Diego as a "true and faithful" individual who gained the Netherlanders' esteem to the point that they "married him to one of their nation, and made him captain of a ship" under "Pie de Palo or Peg-leg" (*id*., 64).[59] Echoing Drake's alliance with Spanish castaways (*cimarrones*) and indigenous populations during his circumnavigation of 1577–80, Gage's rhetoric seems to encourage future projects of English settlement in the Caribbean based on recruitment through cultural, racial, or socioeconomic dissent.[60] Emphasizing the good or average treatment of a captive (Gage, in this case), the narrative showcases the complexity of the debates around piracy in the Caribbean context. Thus, Diego the Mulatto is subsumed into the rhetoric exemplified by Mainwaring and Smith, discussed in Chapter 5: that of those valuable men who undertook piracy and contraband practices because of their humble and somewhat deplorable origins.[61] In Diego's case, he proved to be a dutiful subject of a regime that allowed him to escape the sorrows of the Spanish Crown.

Let us turn the page to explore another Caribbean transatlantic "dutiful subject" who did not openly justify contraband but provided the Spanish Crown with material resources for both economic growth and military defense against its enemies in Puerto Rico. Miguel Enríquez (c1674–1743), born to a formerly enslaved woman (Graciana Enríquez) and an undisclosed father—probably a high clergyman in the city of San Juan—became a prominent businessman in spite of his humble origins and local racial discrimination toward the mulatto population. A former shoemaker and leather tanner, by the decade 1700–1710, Enríquez engaged in lucrative legitimate and illegitimate trading practices (López Cantos, 20–26). That is to say, Enríquez's fortune and purchasing power were less based on selling legitimate corsair captures (*efectos de corso*) than on reselling products from contraband collected by his fleets, which he frequently lent to colonial and ecclesiastical authorities. At age 26 Enríquez was accused of selling contraband merchandise in the city of San Juan. He was sentenced to one year's forced labor without pay in El Morro along with a fine of 100 pesos in silver. Governor Gabriel Gutierrez de la Riba, who had formerly introduced him to "the trade" (smuggling) by making him a *ventero* (seller), commuted his sentence by having him serve as an artilleryman without pay instead of becoming an insular convict. By that time, he was considered a literate individual whose library, containing books in Latin, was confiscated (López Cantos, 22). Besides owning a shipyard and 13 workshops and warehouses in San Juan, as well as an estate in the countryside, he managed to amass an armory of 100 rifles and to provide the island with enough military resources to defend it, along with 25 flags of different nations to be displayed overseas (*id*., 88–89). There are two aspects that make this figure fascinating for his contemporary racially divided society. First, by 1712, King Philip V acknowledged his services awarding him the *Medalla de Su Real Efigie*. This medal granted Enríquez an upper social status: he became a knight and earned the right to be called "don Enríquez." Second, in 1713, the Spanish King granted Enríquez a *Real Cédula Auxiliatoria*, which was a legal protection that gave him the power and right to appeal directly to the Council of Indies without the need of intermediaries (or colonial authorities) in any legal dispute.

Enríquez became a resourceful asset for both peninsular and colonial authorities. He earned the trust of politicians and clergymen of the island through favors, accommodations, and donations. From 1704 to 1735 he was an *armador de corso* (privateer) and his ships were frequently used to deliver important news (*avisos*) sent to the Caribbean zone by the Spanish Crown. He also provided services of transportation, free of charge, to colonial authorities, Jesuits, and Franciscans arriving in the Indies. When there was a lack of royal vessels in the islands, Enríquez's ships carried local products to Spain. In 1718 his ships contributed greatly to ending the English occupation of the small island of Vieques, close to Puerto Rico. During the War of the Spanish Succession (1701–14), Enríquez kept the Antilles out of the hands of Spain's enemies, England and Holland, by guarding the waters and attacking their ships relentlessly (*id.*, 53). Fleeing Abadía's authority in 1735, Enríquez secluded himself in the Carmelite convent of Santo Tomás in the city of San Juan, where he died eight years later in the company of only his accountant Antonio Paris Negro, the Dominican friar Andrés Bravo, and the prioress Sister Mariana de San José. His illegitimate daughter, the Carmelite nun Rosa Enríquez, suspected that her father was poisoned (*id.*, 389–392).

I would like to stress that Enríquez racial condition as a mulatto or *pardo* had a great influence both on his success and failure throughout his career. He was very close to several governors and he had them in his pocket because of his plentiful amount of resources (merchandise, fleets, and contacts with other merchants and political figures in other islands of the non-Hispanic Caribbean). The governors, on their part, provided Enríquez with the authorizations or *licencias de corso* to conduct business, which allowed them to receive a generous cut from these illegal transactions. In other words, Enríquez was in charge of the dirty work whereas the Spanish governors secretly profited from his spoils and remained officially detached from these practices.

On the other hand, Enríquez was representative of the intersection between war and commerce because he participated in both dynamics. Besides loaning or donating his fleet to repel attacks from Spain's rivals, he established a commercial network in the Caribbean. Although he died in disgrace and stripped of his fortune, Enríquez put forward a notion of commerce that did not align with Spanish peninsular mercantilist practices. He wrote to the Spanish king to promote direct commerce with the port of Cádiz in goods exported from Puerto Rico and Santo Domingo.[62] Against the backdrop of economic protectionism and Spanish mercantilism, he seemed to believe in open markets conducted by foreign, multiracial, and international parties in the broader context of the non-Hispanic Caribbean region. He befriended Irish and Jews alike, with whom he engaged in businesses both legitimate and illegitimate.

But Enríquez was unaware of what was coming after him. If, in the past, he had been celebrated by the Spanish king for his hostility against the British enemy in the Caribbean, by the mid-1740s the geopolitical panorama had changed and the diplomatic relations between Spain and England were apparently improving. Historians have speculated that the advisors of King Philip V suggested the restoration of the Spanish naval glory of previous centuries and, to achieve this, they needed England's collaboration. Therefore, it is believed that Enríquez became the pawn to be sacrificed. The two powers granted by the Spanish king in earlier decades, the *Medalla de Su Real Efigie* and the *Real Cédula Auxiliatoria*, were no longer acknowledged by colonial and Spanish Iberian authorities. He died in disgrace with no money while other individuals were granted *licencias de corso*. So, the fact that he was a mulatto with a vast commercial monopoly and a fighter against the former rivals of Spain contributed not only to his economic demise, but also to the removal of this figure and its legacy.

Broadly speaking, the situation of Puerto Rico within the Spanish empire was characterized by economic scarcity both in terms of the lack of enough of currency and the shortage of goods. Also, in relation to the military protection of the island and other Hispanic Caribbean islands, they depended on the *situado mexicano* (established in the 1580s), which was an economic source that had contributed to the construction of military fortresses and systems of defense. Certainly, several appointed governors in Puerto Rico squandered or redirected these funds to promote the local economy instead and privately enrich themselves. In this way, institutional corruption and contraband went hand in hand. Furthermore, during the early 1700s the Spanish *Armada of Barlovento*, a fleet created to protect the Caribbean ports in the past, was relocated into Europe to fight against England and the Low Countries.

Due to these factors and the vulnerable position of the Caribbean islands, there were several English attempts to seize the islands of Cuba and Puerto Rico. In 1702 they landed in the northwestern part of Puerto Rico, in Arecibo with no success, and again they attacked the island in 1703 and in the following years. These hostilities, not only in the Caribbean but also in other Spanish territories, led to the declaration of war between England and Spain in 1739. Then again, another war was declared between the two nations resulting from the Bourbon family compact (a pact between the kings of France and Spain) that lasted from 1761 to 1763 and, in the process, British forces managed to capture trading ports—one in Havana (Cuba) and another one in Manila (the Philippines)—damaging both Spanish transpacific and transatlantic routes. However, as I mentioned earlier, this century was also marked by a multinationally controlled Caribbean archipelago that, in turn, fueled dynamics of contraband and the Spanish crown did not have enough resources to protect the coasts and to contain illegitimate trade.

These problems remained at the heart of local socioeconomic crises in the seventeenth century when, although Puerto Rico swarmed with contraband and "corsairing" practices, the mulatto captain Enríquez alerted one of his

Caribbean business associates, a Jew from Curaçao, about the island's scanty circulation of currency. Exposing the correlation between war and commerce, Enríquez's letter states that "silver is the principal weapon of commerce."[63] Certainly Enríquez belonged to a different era, commonly denominated as the Golden Age of Piracy and characterized by buccaneers and freebooters, in which categories related to maritime predation, while being legally standardized and openly acknowledged by European powers, nonetheless became slippery when dealing with contraband and corsairing (*ir de corso*). In Enríquez's words, he obtained his "merchandise" (*mercaduarías*) through his "corsairing" (*corsos*) at 30 to 50 percent below market.[64] Legal commerce and financial considerations, instead of just war, became the barometer against which piracy was redefined.

From a transatlantic perspective (England, Spain, and the Caribbean) this book has traced, within the framework of cultural studies, the several discursive webs constituted by institutional and individual interests that, while being oppositional at times, nonetheless played a significant role in the conceptualization of piracy and its repercussions. Through the examination of English chronicles by Samuel Purchas and William Camden and their comparison with Spanish diplomatic correspondence, as well as visual imagery (maps and portraits) that celebrated and occasionally debated Drake's legacy after his circumnavigation, Chapter 1 stressed the relations between piracy, property, and the geographical space as represented in English and Spanish cultural productions of the sixteenth century. The chapter charted Drake's cultural construction as a "knight of the seas" and the way piracy became an ambivalent spatial category that reformulated the parameters of property and space as Drake opened up the possibility of English maritime domination. Moving to Drake's first Caribbean raid (1585–1586), which took place during the intermittent military conflict between England and Spain that lasted almost two decades (1585–1604), Chapter 2 scrutinized the narrative mechanisms employed by Spanish colonial and English authors such as Richard Hakluyt, Walter Bigges, and Juan de Castellanos. These authors ultimately took advantage of Drake's raid to craft imperial narratives of power and insert the West Indies into the larger Anglo-Spanish conflict.

Delving into the notion of the Caribbean islands as a space characterized by foreign agents who undertook unlawful practices driven by economic scarcity, political incompetence, and the absence of traditional continental frontiers, Chapter 3 focused on the rhetorical devices employed by early modern authors within the context of the global eagerness of European imperial expansions and rivalries. This chapter analyzed the articulation of European territorial claims in cartographic representations, including the contra-cartographies projected over the Caribbean, and the geopolitical consequences of such assertions. Following Drake's fortunes and misfortunes as described in print, the defeat of King Philip II's Armada (1588), and Drake's last Caribbean raid (1595–1596), Chapter 4 reviewed the inaccurate Spanish reporting of Drake's whereabouts, Spanish poems and ballads distorting his image, and English pamphlets condemning such images as "lies" and "libels." In so doing, the chapter traced the correlation between piracy and libel by demonstrating that the English accusations showcased an entangled narrative—stressing the Spaniards' moral misbehavior, financial ambitions, and military weakness—that ultimately reproduced the Spanish rhetorical model of describing Drake's maritime and territorial predations in Spanish America in the sixteenth century. Turning back to the flexibility of the category of piracy in European and colonial legal treatises, historical accounts, and royal documents, Chapter 5 demonstrated that the plasticity of the concept of piracy stems from an entanglement of the economic, political, legal, and religious realms. Considering seventeenth-century treatises against piracy and juridical agreements between England and Spain that took place after the deaths of Drake, Philip II, and Queen Elizabeth I, the chapter registered the legal standardization of piracy and the adoption of picaresque undertones to justify it and rationalize its prevalence. Considering the proliferation of English, French, and Dutch colonial bases on several islands as these nations made the Caribbean their base of operations, the current chapter has traced the parallel articulations of "dutiful subjects" in the Caribbean as well as the new categories related to maritime predation that related directly to contraband. Through the analysis of the works of Spanish peninsular settlers and Caribbean-born authors, we saw the conjunction of internal corruption and contraband surrounded and protected by the very military fortresses that were supposed to cancel them.

Overall, this book has focused on registering those previous discursively intertwined narratives and visual media employed to portray piracy, which in turn elicited the articulation or negotiation of the limits of property, geographical space, and sovereignty. Aiming to rethink the relevance of early modern piracy to contemporary issues, innovative lines of investigation of piracy from transhistorical and interdisciplinary perspectives have been undertaken. From the study of contemporary pirates in Somalian waters to the analysis of policies related to intellectual property and the conceptual reexamination of terrorism, research on the discursive nature of piracy is more relevant than ever.[65] Focusing on the moral, economic, and political interests behind the narrativization and visual depiction of piracy, this book is intended to shed light on the conformation of ideological concepts that permeate social structures and account for the ways in which individuals and institutions crafted narratives of power. The early modern manipulation of the discourse on piracy and its unstable quality provides a cultural framework to understand the configuration and limits of national, economic and political institutions.

Notes

1 In the short play, *Entremés* (c1588), the character of Proteo states that the monster should be understood as the "República," suggesting that it could refer to the island of Hispaniola: "y así entiendo que se debe entender por esta figura nuestra república" (*Entremés*, Cervantes Virtual).

2 Touching on "Creole discontent," Julie Greer Johnson, in "Cristóbal de Llerena and His Satiric *Entremés*" (1988) argues that "Llerena's satiric perspective, which separates the city's people from their government in the play, is an expression of Creole discontent at being denied the rights and privileges customarily granted to Peninsular Spaniards, and it represents a glimmer of a national consciousness which would eventually spread throughout Spain's possessions and would ultimately result in the dismantling of the Spanish American empire" (44). For more about the analysis on the introduction of classical figures in this short play, see Johnson, 39–45. For more about the historical context related to the economic and moral decay surrounding Llerena's *entremés* and the next century, see the analysis of Ponce Vázquez (Ponce Vázquez, 56–95).
3 About a potential attack on Hispaniola, Calcas states: "Yo siempre he sido consultado en contingentes bélicos; y siempre han tenido mis presagios sucesos correspondientes a mis agüeros. Considerando el nacimiento de este monstruo alcé la figura y socorrióme en el ascendente de Marte el signo de Piscis; por lo cual pronostico guerra y navíos, y por las figuras del monstruo, las prevenciones que debemos tener, porque mujer, caballo y plumas y pece quiere decir que las mujeres se pongan en cobro y se aparejen los caballos para huir, y alas para volar, y naos para navegar, que podrá todo ser menester." (*Entremés*, Cervantes Virtual)
4 Alcalde 1: "A nada deso tenemos miedo, buen caballero; nos tenemos en el río galeras bien reforzadas de gente y municiones, un cubo de matadero que vale su peso de plata; caminos cerrados que no los abrirá un botón de cirujano; deso bien podemos dormir a sueño suelto." (*Entremés*, Cervantes Virtual)
5 The archbishop, Don Alonso de Avila, wrote to King Philip II on behalf of Llerena and attached the script of the *Entremés* to his letter.
6 The English settled in Nevis, 1628, and St. Christopher (now known as St. Kitts), 1630, while the French took control over Tortuga, 1630, and the Dutch occupied Santa Catalina by 1629. By 1658 the Spanish lost Jamaica to the English (see Lane 2016).
7 According to Lane, the purpose of the company was twofold. On the one hand, they were interested in "belligerent commerce" while on the other, they also armed their sailors "for conquest in order to guarantee a high rate of return to the WIC's shareholders" (id., 61).
8 For more about the English, Dutch, and French trading companies, see Latimer (2009), Games (2008), and Lane (2016).
9 The Peace of Westphalia (1648) ended the Eighty Years' War between the Low Countries and Spain. Among the agreements in this treaty we find the recognition of the concept of the sovereign nation-state, which brought peace to belligerent nations (Latimer 2009; Lane 2016). Following that, Oliver Cromwell sent an imperialist mission to the Caribbean in 1654. The fleet arrived on the island of Barbados in 1655 and recruited soldiers and vessels on the islands of St. Christopher and Nevis. Even though more than 9,000 men joined this mission, they failed to accomplish Cromwell's project (Lane *id.*, 95).
10 For more about the debates in Hispaniola regarding the process of depopulation of the northern region, see Lugo (2009).
11 Lane specifies that *boucan* was originally a Tupi-Guaraní term that the French frontiersmen appropriated from Brazil (Lane 2019, xxvi).
12 There are several editions of Labat, and I will be using the ones from 1722 (Paris), 1724 (The Hague), and 1742 (Paris). The full title is *Nouveau voyage aux isles de l'Amerique. Contenant l'histoire naturelle de ces pays, l'origine, les moeurs, la religion & le gouvernement des habitans anciens & modernes: les guerres & les evenemens singuliers qui y sont arrivez pendant le long séjour que l'auteur y a fait: le commerce et les manufactures qui y sont etablies, & les*

moyens de les augmenter. Ouvrage enrichi d'un grand nombre de cartes, plans, & figures en tailles-douces.

13 "Nous arrivames assez tard a leur Boucan, ou nous trouvames leur trois autres camarades ... soit que la viande fut plus tendre, & plus appetissante, je croi que j'en mangeai pres de quatre libres. Nous dormimes a merveille. La faim plutot que le point du jour nous réveilla. J'avois de la peine a concevoir qu'ayant tant mangé pen d'heures auparavant, mon estomach eut déja fait la digestion ... les Chasseurs me di qu'il ne falloit pas que cela nous étonnat, qu'ils avoient autant d'appetit que nous, & que cela leur étoit ordinaire, parce que la viande de Cochon mangée de cette façon se digere plus facilment" (Labat 1742, 235–236).

14 According to Suzanne Toczyski, the term "barbecue" derives from the Arawak term *barbakoa*, which is close to our understanding of grilling meat (Toczyski 2010, 65).

15 Labat stresses that the number of these individuals has increased, mainly on Tortuga: "Enfin le nombre de ces Chasseurs ou Boucaniers, s'étant beaucoup augmenté, quelques-uns juegerent a propos de se retirer sur l'Isle de la Tortue" (Labat, 64).

16 Labat, vol. 5, 73. The term *filibustier* comes from the English "freebooter," which in turn derives from the Dutch *vrijbuiter* ("man with free booty") (Galvin, 7). The term was employed to refer to those seamen who lived by capturing booty instead of receiving regular pay for their services at sea (Latimer, 3).

17 Nominally speaking, the buccaneers were "jerky makers." Labat: "[C]es Chasseurs, qu'on nomma dans la suite Boucaniers du nom des Ajoupas ou Boucans..." (Labat, vol. 5, 62). For more historical context and social dynamics about the buccaneers, see Lane 2016. For the amphibious nature of the buccaneers in relation to that of previous pirates and corsairs, see Galvin (1999) and Latimer (2009). About the Golden Age of Piracy and the nationless character of buccaneers, freebooters, and filibusters, see Rediker (2004).

18 The original work by Exquemelin, *De americaensche zee-roovers* (Amsterdam 1678), was translated into Spanish in 1681 and then anonymously into English (London, W. Crooke, 1684). Fray Íñigo Abbad y Lasierra in his *Historia geográfica, civil y natural de las islas de San Juan Bautista de Puerto Rico* (1788) includes parts of Exquemelin's work, focusing on the dynamics between buccaneers and freebooters, and describes both types of individuals as "foreign barbarians" (*bárbaros forajidos*) (Abbad, 241–245). About the lifestyle of the French buccaneers in Hispaniola, Exquemelin writes: "It is now time to speak of the French who inhabit a great part of this island. We have already told how they came first into these parts; we shall now only describe their manner of living, customs, and ordinary employments. The callings or professions they follow are generally but three, either to hunt or plant, or else to rove the seas as pirates. It is a constant custom among them all to seek out a comrade or companion, whom we may call partner in their fortunes, with whom they join the whole stock of what they possess towards a common gain. This is done by articles agreed to and reciprocally signed. Some constitute their surviving companion absolute heir to what is left by the death of the first. Others, if they be married, leave their estates to their wives and children; others, to other relations. This done, everyone applies himself to his calling, which is always one of the three aforementioned. The hunters are again subdivided into two sorts; for some of these only hunt wild bulls and cows, others only wild boars. The first of these are called Buccaneers, and not long ago were about 600 on this island, but now they are reckoned about 300. The cause has been the great decrease of wild cattle. which has been such, that, far from getting, they now are but poor in their trade ... After the hunt is over and the spoil divided, they commonly sail to Tortuga to provide themselves with guns, powder, and shot, and other necessarys for another

208   *The Aftermath: Conclusion*

      expedition; the rest of their gains they spend prodigally, giving themselves to all manner of vices and debauchery, particularly to drunkenness, which they practise mostly with brandy; this they drink as liberally as the Spaniards do water" (Exquemelin edition of 1853, c1851, Boston: Benjamin B. Mussey & Co., 40–41).

19 Thomas Gage, an English Dominican friar, reports his encounter with Diego de Los Reyes (Diego el Mulato) in his *Travels in the New World* (1648), which was reprinted in 1655 and translated into French in 1676 and Dutch in 1700. Gage is quoted in Lane 2016.

20 "Il n'est permis a acune Nation, sous quelque prétexte que se puisse etre, d'a ller traiter chez Espagnols. Ils confisquen sans misercordie tous les Batiments qu'ils peuvent prendre, soit qu'ils les trouvent moullez sur leurs Cotes, soit qu'ils les recocontrent a une certaine distance, parce qu'ils supposent qu'ils n'y sont que pour faire le Commerce; & pur etre convaincus de l'avoir fait, il suffit qu'ils trouvent dans le Batiment, ou des marchandises fabriquées chez euc. Ou de l'argent de Espagne" (Labat 1742, 221).

21 Original description found in the 1742 edition (222–224): "For instance, if you wish to enter one of their ports to trade, you say that you are short of water, fuel, or victuals, or that you have a split mast, or a leak which cannot be plugged without removing the cargo. An officer is sent to explain all these things to the Governor, and, by giving him a good present, makes him believe what you wish him to believe. His officers can be made blind in the same way if necessary, and then permission is granted to enter the port and unload the ship in order to repair her" (*The Dominican Republic Reader*, 86).

22 "With regard, however, to the smaller cargoes which are more frequently carried by the English, French, and Dutch ships, they are generally disposed of at places some distance from the towns. A few cannons are fired to warn the Spanish settlers in the neighborhood of the arrival of the ship and they come in their canoes to buy what they require. This trade is mostly done at night, and the captain must be careful never to allow more people to come on the ship than his crew can tackle. The word "Credit" is never mentioned in this business, which is called trading a la Pique, and nothing is accepted in payment but cash, or produce actually delivered on board the ship" (*The Dominican Republic Reader*, 87).

23 "Le fusils dont on se sert aux isles sont appellez boucaniers, parce que ce sont les Boucaniers & les chasseurs de l'Isle Saint Domingue qui les ont mis en vogue. Les meilleurs se faisoient autrefois a Dieppe ou a la Rochelle. On en fait present a Nantes, a Bordeaux & autres Ports de mer du Royaume qui sont tres bons" (Labat 1724, vol. 1, 132 [1696]).

24 The term "privateer" was unknown to the Elizabethan era and was first used in the 1600s (Heller-Roazen, 81). For more about the emergence of English privateers, see K. Andrews' seminal study *Elizabethan Privateering* (1964).

25 The 1621 Ordinance for Corsairs was followed by other ordinances enforced in 1674, 1702, 1754, discussed in Chapter 3. By the same token, English maritime and coastal pillaging elicited policies in the New World such as the consolidation of the Spanish Armada of Barlovento in the Caribbean and the mandatory implantation of the Spanish *flotilla* system (fleet system). The project of creating the Barlovento Armada was initiated in the sixteenth century, but it was not until the seventeenth century that it became fully consolidated. In 1627 a royal *cédula* was expedited to the president of the Audiencia of Santo Domingo ordering the conformation of an *armadilla* (a small armada), which fell into disuse by 1647 (mainly because its crew deserted) and reappeared by 1667 and again in 1672. On the other hand, the Spanish *flotilla* system, implemented in 1526, compelled every Spanish merchant ship to navigate with at least 19 other ships. The *flotilla* system was regulated by the House of Trade in Seville, and the navigation route

encompassed the ports of Santo Domingo, Cartagena, Nombre de Dios, Veracruz, Porto Bello, and Havana (Galvin 36–37).
26 The revival of the Drake narrative is found in the following seventeenth-century publications: *Francis Drake Revived: Calling Upon this Dull or Effeminate age* (1628), *Sir Francis Drake Revived* (1652–1653), William D'Avenant's *The History of Sir Francis Drake: Exprest by Instrumentall and Vocall Musick* (1659), Samuel Clarke's *The life & death of the valiant and renowned Sir Francis Drake* (1671), *The Voyages of the Ever Renowned Sr. Francis Drake into the West Indies* (1683), *The English Heroe: or, Sir Francis Drake Revived* (1687), and *The Voyages & Travels of that Renowned Captain, Sir Francis Drake, into the West-Indies, and Round the World* (1707). For more about the development of Drake's legendary legacy, see: Kelsey (1998), Coote (2003), and Jowitt's edited collection *Pirates? The Politics of Plunder, 1550–1650* (2007).
27 Scholarship produced in the Caribbean about piracy is closely related to the writing of Caribbean history, by retrieving primary sources from Spanish archives. Due to the colonial past of the Greater Antilles—Cuba, Hispaniola, and San Juan Bautista (Puerto Rico)—a great part of the documentation related to history and, therefore, piracy (*cédulas,* epistles, and *relaciones*) was transferred to and preserved in both the Archivo de Indias and the Archivo Real de Simancas in Spain.
28 Abbad's *Historia* was later reviewed and edited by the 19th-century historian José Julián Acosta.
29 The Dutch West India Company was founded in 1621 following the model of the Dutch East India Company, created in 1602 under the leadership of Johan Oldenbarnevelt and the support of Prince Maurice of Orange. Dávila was kidnapped by a Portuguese person who brought three Frenchmen from the island of San Cristóbal who, according to the author, pretended to be English captives but in reality were spies and handed him over to Hauspater (Rabell, 29).
30 He was released in May 1630. In this chapter I will consult Carmen Rabell's modernized transcript of Dávila y Lugo's *Discurso,* which is based on a manuscript from 1784.
31 The nine parts are as follows: "Descripción sucinta de la isla;" "Importancia de la plaza de Puerto Rico;" "Motivos que mueven a los holandeses a la empresa de esta plaza;" "Los medios que dispone los holandeses para señorear a Puerto Rico;" "Aquí la descripción del puerto de la Granada;" "Aquí la planta de esta ensenada;" "Estado en que está la plaza de Puerto Rico;" "Como puede remediarse esta plaza tan importante y aún aquellas travesías con poco costo de su Majestad;" and "Cuanto a los mares y travesías."
32 "Esta disposición Francisco Draque, inglés gran corsario, lo notó con experiencias y especulaciones, práctico y sabio informó a la Reina de Inglaterra que poseyendo esta plaza era señora de todas las navegaciones que la corona de Castilla hace en las Indias Occidentales en la mar del norte" (Rabell, 138).
33 See Rabell's introductory study about Dávila y Lugo's "Discurso" in *La isla de Puerto Rico …,* 2016, 15–128.
34 Dávila y Lugo writes: "Estas y otras consideraciones obligaron a la reina Isabel de Inglaterra y su Consejo a hacer armada gruesa que a cargo de Francisco Draque como el que proponía la acción y la tenía bien entendida la ejecutase" (Rabell, 143). For more about the metonymical representation of the island in Dávila y Lugo's *Discurso,* see Rabell, 55–128.
35 Dávila y Lugo writes: "Aunque muerto Francisco Draque, la reina de Inglaterra y su Consejo no desistieron de tal empresa de Puerto Rico fundado en ella la base de todo el poderío que se pretende por el enemigo adquirir en las Indias Occidentales" (Rabell, 155).

36 "Era mas buen soldado para obedecer que para mandar, y así le sucedió la desgracia de tomar la Ciudad á pocos días de su gobierno el conde Jorge Cumberland, inglés de nación y del hábito de la Jarretiera de Inglaterra, que por mandado de su Reina Isabel, vino á solo esta facción, corrida del desaire de Francisco Draque" (Torres Vargas, 564) and included in Alejandro Tapia y Rivera's compilation *Biblioteca histórica de Puerto Rico anotada por Alejandro Tapia y Rivera* (Tapia, 1854).

37 Dávila y Lugo's accusation of Haro states that, instead of working for the king's interests, he tends to: "revender a precios inflados y para lucro personal los bastimentos comprados con el situado que asigna el rey para abastecer el Morro harina, vino, etc" (Rabell, 165).

38 He bore the same name of his grandfather.

39 "En esta ysla ay una villa que llaman la Nueva Salamanca o San Germán el nuebo el qual fundó el governador Francisco de Solís con el despojó que quedó de un pueblo o villa que se dezía Guadanylla que estaba a la banda del sur desta ysla y lo quemaron Caribes, yndios e comarcanos a esta ysla, y rrobaron franceses. Estaba junto a la mar en una sierra como media legua de la mar y a esta causa destar a tanto peligro se pasó la tierra dentro con acuerdo de la audiencia de Santo Domingo," in *Relación de la isla de San Juan de Puerto Rico*, available online at www.mlab.uiah.fi/simultaneous/Text/Rel_Puerto_Rico.html

40 Melgarejo writes: "Y el temperamento y ayres es lo mismo que corre en la ciudad de Puerto Rico. No tiene defensa alguna para corsarios" (*id.*).

41 Benton concludes that "Penal colonies were shaped by several streams of law—the law of exile and the law of emergency—and there was ambiguity in both areas of law" (Benton 2010, 218).

42 For more about the literary and stylistic European influences and innovations found in Balboa's epic poem, see Juana Goergen's (1993) and Raúl Marrero-Fente's (2008) seminal studies.

43 Balboa opens the chivalric poem alluding to the "prison" and "sorrows" of Angélico and the character Orco found in Luis de Barahona de Soto's *Las lágrimas de Angélica*, published in 1586.

44 "Ahora es tiempo que me vayas dando, ¿Musa, una vena muy copiosa y larga, / para que pueda celebrar llorando del buen obispo la prisión amarga. / No se hubo dado a las prisiones, cuando / aquella gente de conciencia larga, / las manos maniató al Pastor doliente, / y el las cruzó por ser más obediente" (Balboa, v 241–248).

45 "Al fin se concertaron en mil cueros / por el rescate del pastor benigno, / y doscientos ducados en dineros, / cien arrobas de carne y tocino" (*id.*, v 417–420).

46 "Estaba el buen obispo muy sentido / de las pobres ovejas de esta villa, / porque del triste caso sucedido/pensó que tenían culpa no sencilla" (*id.*, v 457–460).

47 "[U]no de los nuestros que allí junto / estaba con la mano prevenida, / le corta la cabeza, y con tal gloria" (*id.*, v 957–959); "Y dando por las calles un paseo / llegaron a la plaza dedicada; / donde en un palo alto el rostro feo / pusieron de aquella alma desdichada. / Aquesto hecho se acabó el trofeo / de victoria tan alta y señalada" (*id.*, v 1206–1211).

48 In her recent study of this figure and his *Discurso*, Carmen Rabell has convincingly identified three proposals derived from seventeenth-century lobbyist (*arbitrista*) rhetoric, i.e.: (1) that the anti-Dutch offensive should be conducted through channels of commerce, (2) that Spaniards should learn from their enemies in terms of their courage, stubbornness, and originality, and (3) that Spain should consider the possibility of trading with the enemy (Rabell, 52).

49 Rabell pinpoints in Dávila y Lugo's work the presence of the classical rhetorical figure of *inventio,* which enabled the author to propose solutions or identify an issue based on the selection of historical examples (57–58).

50 "Con que tanto cuanto es fácil socorrer de este puerto los otros, es dificultoso ser socorrido de ellos."
51 "Mas ay del que se atreve a proponer estos u otros daños en el Real Consejo de las Indias. Los ejemplos no solo miedo, mas terror ponen a los tristes vecinos. Yo me atrevo arriesgando mi vida por si con ella comprase muchas."
52 "[E]l ánimo y valor de nuestro buen Gobernador y el que tenían los Españoles y naturales de la isla, cuya memoria merece estar escrita entre los casos memorables."
53 "[O]ro si hoy quieren beneficiarle hay mucho" (Rabell, 139).
54 "[Y] es cierto que si esta granjería del oro no hubiera cessado la tierra estubiera próspera y muy poblada y muy proveyda de las cosas de España porque abiendo oro nada faltara cesso esta grangería rrespeto de acabarse los yndios y de encarecerse los negros y ser pocos los que vienen por que los que pasan a estas partes llabanlos a tierra firme y Nueva España y si su magestad hiziese merced de mandar traer a esta ysla myll negros y bendellos a los vezinos en muy breve tiempo se le pagaran y los vezinos quedaban mmás rricos y las rreales rentas se aumentaran en gran manera y en la venta de los negros sacado el costo dellos quedará gran aprovechamiento a la rreal hazienda porque demas del oro que se saca por los rríos se an hallado muchos nacimientos en esta ysla de que se an sacado de solo uno mmás de ochenta mill ducados y destos a abido hartos y oi en día está por catear" (Melgarejo, unnumbered).
55 "[O]ro que de esta isla tiene gran cantidad y se sacó en abundancia cuando sus naturales vivían y la habitaban que unos muertos, otros huidos a otras islas se han acabado."
56 Dávila y Lugo: "[P]uede sacarse de sal mucha suma y muy buena para todos usos por ser parecida a la de España" (Rabell, 135). Melgarejo's report: "[E]s la sal muy buena sala mucho mmás que la de España y podríanse sacar della cuaja grandísima cantidad de sal porque es muy grande pero como los vezinos de la Nueva Salamanca a cuyo distrito esta la dicha salina son pobres no sacan mmás que lo que an menester y alguna tres o quatro mill hanegas para vender ay otra en dicho termino que llaman las salinas de Guánica que tambien cuaxa y no se aprovechan della por falta de gentes ay otra en el rrío de Abei término de Puerto Rico y no cuaxa por falta de beneficio y con abre tanta sal en esta ysla los vezinos de la ciudad de Puerto Rico no se aprovechan della por que se proveen de la ysla Margarita y salinas de Araya que es en tierra firme en la provincia de Cumaná; respeto de hállalla mmás barata porque aber de traerlas por tierra a esta ysla es dificultosso a causa de los caminos ser ásperos y traéla por la mar mucho mmás porque an de venir barloventeandoy vinyendo de la Margarita corre norte sur y como vientos mmás ordinarios son estes puedese nabegar con ellos con facilidad" (Melgarejo, unnumbered).
57 González de Salcedo quotes the *Second Partida*, Title 23, Law 14,
58 While Cuba's governor mistakenly catalogued the chief pilot Diego "the mulatto" as being born in Seville, Gage—who later converted to Protestantism and advocated for Cromwell's Western Design—described in detail his encounter with the Caribbean-born slave and sailor (Lane and Bialuschewski, 60–62).
59 By the same token, Diego el Mulatto apparently talked about his mother, showing a different side of his character: "[A]nd knowing that I was going toward Havana, besides many other brindis or healths, he drank one unto his mother, desiring me to see her and to remember him unto her; and that how for her sake he had used me well and courteously in what he could" (Lane and Bialuschewski, 64).
60 See Ríos Taboada's analysis about the representation of the alliance between *cimarrones* and Drake as depicted in Lope's *La Dragontea*. (2021, 204–219)
61 For a detailed analysis of Gage's ulterior intention to persuade Oliver Cromwell to invade Spanish American strongholds and the role played by mulattoes and

other subaltern agents in the Western Design's collapse, see Monica Styles's article (2019).
62 "Con motivo de hallarse esta Isla padeciendo el desalivio y desconsuelo de los registros de esa Europa ... me he esforzado a pedir a Vuestra Magestad me conceda licencia para todos los años remitir una balandra de 80 toneladas de este puerto al de Cádiz con frutos de esta isla y de la de Santo Domingo" (AGI Santo Domingo 2296; also quoted in López Cantos, 92).
63 "La plata es la principal arma del comercio."
64 "Hallarme en esta ciudad con más de cincuenta mil pesos de mercadurías, habidas de mis corsos más baratas a un cincuenta, cuarenta y treinta por ciento entre los nacionales" (AGI, Escribanía de Cámara, 140 A; also quoted in López Cantos, 96).
65 Regarding the cultural history of nineteenth-century intellectual property in England and the United States, see Monica F. Cohen's study *Pirating Fictions: Ownership and Creativity in Nineteenth-Century* (2018).

Bibliography

Manuscripts

Anonymous. *Diary of Francis Drake's Last Voyage Containing Colored Images*. BnF, MS Anglais, 51.
Escalante de Mendoza, Juan. *Libro regimiento de la navegación de las Indias occidentales. Itinerario de navegación de los mares y tierras occidentales de 1575, anotado por su hijo Alonso Escalante de Mendoza*. BNE, MS 3104, c1575.
Escalante de Mendoza, Juan. *Libro regimiento de la navegación de las Indias occidentales. Itinerario de navegación de los mares y tierras occidentales de Itinerario de navegación de los mares y tierras occidentales compuesto por el capitán Jhoan de Escalante de Mendoza escrito en modo de diálogo*. AN523, c1623.
Mallet, A.M. *Description de l'Univers*. Paris: Chez Denys Thierry, c1683.
Ptolemy, Claudius. *Geographia vniversalis, vetvs et nova complectens Clavdii Ptolemi Alexandrini enarrationis libros VIII*. RBML, 1549 P95. 1545.
Ptolemy, Claudius. Geographia vniversalis, vetvs et nova complectens Clavdii Ptolemi Alexandrini enarrationis libros VIII. RBML, P959, *La Geografia Di Clavdio Tolomeo Alessandrino, Nuouamente tradotta di Greco in italiano Da Ieronimo Rvscelli*. RBML, B911.3, P951.1511.
Sahagún, Bernardino. "Prólogo al lector." *Historia general de las cosas de la nueva España*. c1540–1577. Original manuscript digitized by the Library of Congress. www.wdl.org/es/item/10621/
Santa Cruz, Alonso de. *Islario general de todas las islas del mundo*. MSS 12638. Biblioteca Digital Hispánica, BNE, 1542–1560.

Manuscript Documents

This book has incorporated a significant portion of primary evidence such as royal cédulas, English, Spanish Peninsular, and Spanish Colonial epistles and reports, plus other miscellaneous documents. What follows is a list of the main archives and their respective collections to facilitate the localization of the consulted primary sources.

AGI (Archivo General de Indias, Seville, Spain)
Estado
Indiferente general
Patronato

Santo Domingo
Santa Fe

AGN-M (Archivo General de la Nación, México)
Inquisición

AGN-SD(Archivo General de la Nación, Dominican Republic)

AGS (Archivo General de Simancas, Spain)
Guerra Antigua
Guerra y Marina (GYM)

BL (British Library)
Additional (Add.)
Cotton
Harleian
Hatfield
Sloane

CCELJ (Centro Cultural Eduardo León Jimenes, Dominican Republic)
Mapoteca

LC (Library of Congress)
Hans P. Kraus

RBML (Rare Book and Manuscript Library, Columbia University, NYC, USA)

BnF (Bibliothèque nationale de France Paris, France)

NMM (National Maritime Museum, Greenwich, UK)

Printed Materials and Editions

Abbad y Lasierra, Fray Íñigo. *Historia geográfica, civil, y natural de las islas de San Juan Bautista de Puerto Rico*. Editorial Doce Calles & Centro de Investigaciones Históricas, 2002.

Alegría, Ricardo E., editor. *Documentos históricos de Puerto Rico: 1493–1599*. 5 vols. San Juan: Centro de Estudios Avanzados, 2009.

Alfonso, X. *Las siete Partidas de Alfonso X el Sabio con las adiciones de Alfonso Díaz de Montalvo*. Sevilla: Pablo de Colonia. Juan Pegnitzer, Magno [Herbst] y Tomás [Glockner], por comisión de Rodrigo de Escobar y Melchor Gorricio, 1491.

Alfonso, X. *Siete partidas del Sabio Rey don Alonso el Nono nueuamente glosadas por el licenciado. Gregorio Lopez*. Salamanca: Andrea de Portonari, 1555.

Alfonso, X. *Las siete partidas del Rey Don Alfonso el Sabio: Cotejadas con varios códices antiguos por la Real Academia de la Historia*. Madrid: Imprenta Real, 1807.

Alfonso, X. *Las siete partidas (el libro del Fuero de las Leyes)* .Edited by José Sánchez-Arcilla, Editorial Reus, 2004.

Anonymous. *A Pack of Spanish Lies, Sent Abroad into the World, Now Ripp'd Up, Unfolded, and by Just Examination Condemned, as Containing False, Corrupt, and Detestable Wares, Worthy to Be Damn'd and Burn'd*. London: Deputies of Christopher Barker, printer to the Queens Most Excellent Majestie, 1588.

Ayala, Balthazar. *Three Books on the Law of War and on the Duties Connected with War and on Military Discipline*. Translated by John Pawley Bate. Buffalo: William S. Hein & Co., Inc., 1995.

Bacon, Francis. *The Works of Francis Bacon*. Edited by James Spedding, Robert Leslie Ellis and Douglas Denon Heath. London: Longmans, 1857–1874.

Balboa Troya Quesada, Silvestre de. *Espejo de paciencia*. Editorial Pueblo y Educación de la Habana, 1976.

de Berwick y de Alba, D., Conde y Luque, R., de Zúñiga, J., Marín, A., et al. *Coleccion de los tratados de paz, alianza, neutralidad, garantia ... hechos por los pueblos, reyes y principes de España con los pueblos, reyes, principes, republicas y demás potencias de Europa ...* Madrid: Antonio Marin, Juan de Zúñiga y la Viuda de Diego Peralta, 1740.

Beccari, Bernardino. *Avviso della morte di Francesco Drac e del mal successo dell'armata inglese piche parti` dal Nome di Dio, dove s'intende como e in qual luoco detta armata fu giunta dall'armata del Re Catolico e il combattimento che fecero alli 11 del mese di marzo 1596*. Roma: Nicolo Mutii, 1596.

Bigges, Walter. *A Summarie and True Discourse of Sir Francis Drake's West Indian Voyage. Wherein Were Taken, the Twones of Saint Iago, Sancto Domingo, Cartagena, and Saint Augustine*. London: Richard Field, 1589.

Bigges, Walter. *Sir Francis Drake's West Indian Voyage, 1585–86*. Edited by Mary Frear Keeler. London: Hakluyt Society, 2010.

Blundeville, Thomas. *M. Blundeville: His Exercises*. London: Imprinted by William Stansby, 1613.

Bodin, Jean. *On Sovereignty: Four Chapters from the Six Books of the Commonwealth*. Edited and translated by Julian H. Franklin. Cambridge: Cambridge University Press, 1992.

Borough, William. *A Discourse of the Variation of the Magneticall Needle*. London: J. Kyngston for Richard Ballard, 1581.

Breton, Nicholas. *A Discourse in Commendation of the Valiant as Virtuous Minded Gentleman Mister Frauncis Drake: With a Rejoicing of His Happy Adventures*. London: John Charlewood, 1581.

Brown, Horatio F., editor. *Calendar of State Papers Relating to English Affairs in the Archives of Venice*. Vol. 8. Edited by Horatio F.Brown. London: Her Majesty's Stationary Office, 1894.

Bry, Theodor de. *Grand Voyages*. Frankfurt: M. Becker, 1599.

Camden, William. *Annales the True and Royal History of the Famous Empresse Elizabeth Queene of England France and Ireland ...*London: Printed by George Purslowe, Humphrey Lownes, and Miles Flesher, for Beniamin Fisher, 1625.

Capmany, D. Antonio de, copied by. *Ordenanzas de las armadas navales de la Corona de Aragón*. Madrid: Imprenta Real, 1787.

Capitulaciones de la paz, entre el Rey nuestro señor, los ... archiduques de Borgoña, sus hermanos y el Rey de Gran Bretaña. Valladolid: Luis Sánchez, 1605.

Capmany y de Montpalau, Antonio, editor. *Memorias históricas sobre la marina, comercio y artes de la antigua ciudad de Barcelona*. Vol. 3. Barcelona: Imprenta de D. Antonio de Sancha, 1792.

Castellanos, Juan de. *Elegías de varones ilustres de Indias*. Madrid: M. Rivadeneyra, 1847.

Castellanos, Juan de. *Discurso del capitán Francisco Draque*. Edited by Ángel González Palencia. Madrid: Instituto de Valencia de D. Juan, 1921.

Covarrubias Horozco, Sebastián, de. *Tesoro de la lengua española (1611)*. Edited by Ignacio Arellano and Rafael Zafra. Iberoamericana: Vervuert, 2006.

Cawdrey, Robert. *A Table Alphabeticall*, 4th edn. London: Printed by W.I. for Edmund Weauer at North doore of Paules Church, 1617.

Collectanea Juridica. Vol. 2. London: Printed for E. and R. Brooke: Bell-Yard, 1792.

Controversia Las Casas-Sepúlveda. Biblioteca Universal Virtual: Editorial del Cardo, 2006. www.biblioteca.org.ar

D. F. R de M. *Respuesta y desengaño contra las falsedades publicadas é impresas en España en vituperio de la Armada inglesa... y del muy ilustre y valeroso caballero don Francisco Draque, y de los más nobles y caballeros, dirigida á la sacra Catholica y Real Magestad de la Reyna doña Isabel*. London: Arnoldo Hatfildo, por Thomo Cadmano, 1589. Transcribed and printed by Cesáreo Fernández-Duro in *La Armada Invencible*, 1884.

Diccionario de autoridades. Madrid: Real Academia Española, 1734.

Drake, Francis. *The World Encompassed* (1628). London: Nicholas Bovrne, Hakluyt Society, 1854.

Elizabeth, I. *By the Queene: A Proclamation Agaynst the Maintenaunce of Pirates*. London: Richarde Iugge and Iohn Cawood, 1569.

Elizabeth, I. "Queen Elizabeth's Song, Composed by Queen Elizabeth after the Defeat of the Armada," NMM, SNG/4, 1588.

Eliot, Charles W. *Voyages and Travels: Ancient and Modern*. Vol. 33. *The Harvard Classics*. New York: P.F. Collier & Son, 1909–1914.

Encinas, Diego de. *Cedulario indiano*. Vol. 4. Madrid: Imprenta Real, 1596.

Escalante de Mendoza, Juan. *Itinerario de navegación de los mares y tierras occidentales, según la edición anotada por Martín en Fernández de Navarrete 1791*. Madrid: Museo Naval, 1985.

Fernández de Navarrete, Martín, ed. *Colección de los viajes y descubrimientos que hicieron por la mar los españoles desde fines del siglo XV: Con varios documentos inéditos concernientes á la historia de la marina castellana y de los establecimientos españoles en indias*. Vol. 3. Madrid: Imprenta Real, 1829.

Fernández Oviedo y Valdés, Gonzalo. *Historia general y natural de las Indias, islas y tierra firme del mar océano*. Madrid: Imprenta de la Real Academia de la Historia, 1851–1855 [1525].

Fernández Oviedo y Valdés, Gonzalo. *Sumario de la historia natural de las Indias*, 1525. Barcelona: Linkgua, 2011.

Freitas, Serafim. *Do justo império asiático dos Portugueses*. Lisboa: Instituto de Alta Cultura, Universidad de Lisboa, 1959.

Gesner, Konrad. *Historia animaliaum*. Tigvri [Zurich], Apvd Christ. Froschovervm, 1587 [1551–1587].

Gentili, Alberico. *Hispanicae advocationis Libri Duo*. Translated by Frank Frost Abbott. Oxford: Oxford University Press, 1921.

Góngora y Argote, Luis de. *Sonetos completos*. Edited by Birute Ciplijauskaité. Barcelona: Castalia, 1969.

González de Salcedo, Pedro. *Tratado iuridico político del contra-bando*. Madrid: Diego Diaz de la Carrega, 1654.

Greepe, Thomas. *The True and Perfecte News of the Worthy and Valiant Exploits, Performed and Done by that Valiant Knight Syr Francis Drake: not Onely at*

Sancto Domingo, and Carthagena, but also nowe at Cales, and upon the coast of Spayne. London: I. Charlewood, 1587.

Grotius, Hugo. *Mare liberum (The Free Sea).* Translated by Richard Hakluyt with William Welwod's Critique and Grotius Reply. Edited by David Armitage. Indianapolis, IL: Liberty Fund, 2004.

Hakluyt, Richard. *The Principall Navigations, Voiages, Traffiques and Discoueries of the English Nation.* London: G. Bishop, R. Newberie, and R. Barker, 1589–1590.

Hakluyt, Richard. *The Principall Navigations, Voiages, Traffiques and Discoveries of the English Nation*, 3 vols. London: George Bishop, Ralph Newberie and Robert Barker, 1598/99–1600.

Hawkins, Richard. *The Observations of Sir Richard Hawkins Knight, in His Voyage into the South Sea: Anno Domini 1593.* London: Printed by I.D. for I. Iaggard, 1622.

Hawkins, Richard. *The Observations of Sir Richard Hawkins.* 1622. Edited by James A. Williamson. Madison: Argonaut Press, 1933.

Herrera y Tordesillas, Antonio de. *Historia general.* Madrid: En la Emplenta Real, 1601–1615.

Holinshed, Raphael. *Chronicles of England, Scotland, and Ireland.* Edited by John Stow. London: Printed by Henry Denham in Aldersgate Street at the Signe of the Starre, 1587.

Holinshed, Raphael. *Holinshed's Chronicles of England, Scotland, and Ireland.* Edited by Sir Henry Ellis. London: J. Johnson and J. Rivington; T. Payne; Wilkie and Robinson; Longman, Hurst, Rees, and Orme; Cadell and Davies; and J. Mawman, 1808.

Hotman de Villiers, Jean. "The Ambassador (De la Charge et Dignité de l'Ambassadeur)." *Inmemoriam celeberrimi viri Domini Francisci Drake.* London: J. Windet. London: Valentine Simmes for Iames Shawe, 1596, 1603.

Hudson, William. "A Treatise on the Court of Star Chamber." *Collectanea Juridica.* Vol. 2. London: Printed for E. and R. Brooke, Bell-Yard, 1792, 1–241.

Jonson, Ben, George Chapman, and John Marston. *Eastward Hoe.* London: Printed by George Eld for William Aspley, 1605.

Labat, Jean-Baptiste. *Nouveau voyage aux isles de l'Amerique. Contenant l'histoire naturelle de ces pays, l'origine, les moeurs, la religion & le gouvernement des habitans anciens & modernes ...* 2 vols. The Hague: P. Husson ..., 1724.

Labat, Jean-Baptiste. *Nouveau voyage aux isles de l'Amérique.* Paris: Ch. J.B. Delespine, 1742.

Las Casas, Bartolomé de. *Apologética historia summaria de las gentes destas Indias.* Edited by Edmundo O'Gorman. Ciudad de México: Universidad Autónoma de México, 1967.

Las Casas, Bartolomé de. *Tratados de 1552.* Edited by Ramón Hernández and Lorenzo Galmés. Madrid: Alianza Editorial, 1992.

Las Casas, Bartolomé de. *Historia de las Indias.* Edited by Paulino Castañeda Delgado. Madrid: Alianza, 1994.

Llerena, Cristóbal de. *Entremés*, Cervantes Virtual. No date. www.cervantesvirtual.com/obra-visor/entremes–1/html/fef00ff0-82b1-11df-acc7-002185ce6064_1.html#I_1_

Lodge, Thomas. *The Complete Works of Thomas Lodge 1580–1623.* New York: Russell & Russell, 1963.

López de Velasco, J., *Demarcacion y Diuision de las Yndias: Codex Sp7.* Map Collection, John Carter Brown Library, 1575.

Mack, John. *The Sea. A Cultural History.* London: Reaktion Books, 2011.

Mainwaring, Henry. *The Life and Works of Sir Henry Mainwaring*. Edited by G.E. Manwaring. 2 vols. London: Navy Records Society, 1920–1922.
Marsden, Reginald Godfrey. *Documents Relating to Law and Custom of the Sea*. London: Navy Records Society, 1915–1916.
Maynarde, Thomas. *Sir Francis Drake, His Voyage, 1595*. London: Hakluyt Society, 1849.
Melgarejo, Juan. *Relación de la isla de San Juan de Puerto Rico*, 1582. www.mlab.uiah.fi/simultaneous/Text/Rel_Puerto_Rico.html
Mercado, Tomás. *Suma de tratos y contratos*. Edited by Nicolás Sánchez-Albornoz. Instituto de Estudios Fiscales, Ministerio de Economía y Hacienda, 1977.
Minsheu, John. *Vocabularium Hispanicum Latinum et anglicum*. London: Joanum Browne, 1617.
Nebrija, Antonio de. *Vocabulario de Romance en Latin*. Salamanca, 1495.
Nebrija, Antonio de. *Vocabulario de Romance en Latin*. Sevilla, 1516.
Nichols, Philip. *Sir Francis Drake Revived. Who Is or May Be a Pattern to Stirre up All Heroicke and Active Spirits of These Times, to Benefit Their Country and Eternize Their Names by Like Noble Attempts*…London: For Nicholas Bovrne, 1628.
Ortelius, Abraham. *Theatrum orbis terrarum*. Antwerp: Ioannes Bapt. Vrintius, 1603.
Ortelius, Abraham. *Theatri orbis terrarum parergon*. Antwerp: Officina Plantiniana, Balthasar Moretus, 1624.
Oudin, César. *Thresor des Deux Languages Françoise at Espagnolle*. Paris: Marc Orry, 1607.
Palleja, Cayetano de, translator. *Consulado Del Mar de Barcelona*. Barcelona: Imprenta de J. Piferrer, 1732. Percival, Richard. *Bibliothecae Hispanicae Pars altera*. London: John Jackson and Richard Watkins, 1591.
Pérez de Soto, Antonio. *Recopilación de las leyes de los reynos de Indias*. Vol. 2. 3rd edn. Madrid: A. Ortega, 1774.
Philip II. *Ordenanças para remedio de los daños e inconuenientes, que se siguen de los descaminos, y arribadas maliciosas de los nauios que nauegan a las Indias occidentales, 1590*. Madrid: Viuda de Alonso Martínez de Balboa, 1619.
Purchas, Samuel. *Hakluyt's Posthumus or Purchas His Pilgrimes: Containing a History of the World in Sea Voyages and Lande Travells by Englishmen and Others*. Glasgow: James MacLehose, 1905.
Raleigh, Sir Walter. *The History of the World*, 2 vols. London: William Stansby, 1614.
Ray, John. *A Complete Collection of English Proverbs*. London: G. Cowie and Co., 1813.
Roberts, Henry. *A Most Friendly Farewell to Sir Francis Drake*. Transcribed with a short introduction by E.M. Blackie. Cambridge, MA: Harvard University Press, 1924.
Savile, Henry. *A Libell of Spanish Lies*. London: John Windet, 1596.
Selden, John. *Mare clausum (Dominion or Ownership of the Sea Two Books)*. London: William Dugard, 1652.
Simón, Fray Pedro. *Noticias Historiales de las Conquistas de Tierra Firme en las Indias occidentales.1624–25*. Biblioteca de Autores Colombianos, 1953.
Smith, John. *The True Travels, Adventures, and Observations of Captain Iohn Smith, into Europe, Affrica, and America From Anno Domini 1593 to 1629*. London: J.H. for Thomas Slater, 1630.
Soto, Antonio Pérez de, editor. *Recopilación de las leyes de los reynos de Indias*. 3rd edition. Madrid: A. Ortega, 1774.

Spenser, Edmund. "Book VI." In *The Complete Works in Verse and Prose of Edmund Spenser* (1882). Prepared by Risa S. Bear. Eugene, OR: University of Oregon, 1995.

Stow, John. *A Summary of the Chronicles of Englande, Diligently Collected and Continued unto This Present Yeare of Christ, 1587*. London: Imprinted by Rap Newberie and Henrie Denham, 1590.

Suárez de Figueroa, Cristóbal. *Hechos de don García Hurtado de Mendoza. 1613*. Edited by Enrique Suárez Figaredo. Cervantes Virtual, 2006.

Tapia y Rivera, Alejandro. *Biblioteca histórica de Puerto Rico anotada por Alejandro Tapia y Rivera*. Puerto Rico: Imprenta de Márquez, 1854.

Torres y Vargas, Diego de. *Descripción de la isla y ciudad de Puerto Rico, y de su vecindad y poblaciones, presidio, gobernadores y obispos; frutos y minerales*. Edited by Ángel Rodríguez Álvarez. Editorial Nuevo Mundo, 2010. (Place of publication not available.)

van Linschoten, Jan Huygen. *Itinerario*. Amsterdam: Cornelis Claesz, 1596.

Vega y Carpio, Félix Lope de. *La Dragontea (1598)*. Edited by Antonio Sánchez Jiménez. Madrid: Cátedra, 2007.

Veitia-Linage, José. *Norte de la contratación de las Indias Occidentales*. Buenos Aires: Comisión Argentina de Fomento Interamericano, 1945.

Vellerino de Villalobos, Baltasar. *Luz de navegantes*. Edited by María Luisa Martín-Merás Verdejo. Madrid: Museo Naval, 1984.

Verstegan, Richard. *A Declaration of the True Causes of the Great Troubles* .... Antwerp: J. Trognesius, 1592.

Vitoria, Francisco de. *Political Writings*. Edited and translated by Anthony Pagden and Jeremy Lawrence. Cambridge: Cambridge University Press, 2010.

Vittori, Girolamo. *Tesoro de las tres lenguas francesa, italiana y española*. Geneva: Philippe Albert and Alexandre Pernet, 1609.

Critical Readings

Acosta, Diego. *The National versus the Foreigner in South America*. Cambridge: Cambridge University Press, 2018.

Adorno, Rolena. *The Polemics of Possession in Spanish American Narrative*. New Haven: Yale University Press, 2007.

Altman, Ida. *Transatlantic Ties in the Spanish Empire: Brihuega, Spain, and Puebla, Mexico, 1560–1620*. Redwood City, CA: Stanford University Press, 2000.

Alves, Andre and José M. Moreira. *The School of Salamanca*. New York: Continuum, 2010.

Anderson, John L. "Piracy and World History: An Economic Perspective on Maritime Predation." *Journal of World History*, 6, no. 2, 1995, 175–199.

Andrews, Kenneth R. *English Privateering to the West Indies, 1588–1595*. London: Hakluyt Society, 1959.

Andrews, Kenneth, R. *Elizabethan Privateering. English Privateering During the Spanish War, 1585–1603*. Cambridge: Cambridge University Press, 1964.

Andrews, Kenneth R. *The Last Voyage of Drake and Hawkins*. Cambridge: Cambridge University Press, 1972.

Andrews, Kenneth R. *The Spanish Caribbean*. New Haven: Yale University Press, 1978.

Andrews, Kenneth R. *Trade Plunder, and Settlement: Maritime Enterprise and the Genesis of the British Empire, 1480–1630*. Cambridge: Cambridge University Press, 1984.

Andrews, Sean Johnson. "Property, Sovereignty, Piracy and the Commons." *Property, Place, and Piracy*. Edited by James Arvanitakis and Martin Fredriksson. New York: Routledge, 2018, 36–49.
Armitage, David. *The British Atlantic World, 1500–1800*. London: Palgrave Macmillan, 2012.
Bagrow, Leo. *History of Cartography*. 2nd English edition. Tampa, FL: Precedent Publishing, 1985.
Barrow, John. *The Life, Voyages, and Exploits of Sir Francis Drake*. London: John Murray, 1844.
Bauer, Ralph. *The Cultural Geography of Colonial American Literatures: Empire, Travel, and Modernity*. Cambridge: Cambridge University Press, 2003.
Bauer, Ralph and Marcy Norton. "Introduction: Entangled trajectories: Indigenous and European histories." *Colonial Latin American Review*, 26, no. 1, 2017, 1–17.
Bentancor, Orlando. *The Matter of Empire*. Pittsburg: University of Pittsburg Press, 2017.
Bentley, Jerry, Renate Bridenthal, and Anand A.Yang, editors. *Interactions: Transregional Perspectives on World History*. Honolulu: University of Hawaii Press, 2005.
Benton, Lauren. *A Search for Sovereignty: Law and Geography in European Empires (1400–1900)*. Cambridge: Cambridge University Press, 2010.
Benton, Lauren. "Toward a New Legal History of Piracy: Maritime Legalities and the Myth of Universal Jurisdiction." *International Journal of Maritime History*, 23, no. 1, 2011, 224–240.
Blanco, Enrique T. *Los tres ataques británicos a la ciudad de San Juan Bautista de Puerto Rico*. San Juan: Editorial Coquí, 1969.
Blitch, Alice Fox. "Prosperpina Preserved: Book VJ of the Faierie Queene." *Studies in English Literature, 1500–1900*, 13, no. 1, 1973, 15–30.
Block, Kristen. *Ordinary Lives in the Early Caribbean: Religion, Colonial Competition, and the Politics of Profit*. Athens: University of Georgia Press, 2012.
Blom, Hans, editor. *Property, Piracy and Punishment: Hugo Grotius on War and Booty in De Iure Praedae: Concepts and Contexts*. Leiden, NL and Boston, MA: Brill, 2009.
Braudy, Leo. *The Frenzy of Renown. Fame and Its History*. New York: Vintage Books, 1986.
Bravo Ugarte, José. *Historia de México, La Nueva España*. Vol. 2. Ciudad de México: Editorial Jus, 1953.
Brendecke, Arndt. *Imperio e información. Funciones del saber en el dominio colonial español*. Translated by Griselda Mársico. Madrid: Iberoamericana/Vervuert, 2012.
Brito Vieira, Monica. "Mare Liberum vs. Mare Clausum: Grotius, Freitas, and Selden's Debate on Dominium over the Seas." *Journal of the History of Ideas*, 64, no. 3, 2003, 361–377.
Brody, Saul Nathaniel. *The Disease of the Soul: Leprosy in Medieval Literature (1971)*. Ithaca: Cornell University Press, 1974.
Bueguer, Christian. "Making Things Known: Epistemic Practices, the United Nations, and the Translation of Piracy." *International Political Sociology*, no. 9, 2015, 1–18.
Buisseret, David. "Spanish Colonial Cartography, 1450–1700." In *The History of Cartography, Cartography in the European Renaissance*, Vol 3. Edited by David Woodward. Chicago, IL: Chicago University Press, 2007, 1069–1094.

Burckhardt, Jacob. *The Civilization of the Renaissance in Italy*. London & New York: George Allen; Macmillan, 1914.
Burgess, Douglas R. *The Politics of Piracy: Crime and Civil Disobedience in Colonial America, 1600–1730*. Lebanon, NH: University Press of New England, 2014.
Cañizares-Esguerra, Jorge. *Puritan Conquistadors: Iberianizing the Atlantic, 1550–1700*. Stanford: Stanford University Press, 2006.
Certeau, Michel de. *The Practice of Everyday Life*, translated by Steven Rendall. Berkeley: University of California Press, 1984.
Chet, Guy. *The Ocean is a Wilderness*. Amherst, MA: University of Massachusetts Press, 2014.
Cohen, Monica F. *Pirating Fictions: Ownership and Creativity in Nineteenth-Century*. Charlottesville: University of Virginia Press, 2017.
Conley, Tom. "Early Modern Literature and Cartography: An Overview." In *The History of Cartography*, Vol. 3. Edited by David Woodward. Chicago, IL: Chicago University Press, 2007, 401–411.
Coote, Stephen. *Drake: The Life and Legend of an Elizabethan Hero*. New York: Simon & Schuster, 2003.
Cormack, Lesley B. "Britannia Rules the Waves?: Images of Empire in Elizabethan England." In *Literature, Mapping, and the Politics of Space in Early Modern Britain*. Edited by Andrew Gordon and Bernhard Klein. Cambridge: Cambridge University Press, 2001, 45–68.
Crang, Mike and Nigel Thrift, editors. *Thinking Space*. London: Routledge, 2000.
Croft, Pauline. "*Rex Pacificus*, Robert Cecil and the 1604 Peace with Spain." *The Accession of James I: Historical and Cultural Consequences*, edited by Glenn Burgess. Basingstoke: Palgrave Macmillan, 2006, 140–154.
Cruz, Anne, J. "Arms versus Letters: The Poetics of War and the Career of the Poet in Early Modern Spain." *In European Literary Careers: The Author from Antiquity to the Renaissance*. Edited by Frederick A. de Armas and Patrick Cheney. Toronto: University of Toronto Press, 2002, 186–205.
Cruz Barney, Oscar. *El combate a la piratería en indias: 1555–1700*. Oxford: Oxford University Press, 1999.
Cruz Barney, Oscar. *El corso marítimo*. Mexico: Universidad Nacional Autónoma de México, 2013.
DeGuzmán, Maria. *Spain's Long Shadow: The Black Legend, Off-Whiteness, and Anglo-American Empire*. Minneapolis, MN: University of Minnesota Press, 2005.
Deive, Carlos Esteban. *Tangomangos: Contrabando y piratería en Santo Domingo*. Santo Domingio: Corripio, 1996.
Delano-Smith, Catherine. "Signs on Printed Topographical Maps ca.1470-ca. 1640." In *The History of Cartography*. Edited by David Woodward. Chicago, IL: Chicago University Press, 2007, 528–590.
Delano-Smith, Catherine. "Cartographic Signs on European Maps and Their Explanation before 1700." *Imago Mundi*, 37, no. 1, 1985, 9–29.
Dietz, James L. *Economic History of Puerto Rico: Institutional Change and Capitalist Development*. Princeton: Princeton University Press, 1986.
Dodds, Klaus. *Geopolitics: A Very Short Introduction*. Oxford: University of Oxford Press, 2007.
Eissa-Barroso, Francisco, A. *The Spanish Monarchy and the Creation of the Viceroyalty of New Granada (1717–1739). The Politics of Early Bourbon Reform in Spain and Spanish America*. Leiden and London: Brill, 2016.

Elliott, John H. *Empires of the Atlantic World: Britain and Spain America 1492–1830.* New Haven, CT: Yale University Press, 2006.

Espinosa, Aurelio. *The Empire of the Cities: Emperor Charles V, the Comunero Revolt, and the Transformation of the Spanish System.* Leiden and London: Brill, 2008.

Ezell, Margaret J.M. *Literary Pirates and Reluctant Authors: Social Authorship and the Advent of Print.* Baltimore, MA: John Hopkins University Press, 1999.

Feenstra, Robert and Jeroen Vervliet, editors and translators. *Hugo Grotius Mare Liberum 1609–2009: Original Latin Text and English Translation.* Leiden: Brill, 2009.

Fernández-Armesto, Felipe. *Before Columbus.* Philadelphia, PA: University of Philadelphia Press, 1987.

Fernández-Duro, Cesáreo. *Nociones de derecho internacional marítimo.* La Habana: Imprenta del Tiempo, 1863.

Fernández-Duro, Cesáreo. *La Armada invencible.* Vol. 2. Madrid: Est. tipográfico Sucesores de Rivadeneyra, 1884–1885.

Finucane. Adrian. *The Temptations of Trade: Britain, Spain and the Struggle for Empire.* Philadelphia: University of Pennsylvania Press, 2016.

Lorenzo, Franciosini. *Vocabulario español e italiano ahora nuevamente sacado a luz.* Rome: Iuan Angel Rufineli and Angel Manni, 1620.

Fuchs, Barbara. *Mimesis and Empire: The New World, Islam, and European Identities.* Cambridge: Cambridge University Press, 2001.

Fuchs, Barbara. *The Poetics of Piracy. Emulating Spain in English Literature.* Philadelphia: University of Pennsylvania Press, 2013.

Gallardo, Bartolomé José. *Ensayo de una biblioteca española de libros raros y curiosos.* Madrid: M. Rivadeneyra, 1863–1889.

Galvin, P.R. *Patterns of Pillage: A Geography of Caribbean-Based Piracy in Spanish America, 1536–1718.* New York: Peter Lang Publishing, 1999.

Games, Alison. *The Web of Empire: English Cosmopolitans in an Age of Expansion, 1560–1600.* Oxford: Oxford University Press, 2008.

García del Pino, César. "Corsarios, piratas y Santiago de Cuba." *Revista Santiago.* 26–27, 1977, 101–178.

García-Redondo, José María and Consuelo Varela. "Ecos literarios y memoria cartográfica del *Famous Voyage* de Francis Drake." *Anuario de estudios Americanos,* 70, no. 2, 2013, 441–478.

Garrido Ardila, J.A., editor. *A History of the Spanish Novel.* Oxford: Oxford University Press, 2015a.

Garrido Ardila, J.A., editor. *The Picaresque Novel in Western Literature: from Sixteenth century to Neopicaresque.* Cambridge: Cambridge University Press, 2015b.

Gerassi-Navarro, Nina. *Pirate Novels: Fictions of Nation Building in Spanish America.* Durham, NC: Duke University Press, 1999.

Gil-Ayuso, Faustino. *Noticia Bibliográfica de textos y disposiciones legales de los reinos de Castilla impresos en los siglos XVI y XVII.* Junta de Castilla y León: Consejería de Educación y Cultura, 2001.

Goergen, Juana. *Literatura fundacional americana: El espejo de paciencia.* Madrid: Editorial Pliegos, 1993.

González Ferrando, José M. "La idea de 'usura' en la España del siglo XVI: Consideración especial de los cambios, juros y asientos." *Pecvnia,* 15, 2012, 1–57.

Goslinga, Cornelius. *The Dutch in the Caribbean and on the Wild Coast (1580–1680)*. Florida, FL: University Press of Florida, 1971.
Gosse, Philip. *The History of Piracy*. New York: Tudor Publishing Company, 1934.
Gould, Eliga H. "Entangled Atlantic Histories: A Response from the Anglo-American Periphery." *American Historical Review*, 112, no. 5, 2007, 1415–1422.
Grieve, Patricia E. *The Eve of Spain: Myths of Origins in the History of Christian, Muslim and Jewish Conflict*. Baltimore, MA: John Hopkins University Press, 2009.
Gruzinski, Serge. *Las cuatro partes del mundo. Historia de una mundialización*. Ciudad de México: Fondo de Cultura Económica, 2010.
Guillén, Claudio. "Toward a Definition of the Picaresque." *Literature as a System: Essays Toward the Theory of Literary History*. Princeton, NJ: Princeton University Press, 1971.
Hale, J., "Warfare and Cartography, ca. 1450 to ca. 1640." In *The History of Cartography, Cartography in the European Renaissance*. Vol. 3. Edited by D. Woodward. Chicago, IL: Chicago University Press, 2007, 719–737.
Hampton, Timothy. *Fictions of Embassy: Literature and Diplomacy in Early Modern Europe*. Ithaca, NY: Cornell University Press, 2009.
Hanna, Mark G. *Pirate Nests and the Rise of the British Empire, 1570–1740*. Chapel Hill, NC: University of North Carolina Press, 2015.
Haring, Clarence. *Comercio y navegación entre España y las Indias*. Ciudad de México: Fondo de Cultura Económica, 1939.
Haring, Clarence. *The Buccaneers in the West Indies in the XVII Century*. North Yorkshire: Methuen, 1910.
Helgerson, Richard. *Forms of Nationhood. The Elizabethan Writing of England*. Chicago & London: University of Chicago Press, 1992.
Heller-Roazen, Daniel. *The Enemy of All: Piracy and the Law of Nations*. New York: Zone, 2009.
Hershenzon, Daniel. "The Political Economy of Ransom in the Early Modern Mediterranean." *Past and Present*, 231, no. 1, 2016, 61–95.
Herzog, Tamar. *Defining Nations: Immigrants and Citizens in Early Modern Spain and Spanish America*. New Haven, CT: Yale University Press, 2003.
Herzog, Tamar. *Frontiers of Possession: Spain and Portugal in Europe and the Americas*. Cambridge, MA: Harvard University Press, 2015.
Hoffman, Paul. *The Spanish Crown and the Defense of the Caribbean, 1535–1585: Precedent, Patrimonialism, and Royal Parsimony*. Baton Rouge, LA: Louisiana State University Press, 1980.
Houliston, Victor. *Catholic Resistance in Elizabeth, England: Robert Person's Jesuit Polemic, 1580–1610*. Burlington: Ashgate, Institutum Historicum Societatis Iesu, c2007.
Hulme, Peter. *Colonial Encounters: Europe and the Native Caribbean, 1492–1797*. North Yorkshire: Methuen, 1986.
Ish-Shalom, Piki. "The Rhetorical Capital of Theories: The Democratic Peace and the Road to the Roadmap." *International Political Science Review*, 29, no. 3, 2008, 281–301.
Ita Rubio, Lourdes de. "La presencia británica en el caribe durante el siglo XVI y principios de XVII." In *Comercio y piratería y vida cotidiana en el caribe*. Edited by Yolanda Juárez and Leticia Bobadilla. Morelia, Michoacán: Universidad Michoacana de San Nicolás de Hidalgo, 2009, 17–45.
Jacob, C. *The Sovereign Map*. Translated by Tom Conley. Chicago, IL: University of Chicago Press, 2006.

Jameson, A.K. "Lope de Vega's Knowledge of Classical Literature." *Bulletin Hispanique*, 38, no. 4, 1936, 444–501.
Jardine, Lisa. *Worldly Goods: A New History of Renaissance*. New York: Doubleday, 1996.
Johnson, Julie Greer. "Cristóbal de Llerena and his Satiric *Entremés*." *Latin American Theatre Review*, 1988, 39–45.
Jowitt, Claire. *Pirates? The Politics of Plunder, 1550–1650*. Basingstoke: Palgrave Macmillan, 2007.
Jowitt, Claire. *The Culture of Piracy, 1580–1630: English Literature and Seaborne Crime*. Burlington: Ashgate, 2010.
Jutte, Robert. *A History of the Senses: From Antiquity to Cyberspace*. Cambridge, MA: Polity Press, 2005.
Kagan, R.L. *Clio and the Crown: The Politics of History in Medieval and Early Modern Spain*. Baltimore, MA: Johns Hopkins University Press, 2009.
Kagan, R.L. and B. Schmidt. "Maps and the Early Modern State: Official Cartography." In *The History of Cartography, Cartography in the European Renaissance*. Vol. 3. Edited by D. Woodward. Chicago, IL: University of Chicago Press, 2007, 661–679.
Keen, B. "The Black Legend Revisited: Assumptions and Realities." *Hispanic American Historical Review*, 49, no. 4, 1969, 703–719. doi:10.1215/00182168-00182149.4.703.
Kelsey, Harry. *Sir Francis Drake: The Queen's Pirate*. New Haven, CT and London: Yale University Press, 1998.
Kempe, Michael. "Beyond the Law: The Image of Piracy in the Legal Writings of Hugo Grotius." In *Property, Piracy and Punishment: Hugo Grotius on War and Booty in De Iure Praedae: Concepts and Contexts*. Edited by Hans Blom. Leiden, NL: Brill, 2009, 379–395.
Kempe, Michael. "'Even in the remotest corners of the world': globalized piracy and international law, 1500–1900." *Journal of Global History*, 5, no. 3, 2010, 353–372. doi:10.1017/S1740022810000185.
Knorr Cetina, Karin. "Objectual Practice." In *The Practice Turn in Contemporary Theory*, edited by Theodore R. Schatzki, Karin Knorr Cetina, and Eike von Savigny, London: Routledge, 2001, 184–197.
Lane, Kris. *Pillaging the Empire: Global Piracy on the High Seas, 1500–1750*. 2nd edition. New York: Routledge, 2016.
Lane, Kris and Arne Bialuschewski, editors and translators. *Piracy in the Early Modern Era: An Anthology of Sources*. Indianapolis: Hackett Publishing Company, 2019.
Latimer, J. *Buccaneers of the Caribbean: How Piracy Forged an Empire*. Cambridge, MA: Harvard University Press, 2009.
Laures, Johannes. *The Political Economy of Juan de Mariana*. New York: Fordham University Press, 1928.
LeGear, Clara Egli. "Sixteenth-Century Maps Presented by Lessing J. Rosenwald." *Quarterly Journal of the Library of Congress*, 6, no. 1, 1949, 18–22.
Le Goff, Jacques and Nicolas Truong. *Una historia del Cuerpo en la Edad Media*. Translated by Josep M. Pinto. Barcelona: Paidós Ibérica, 2005.
León-Borja, István Szásdi. *Los viajes de rescate de Ojeda y las rutas comerciales indias*. Santo Domingo: Fundación García Arévalo, 2001.
Lewis, M.W. *The Myth of Continents: A Critique of Metageography*. Berkeley, CA: University of California Press, 1997.
López Cantos, Ángel. *Miguel Enríquez*. Third Edition. San Juan: Ediciones Puerto, 2017.

López Lázaro, Fabio. "Predation's Place within Profit: Pirates and Capitalists within the Seventeenth-Century Rise of Lockean Liberalism." *International Journal of Maritime History*, 23, no. 1, 2011, 241–276. doi:10.1177/084387141102300114.

López de León, Dorian. *Entre piratas y corsarios: La imposibilidad categórica en la multiplicidad discursiva hispánica en el caribe, siglos XVI y XVII*. Puerto Rico: Universidad de Puerto Rico (PhD dissertation), 2014.

López Nadal, Gonçal. "Corsairing as a Commercial System: The Edges of Legitimate Trade." In *Bandits at Sea: A Pirates Reader*. Edited by C.R. Pennell. New York: New York University Press, 2001, 125–136.

Lugo, Américo. *Escritos Históricos*. Edited by Andrés Blanco Díaz. Santo Domingo: BanReservas, 2009.

Macdonald, Lauren. "The Cemí and the Cross. Hispaniola Indians and the Regular Clergy,1494–1517." In *The Spanish Caribbean and the Atlantic World in the Long Sixteenth Century*. Edited by Ida Altman and David Wheat. Lincoln, NE: University of Nebraska Press, 2019, 3–24.

Márquez, Roberto, editor. "The Colonial Crucible, 1580–1820." In *Puerto Rican Poetry: A Selection from Aboriginal to Contemporary Times*. Amherst, MA: University of Massachusetts Press, 2006.

Marrero-Fente, Raúl. *Epic, Empire, and Community in the Atlantic World*. Lewisburg, PA: Bucknell University Press, 2008.

Martín-Merás Verdejo, María Luisa. *Cartografía marítima hispana: La imagen de América*. Barcelona: Lunwerg, 1993.

Martínez-Osorio, Emiro. "'En éste nuestro rezental aprisco': Piracy, Epic, and Identity in Cantos I-II of *Discurso del capitán Francisco Draque* by Juan de Castellanos." *Calíope*, 17, no. 2, 2011, 5–34.

Martínez-Osorio, Emiro. *Authority, Piracy, and Captivity in Spanish American Writing: Juan de Castellanos' Elegies of Illustrious Men of the Indies*. Lewisburg, PA: Bucknell University Press, 2016.

Martínez-San Miguel, Yolanda. "'La gran colonia': Piracy and Coloniality of Diasporas in the Spanish and French Caribbean in the Seventeenth Century." In *Coloniality of Diasporas: Rethinking Intra-Colonial Migrations in a Pan-Caribbean Context*. London:Palgrave Macmillan, 2014, 19–36.

Marx, Karl. "The General Formula of Capital." In *Capital*, Vol. 1. Chicago, IL: C. H. Kerr & Company, 1906–1909.

Mathew, Johan. *Margins of the Market: Trafficking and Capitalism across the Arabian Sea*. Berkeley, CA: University of California Press, 2016.

Mattingly, Garrett. *The Defeat of the Spanish Armada (1959)*, 2nd edition. Boston, MA: Houghton Mifflin, 1984.

Mazzotti, José Antonio. "The Dragon and the Seashell." In *Colonialism Past and Present: Reading and Writing About Colonial Latin America Today*. Edited by Alvaro Félix Bolaños and Gustavo Verdesio. Albany, NY: State University of New York Press, 2002.

McCarl, Clayton. "Carlos Enriques Clerque as crypto-Jewish confidence man in Francisco de Seyxas y Lovera's *Piratas y contrabandistas (1693)*." *Colonial Latin American Review*, 24, no. 3, 2015, 406–420.

McCloskey, Jason. "Crossing the Line in the Sand: Francis Drake Imitating Ferdinand Magellan in Juan de Miramontes' *Armas antárticas*." *Hispanic Review*, 81, no. 4, 2013, 393–415.

McCloskey, Jason. "Cosmographical warfare: secrecy and heroism in Juan de Miramontes's *Armas antárticas*." *Journal of Spanish Cultural Studies*, 21, no. 2, 2020, 171–185.
McRae, Andrew. "The Literary Culture of Early Stuart Libeling." *Modern Philology*, 97, no. 3, 2000, 364–392.
Mignolo, Walter. *The Darker Side of Renaissance: Literacy, Territoriality, and Colonization, 1995*. Ann Arbor, MI: University of Michigan Press, c2003.
Mira-Caballos, Esteban. *La Española: Epicentro del caribe en el siglo XVI*. Santo Domingo: Academia Dominicana de la Historia, 2010.
Montcher, Fabien. "The Transatlantic Mediation of Historical Knowledge across the Iberian Empire (c1580–c1640)." *E-Spania Revue Interdisciplinaire d'Études Hispaniques Médiévales et Modernes*, 2014. http://e-spania.revues.org/23697
Moore, Roger I., 1983. "Heresy as Disease." In *The Concept of Heresy in the Middle Ages*. Edited by Willem Lourdaux and Daniel Verhelst. Leuven: Leuven University Press, 1983, 1–11.
Mundy, Barbara E. *The Mapping of New Spain: Indigenous Cartography and the Maps of the Relaciones Geográficas*. Chicago, IL: University of Chicago Press, 1996.
Neale, John Ernest. *Queen Elizabeth I*. Chicago, IL: Academy Chicago Publishers, 1972.
Nemser, Daniel. "Introduction: Iberian Empire and the History of Capitalism." *Journal for Early Modern Cultural Studies*, 19, no. 2, 2019a, 1–15.
Nemser, Daniel. "Possessive Individualism and the Spirit of Capitalism in the Iberian Slave Trade." *Journal for Early Modern Cultural Studies*, 19, no. 2, 2019b, 101–129.
Nemser, Daniel, and John D. Blanco, eds. "Capitalism-Catholicism-Colonialism." Special issue of the *Journal for Early Modern Cultural Studies* 19, no. 2. 2019, 1–161.
Nievergelt, Marco. "Francis Drake: Merchant, Knight, and Pilgrim." *Renaissance Studies* 23, no. 1, 2009, 53–70.
Nirenberg, David. *Communities of Violence: Persecution of Minorities in the Middle Ages*. Princeton, NJ: Princeton University Press, c1996.
Norton, Marcy. "Subaltern Technologies and Early Modernity in the Atlantic World." *Colonial Latin American Review*, 26, no. 1, 2017, 18–38.
Nutall, Zelia. *New Light on Drake; A Collection of Documents Relating to His Voyage of Circumnavigation, 1577–1580*. London: Hakluyt Society, 1967 [1914].
Padrón, Ricardo. *The Spacious Word: Cartography, Literature, and Empire in Early Modern Spain*. Chicago, IL: University of Chicago Press, 2004.
Pagden, Anthony. *Lords of All the World: Ideologies of Empire in Spain, Britain, and France (c. 1500-c. 1800)*. New Haven, CT: Yale University Press, 1995.
Pagden, Anthony. *The Burdens of Empire: 1539 to the Present*. Cambridge University Press, 2015.
Parker, Geoffrey. *The Military Revolution*. Cambridge: Cambridge University Press, 1988.
Parry, J. H. *The Age of Reconnaissance*. Berkeley, CA: University of California Press, 1981.
Peralta, Manuel. *Costa Rica, Nicaragua y Panamá en el siglo XVI*. Madrid: M. Murillo, 1883.
Pérotin-Dumon, Anne. "The Pirate and the Emperor: Power and the Law on the Seas, 1450–1850." In *Bandits at Sea: A Pirates Reader*. Edited by C.R. Pennell. New York: New York University Press, 2001, 25–54.
Perruso, Richard. "The Development of the Doctrine of Res Communes in Medieval and Early Modern Europe." *Tijdschrift voor Rechtsgeschiedenis*, 70, 2002, 69–94.

Ponce Vázquez, Juan José. *Islanders and Empire*. Cambridge: Cambridge University, Press, 2020.
Portuondo, María. *Secret Science: Spanish Cosmography and the New World*. Chicago, IL: University of Chicago Press, 2009.
Probasco, Nathan J. "Cartography as a Tool of Colonization: Sir Humphrey Gilbert's 1583 Voyage to North America." *Renaissance Quarterly* 67, no. 2, 2014, 425–472.
Quinn, David. "Early Accounts of the Famous Voyage." In *Sir Francis Drake and the Famous Voyage, 1577–1580, Essays Commemorating the Quadricentennial of Drake's Circumnavigation of the Earth*. Edited by Norman J W. Thrower. Berkeley, CA: University of California Press, 1984, 33–48.
Quinn, David. *Sir Francis Drake as Seen by His Contemporaries*. John Carter Brown Library, 1996.
Quint, David. *Epic and Empire*. Princeton, NJ: Princeton University Press, 1993.
Rabell, Carmen Rita. *La isla de Puerto Rico se la lleva el holandés. Discurso de Don Francisco Dávila y Lugo al Rey Felipe IV (1630)*. San Juan: ICP, 2016.
Rahn Phillips, Carla Rahn. "Visualizing Imperium: The Virgin of the Seafarers and Spain's Self-Image in the Early Sixteenth Century." *Renaissance Quarterly*, 58, no. 3, 2005, 815–856.
Rahn Phillips, Carla Rahn. "Libels and Other Weapons: The Written Word as an Adjunct to Naval Warfare." In *Material and Symbolic Circulation between Spain and England, 1554–1604*. Edited by Anne Cruz. Aldershot:Ashgate Publishing, Ltd., 2008, 123–134.
Ray, John Arthur. *Drake dans la poésie espagnole*. Paris:Université de Paris (PhD dissertation) 1906.
Rediker, Marcus. *Villains of All Nations: Atlantic Pirates in the Golden Age*. Boston, MA: Beacon Press, 2004.
Rediker, Marcus. *Outlaws of the Atlantic: Sailors, Pirates, and Motley Crews in the Age of Sail*. Boston, MA: Beacon Press, 2014.
Restall, Matthew. *Seven Myths of the Spanish Conquest (1964)*. Oxford: Oxford University Press, 2003.
Restrepo, Luis Fernando. *Un nuevo mundo imaginado: Elegías de varones ilustres de Juan de Castellanos (1999)*. Bogotá: Instituto colombiano de cultura hispánica, 2020.
Ríos Taboada, María Gracia. "'No hubo tal cosa, que yo estaba allí': Pedro Sarmiento, censor de Juan de Castellanos." *Revista Hispánica Moderna*, 70, no. 2, 2017, 161–177.
Ríos Taboada, María Gracia. *Disputas de altamar. Sir Francis Drake en la polémica española-inglesa sobre las Indias*. Madrid/Frankfurt: Iberoamericana/Vervuert, 2021.
Rodríguez Demorizi, Emilio. *Relaciones históricas de Santo Domingo*. Vol. 2. Santo Domingo: Editora Montalvo, 1945.
Rodríguez-Moñino, Antonio. "Cristóbal Bravo, ruiseñor popular del siglo XVI." In *La transmisión de la poesía española en los siglos de oro. Doce estudios, con poesías inéditas o poco conocidas*. Edited by Edward M. Wilson. Barcelona: Ariel (Planeta de Libros), 1976, 255–283.
Rosales, Luis. *El sentimiento del desengaño en la poesía barroca*. Madrid: Cultura Hispánica, 1966.
Rubin, Alfred. *The Law of Piracy*. Newport: Naval War College Press, 1988.
Rumeu de Armas, Antonio. *Nueva luz sobre las capitulaciones de Santa Fe de 1492 concertadas entre los Reyes Católicos y Cristóbal Colón: Estudio institucional y diplomático*. Madrid: CSIC, 1985.

Toczyski, Suzanne. "Jean-Baptiste Labat and the Buccaneeer Barbecue in Seventeenth-Century Martinique." *Gastronomica* 10, no. 1, 2010, 61–69.
Salzman, Paul. "Traveling or Staying in Spain and the Picaresque in the Early 1620s." *YES* 41, no. 2, 2011, 143–155.
Sánchez-Martínez, Antonio. "La institucionalización de la cosmografía americana." *Revista de Indias*, 70, 2010, 715–748. doi:10.3989/revindias.2010.23.
Sanders, Julie. *The Cultural Geography of Early Modern Drama, 1620–1650*. Cambridge: Cambridge University Press, 2011.
Sandman, Alison. "Controlling Knowledge: Navigation, Cartography, and Secrecy in the Early Modern Spanish Atlantic." In *Science and Empire in the Atlantic World*. Edited by James Delbourgo and Nicholas Dew. New York: Routledge, 2008, 31–52.
Scammell, G. V. *Ships, Oceans and Empire: Studies in European Maritime and Colonial History, 1400–1750*. Burlington, VT: Variorum/Ashgate, 1995.
Schmitt, Carl. "Cinco corolarios a modo de introducción","La toma de la tierra en un nuevo mundo." In *El nomos de la tierra*. Translated by Dora Schilling Thon. Buenos Aires: Ed. Struhart y Cía, 2002.
Schmitt, Carl. *The Nomos of the Earth in the International Law of Jus Publicum Europaeum*. Translated by G.L. Ulmen. 1950. Candor: Telos Press, 2006.
Seed, Patricia. *Ceremonies of Possession in Europe's Conquest of the New World, 1492–1640*. Cambridge: Cambridge University Press, 1995.
Shields, David. "Sons of the Dragon; or, The English Hero Revived." In *Creole Subjects in the Colonial Americas: Empires, Texts, Identities*. Edited by Ralph Bauer and José Antonio Mazzoti. Chapel Hill, NC: University of North Carolina Press, 2009, 101–117.
Slöterdijk, Peter. *En el mundo interior capital*. Translated by Isidoro Reguera Sello. Madrid: Siruela, 2010.
Styles, Monica. "Foreshadowing Failure: Mulatto and Black Oral Discourse and the Upending of The Western Design in Thomas Gage's *A New Survey* (1648)." *Hispania*, 102, no. 4, 2019, 483–600.
Sutton, James. *Materializing Space an Early Modern Prodigy House: The Cecils at Theobalds, 1564–1607*. Aldershot, UK and Burlington, VT: Ashgate, 2004.
Tai, Emily Sohmer. "Marking Water: Piracy and Property in the Premodern West." In *Maritime Histories, Littoral Cultures, and Transoceanic Exchanges*. Edited by Jerry H. Bentley, Renate Bridenthal, and Kären Wigen. Honolulu, HI: University of Hawaii Press, 2007, 205–220.
Thomson, Janice. *Mercenaries, Pirates, and Sovereigns: State-Building and Extraterritorial Violence in Early Modern Europe*. Princeton: Princeton University Press, 1994.
Thrower, Norman J.W., editor. "Sir Francis Drake and the Famous Voyage, 1577–1580." In *Essays Commemorating the Quadricentennial of Drake's Circumnavigation of the Earth*. Berkeley, CA: University of California Press, 1984.
Tubau, Xavier. "Temas e ideas de una obra Perdida: La Spongia (1617) de Pedro de Torres Rámila." *Revista de filología española*, 90, no. 2, 2010, 303–330.
Ungerer, Gustav. *A Spaniard in Elizabethan England*. Vol. 1. Rochester and Suffolk: Tamesis Books Limited, 1975.
United Nations Convention on the Law of the Sea, 1982. www.un.org/depts/los/convention_agreements/texts/unclos/unclos_e.pdf
Valdivieso, Enrique. *Vanidades y desengaños en la pintura española en el Siglo de Oro*. Madrid: Fundación de Apoyo a la Historia del Arte Hispánico, 2002.

van Deusen, Nancy E. "Indios on the Move in the Sixteenth Century Iberian World." *Journal of Global History*, 10, no. 3, 2015, 387–409.

van Eijnatten, Joris. "War, Piracy and Religion: Godfried Udemans' Spiritual Helm (1638)." *Grotiana* 26, no. 1, 2007, 192–214.

Varela, C. and I. Aguirre. *La caída de Cristóbal Colón: El juicio de Bobadilla*. Madrid: Marcial Pons, 2006.

Veeder, Van Vechten. "The History and Theory of the Law of Defamation, I." *Columbia Law Review*, 3, no. 8, 1903, 546–573.

Viktus, Daniel, and Nabil Matar, editors. *Piracy, Slavery, and Redemption: Barbary Captivity Narratives from Early Modern England*. New York: Columbia University Press, 2001.

Vilches, Elvira. *New World Gold: Cultural Anxiety and Monetary Disorder in Early Modern Spain*. Chicago, IL: University of Chicago Press, 2010.

Voigt, Lisa. *Writing Captivity in the Early Modern Atlantic: Circulations of Knowledge and Authority in the Iberian and English Imperial Worlds*. Chapel Hill, NC: University of North Carolina Press, 2009.

Walerich, Alicja. "La imaginación en la tradición metafísico-mística: de Platón a Marsilio Ficino." *Veritas*, 23, 2015, 122–142.

Wallerstein, Immanuel. *World-Systems Analysis*. Durham, NC: Duke University Press, 2004.

Wallis, Helen. "The Cartography of Drake's Voyage." *Sir Francis Drake and the Famous Voyage, 1577–1580. Essays Commemorating the Quadricentennial of Drake's Circumnavigation of the Earth*, edited by Norman J.W.Thrower. Berkeley, Los Angeles, and London: University of California Press. 1984, 121–163.

Weber, Max. *General Economic History*. London: Allen & Unwin, 1923/27.

Wright, Elizabeth. *Pilgrimage to Patronage. Lope de Vega and the Court of Philip III, 1598–1621*. Lewisburg, PA: Bucknell University Press, 2001.

Wright, Elizabeth. "From Drake to Draque: A Spanish Hero with an English Accent." In *Transculturalisms, 1400–1700*. Edited by Minhoko Sucuki, Ann Rosalind Jones, and Jyotsna Singh. Burlington, VT: Ashgate, 2008, 29–38.

Wright, Irene A. *Further English Voyages to Spanish America*. London: Hakluyt Society, 1951.

Index

Abbad y Lasierra, Íñigo 191
Acosta, Diego de 125n75
Adorno, Rolena 11, 51–52, 64, 78n39
Alciato, Andrea 163
Alemán, Mateo 174–175, 185n55
Alexander VI, Pope 17n17, 40, 91
Alfonso V, King of Aragon 124n67
Alfonso X, King of Castile 180n8
Aliaga, Francisco de 186n66
Anderson, J.L. 103
Andrews, Kenneth 16n9, 94, 121n45, 125n80
Andrews, Sean Johnson 14–15, 76n12, 120n28, 123n63
Ardila, Garrido 185n53
Arias de Ávila, Pedro 182n19
Aristotle 153n51
Ark Royal 134
Armada *see* Spanish Armada, defeat of
Armitage, David 16n6
Arrianus, Lucius Flavius 8
Avellaneda, Bernardino Delgadillo de 149n5
Ávila, Alonso de 206n5
Ayala, Balthazar 2, 71, 81n68, 164–166, 181n17, 183n31, 199

Bacon, Francis 45n26, 131–133
Bahamonde de Lugo, Francisco 192
Balboa, Silvestre de 52, 62–63, 77n29, 77n31, 196, 199, 210n43
Baskerville, Thomas 135, 138, 149n5
Bejaramo, Gabriel Ramos 140
Benton, Lauren 32, 80n67, 86, 96, 100, 126n85, 163, 167, 182n23–25, 182n26, 183n27, 193–194, 210n41
Bermúdez, Pedro 53–54, 75n9

Bigges, Walter 13, 50, 52–53, 55–57, 59, 63, 66, 68, 73–74, 75n3, 95, 109, 113–114, 126n86, 127n93, 204
Black Legend 76n18, 126n91
Blackbeard 16n12
Block, Kristen 86
Bluq, Vincent 137
Boazio, Giovanni Battista 84, 95, 109–114, 117
Bodin, Jean 71, 80n66, 166, 169, 182n21
booty 2–3, 160, 162–165, 168–169, 177, 180n8, 182n19, 190, 194–195, 207n16; Drake's 20, 26, 30–33, 42, 145
Borja y Aragón, Francisco de 144
Braudel, Fernand 80n63
Braudy, Leo 21, 28
Bravo, Alonso 66, 79n48, 82n76
Bravo, Andrés 202
Bravo, Cristóbal 129, 139–142, 152n46, 153n50, 153n51
Bravo Ugarte, José 16n9
Brendecke, Arndt 155n73
Breton, Nicholas 25–26, 45n24
Bry, Theodor de 33, 35, 48n51, 95, 112–113, 126n91, 155n80
buccaneers 4, 12, 14, 16n9, 62, 188–189, 207n17–18
Bueguer, Christian 160, 180n7
Burckhardt, Jacob 26
Busto, Pedro Fernández de 52, 54, 57–58, 64–65, 68, 70–71, 73
Bustos de Villegas, Juan de 88

Cabezas de Altamirano, Juan de las 63, 195
Cairasco de Figueroa, Bartolomé 129, 142, 153n60
Camden, William 19–20, 22, 31, 43n2, 44n12, 204

Index 231

Cañizares-Esguerra, Jorge 76n18
Cano, Francisco 156n92
Carleill, Christopher 53–54
Caro de Torres, Francisco 155n74
cartography: of the Caribbean 84, 93–117, 125n81; of Drake's circumnavigation 21, 28–30, 32–40, 42, 46–47n38, 46n37; mapping piratical spaces 6–10, 17n16
Castellanos, Juan de 13, 28, 50–53, 60–61, 63–64, 66–69, 71–74, 78n34–36, 78n40, 79n50, 80n53, 80n56, 81n71, 83, 85–86, 88–93, 117n1, 134–135, 139, 204
Cavendish, Thomas 34, 36, 46n32
Cecil, Robert 21
Certeau, Michel de 113, 126n92
Chaparro, Guillén 66
Chapman, George 45n26
Charles I, King of Great Britain and Ireland 175–176, 180n6
Charles I, King of Spain 87, 90, 96, 118n8, 122n51, 122n53, 126n91, 149n1
Chet, Guy 17n12
Cibo de Sopranis, Ana 143
Cid, Francisco de 154n71
Clare, Janet 158n113
Cliffe, Edward 31
Clifford, George 170, 184n36, 184n38, 192
Coke, Edward 128, 132–133
Columbus, Bartholomew 88
Columbus, Christopher 35, 48n52, 83–85
Columbus, Diego 118n8
Conley, Tom 123n61
conquistadors 11–12, 83
contraband 199–201
Cooke, John 31, 44n19, 49n61
Coronelli, Vicenzo 117, 123n61
corsairs 4–5, 14, 53, 57, 60, 62, 71–73, 81n71, 92, 135, 144, 159, 161–163, 169, 173, 180n8–9, 189–190, 192–193, 204, 208n25
Cortés, Hernán 35, 86, 113
Cote, Martin 88
Covarrubias de Orozco, Sebastián 53, 56–57, 61, 76n13, 147, 156n91, 157n99
Crang, Mike 44n13
Cromwell, Oliver 188, 206n9, 211n58, 211n61
Cruz, Anne J. 55, 137
Cusack, George 77n28

Davenant, William 158n113
Dávila y Lugo, Francisco 191–193, 196–199, 209n29, 210n37, 210n49
Day, John 173
Delgadillo de Avellaneda, Bernardino 135–138, 142, 148, 151n26, 153n59
Deusen, Nancy van 123n64
Diego the Mulatto 189, 200–201, 208n18, 211n58–59
Dodds, Klaus 118n13
dominium 166–167
Doughty, John 49n62
Doughty, Thomas 41–42, 49n62
Drake, Francis 4–5, 8, 11–13, 16n10, 17n12, 18n23, 172; booty collected by 20, 26, 30–33, 42, 145; as a brand 190; Caribbean raids (1585–1586) 42–43, 50–82, 95–96, 103, 109–114, 125n80, 129, 139, 160, 173, 181n12, 187, 190, 204; circumnavigation (1577–1580) 19–49, 51, 101, 103, 144, 173, 201, 204; death of 128–131, 133, 135, 137–139, 141, 143–144, 146–148, 149n6, 152n37, 156n91, 160; diary of 31, 33, 35, 40, 42, 47n43, 47n46; discovery of Nova Albion 22, 27, 38–40, 48n48, 48n51, 48n55; fame of 26–27, 190; final raid of 128–129, 135–139, 142–144, 149, 170, 191, 193, 204; knighting of 19–20, 22–24, 28, 30–31, 43, 44n9; portraits of 28, 30; revival in historical narratives 191–193, 209n27; role in the Spanish Armada battles 130–131, 133–135, 139–142, 144, 149, 150n8, 205; royal commissions of 41–42, 61–62, 136–137, 173, 178; secrecy regarding 19–20, 28, 30–33, 35–36, 38–43, 101; slave-trading 5, 103
Drake "the Younger" 21, 46n31, 47n46, 51, 158n113
Dutch East India Company 3, 15n4, 209n29
Dutch West India Company 188, 191, 209n29
dutiful subjects 201–205

Eijnatten, Joris van 181n16
Elcano, Juan Sebastián 30, 43n1
Elizabeth I, Queen of England 4, 13, 17n12, 19–21, 25–26, 31–32, 38–43, 44n12, 49n62, 55, 58, 61–62, 68, 75, 75n1, 76n12, 82n76, 114, 129, 131–133, 136, 148, 149n1, 150n14, 159, 169–171, 173, 175, 178, 179n5, 192

Index

Elizabeth's Island 22, 27, 36, 48n50
Elliott, John H. 122n53, 167
Ellis, Henry 22
Encinas, Diego de 182n19
Enríquez, Miguel 200–204
Enríquez, Rosa 202
enterprise 56–57, 60
Equisman, Daniel 137
Ercilla, Alsonso de 32, 117n1
Escalante de Mendoza, Juan 84, 95, 100–102, 114, 124n70, 124n72
Exquemelin, Alexandre 189, 207n18

fake news *see* libel; misinformation
Ferdinand II, King of Aragon 84–85, 96, 98–99, 118n8, 124n67
Ficino, Marsilio 153n51
filibusters 4, 12, 14, 16n9, 189, 207n16
Fletcher, Francis 31, 36, 46n31
Flores, Alvaro 149n7
Flores, Pedro 135
fortified lines 168
Frampton, John 43n8
freedom of navigation 1, 3–4, 38, 42
freedom of trade 1, 3
Freitas, Serafim de 90–92
French West India Company 188
Frobisher, Martin 130
Fuchs, Barbara 11, 28, 35, 155n83, 156n89

Gage, Thomas 200–201, 208n18, 211n58, 211n61
Gager, William 45n25
Galvin, Peter 10–11
Gama, Antonio de 163
Gamarra, John 133–134
Gastaldi, Giacomo 104
Gaulle, Philip 33
Gentili, Alberico 2, 5, 42, 71, 80n67, 81n68, 163–169, 182n23, 194–195, 199
Gerassi-Navarro, Nina 79n43
Gheeraerts, Marcus 30
Gilbert, Humphrey 26–27, 45n27, 184n38
Girón, Gilberto 63, 195–196
Golden Age of Piracy 189, 204, 207n17
Golden Hind 19–20, 22–24, 26, 39, 44–45n20, 45n26
Góngora y Argot, Luis de 144
Gonson, Benjamin 125n79
González, Ángel 73
González de Mendoza, Juan 73
González de Salcedo, Pedro 183n28, 199

Gosse, Philip 10, 16n9, 16n10, 17n20
Griego, Juan 40
Grieve, Patricia 79n43
Grotius, Hugo 2–3, 5, 15–16n4–6, 42, 45n26, 91, 164–165, 167, 169, 181n13, 182n25, 183n28, 199
Guillén, Claudio 174, 185n55
Gutierrez de la Riba, Gabriel 201

Hakluyt, Richard 13, 15n4, 21–23, 30–31, 39, 43n5, 46n31–32, 47n46, 48n52, 51–52, 56, 75n5, 204
Haring, Clarence 182n23
Haro, Juan de 197
Hauspater, Johann Adrián 191, 209n29
Hawkins, John 35–36, 75n1, 102–103, 125n79, 136–137, 143, 152n33, 158n110, 160, 175, 181n12, 189
Hawkins, Richard 48n49, 162–163, 169, 181n12
Hawkins, William 75n1
Heemskerk, Jacob van 2–3
Heller-Roazen, Daniel 80n67, 165–166
Hendricksz, Boudewijn 192–193, 196–197
Henry III, King of France 150n12
Henry IV, King of France 33, 35, 156–157n94
Henry VIII, King of England 133
heroic figures, pirates as 14, 21–22
Herrera y Tordesillas, Antonio de 48n51, 98, 155n74, 191
Herzog, Tamar 102, 124n73, 125n74
Heyn, Piet 188
Hidalgo de Montemayor, Diego 64, 66–67, 78n37
Hilliard, Nicholas 28
Holinshed, Raphael 22–23, 30, 44n14–15
Homer 140, 145
Hondius, Hendrik 21, 30
Hondius, Jodocus 33–34, 39, 45n24, 48n51, 108
House of Trade 96, 103
Howard, Charles 130–131, 134
Hudson, William 128, 132–133, 139, 152n40–42, 153n50
Hulsius, Levinus 30, 37
Hurtado de Mendoza, García 35

indigenous people of the Caribbean 68, 78n40, 83–90, 93–94, 99, 102, 193
infestation 86–89, 91–92, 120n32, 139
intellectual property 205, 212n65

Index   233

International Maritime Organization 180n7
Isabella I, Queen of Castile 84–85, 96, 98–99, 124n67
Ish-Shalom, Piki 82n78

James I, King of Great Britain and Ireland 14, 91, 132–133, 149n1, 170–176, 185n51–52, 186n62, 187
Jameson, A.K. 158n109
Johnson, Julie Greer 206n2
Jonson, Ben 45n26
Jowitt, Claire 11, 16n10, 21, 23, 44n9, 51, 71, 78n38, 173–174, 185n51
Judith 103
Julius II, Pope 17n17
just war 2, 73, 144, 157n108, 160, 162, 164–166, 169, 204

Keeler, Mary Frear 75n7, 127n93
Kelsey, Harry 5, 47–48n48, 48n52, 51, 69, 76n12, 80n61, 82n76–77, 150n10
Kempe, Michael 58, 77n28
Knorr Cetina, Karin 160

Labat, Jean-Baptiste 188–189, 195, 206n12, 207n15
Lane, Kris 5, 16n9, 206n7
Larrasa, Diego de 197
Las Casas, Bartolomé de 87–88, 93–94, 113, 119n18–119n19
Latimer, Jon 94
Laures, Johannes 157n95
León, Luis de 86–87, 191
leprosy 88, 119n22
letters of marque 5–6, 76n12, 120n33, 172, 185n47, 185n52
Leu, Thomas de 28
Lewis, Martin 95
libel 129, 131–136, 138–139, 141–142, 145, 149, 149n1, 155n84, 204–205, *see also* misinformation
licentia marcandi 6, 172, 185n47
Linschoten, Jan Huygen van 30
Llerena, Cristóbal 187
Lodge, Thomas 151n29
Lope de Vega y Carpio, Félix 28, 64, 129, 143–149, 155n73, 155n84, 156n89, 156n92, 157n108, 158n109–110, 211n60
Lope de Vega y Fonseca, Hernando 68, 84
López de Velasco, Juan 95, 98, 123n64
López Lázaro, Fabio 5

López Nadal, Gonçal 5
Los Reyes, Diego de *see* Diego the Mulatto
Lovell, John 103
Lucan 69

Mabbe, James 174
Macdonald, Lauren 118n9
Mack, John 23–25, 44n20, 86
Madox, Richard 48n48
Magellan, Ferdinand 19, 27–28, 30, 35–36, 40, 43n1
Mainwaring, Henry 14, 160–161, 173–178, 180n6, 185n50, 185n56, 186n59, 186n61, 188, 190, 200–201
Mallet, Allain Malleson 114, 116–117
Mancing, Howard 185n53
Manwaring, G.E. 180n6, 185n50, 186n63
maps *see* cartography
Mariana, Juan de 146, 156–157n94
maritime law 1–2, 15n2, 16n11, 168–169
Marston, John 45n26
Martines, Joan 33
Martínez-Osorio, Emiro 11, 51, 64, 75n4, 79n47
Martyr, Peter 33
Mary, Queen of Scotland 42
Massinger, Philip 174
Mattingly, Garrett 150n12
Maynarde, Thomas 128–129, 148, 151–152n33, 158n110–112
McCloskey, Jason 27–28, 40, 43n6, 45n28
Melgarejo, Juan 191, 193, 198
Mendaña, Alvaro de 35
Mendoza, Bernardino de 22, 31–33, 42–43, 44n10, 44n12, 46n36, 128, 130–131, 133–136, 138, 140, 150n12
Mercado, Alonso de 194
Mercado, Tomás de 86
Mercator, Gerardus 21, 32–33, 47n39, 84, 95, 101, 104–109, 126n83
Merian, Matthäus 114–115, 117
Mesia, Pedro 92
Mignolo, Walter 118n5
Milio, Juan 73
Miramontes, Juan de 21, 27–28, 33, 40
misinformation 128–143, 149, 204–205, *see also* libel
Montcher, Fabien 155n73
Morgan, Henry 189
Mosquera, Antonio de 170
Mundy, Barbara 123n59

234 Index

Nebrija, Antonio de 61
Negro, Antonio Paris 202
Nemser, Daniel 57, 76n19, 77n27
Nicholls, Thomas 43–44n8
Nichols, Philip 158n113
Nievergelt, Marco 18n23, 45n25
Nirenberg, David 88, 119n21
Noort, Oliver van 30
Norman, Robert 45n25
Nova Albion 22, 27, 38–40, 48n48, 48n51, 48n55

Ochoa de Villanueva, Melchor 68
Oldenbarnevelt, Johan 209n29
Ortelius, Abraham 8–10, 32, 101
Osorio, Elena 155n84
Osorio Villegas, Diego 178
Ovalle, Cristóbal de 52, 57–58, 64, 67–68, 70–71, 73, 95, 186n65
Ovando y Cáceres, Nicolás de 83, 118n9
Oviedo y Valdés, Gonzalo Fernández 93, 113, 121n40

Packe of Spanish Lyes, A 128, 131, 133–136, 138–139, 142, 150n16
Padrón, Ricardo 93–94, 113, 121n41, 122n49
Pagden, Anthony 121–122n47, 121n46
pardons 173, 175–178, 181n10, 185n51, 186n59–61
Parker, Geoffrey 126n87
Pascual, Juan 40
Passe, Crispin van de 30
Peace of Ryswick 189
Peace of Westphalia 4–5, 19, 188, 206n9
Peckham, George 26
penal colonies 193–194, 198, 210n41
Pérotin-Dumon, Anne 125n78
Perruso, Richard 183n27
Peter IV, King of Aragon 161
Petrarch, Francesco 26
Philip II, King of Spain 13, 22, 38, 40–43, 45n22, 46n38, 52, 55, 64, 70–72, 75, 78n40, 80n63–64, 81n68, 87, 96–97, 100, 113–114, 122n53, 122n56, 129–130, 132, 136–137, 142, 146, 159, 164, 169–170, 173, 193, 204
Philip III, King of Spain 14, 146, 157n94, 170–173, 187–188
Philip IV, King of Spain 8, 192
Philip V, King of Spain 201–203
Phillips, Carla Rahn 149n5, 149n6, 151n26, 152n37
picaros 174, 185n55

piracy, categories of *see* buccaneers; corsairs; filibusters
piracy, changing winds of 159–186
piracy, criminalization of 4, *see also* maritime law
piracy, definition of 5–12, 14–15, 16n10, 27, 43, 53, 71, 80n67, 135, 159, 162–164, 169, 173, 204; in the UN Convention 1, 15n2
piracy, Somalian 180n7, 205
piracy cycles 10–11, 16n9, 17n21, 18n22
pirates, execution of 23, 159, 177–178
Pizarro, Francisco 35
Plantijn, Christoffel 46n38
Plutarch 6
Policante, Amedeo 120n28
Ponce de León, Juan 193
Ponce-Vázquez, Juan José 186n64, 186n66
ports 85–88, 94, 101–103, 105–107, 112, 117, 121n44, 160, 196
Portuondo, M. 32, 40, 46n38
privateering 5, 11, 16n9, 16n11, 190, 202, 208n24
property ownership 3, 99, 146, 160, 162, 164–169, 204–205; intellectual property 205, 212n65
Ptolemy, Claudius 6–7
Purchas, Samuel 20–22, 26, 140, 162, 204

Quinn, David 46n31
Quint, David 44n9, 69, 72

Rabel, Jean 28
Rabell, Carmen 192, 210n48–49
Raleigh, Walter 16n10, 36, 38, 40, 75n1, 172
Ramusio, Giovanni Battista 104
Rediker, Marcus 16–17n12
religion 3–4, 23–25, 40, 55, 61, 65–66, 86–89, 91, 130, 132, 144, 147–148, 156n89, 165–166, 170–174, 179, 196
Restall, Matthew 118n8
Restrepo, Luis 67, 78n36
Riaño y Gamboa, Francisco 200
Ríos Taboada, María Gracia 11–12, 21–22, 27, 36, 39, 41, 43n8, 144, 211n60
Rowland, David 174, 185n54
Rowley, William 173
Rubin, Alfred 6, 11, 16n11, 17n13, 181n14, 185n48
Ruscelli, Girolamo 104

Sahagún, Bernardino de 87, 119n14
Salas, Juan de 85
Salzman, Paul 175
Sampson, Captain 53–54
Samson, Alexander 200
San José, Mariana de 202
Sánchez Colchero, Alonso 40
Sanders, Julie 44n13
Sandman, Alison 121n44
Santa Catarina 2–3
Santa Clara, Antonio de 193
Santa Cruz, Alonso de 95, 97–98, 101, 121n39, 122n49, 123n60, 123n62, 123n64
Sarmiento de Gamboa, Pedro 36, 40–41, 64, 117n1
Savile, Henry 128, 135–138, 141, 148, 149n5, 152n38, 153n59, 156n91
Schmitt, Carl 166–167, 181n16, 182n18, 182n24
Seed, Patricia 123n66
Selden, John 2–5, 42, 45n26, 91–92
Sepúlveda, Juan Ginés de 87
Shields, David 27
Silva, Nuño da 30, 35–36, 39–40, 45–46n30
Simón, Pedro 78n40
slavery 5, 17n12, 102–103, 125n79, 156n92, 163–164, 189, 193, 200–201, 211n58
Smith, John 161, 173–176, 178, 186n62, 190, 200–201
smuggling 1, 5, 11, 62, 102–103, 125n79, 178
Sores, Jacques de 102
Soto, Domingo de 165
Sotomayor, Alonso de 143
sovereignty 1–2, 4, 6, 14, 53, 84, 91, 96, 162, 166–167, 169, 179, 182n22, 182n24, 205
Spanish Armada, defeat of 13, 128–131, 133–136, 138–142, 144, 149, 150n14, 169, 181n12, 204–205
Spenser, Edward 81n71
stereotypes 84–85, 142
Stow, John 23–24, 44n18–19

Strait of Magellan 20–21, 32, 36, 40–41, 43n5, 47n40
Suárez, Pedro 95, 143
Suárez de Amaya, Diego 143–145
Sutton, James 44n13
Sype, Nicola van 28–29, 33, 48n51

Tai, Emily Sohmer 6, 17n17, 96, 123n57
Thomson, Janice 182n22
Toczyski, Suzanne 207n14
Toledo, Francisco de 40
Torres Rámila, Pedro de 145
Torres Vargas, Diego de 191, 193
Tossigno, Pietro 88
Treaty of London 14, 160, 171–172
Tubau, Xavier 156n85

Ubaldino, Petrucci 150n10
UN Convention on the Law of the Sea 1–2, 15n2
Undemans, Godfried 181n16

Valdés, Pedro de 169–170, 183n32–35
Veitía-Linage, José 182n19
Vellerino de Villalobos, Baltasar 95, 100–102, 124n70, 124n71
Verstegan, Richard 24, 45n22, 45n26
Vilches, Elvira 86
Vique, Pedro 64, 67, 73
Virgil 69, 145
Vitoria, Francisco de 99, 102
Volosinov, Matejka 14

Wallis, Helen 46n31, 47n42, 47n46, 47n48, 48n50
Walsingham, Francis 46n31
Weber, Max 57
Welser, Mark 8
Welwod, William 2–3, 5
Wilkin, George 173
Wright, Elizabeth 56, 70, 80n63
Wroth, Mary 174
Wynter, John 41

Zárate, Agustín de 83, 85, 117n1–4
Zárate, Francisco de 35
Zerpa, Antonion Romero 143